THE FINAL SOLUTION

Origins and Implementation

Edited by
David Cesarani

London and New York

First published 1994
First published in paperback 1996
by Routledge
11 New Fetter Lane, London EC4P 4EE

Simultaneously published in the USA and Canada
by Routledge
29 West 35th Street, New York, NY 10001

Reprinted 1997

The collection as a whole © 1994, 1996 David Cesarani
The individual chapters © 1994, 1996 the respective authors

Typeset in Garamond by Florencetype Ltd, Stoodleigh, Devon
Printed and bound in Great Britain by
TJ Press (Padstow) Ltd, Padstow, Cornwall

British Library Cataloguing in Publication Data
A catalogue record for this book is available from the British Library

Library of Congress Cataloguing in Publication Data
A catalogue record for this book has been requested

ISBN 0–415–15232–1 (pbk)
ISBN 0–415–09954–4 (hbk)

THE FINAL SOLUTION

CONTENTS

NOTES ON CONTRIBUTORS

Avraham Barkai is a member of the executive committee and on the research staff of the Leo Baeck Institute, Jerusalem, and the author of *From Boycott to Annihilation. The Economic Struggle of German Jews, 1933–1943* (London, 1989).

Henry Friedlander is Professor of History in the Department of Judaic Studies at Brooklyn College, City University of New York. He is the author of numerous articles in German and English on aspects of the Holocaust and served most recently as co-editor of the twenty-six volume documentary series *Archives of the Holocaust*.

Benno Müller-Hill is a professor at the Institut für Genetic der Universität zu Köln and the author of *Murderous Science. Elimination by Scientific selection of Jews, Gypsies and Others, Germany 1933–1945* (Oxford, 1988) among other works.

Richard Breitman is Professor of History at the American University, Washington, DC, and has recently published *The Architect of Genocide: Himmler and the Final Solution* (New York, 1991).

Jürgen Förster is a member of the Militärgeschichtliches Forschungsamt, Freiburg in Breisgau. His work, which has been published extensively in Germany, can be sampled in 'The German Army and the ideological war of extermination against the Soviet Union' in Gehard Hirschfeld (ed.) *The Policies of Genocide: Jews and Soviet Prisoners of War in Nazi Germany* (London, 1986).

Christian Streit teaches at a grammar school in Mannheim, and published *Keine Kameraden. Die Wehrmacht und die sowjetischen Kriegsgefangenen 1941–1945* in 1978 (3rd edn 1991), a summary version of which may be found in 'The German Army and the policies of genocide', in Hirschfeld (ed.) *The Policies of Genocide*.

Omer Bartov is Associate Professor of History at Rutgers University. His most recent book is *Hitler's Army: Soldiers, Nazis, and War in the Third Reich* (Oxford, 1991).

Christopher R. Browning is Professor of History at Pacific Lutheran University in Tacoma, Washington. He has published many books and articles on the Final Solution of which the latest is *Ordinary Men. Reserve Police Battalion 101 and the Final Solution in Poland* (New York, 1992).

Yisrael Gutman, is head of Yad Vashem, Jerusalem, the author of *The Jews of Warsaw, 1939–1943: Ghetto, Underground, Revolt* (Bloomington, Ind., 1982) and editor-in-chief of the *Encyclopedia of the Holocaust* (London, 1990).

Dina Porat is Senior Lecturer in the Department of Jewish History, Tel Aviv University. Among her publications in Hebrew and English is *The Blue and the Yellow Stars of David. The Zionist Leadership in Palestine and the Holocaust* (London, 1991).

Jonathan Steinberg is Reader in Modern European History and Vice-master of Trinity Hall, Cambridge. He is the author of *All or Nothing: The Axis and the Holocaust 1941–1943* (London, 1990).

John P. Fox is editor of the *British Journal of Holocaust Education*. He has published numerous articles on the Holocaust, including the recent 'German bureaucrat or Nazified ideologue? Ambassador Otto Abetz and Hitler's anti-Jewish policies 1940–44' in M. G. Fry (ed.) *Power, Personalities and Policies* (London, 1992).

David Bankier is Senior Lecturer in Holocaust Studies at the Institute of Contemporary Jewry, Hebrew University of Jerusalem, and is the author of *The Germans and the Final Solution. Public Opinion under Nazism* (Oxford, 1992).

Aaron Berman teaches in the school of Social Science, Hampshire College, in Amhurst, Massachusetts, and is the author of *Nazism, The Jews and American Zionism 1933–1948* (Detroit, 1990).

Tony Kushner is Parkes Fellow in the Department of History at Southampton University and the author of *The Persistence of Prejudice* (Manchester, 1989) as well as many articles on anti-Semitism, refugees and responses to the Holocaust in Britain.

Dalia Ofer is affiliated to the Institute of Contemporary Jewry, Hebrew University of Jerusalem, and is the author of *Escaping the Holocaust: Illegal Immigration to the Land of Israel 1939–1944* (Oxford, 1990).

Shmuel Krakowski is head of archives at Yad Vashem, Jerusalem, and author of *The War of the Doomed: Jewish Armed Resistance in Poland, 1942–1944* (New York, 1984). With Yitzhak Arad and Shmuel Spector, he edited *The Einsatzgruppen Reports* (New York, 1989).

Yehuda Bauer is the Jona M. Machover Professor of Holocaust Studies at the Institute of Contemporary Jewry at the Hebrew University of Jerusalem. He has published many books and articles on the Holocaust including *The Holocaust in Historical Perspective* (Seattle, 1973) and *A History of the Holocaust* (New York, 1982).

ACKNOWLEDGEMENTS

The contributions to this volume arose out of an international conference on 'The Final Solution: origins and implementation' held in London on 18–20 January 1992. The conference was organized by the Institute for Contemporary History and Wiener Library, London; the Institute of Jewish Studies, University College London; and the Tauber Institute for the Study of European Jewry, Brandeis University, USA. It was planned by Dr David Cesarani, Wiener Library, Professor Mark Geller, Institute of Jewish Studies, and Professor Jehuda Reinharz, Tauber Institute. The conference coordinators were Gerta Regensburger, Wiener Library, Katie Edwards and Tessa Richards, University College London, and Sylvia Fuks Fried, Tauber Institute. Without the support of several trusts and foundations around the world the conference would not have been possible. The organizers gratefully acknowledge the support of the Doron Foundation for Education and Welfare, the Harold and Hyam Wingate Foundation, the Lord Ashdown Charitable Trust, the Maxwell Foundation, the Valya and Robert Shapiro Endowment, and the Yad Vashem Charitable Trust. Sylvia Fuks Fried assisted greatly in the preparation of this volume, but the final responsibility for it lies with the editor alone.

INTRODUCTION

The literature on the 'Final Solution', the attempted genocide of the Jews during the Second World War, is already enormous, but many of the critical questions within this tragic chapter remain clouded or unresolved.[1] At the same time the subject is being taught at an ever-growing number of institutions around the world to a swelling band of students.[2] In several countries the Holocaust has also become the focus of heated public debate. This has been most notable in Germany where the place of the Third Reich and the persecution of the Jews in German history naturally assumes a highly charged significance.[3] Meanwhile, attempts have been made by practitioners of Holocaust Denial to exploit the fractures in the historiography and so undermine the veracity of the Final Solution.[4]

This collection of essays is intended as a contribution to the central historical debates and an aid to teachers and students of the subject. It introduces important new research by leading scholars in the field in a concise but accessible form. One criterion for the selection has been to elucidate the major interpretative tendencies among historians. All the essays were produced in connection with an international gathering of scholars held in London on 18–20 January 1992 to mark the fiftieth anniversary of the Wannsee Conference on 20 January 1942.

The Wannsee Conference was summoned by SS-Obergruppenführer Reinhard Heydrich, head of the Nazi Security Police, who was charged with implementing Nazi policy towards the Jews. On 29 November 1941, Heydrich sent out invitations to a selection of senior SS figures and secretaries of state in key ministries requesting their presence at a meeting to arrange cooperation between the agencies necessary to the pursuit of the Final Solution of the Jewish question. Originally scheduled for 9 December 1941, the meeting was delayed to 20 January 1942. It was attended by representatives of seven ministries of state and Nazi Party offices, including the Ministry for Occupied Eastern Territories, the Interior Ministry, the Office of the Four Year Plan, the Ministry of Justice, the Generalgouvernement (General Government – controlling central-southern Poland), the Foreign Ministry, the Party Chancellery, the Reich Chancellery, and five

1

high-ranking SS officers from the central SS apparatus and its operations in the occupied eastern areas including the Generalgouvernement and the Baltic/White Russia. Heydrich opened the proceedings, sandwiched between noon and lunch, with an address in which he established the authority of the SS over Jewish policy and within it his personal hegemony in the matter. He announced that emigration had failed to solve the Jewish question so that a new method would be used: 'evacuation to the east'. To achieve this it would be necessary for all government agencies to coordinate their activities. Heydrich summarized the numbers of Jews involved, including the Jewish populations in Britain and neutral countries, and explained that once deported to the east they would be set to work, an ordeal which it was expected few would survive. Those who did remain alive would be 'dealt with appropriately', so as to avoid the reconstitution of the Jewish people. After some discussion of how to enact this pro-gramme in conquered countries so that all Europe would be 'combed from west to east', there was a long debate on the status and treatment of *Mischlinge*, the products of marriages between Jews and non-Jews.[5]

Although the significance of the Wannsee Conference was overrated for many years and has since been downgraded to little more than a platform for Heydrich to display his new powers, its fiftieth anniversary provided a point of departure for scrutinizing the origins and implementation of the Final Solution.[6] The intention, as reflected in these essays, was to concen-trate on the immediate sources of the genocidal project, the precise nature of the decision-making process which led to it, the manner of its implemen-tation and the responses it aroused among a selection of Germany's allies and client states, in German public opinion itself, among the democratic powers and among Jews in Europe and Palestine. These areas were chosen so as to give a broad overview and a sense of the main points in the current historical debates. Each topic is the centre of important developments in the historiography, either as an emergent new subject or one which is the object of major reinterpretation. This introduction will summarize the gist of each contribution, signalling the particular issues they present, and indicating their place in the historiography.

PRECONDITIONS AND ANTECEDENTS

The first three essays, by Dr Avraham Barkai, Professor Henry Fried-lander, and Professor Benno Müller-Hill, deal with the antecedents of the Final Solution, the preconditions which made its instigation possible and the ideology which legitimated mass murder. Anti-Semitism was the most obvious precondition for Nazi genocide and as such has rightly received a great deal of attention.[7] It was also recognized many years ago that racial thinking was an essential ingredient of Nazi anti-Semitism.[8] More recently, efforts have been made to integrate anti-Semitism and racism with the socio-biological thought that predated the Nazi regime but informed and underpinned its policies.⁹ In the immediate aftermath of the war Nazi atrocities, including those committed by trained scientists, were treated as the outcome of sadism, brutalization and unfettered hatred. Later, this perspective was modified by an understanding of the role played by bureaucracies and 'experts' in the process of persecution and extermination. Historians of widely different disciplines are now striving to demonstrate the relationship between racism, anti-Semitism, eugenics and social policy, and the dynamic between individual motivations, ideology and impersonal technologies.¹⁰

This interaction is explored by Dr Avraham Barkai who stresses the importance of *völkisch* ideology in creating popular consent for the Nazi regime and preparing the ground for the despoliation and eventual destruction of the Jews. The notion of a people united by blood and mystical ties displaced rival ideas of class unity and, simultaneously, excluded the Jews from society. Racial exclusivity legitimated the economic extrusion of the Jews which, in turn, provided precedents for more lethal forms of expulsion. In studying these steps towards exclusion and destruction, Barkai rejects 'functionalist' interpretations of the Holocaust according to which Nazi policy evolved in a piecemeal fashion without any marked ideological input.¹¹ Avoiding the other extreme, he maintains that ideology did not operate in a vacuum: propaganda functioned in relationship to the practices of the regime and public responses. This approach leads him to a consideration of the attitudes of the German public. Describing the progressive isolation of the Jewish population and the absence of protests from Gentile Germans, Barkai gives a schematic analysis of the reasons for antipathy or even sympathy towards the Jews. From his discussion of anti-Semitism he goes on to argue that ideology, the construction of the mythic Jew, legitimated the expropriation and destruction of real Jews.

In his contribution, Professor Henry Friedlander argues that the doctrine and practice of racial exclusion, as applied to Jews and Gypsies, created the essential preconditions for scientifically conducted, industrially organized and bureaucratically managed mass murder. This may be illustrated by the strong connections in terms of personnel and killing techniques between the earlier Nazi 'euthanasia' programme and the implementation of the Final Solution. On this basis, Friedlander suggests that the 'euthanasia' programme was the model for the planned extermination of the Jews. The way in which it was set in motion and authorized may be taken, equally, as a model for the instigation and sanctioning of the Final Solution. In the course of his argument, he throws light on the vexed issue of how such programmes gained official approval, and the role of the Reich Chancellery in this process.

Völkisch ideology may have had a crucial role in the process of racial exclusion and prepared the way for the deliberate impoverishment and eventual annihilation of the Jews, but 'value-free' scientific and objective discourse could prove equally dangerous. Professor Benno Müller-Hill is disturbed by the evidence that university qualifications served to legitimate horrifying and criminal acts. The Nazis' sterilization programme in Germany required the mobilization of many trained legal officials. Their involvement helped to mute opposition to this brutal process and encouraged German citizens, accustomed to respect academics and experts, to feel that all was in order. After briefly discussing the role of such experts in the 'euthanasia' programme and in the selections at Auschwitz, Müller-Hill focuses on the leaders of the *Einsatzgruppen*, the mobile killing squads responsible for murdering hundreds of thousands of Jews, Gypsies, communists and the mentally ill in the wake of the advancing German Army in Russia in 1941–2. An astonishingly high proportion of the men commanding the *Einsatzgruppen* and their sub-units or *Einsatzkommandos* possessed legal training and had completed law doctorates. Such impressive qualifications, he maintains, legitimated the commission of acts that were grossly illegal and helped to create popular acquiescence. That such men could behave in this way calls into question the ethical scope of such expertise, and suggests that scientific specialization may be one way in which the usual standards of human decency can be short-circuited.

THE HISTORIANS' DEBATE OVER THE ORIGINS OF THE FINAL SOLUTION

To move from a discussion of the preconditions and antecedents of the Final Solution to the decision to embark on genocide involves entry into a different historiographical milieu. Debate revolves more around the interpretation of certain documents, particular dates and individual actions. The sheer amount of detail and the proliferation of conflicting interpretations can appear bewildering, yet the issues involved are crucial. The contributions to this volume can be read and appreciated in their own right, but since they refer to and take their place within a long-running debate it may help to summarize its main points.

In 1951, Leon Poliakov, one of the first historians of the Final Solution, noted that the origin of the overall plan of extermination 'remains shrouded in darkness'. With the help of material collected for the International Military Tribunal at Nuremberg he maintained that it was possible to reconstruct the chain of events with some accuracy although certain details would remain unknown. 'The three or four people chiefly involved in the actual drawing up of the plan for total extermination are dead and no documents have survived; perhaps none ever existed.' Poliakov deduced that the step to extermination was taken 'some time between the end of the Western campaign in June 1940 and the attack on Russia a year later'.[12] Gerald Reitlinger, another pioneer in the field, concluded in his 1953 study that the existing evidence pointed to 'an actual Führer order' in early 1941 and suggested March 1941 as the likeliest date.[13] Some years later, the German historian Wolfgang Scheffler dated the onset of the genocidal campaign from the end of July 1941.[14] Raul Hilberg, whose massive study *The Destruction of the European Jews* appeared in 1961 and quickly became the standard work, was more cautious.

> Shortly after the Einsatzgruppen crossed the June 22, 1941 line into the USSR, Hitler ordered the commencement of the 'final solution of the Jewish question' on the entire European continent. The history of the Final Solution is not easy to reconstruct. We are dealing not with a sudden decision but with the emergence of an idea.

However, he regarded an infamous letter of 31 July 1941 from Hermann Goering, Commander of the *Luftwaffe*, President of the Reichstag, Prime Minister of Prussia and 'number two' after Hitler in the Nazi hierarchy, to Heydrich as a critical 'turning point'. This letter gave Heydrich the plenipotentiary powers which he had solicited for the 'overall solution of the Jewish question in the German sphere of influence in Europe'.[15]

By contrast, Helmut Krausnick, who acted as an expert witness in German war crimes trials in the 1960s, acknowledged in 1965 that 'The exact moment at which Hitler made up his mind that the Jews must be physically destroyed cannot be precisely determined from the evidence available.' But he reasoned that this decision could not have occurred later than March 1941 and saw the cancellation of Jewish emigration, in May 1941, from certain areas under German control as crucial. The Goering letter of 31 July 1941 only 'set the seal of approval on the procedure – to "legalize" it so to speak'.[16]

Not only do these dates differ, but inescapable contradictions existed within these narratives that even their authors found hard to explain. There were also statements by elements of the Nazi leadership that seemed to point in another direction. For example, Poliakov noted that up to 1939 the main thrust of Nazi policy towards the Jews was emigration, voluntary and then forced. In 1940, the German Foreign Ministry was studying a plan to deport Europe's Jews to the East African island of Madagascar, while Jews were being expelled from the Reich to available adjacent territories.[17] Reitlinger likewise noted that Jewish emigration from all areas of German control was not halted until October 1941.[18] Hilberg sought to resolve the apparent contradiction by stating that 'there was a gap between the beginnings of the deportations and the actual construction of facilities for killing the Jews'.[19] Krausnick could only suggest that the *Einsatzgruppen* commanders received verbal orders to kill all Jews since the only written evidence, a letter from Heydrich to SS commanders on 2 July 1941, pointed to the limited category of Russian Jews in the Communist Party and state apparatus.[20]

In two of the most important works of the 1970s, the interpretative gap widened. Uwe Dietrich Adam argued that in the spring and summer of 1941 various 'solutions' to the Jewish question existed, including pushing the Russian Jews beyond the Urals and deporting the rest of Europe's Jews to the east. It was only when military reverses on the Eastern Front in the autumn of 1941, 'between September and November', made such plans unviable that Hitler turned to mass murder.[21] Adam's analysis paralleled the view of the American scholar Karl Schleunes, that Nazi policy towards the Jews prior to 1939 was improvised and frequently incoherent.[22] His approach anticipated the emerging view of certain German historians that the Third Reich was less an autocratic, totalitarian regime, and more of a repressive police state dominated by feuding barons competing for Hitler's ear, each trying to outdo the other in achieving what they divined to be his wishes.[23] In stark opposition to this conception stood Lucy Dawidowicz whose approach has been dubbed 'intentionalist' as against that of the 'functionalists'. In her book *The War Against the Jews*, published in 1975, she held that Hitler had intended to exterminate the Jews from the moment the First World War ended. He launched Germany on a war of expansion to achieve his fundamental goal of destroying the Jewish people. Since Hitler conflated the Jews with the Bolsheviks and regarded the Soviet Union as their base, his attack on Russia was part and parcel of this mission. According to Dawidowicz it was after December 1940, when Hitler issued the first orders to prepare for the invasion of Russia, and before March 1941, when he told his generals that it would be 'an ideological war of extermination', that 'the decision for the practical implementation of the plan to kill the Jews was reached'.[24]

The divergence of interpretations became even more extreme with the appearance of studies by Martin Broszat in 1977, Christopher Browning in 1978, and Hans Mommsen in 1983. Broszat stated his considered view on the 'genesis of the Final Solution' in the course of a decisive rebuttal of the claims made by the extreme right-wing author, David Irving, that Hitler was unaware of the genocidal policy until late in the war. He confronted the difficulties, malevolently exploited by Irving, that flowed from the absence of a written order linking Hitler to the extermination policy.[25] Although Broszat showed convincingly that Hitler must have known about the massacres in Russia in the summer of 1941, he did not detect indications that these were part of a Europe-wide plan. Moreover, he argued that deportations of Jews from the Reich to the east were carried out *ad hoc* and the possibility still existed of using Madagascar as a dumping site. However, as the German Army's advance in Russia bogged down, deportations to eastern occupied zones became impracticable. The Nazis were in a frustrating situation. Their conquests in 1939, 1940 and early 1941 had brought millions more Jews under their control, but had not resulted in making anywhere available to send them in order to 'cleanse' the Reich and other occupied lands of the Jewish presence.

It thus seems that the liquidation of the Jews began not solely as the result of an ostensible will for extermination but also as a 'way out' of a blind alley into which the Nazis had manoeuvred themselves. The practice of liquidation, once initiated and established, gained prominence and evolved in the end into a comprehensive 'programme'.

Broszat added that

It appears to me that no comprehensive order for the extermination existed and that the 'programme' for the extermination of the Jews developed through individual actions and gradually attained its institutional and factual character by the spring of 1942 after the construction of the extermination camps in Poland.[26]

He maintained that the first mass killings, including by the use of poison gas, were local initiatives. They were intended to deal with overcrowding in particular Polish ghettos which were designated to receive Jews from the west. But once local commanders had resorted *ad hoc* to mass murder they turned to it on a routinized basis to solve the problems of disease in the ghettos and to deal with Jews arriving from the west with nowhere else to go. In Broszat's view Hitler would indubitably have known about these measures, but need not necessarily have instigated them.[27]

Broszat's article opened a long-running historical debate that threatened to polarize research by focusing it on a single issue. Yet, in the longer term it fructified and enhanced scholarship. His thesis stimulated a reply from Christopher Browning, author of an important 'functionalist' study of the German Foreign Office and the Final Solution.[28] Browning attempted to narrow the distance between the 'intentionalist' and 'functionalist' interpretations and to show that neither sufficed on its own.[29] He admonished that it was pointless to expect to find a document ordering the Final Solution signed by Hitler since this was not how he operated. Hitler 'ordered, or to be more precise, incited or solicited the preparation of an extermination plan in the summer of 1941'. It would have been inconceivable that it could have proceeded without his desire or knowledge, but it would have taken many months for his aides to give his wishes practical effect. In the period before the killing sites were ready, it was not surprising to detect improvisations and contradictory policies. Yet the notion that labour in the east was a serious option for the old, women and children was ridiculous and exposed the hollowness of alternative explanations of what was intended by the deportations.[30] In Browning's view, the activities of the *Einsatzgruppen* marked a transformative moment in Nazi policy. The Nazi leadership would no longer accept an increase in the number of Jews under their control as a necessary concomitant of expansion. Moreover, since mass killings were already in motion in Russia by July 1941, Goering's letter to Heydrich signalled a new step. This required better methods than those practised so far and it was not until October–November that these were decided upon. At this time, deportations of German Jews to the east, leading to instant destruction, the stop to emigration throughout Europe, the construction of the death camps, and the first gassings of Polish Jews at Chelmno in the first week of December, all indicated 'a late October or November approval by Hitler of the extermination plan which he had solicited the previous summer'.[31]

Broszat's thesis was subsequently developed and extended by Hans Mommsen in 1983. Mommsen characterized Hitler as indecisive on Jewish matters as on much else and detected signs of drift and compromise in the development of policy. Hitler's rhetoric about destroying the Jews was more in the nature of threats aimed at hostages with the purpose of intimidating the western democracies; he was 'out of the loop' of policy making until a very late stage.[32] There was no Führer order to destroy all the east European Jews at the time of Operation Barbarossa, the invasion of Russia on 22 June 1941, and 'we must conclude that Hitler gave no formal order to carry out the Final Solution of the "European Jewish question".'[33] Mommsen attributed Jewish policy to Himmler, head of the Gestapo and the SS, and Heydrich, and suggested that it was incrementally radicalized because of rivalries between the satraps in Hitler's court. Competing factions drove it forward as powerfully as any ideological input. The main strategy in dealing with the Jews up to July 1941 was emigration, and even after that had been cancelled there was still an element of experimentation with various 'solutions'. At the Wannsee Conference it was indicated that mass killing was only one experimental solution. The use of Jews for labour was a serious policy that became a cover for a generalized extermination only later.

> The Holocaust was not based upon a programme that had been developed over a long period. It was founded upon improvised measures that were rooted in earlier stages of planning and also escalated them. Once it had been set in motion, the extermination of those people who were declared unfit for work developed a dynamic of its own.[34]

Mommsen's explanation was subsequently challenged by Saul Friedländer who pointed to the illogicalities and dangers which resulted from abstracting Hitler so completely from the decision-making process. Friedländer countered by illustrating Hitler's persistent and detailed interventions in the formulation and conduct of Jewish policy. Although he acknowledged the important work of the 'functionalists', Friedländer argued that it actually bolstered the 'intentionalist' position. He expressed concern at the approach which sought to 'stress autonomous processes to such a degree that the role of Hitler was almost eliminated' and created the impression that the events in question were characterized by 'improvization and haphazardness'.[35]

The logic of this argument reached an apex of controversy in 1988 with the appearance of *Why Did the Heavens Not Darken?* by the American historian Arno Mayer. He constructed the German invasion of Russia as a crusade on the model of the Christian crusades in the Middle Ages. The fate of the Jews in Russia was a collateral effect of this war, in much the same way as had been the case with the devastation of Jewish communities by crusaders in .the Rhineland in the eleventh century.[36] According to Mayer, the *Einsatzgruppen* only incited pogroms, leaving their conduct mainly to locals, and merely shot small groups of selected Jews themselves. The systematized slaughter of whole communities came only once the blitzkrieg had broken down and the bitter German forces lashed out at the 'enemy' in their rear. Indeed, the massacres of Jews were always related to military perturbations.[37] Mayer did not regard the Wannsee Conference as indicative of a decisive shift in policy. Rather, he detected a 'tension' between the desire to exploit Jews for their labour and the desire to murder them as punishment for the failures of German arms. At Auschwitz, he argued, work details vied with the gas chambers to claim Jewish arrivals. Even those Jews who were transported from Polish and Russian ghettos to Belzec, Sobibor and Treblinka to be gassed immediately were only those 'unfit for work'.[38]

In the crucial debate over responsibility for, and the timing of, the decision for the Final Solution a great deal hinged on the activities of the *Einsatzgruppen*. Hilberg had depicted the assault on Russian Jewry as a 'prelude' to the destruction of the European Jews. The fact that some Russian Jews survived the first onslaught and were placed in ghettos was evidence only of an 'intermediary stage' before the Nazis had amassed sufficient resources or developed the technology to finish the job.[39] Krausnick, it will be recalled, inferred that a verbal order existed for the murder of all Jews, and pointed to the agreement between the SS and the army to select and deal with every Jew found among Soviet prisoners-of-war (POWs).[40] He maintained that the existence of a general order was self-evident from the vast toll of lives which the *Einsatzgruppen* exacted on the Jewish population in the areas overrun by the Nazi forces. Even so, Krausnick acknowledged certain inconsistencies such as the preservation of some Jews for labour in ghettos and conflicts over their use between the SS, the army and the occupation authorities.[41] By contrast, Adam, Broszat and Mommsen saw the *Einsatzgruppen* as engaged in limited operations, confined to certain categories of Jews in the eastern occupied territories. It was only once the killing operations had begun that a process of radicalization followed which, in turn, made practicable and conceivable the decision to murder all the Jews of Europe.[42]

For historiographical and also judicial reasons, it was consequently important to establish whether the members of the *Einsatzgruppen* were following an order to kill all Jews in Russia and, hence, were in the vanguard of a Europe-wide programme of destruction, or whether they had limited orders at first which were only expanded later. In their authoritative study of the *Einsatzgruppen*, Helmut Krausnick and Hans-Heinrich Wilhelm indicated that their commanders ordered the murder of Jews more or less indiscriminately, although not as part of a preordained and self-conscious extermination programme. The fact that the only surviving written order, from Heydrich to his field commanders on 2 July 1941, stipulated the execution of Jews who held positions in the Soviet state and Communist Party had to be set against the actual killing of women, children and the aged. Since *Einsatzgruppen* personnel would have been unlikely to exceed their orders, they argued that this indicated a prior verbal instruction to murder all Jews.[43]

However, it was the conviction of Alfred Streim, the head of the West German office for the prosecution of war criminals, that no such prior order was delivered: its existence was fabricated by defendants in post-war trials so that they could claim obedience to superior orders. Streim maintained that immediately after the invasion began the *Einsatzgruppen* confined themselves, as instructed, to inciting programs and shooting certain groups of Jews who fell within categories that might have been considered 'permissible' under martial law. The written order from Heydrich on 2 July 1941 giving instructions to shoot Jews in the state and party apparatus meant just that; it was not superseded until the end of July when the scale of killings escalated dramatically.

> The general order for the destruction of the Jews was not issued to the *Einsatzgruppen* prior to the invasion of the Soviet Union; rather, it was issued weeks later, approximately between the beginning of August 1941 at the earliest and September 1941 at the latest.[44]

Once again, Christopher Browning made a telling intervention in the debate. He suggested that among the *Einsatzgruppen* knowledge of the orders to kill Jews was likely to have been compartmentalized: not all the SS commanders need have known the details. Gradually, as the procedures were tried out in the field, the scope of the killing was expanded.[45] Subsequently, research has moved away from this concentration on the provenance, dating and content of the orders issued by the centre and paid greater attention to what occurred in the field. This tends to show that the killings did, indeed, start slowly and escalate after July 1941. But this might have reflected a natural caution on the part of the *Einsatzgruppen* commanders who were testing their men and the response of the local populations. There were also technical difficulties to overcome, such as finding suitably discreet locations for the killing sites, and the sheer size of the task. It was only after more personnel were drafted in that the scale of the murders jumps sharply. This signified the assurance which the *Einsatzgruppen* and SS commanders had gained through their operations, their confidence in a successful military outcome to the war, and a willingness to commit the resources needed for an expanded set of objectives.[46]

None of this need have precluded an overall plan of extermination at the centre which was shared with the highest SS field operatives, but the evidence remains far from conclusive. As the Swiss historian Philippe Burrin has pointed out, if it was always intended that the *Einsatzgruppen* would embark on the extermination of Russian Jewry, why was it necessary for the SS leadership to start looking for new, more 'efficient' methods of mass killing? He answers with a blend of the 'intentionalist' and 'functionalist' explanations. Burrin suggests that Hitler always intended to kill the Jews of Europe, but only if Germany was forced into a world war and only then if the conditions made this practicable. Hitler was haunted by Germany's defeat in 1918 which he blamed on the Jews. When, in the late summer of 1941, it looked as if the Soviet Union would not be a pushover and there were menacing signs of a rapprochement between Britain, the USSR and the United States of America, Hitler concluded that the Jews were responsible. He ordered the escalation of the murders in Russia and preparations for the extermination of Europe's Jews both as revenge for the setbacks at the front and to pre-empt 'Jewish treachery' of the sort that occurred in November 1918.[47]

OPERATION BARBAROSSA AND THE TIMING OF THE FINAL SOLUTION

As the above discussion illustrates, there has been some convergence of views on several key issues regarding the origin and timing of the Final Solution. However, the argument between the various schools of thought concerning the dating of the decision to implement the Final Solution and its relationship to the German invasion of Russia is by no means resolved. Those divergences and controversies are represented in the contributions to this collection. But Operation Barbarossa and the war in the east raise other important questions. To what extent was the leadership of the German Army, the *Wehrmacht*, implicated in the murderous attack on Russian Jews? And how did the lower echelons as well as the rank and file respond to the evidence of this genocidal enterprise?

The dating of the decision to embark on genocide is tackled by Professor Richard Breitman through a close study of the activities of Reichsführer-SS Heinrich Himmler. Breitman begins by establishing the importance of Himmler in the Nazi hierarchy and the implementation of Jewish policy.

It was Himmler who had control over the SS and the main agencies responsible for anti-Jewish measures; he made many personal interventions in this sphere. Breitman then examines the twists and turns in Nazi policy regarding the Jews between 1939 and 1941, seeking to identify the turning point which led to the Final Solution. In so doing, he stresses that the appearance of contradictions between policy and practice may be explained by the sheer amount of time taken up in planning major departures and the euphemisms in which they were cloaked. Breitman argues that the decision to 'purify' Europe of the Jews was taken in the course of December 1940–January 1941 at the same time as Hitler issued the orders to prepare for the attack on Russia. The persistence for several months of projects such as the Madagascar Plan and local expulsions of Jews from Germany to adjacent territories has been cited by some historians as evidence that, at this stage, there was no preconceived notion of mass annihilation. However, Breitman argues that such initiatives did not cut across plans for an ultimate exterminatory drive. What was possible in the east was not necessarily suitable in the west; Jews expelled from one place and interned somewhere else could be caught up with later on. This argument is supported in part by documentary evidence which was discovered in newly opened east European archives.

In his essay, Professor Jürgen Förster emphasizes the critical nexus between Hitler's racial thinking, the war for 'living space' and the extermination of Jewish Bolshevism in the east, and the beginning of the genocide. The instrumentality of warfare inevitably sucked the German Army into the realm of Hitler's world vision. However, Förster rejects the once fashionable argument that the German Army remained untainted by Hitler's racism and the policy of exterminating civilians. Förster shows that by 1939 the officer corps was permeated by racist ideology. Its conduct in Poland was marked by tolerance towards the brutal measures of the SS against the population; the only concern of the military leadership was to ensure discipline among its troops. Hitler's generals were left in no doubt that the war against the USSR would be a war of extermination. This did not arouse protests or misgivings because the racist, anti-Bolshevik and Social Darwinist outlook of the officer corps coincided with that of the Nazis and enabled them to work in harmony. This ideological affinity played a decisive role in enabling officers and soldiers to make the leap into abetting genocide. Anti-Bolshevism and racism were prominent in army propaganda and received official sanction in the orders of the day issued to the troops during Operation Barbarossa. It found practical expression in cooperation between the army and the *Einsatzgruppen*. Anti-partisan warfare further facilitated and deepened the ideological and day-to-day complicity of the army in the massacre of the Jews. Förster ends with reflections on the timing of the Final Solution from the standpoint of Operation Barbarossa. He concludes that the general extermination plan was arrived at in the summer of 1941, when the war against Russia fused racism, anti-Bolshevism and notions of *Lebensraum* to make possible the conceptualization and implementation of genocide.

Dr Christian Streit shares with Förster the belief that a shared racism and anti-Bolshevism secured the collaboration of the German Army in the murder of the Jews and, likewise, sees the war in the east as a vital step towards an overall plan for the destruction of the European Jews. However, he differs from Förster on the role of the *Einsatzgruppen* and the timing of the decision to kill all Jews in Russia and then Europe. Streit, following Streim, describes a process of radicalization in the killing. At first, the *Einsatzgruppen* proceeded cautiously since they were nervous about the army's response. It was, in any case, unrealistic of them to attempt to kill all Jews in the territories which they overran. For this reason they were happy to observe the flight of Jews to the Russian interior. It was only at the end of July 1941, once the German advance had slowed and the *Einsatzgruppen* had more time to murder large numbers of Jews, and in the knowledge that at the very least the army would acquiesce, that the scope of the shootings was expanded. Streit further argues that anti-Bolshevism, even more than Hitler's personality or interventions, propelled the liquidation of civilians in the east. It was buttressed by the nature of the anti-partisan war: inhibitions about the slaughter of non-combatants were eroded by a military campaign in which it was all too easy to blur the distinctions between Jews, Bolsheviks, partisans and civilians. Streit notes that non-Jewish Russians, identified automatically as Bolsheviks, were among the earliest victims of Nazi mass murder operations and offers this as proof that anti-Bolshevism was essential to both the compliance of the army and the transition to genocide.

Further evidence of the racism which permeated the *Wehrmacht*, enabling it to become an adjunct to the Final Solution, is presented here by Professor Omer Bartov. The complicity of the army was essential since the *Wehrmacht* conquered the areas in which the *Einsatzgruppen* roamed, supplied personnel and logistics in support of their killing operations, and directed its own units to undertake brutal 'cleansing' operations. The army was responsible for the deaths of half a million Soviet POWs and played its part in the brutal exploitation of the occupied territories. This could be accomplished without qualms because officers and men were previously indoctrinated with Nazi ideology when they were civilians, a process which continued once they became soldiers and to which the army command made no objection. Turning away from the debate over relations between the general staff and the SS, Bartov examines the attitudes of ordinary German troops and so illuminates the response of the civilians-turned-soldiers. He also graphically illustrates the effects of the barbarization of warfare on the Eastern Front and its repercussions on the sensitivities of soldiers regarding the murder of Jews, other civilians and POWs. In his view the German historian Andreas Hillgruber is quite wrong in suggesting that the Final Solution and the war in the east need to be confined to separate spheres. There was, he argues, a symbiotic relationship between the two.[48]

In a response to the thesis advanced by Adam, Broszat, Mommsen and Arno Mayer that the Final Solution was unleashed by Hitler as a reaction to military setbacks in Russia late in 1941, Professor Christopher Browning makes use of new documentation to date the Final Solution decision precisely to between mid-September and mid-October 1941 in the 'euphoria of victory'. Browning recapitulates the vicissitudes of German planning regarding the Jews in 1940, culminating in the collapse of the Madagascar Plan early in 1941. He then turns to the debate over the *Einsatzgruppen*, but highlights the behaviour of units at the 'sharp end' and what this tells us about their instructions. The killing process undoubtedly escalated sharply from mid-July, reflecting new orders to kill all Jews. The time-lag between the opening of the campaign and the increase in the figures for Jews who were murdered may be explained by the practical question of manpower which, in turn, illuminates the timing of the decision. It was only once Himmler had resolved to widen the net of the *Einsatzgruppen* to achieve the total annihilation of the Jews in Russia that sufficient resources were allocated to the task. By the end of July, the number of men assigned to the killing had jumped from the initial 4,000 personnel of the *Einsatzgruppen* to around 20,000 in various units. By the end of the year, the total stood at over 60,000. But not all of these units learned of their new tasks at the same time, hence the contradictory patterns of behaviour. Browning goes on to ask when the second decision to exterminate the Jews of Europe was made. He maintains that one consequence of the mid-July escalation was Goering's letter of 31 July 1941 charging Heydrich with the preparation of a Europe-wide plan for eliminating the Jews. Heydrich then instigated a 'feasibility study', but Hitler vacillated before taking the necessary practical steps. Hitler waited for the outcome of the war to be settled and repeatedly delayed the deportation of Jews from Germany 'to the east', where the killing system was ready to operate, until the German army stood at the gates of Moscow in September–October 1941. Then, in the flush of victory, he unleashed the Final Solution.

RESPONSES TO THE IMPLEMENTATION OF THE FINAL SOLUTION: THE JEWS IN OCCUPIED EUROPE

If we can see how hard it is for historians, writing with the benefit of hindsight and with access to a mass of documents, to pin down the origins and timing of the decision for the Final Solution it should be clear how terribly difficult, if not impossible, it was for people at the time to understand what was happening. The debate over timing is thus less than abstract: it fundamentally affects the way historians evaluate Jewish responses to Nazi persecution and the behaviour of the public in occupied Europe as well as that of the governments and populations in the free world. Yet in the early historiography it was common to take a harshly judgemental line towards the Jews. Poliakov wrote sympathetically of the struggle of the Nazi-appointed Jewish Councils in the ghettos to maintain a semblance of normal life. He praised the vitality of the incarcerated Jews who carried on social, cultural and religious activities regardless of their suffering. But he observed that when they were finally murdered they succumbed with the 'quiet and resigned courage' which typified the Jewish reaction to persecution from medieval times. Jews in the west were simply fooled by the Nazis and unable, naturally, to comprehend something unprecedented and so evil. He devoted a chapter to Jewish resistance, built around the story of the Warsaw Ghetto uprising and mentioned the Jewish partisans, but on the whole treated this as a stark exception to the pattern of Jewish responses.[49] Gerald Reitlinger commented on the 'blind fatalism of the Polish Jews' and the equal 'fatalism' of the Galician Jews. He, too, wrote of the Warsaw Ghetto revolt, though in caustic tones as a setback to the smooth running of German plans.[50]

Although Raul Hilberg disavowed an intention to write about Jews, in the opening pages of his classic study and towards the end he delivered several harsh and critical judgements on Jewish behaviour. The 'Jewish collapse' under the Nazi assault was 'a manifestation of failure'. He detected a 'Jewish reaction pattern' of alleviation-compliance that he traced to the medieval Jewish paradigm. In short, Jewish leadership during the Nazi crisis was seriously inadequate and Jewish responses were so inept as to make the Germans' task much easier for them.[51] Hilberg's damning comments were taken up by the German-Jewish émigré writer Hannah Arendt who covered the Eichmann trial in Jerusalem in 1961 for the *New Yorker* magazine. In the book based on her articles she complimented Hilberg who had 'exposed for the first time in all its pathetic and sordid detail' the failure of the Jewish reaction. But she went still further. Reviewing the conduct of the Jewish Councils established by German fiat in the ghettos of Russia and Poland, and the cognate bodies acting as intermediaries between the Jews in western countries and the Nazis, she concluded that more Jews would have survived if there had been no Jewish leaders at all.[52]

This rebuke triggered an avalanche of articles and books on Jewish behaviour in Nazi Europe. It was mostly hostile to Arendt and heavily polemical.[53] Eventually, however, the controversy resulted in a rich body of work on the dilemmas of Jewish life in occupied Europe, threw light on the widely diverse patterns of Jewish behaviour, and resulted in a deeper understanding of the term 'resistance'. Historians writing against the Hilberg–Arendt interpretation pointed out that it depended almost exclusively on German sources which were predisposed to depict the Jews as hapless victims or incompetent. Rather, they turned to Jewish sources – ghetto diaries, memoirs in Yiddish and Hebrew and oral history – to illuminate for the first time the inner world of the ghettos. This revealed a high level of cultural activity and a remarkable spiritual resilience that signified defiance of Nazi efforts to dehumanize and humiliate the Jews.[54] They also directed greater attention to the Jewish partisans and the participation of Jews in the western European resistance movements, using more sensitive readings of German documents to show the extent of Jewish armed opposition.[55]

Professor Yisrael Gutman, himself a survivor of the Warsaw Ghetto, played a leading role in the debate over the 'Arendt thesis' and the research which provided a reply to it. He begins his overview of Polish Jewish responses to the implementation of the Final Solution by noting that in the early historiography, the behaviour of the Jews was either misunderstood, marginalized or ignored totally. Hilberg, for example, did not include in his study any background material on the history, society or structure of Polish Jewry which had such an important impact on their reactions to Nazi rule. Gutman points out that unlike the Jews in Germany, Polish Jews did not have the luxury of time in which to adapt to Nazi policy. They were immediately placed under the lash of oppressive regulations leading to ghettoization. Polish Jews subverted these regulations in myriad ways and constructed a vibrant underground life in the ghettos. They defied the Nazis by procuring food illegally, establishing an illicit press and conducting political and cultural activities. By the summer of 1941, Jews in the ghettos had developed a *modus vivendi* with the local German administrations and there was no sign of imminent destruction. Operation Barbarossa and the radicalization of Nazi policy by the centre, on ideological grounds, reversed trends towards the stabilization of life in the ghettos. Polish Jewry soon learned the truth about the 'deportations', but still found it hard to grasp that a programme of complete annihilation was in full swing. The Nazis fostered their confusion and reluctance to see the worst by selecting only certain groups for 'resettlement' and proceeding in stages. Many, especially among the leadership, believed that working for the Germans would guarantee the survival of at least a proportion of the Jews. Others, notably among the young and the political activists, resolved on physical resistance. They did so despite the enormous obstacles and in the knowledge that it could not serve as a means of rescue.

For nearly three years, Polish Jewry existed under the Nazis, traversing the gradations of Nazi persecution from the confiscation of property, ghettoization, elimination from the economy, forced labour, starvation and disease until the onset of the Final Solution and the deportations. In her contribution, Professor Dina Porat points out that the experience of Lithuanian Jews was unique because they were plunged immediately into the maelstrom of death and destruction. The impact of German policy in Lithuania was singular because of its geographical proximity to German-controlled territory in 1941 and the enthusiastic participation of the local population. As a consequence, the blow was felt sooner, more swiftly and more harshly than elsewhere: approximately 80 per cent of Lithuania's 175,000 Jews had been killed by the close of 1941. Porat proposes that the *Einsatzgruppen* learned from the Lithuanians' savage assault on the Jews: the pogroms in Kovno and Vilna helped to habituate the Germans to massive slaughter. Turning to the Jewish response, she argues that Lithuanian Jews perceived the nature of German plans before any other Jewish community. Due to the inclusion of Vilna in Lithuania in 1939 and the relative freedom prevailing in the country until June 1940, Lithuanian Jews had gained a deeper insight into German behaviour than Jews in the USSR. In addition, they were well organized, especially the youth movements. Because they realized the nature of the Final Solution sooner, Lithuanian Jews also prepared for armed resistance earlier. Furthermore, she suggests that this resolve was fostered by the distinctive cultural heritage of Lithuanian Jewry. Professor Porat concludes by summarizing the events in the Vilna ghetto which culminated in the abortive rising there.

Both Gutman and Porat observe that Jewish responses to Nazi persecution must be placed in the context of local conditions and the reaction of local populations. The *Einsatzgruppen* in Lithuania were highly satisfied with the cooperation of the local population and recruited thousands of Lithuanians into auxiliary units. Few Poles helped the Jews during the Warsaw Ghetto revolt which rendered the possibilities for effective Jewish resistance even more remote.

RESPONSES TO THE FINAL SOLUTION IN GERMANY, AXIS AND CLIENT STATES AND CONQUERED COUNTRIES

Once the Final Solution was set in motion, and Jews were being 'combed out' from west to east throughout Europe, the Nazis had to deal with the regimes of their allies and client states, and the administrations of the conquered states. The fate of the Jews depended, in turn, upon the way the authorities and the public reacted to Nazi demands for their deportation. Each case was different and each has its own historiography, frequently riven by controversies that bear on and are inflamed by present-day political disputes.[56] Two examples are presented here, each highlighting different strands in the contemporary debate.

Doctor Jonathan Steinberg looks at the experience of Croatia, a classic German client state, and includes within the ambit of his inquiry the response of the Roman Catholic church locally and its relations with the Vatican. His discussion of Croatia thus introduces a separate debate over the role of the Vatican during the Final Solution.[57] The Croats needed little encouragement to enact anti-Jewish laws after the Germans created the new, officially Roman Catholic Croat state out of the ruins of Yugoslavia in April 1941. However, although the Jews were prominent among the victims of the nationalist and fascist regime, the Orthodox Serbs were the chief object of Croat attentions. Steinberg elucidates the role of the Roman Catholic clergy in inciting and sanctioning the attempted genocide of Serbs in Croatia. He suggests that the Catholic leadership suffered a moral short-circuiting due to an overriding nationalist fervour. In this border region, religion and national identity fused. Genocide became policy for reasons of state and national survival, and the national church could not disengage from the process. Since the Croat state embraced Roman Catholicism, the Vatican was disinclined to protest overmuch about its conduct even though it was well informed about what was going on there. Finally, Steinberg throws light on German conduct in Europe by comparing it to the actions of the Croats. Contrary to the common presumptions about the singularity of Nazi atrocities, he shows that the Croats were just as barbarous. The form of genocide they practised may not have been technically as sophisticated as that evolved by the Germans, but methodologically it was hardly different from the work of the *Einsatzgruppen* in Poland and Russia. He observes that the distinction was visceral: the Croats hated Serbs, feared them and so murdered them, while the SS apparatus, once set up, acted mechanically and unemotionally.

Vichy France was nominally a sovereign state with an ambiguous role in the governance of the part of France occupied by Germany after the French capitulation in June 1940. Since the early 1980s there has been heated debate over the extent to which the Vichy regime autonomously anticipated Nazi ordinances for the persecution of Jews, collaborated willingly with the deportations of Jews from French territory or acted prudently to protect the interests of all French citizens, regardless of their religious denomination.[58] The interpretation of collaboration and the treatment of the Jews remains a deeply divisive issue in French society and politics. A succession of war crimes trials, most notably those of Klaus Barbie and Paul Touvier, has kept alive controversy about France's wartime past.[59]

Dr John Fox joins the debate by challenging the view of Vichy as an unequivocally collaborationist regime that was infused with anti-Semitism and keen to hand over Jews to the Nazis for deportation to death camps. He argues that initially Vichy officials did not know for certain about the Final Solution, and cannot therefore be accused of complicity in the extermination programme. They certainly did want to get rid of thousands of stateless and foreign Jews in their territory and so were only too happy to round up these categories to meet German requests for Jews to 'work' in the east. Once they had a firmer grasp of what was occurring in 'the east' they were still prepared to hand over foreign Jews, but resisted the inclusion of French Jews in the transportations. The reasons for this stubbornness stemmed from the defence of domestic sovereignty, but were reinforced by prudence as the tide of war turned against the Third Reich. Thus, the numbers of Jews seized by the Nazis decreased following the German military reverses in November 1942 although the Germans now actually occupied the Free Zone (as Vichy was also known). Fox concludes that since Vichy and the Germans had different goals their actions cannot be equated.

Part of Fox's argument rests on the evaluation of how much French officials knew about German intentions towards the Jews and the line between knowing and believing, a distinction first elaborated in this context by Walter Laqueur.[60] He makes the point that the extent of knowledge about the Final Solution is central to assessing the responses of governments and public opinion in the occupied countries and the free world. This caveat applies equally well to the German people themselves.

The question of 'what the Germans knew' was relatively neglected in historiography until quite recently. The Nuremberg Tribunal presumed the collective guilt of the German people, while the assumption that no such thing as 'public opinion' could exist in a totalitarian state deterred further inquiry. This changed with the belated 'discovery' of the secret police reports on the public mood in Germany throughout the Nazi period. The publication of these reports and commentaries on them stimulated a lively debate. Lawrence Stokes in 1973 established that knowledge of the *Einsatzgruppen* operations was widespread, but information about such atrocities helped to cow the population into silence. He detected a 'mixture of private sympathy and public passivity' in the face of the deportations of the Jews from Germany.[61] Otto Dov Kulka argued that the Nazi regime succeeded in totally depersonalizing the Jews, but not sufficiently to avoid Germans experiencing apprehension and the fear of reprisals. Yet this was a 'pragmatic response' and only threw into relief 'a striking abysmal indifference to the fate of the Jews as human beings'.[62] Ian Kershaw drew quite different conclusions from his research for a major study of Bavaria under the Nazis. According to his findings, Germans showed a 'minimal interest' in the mass slaughter of the Jews. They were more concerned with anxieties about the outcome of the war and the daily struggle to survive. Retreating into a 'private sphere', they 'thought little and asked less about the fate of the Jews in the East'.[63]

Kershaw was taken to task by Otto Dov Kulka and Aron Rodrigue in a joint article that criticized his value-free notion of 'indifference' and inner retreat. Instead, they suggested that Germans internalized the negative stereotypes of the Jews purveyed in Nazi propaganda. This produced 'passive complicity' in the destruction of the Jews.[64] In a later article, Kershaw qualified his concept of 'indifference' but insisted that there was a range of responses. Apathy and neutrality could coexist with either hostility or sympathy towards the Jews.[65] Hans Mommsen considered that Germans at all levels of the population were willingly desensitized to the suffering of the Jews. They allowed themselves to accept the progressive isolation of the Jews and the euphemisms about their fate which, at each stage of persecution, enabled Germans to indulge in 'collective suppression'.[66]

In this volume, Professor David Bankier traverses such well-trodden ground, but makes many fresh points based on his original work with widely diverse sources. In particular, he investigates the relatively unexplored question of how Germans responded to information about the Final Solution. Bankier reveals that Nazi propaganda about the Jews, and protests against their treatment broadcast by the Allies, made Germans aware of the crimes being committed. By 1943, church leaders were aware of the unease among the population, but it was hard for Germans to break with the world outlook of the regime which they had supported for ten years. Ironically, Nazi propaganda prevented the population from pushing the Jewish issue out of their thoughts. Instead, it preyed on their minds. Goebbels's assertions that the Jews were behind the Allies induced fear and guilt among a people with more than an inkling of what had befallen them. The way in which ordinary Germans analysed the *Wehrmacht*'s military reverses and the punishing bombing of German cities betrayed feelings of guilt and the fear of revenge. Yet the pervasiveness of Nazi anti-Jewish propaganda, the statements by leaders of the regime and awareness of what was happening to the Jews provoked 'alienation' or withdrawal and denial. The more evident the truth, the more it was evaded by psychological devices.

RESPONSES TO THE IMPLEMENTATION OF THE FINAL SOLUTION: THE FREE WORLD

It has already been noted that knowledge about the Final Solution or, rather, belief in the information that an extermination programme was being carried out, determined the response of public opinion and governments in the free world. From the mid-1960s, a growing familiarity with the history of the Final Solution caused writers and scholars in various fields to ask what the Allies had been doing at the time. By the 1980s a whole new field of research into the behaviour of the Allied governments along with Jewish and non-Jewish responses to news of the Final Solution had been opened up.

In the United States, a heated debate was set off by Arthur D. Morse, the title of whose book *While Six Million Died: A Chronicle of American Apathy* tells its own story succinctly. It triggered similarly polemical inquiries into the activity of the Jewish community in America, which proved an even more explosive subject.[67] Subsequent scholarly debate was polarized around two questions. First, did the Roosevelt administration do enough to assist the Jews in Nazi Europe once the truth about the annihilation plan was known? Second, could American Jews have done more to help their brethren by pressing the American government to take some form of action?

Henry Feingold questioned whether it made sense to accuse the US administration of being 'callously indifferent' or subject to anti-Semitic influences if the fate of the Jews hardly came to its attention. He argued that prior to the spring of 1943, the western Allies were totally preoccupied with gaining the initiative in the war and not losing it. When the Roosevelt administration had the opportunity to ponder the Jewish issue, the range of options available to it was limited by the extent of Nazi domination over Europe. Moreover, Roosevelt considered that American public opinion would not tolerate extensive resources being put at the disposal of rescue measures. Feingold argued that, in any case, by the time the administration could have achieved positive results by threatening reprisals against the Nazis or bombing the railway lines to Auschwitz it was almost too late to make any difference. American Jewish leaders failed not because they did too little, but because they had an unrealistic perception of the humanitarianism of Roosevelt and the administration.[68] Feingold's study was followed by two volumes by David S. Wyman who offered a comprehensive and damning indictment of Roosevelt, the administration, the news media and the churches. They were accused of indifference at best, and anti-Semitic disdain of the Jewish plight at worst. Wyman was no less scathing towards the official Jewish leadership.[69] Subsequently, Richard Breitman and Alan M. Kraut sought to modify this picture of monolithic indifference with a more nuanced one that stressed the fluctuating dynamic between military possibilities, ideology and domestic politics. They questioned the extent to which anti-Semitic currents decisively influenced the administration or public opinion.[70]

A similar, if muted, version of this debate took place in Britain. It was opened in 1973 by A. J. Sherman's *Island Refuge*, a study of British policy towards Jewish refugees from Nazism up to the outbreak of the war, and Bernard Wasserstein's *Britain and the Jews of Europe*, published six years later. Wasserstein revealed Britain's dismal wartime record on Jewish refugees and rescue attempts. He showed that the reluctance to admit refugees to the United Kingdom, the colonies or the dominions was related to the government's determination to keep Jews out of Palestine. Wasserstein also chronicled the scepticism with which Foreign Office personnel greeted information about the massacre of Jews in Europe, often informed by a disparaging attitude towards the behaviour of Jewish people in general. However, he concluded that the low priority assigned to rescue plans, including the refusal to bomb Auschwitz in 1944 when the air force had the capacity to do so, stemmed chiefly from 'imaginative failure', and a refusal to treat the Jews as a 'special case' due to a 'collective paranoia' about the implications of recognizing them as a national group.[71] Martin Gilbert added to the analysis of Allied responses in his close examination of how news of Auschwitz reached the west and how the Allied governments reacted or, rather, failed to react. He made the point that Nazi deception blurred the truth about Auschwitz until mid-1944, although before then the Allies could not have done much to stop its dreadful operations. After that time, he attributed Allied inaction to failures of 'imagination, of response, of Intelligence, of piecing together and evaluating what was known, of co-ordination, of initiative, and even at times sympathy'.[72]

Wasserstein was criticized by John Fox who cautioned that Britain's refusal to accept refugees from Europe before the instigation of the Final Solution should not be evaluated with hindsight. Once the British government was convinced of the Nazi extermination programme, its scope for a response was greatly limited by the Allies' military position. In any case, the Allies reasonably saw the salvation of the Jews as part and parcel of the liberation of all of occupied Europe.[73] Fox had earlier also argued that the British government had been understandably cautious when confronted by evidence of the Final Solution, but went on to play a leading role in developing a war crimes policy intended, in part, to admonish the Germans.[74] The controversies over governmental and public responses to news of the Final Solution in America and Britain are important in their own right, but they are especially significant as the context in which to evaluate the reaction of the Jews of these countries.

In this collection, Professor Aaron Berman offers an insight into the response of Jews in the United States under the impact of US policy. In particular he focuses on the actions of the American Zionists. They had learned in the 1930s that the administration would not open the country's doors to Jewish refugees, so they poured their energies and resources into building up the Jewish National Home in Palestine. This positive work enhanced their profile and prestige in the American Jewish community. After Britain sealed Palestine to Jewish refugees from Europe, the leaders of the Zionist movement in Palestine turned to American Jews to mount a political campaign for immediate Jewish statehood, thus removing British control over immigration. The rescue of Europe's Jews, Zionist political goals and the domestic aims of the American Zionists appeared to dovetail. When the news of the Final Solution reached the public in the USA, it provoked a wave of anguish and protest. Zionist leaders lobbied the administration to secure some form of Allied intervention and succeeded in obtaining the Bermuda Conference on refugees. The lacklustre outcome of the conference confirmed the majority of American Zionists in the tactics they had adopted before 1939. If America would not open its doors, the only alternative was to campaign for immediate Jewish statehood. Few recognized that this policy was now out of kilter with reality and that a 'rescue first' campaign would have been more appropriate.

In his essay on the responses of the British government, public and Anglo-Jewry to information about the Final Solution, Dr Tony Kushner challenges what he sees as the overly reductive character of the debate up to now. He argues that the raw information about the events in Europe was interpreted within a pre-existing ideological matrix, in this case liberalism. According to liberal thinking the Jews were a religious group and not a nation and so stood outside Allied war aims. Moreover, the universalistic basis of liberalism made it difficult to see or treat Jews as a 'special case'. This ideologically determined approach coincided with, and reinforced, the belief that the Jews could only be saved by winning the war. Kushner also criticizes the over-concentration on political leaders, church spokesmen and opinion formers to the exclusion of how ordinary people in all walks of life received information about the mass murder of the Jews. To correct this imbalance he sets out to provide a social history of knowledge about the Final Solution written 'from below'. His study draws on a wide range of sources, including the hitherto neglected raw material collected by Mass-Observation. Kushner shows that governmental leadership was essential in shaping popular attitudes towards the terrible news from Europe. Without a lead from official agencies explaining why it was significant and urgent, boredom set in and the statistics of murder became meaningless. Failure to associate the alleviation of Jewish suffering with the war effort left the public with little reason to identify with the victims of the Final Solution. The agitation that followed the revelation of the Nazi extermination plan in November–December 1942 quickly subsided. British Jews had plenty of information, too, but their response was inflected by the particular pressures which they felt themselves to be under. Afraid of seeming only interested in the suffering of their own people, preoccupied by the scale of wartime anti-Semitism on the Home Front, and drained by various calls on their philanthropy, only a handful possessed the capacity to realize the enormity of the catastrophe on the continent.

Wasserstein and Gilbert, as well as American historians such as Monty Noam Penkower, have related the paucity of the official British response to the extermination of the Jews to the apprehension that Jews who escaped from Nazi Europe might seek refuge in Palestine. This territory occupied by Britain in the First World War, had been a British Mandate under the League of Nations since 1922. Since the Balfour Declaration in 1917, the British government had a nominal commitment to assist the creation of a Jewish National Home there, an obligation embodied in the terms of the Mandate. From the outset, however, this project aroused bitter Arab opposition. Afraid of alienating the Arab world by actively pursuing the creation of a Jewish National Home in Palestine, since 1939 the British authorities had drastically curbed Jewish immigration. For similar reasons, during the war they prevaricated over the creation of a Jewish fighting force.[75] Thus the response of the *Yishuv*, the Jewish community of Mandatory Palestine, was framed within what it knew about the Final Solution and what their British rulers would permit them to do in response.

In 1986 the Israeli historian, Dina Porat, published the first major study of how the Zionist leadership in the *Yishuv* responded to news of the systematic murder of Europe's Jews. She revealed trends that were close to those evident among diaspora Jewish communities in the free world. They, too, faced the initial problem of obtaining information and then of comprehending it, although in this case it was modified by unflattering preconceptions about the behaviour of Jews in the *galut* or exile. Once the seriousness of the crisis was grasped, there was an agonizing debate over how to respond in a situation not of their making, and in which they were treated by the Allies as 'a tolerated annoyance'. Yet Porat exposed the unwillingness to elevate rescue above the established goals of the Zionist movement. She also drew attention to the continuity of everyday life in the *Yishuv* despite the extensive knowledge of the disaster befalling the Jews in Europe.[76]

Professor Dalia Ofer's essay combines the response of both the Jews of the *Yishuv* and the Allies. She details how Jews in Palestine were well informed about events in Europe, but still unable to come to terms with the extent and meaning of the destruction unfolding before them. Rather, they adhered to the pre-1939 policies of fostering legal and illegal immigration and working towards political independence. At first, they placed great faith in the Allies to help the Jews of Europe. It was only once they were disillusioned that they hesitantly set out on their own rescue projects. Ofer reveals the way a mutuality of interests then developed, quite by accident, between the Allied intelligence services and the Mossad, the body which was conducting the rescue missions sent out from the *Yishuv*. The possibility that Jewish refugees from Nazi-occupied Europe might supply intelligence to the Allies enabled the *Yishuv* to gain a measure of Allied cooperation in rescue efforts. But Ofer exposes the limits to the real sympathy or merely pragmatic attitude of British military personnel. Time and again promising initiatives foundered when British Foreign Office officials and embassy staff placed obstacles in their way.

HISTORIOGRAPHY AND SOME ATTEMPTS AT A CONCLUSION

Several of the contributions to this collection make use of documents which have been discovered in archives in the former Soviet Union which were closed to Western researchers until the era of glasnost. The collapse and fragmentation of the Soviet empire has increased still further the opportunities for research in these collections. Professor Shmuel Krakow-ski, head of the Yad Vashem Archive in Jerusalem, has led several dele-gations of academics to the former USSR in the search for material on the Final Solution. In his essay, he summarizes the main features of the massive reservoir of documentation that lies there. Krakowski concludes that in the light of these newly revealed archives, the historiography of the Final Solution may yet undergo further mutations.

The notion that the current corpus of work must, necessarily, be treated as partial is taken up by Professor Yehuda Bauer in his reflections on the meaning of the Wannsee Conference. Bauer argues that historians must delve for the significance of the Final Solution as a product of human agency. They need to understand the victims, the bystanders and the perpetrators in order to come closer to comprehending humankind's behaviour. But he balks at the notion of drawing 'lessons' from this awful period of history. Such 'lessons' inevitably mutate with each generation and, anyway, tend towards either banality or the self-serving purposes of those drawing them. Indeed, there are any number of attempts to misrep-resent the Final Solution or to use it as an essentially empty, free-floating symbol of evil. Bauer protests against attempts either to drain the Final Solution of specific meaning or to freeze it in history. He warns that the new documents may anyway shake up the received wisdom of the his-torians. Above all, he admonishes that the attempted genocide of the Jews is a part of human history, something which humans made. As such, no effort should be spared to learn about the Final Solution and to come to terms with it lest such a thing be repeated.

NOTES

I would like to thank Professor Ian Kershaw, Dr John Fox and Dr Tony Kushner for their comments on an earlier draft of this introduction.

1 The outstanding guide to this literature up to the late 1980s is Michael Marrus, *The Holocaust in History* (Toronto, 1987; published in paperback by Penguin Books, London, 1989).
2 Gideon Shimoni (ed.) *The Holocaust in University Teaching* (Oxford, 1991).
3 Richard Evans, *In Hitler's Shadow: West German Historians and the Attempt to Escape from the Nazi Past* (London, 1987); Charles Maier, *The Unmasterable Past: History, Holocaust and German National Identity* (Cambridge, Mass., 1988); Peter Baldwin (ed.) *Reworking the Past. Hitler, the Holocaust and the Historians' Debate* (Boston, Mass., 1990).
4 Roger Eatwell, 'The Holocaust denial: a study in propaganda technique', in L. Cheles, R. Ferguson and M. Vaughan (eds) *Neo-Fascism in Europe* (London, 1991).
5 The most recent, exhaustive study of this meeting is Kurt Pätzold and Erika Schwarz, *Tagesordnung: Judenmord. Die Wannsee-Konferenz am 20. Januar 1942* (Berlin, 1992).

6 Eberhard Jäckel, *Hitler in History* (Hanover, NH, 1984), p. 55, and the contribution to this volume by Yehuda Bauer.

7 Jacob Katz, *From Prejudice to Destruction: Anti-Semitism, 1700–1933* (Cambridge, Mass., 1980), gives a comprehensive overview while Peter Pulzer, *The Rise of Political Antisemitism in Germany and Austria* (Oxford, second edn, 1992), focuses on the German-speaking world. Both have wide-ranging bibliographies.

8 Hannah Arendt, *The Origins of Totalitarianism*, Pt 2, *Imperialism*, (New York, 1951); Leon Poliakov, *The Aryan Myth. A History of Racist and Nationalist Ideas in Europe* (London, 1974); George L. Mosse, *Toward the Final Solution: A History of European Racism* (London, 1978).

9 Gitta Sereny, *Into that Darkness. From Mercy Killing to Mass Murder* (London, 1974); Ernst Klee, *'Euthanasia' im NS-Staat. Die 'Vernichtung lebensunwerten Lebens'* (Frankfurt am Main, 1983); Benno Müller-Hill, *Tödliche Wissenschaft. Die Aussonderung von Juden, Zigeunern und Geisteskranken 1933–1945* (Hamburg, 1984), published in English as *Murderous Science. Elimination by Scientific Selection of Jews, Gypsies, and Others, Germany 1933–1945* (Oxford, 1988); Robert Jay Lifton, *The Nazi Doctors. Medical Killing and the Psychology of Genocide* (New York, 1986).

10 Lifton, *The Nazi Doctors*, pp. 14–18. For an excellent synthesis, see Michael Burleigh and Wolfgang Wipperman, *The Racial State. Germany 1933–1945* (Cambridge, 1991).

11 Marrus, *Holocaust in History*, pp. 31–46, gives a lucid exposition of the rival schools which dominated interpretations of the Final Solution from the early 1970s to the late 1980s.

12 Leon Poliakov, *Harvest of Hate* (London, 1956; first published in French in 1951), p. 106.

13 Gerald Reitlinger, *The Final Solution: The Attempt to Exterminate the Jews of Europe, 1939–1945* (London, 1953), pp. 80–1.

14 Wolfgang Scheffler, *Judenverfolgung im Dritten Reich 1933–45* (Berlin, 1960), pp. 35–6.

15 Raul Hilberg, *The Destruction of the European Jews* (Chicago, Ill., 1961), pp. 257, 262.

16 Helmut Krausnick and Martin Broszat, *Anatomy of the SS State* (London, 1970; first published in Germany in 1965), pp. 78–85.

17 Poliakov, *Harvest of Hate*, pp. 15–57.

18 Reitlinger, *The Final Solution*, pp. 30–2.

19 Hilberg, *The Destruction of the European Jews*, p. 263.

20 Krausnick and Broszat, *Anatomy of the SS State*, pp. 79–81.

21 Uwe Dietrich Adam, *Judenpolitik im Dritten Reich* (Düsseldorf, 1972), pp. 306–12.

22 Karl Schleunes, *The Twisted Road to Auschwitz: Nazi Policy Towards the Jews, 1933–1939* (Urbana, Ill., 1970).

23 For an incisive summary of the various schools of thought, see Ian Kershaw, *The Nazi Dictatorship* (London, 1985), Chapter 4.

24 Lucy S. Dawidowicz, *The War Against the Jews* (New York, 1975), pp. 147–65. See also Gerald Fleming, *Hitler and the Final Solution* (London, 1985; first published in German in 1982), a stern corrective to David Irving's distortion of history in his book *Hitler's War* (London, 1977) and a powerful statement of the 'intentionalist' case.

25 Martin Broszat, 'Hitler and the genesis of the 'Final Solution': an assessment

of David Irving's theses', *Yad Vashem Studies*, 13 (1979), pp. 73–125. The article first appeared in German in 1977.

26 ibid., pp. 92–3, fn. 26.

27 ibid., pp. 93–102.

28 Christopher R. Browning, *The Final Solution and the German Foreign Office: A Study of Referat D III of Abteilung Deutschland, 1940–1943* (New York, 1978).

29 Christopher R. Browning, 'A reply to Martin Broszat regarding the origins of the Final Solution', *Simon Wiesenthal Centre Annual*, 1 (1984), pp. 113–32. The article first appeared in German in 1981.

30 ibid., pp. 114, 120–1, 122.

31 ibid., pp. 124–7.

32 Hans Mommsen, 'The realization of the unthinkable: the Final Solution of the Jewish question in the Third Reich', in idem, *From Weimar to Auschwitz* (Oxford, 1991), pp. 233, 237. The article first appeared in German in 1983 and in English in Gerhard Hirschfeld (ed.), *The Policies of Genocide: Jews and Soviet Prisoners of War in Nazi Germany* (London, 1986).

33 ibid., pp. 234–6.

34 ibid., pp. 245–6, 248–9, 250.

35 Saul Friedländer, 'From anti-Semitism to extermination: a historiographical study of Nazi policy towards the Jews and an essay in interpretation', *Yad Vashem Studies*, 16 (1984), pp. 1–50.

36 Arno Mayer, *Why Did the Heavens Not Darken?* (New York, 1988), pp. 217–26.

37 ibid., pp. 234–5, 257–9.

38 ibid., pp. 310–12, 348–75, 400–2.

39 Hilberg, *The Destruction of the European Jews*, pp. 224–42.

40 See also Christian Streit, *Keine Kameraden. Die Wehrmacht und die sowjetischen Kriegsgefangenen 1941–1945* (Stuttgart, 1978) and Chapter 6 of this volume.

41 Krausnick and Broszat, *Anatomy of the SS State*, pp. 79–81, 86–8.

42 Adam, *Judenpolitik im Dritten Reich*, pp. 306–12; Broszat, 'Hitler and the genesis of the "Final Solution"', p. 85; Mommsen, 'The realization of the unthinkable', p. 235.

43 Helmut Krausnick and Hans-Heinrich Wilhelm, *Die Truppen des Weltanschauungskrieges* (Stuttgart, 1981), pp. 533–47, 618–35; Helmut Krausnick, 'Hitler und die Befehle an die Einsatzgruppen im Sommer 1941', in Eberhard Jäckel and Jürgen Rohwer (eds) *Der Mord an den Juden im Zweiten Weltkrieg* (Stuttgart, 1985), pp. 96–103.

44 Alfred Streim, 'Zur Eröffnung des allgemeinen Judenvernichtungsbefehls gegenüber den Einsatzgruppen', in Jäckel and Rohwer, *Der Mord an den Juden*, pp. 107–19 and idem, 'The tasks of the SS Einsatzgruppen', *Simon Wiesenthal Centre Annual* 4 (1987), pp. 309–28. See also the exchange between Krausnick and Streim, *Simon Wiesenthal Centre Annual*, 6 (1989), pp. 311–29.

45 Christopher R. Browning, *Fateful Months. Essays on the Emergence of the Final Solution* (New York, 1991; first published in 1985), pp. 16–20.

46 Yehoshua Büchler, 'Kommandostab Reichsführer-SS: Himmler's personal murder brigades in 1941', *Holocaust and Genocide Studies*, 1:1 (1986), pp. 11–25; Yaacov Lozowick, 'Rollbahn Mord: The early Activities of Einsatzgruppe C', *Holocaust and Genocide Studies*, 2:2 (1987), pp. 221–41; Ronald Headland, 'The *Einsatzgruppen*: the question of their initial operations',

Holocaust and Genocide Studies, 4:4 (1989), pp. 401–12. And see the contribution to this volume by Christopher R. Browning.

47 Philippe Burrin, *Hitler et les Juifs. Genèse d'un génocide* (Paris, 1989), pp. 17–18, 32–3, 117–18, 127–8.

48 Andreas Hillgruber, *Zweierlei Untergang: Die Zerschlagung des Deutschen Reiches und das Ende des europäischen Judentums* (Berlin, 1986).

49 Poliakov, *Harvest of Hate*, pp. 88–90, 95–8, 117, 155, 189–92.

50 Reitlinger, *The Final Solution*, pp. 270–1.

51 Hilberg, *The Destruction of the European Jews*, pp. v, 1, 14–17, 206–8, 316–18.

52 Hannah Arendt, *Eichmann in Jerusalem. A Report on the Banality of Evil* (New York, 1963), pp. 104, 110–11, 117–18.

53 For a characteristically trenchant rebuttal of Arendt, see Jacob Robinson, *And The Crooked Shall Be Made Straight* (Philadelphia, Pa, 1975).

54 Isaiah Trunk, *Judenrat: The Jewish Councils in Eastern Europe under Nazi Occupation* (New York, 1972); Emmanuel Ringelblum, *Notes from the Warsaw Ghetto*, ed. Jacob Sloan (New York, 1974); Dawidowicz, *The War Against the Jews*, Pt 2; Isaiah Trunk, *Jewish Responses to Nazi Persecution: Collective and Individual Behaviour in Extremis* (New York, 1982); Yisrael Gutman, *The Jews of Warsaw, 1939–1943: Ghetto, Underground, Revolt* (Bloomington, Ind., 1983); Lucjan Dobroszycki (ed.) *The Chronicle of the Lodz Ghetto, 1941–1944* (New Haven, 1984); Shimon Huberband, *Kiddush Hashem: Jewish Religious and Cultural Life in Poland During the Holocaust* (New York, 1987).

55 Reuben Ainsztein, *Jewish Resistance in Nazi-Occupied Europe* (New York, 1974); Yuri Suhl (ed.) *They Fought Back: The Story of the Jewish Resistance in Nazi Europe* (New York, 1975); Shmuel Krakowski, *The War of the Doomed: Jewish Armed Resistance in Poland, 1942–1944* (New York, 1984); Dov Levin, *Fighting Back: Lithuanian Jewry's Armed Resistance to the Nazis, 1941–1944* (New York, 1985).

56 Marrus, *The Holocaust in History*, pp. 55–84, 99–107; Helen Fein, *Accounting for Genocide: National Responses and Jewish Victimisation during the Holocaust* (New York, 1979).

57 See, for example, Saul Friedländer, *Pius XII and the Third Reich: A Documentation* (New York, 1966); John F. Morley, *Vatican Diplomacy and the Holocaust, 1939–1943* (New York, 1980); Owen Chadwick, *Britain and the Vatican During the Second World War* (Cambridge, 1986).

58 Serge Klarsfeld, *Le Mémorial de la déportation des Juifs de France* (Paris, 1978); Michael R. Marrus and Robert O. Paxton, *Vichy France and the Jews* (New York, 1981); Serge Klarsfeld, *Vichy-Auschwitz: le Rôle de Vichy dans la solution de la question juive en France* (Paris, 1983).

59 Henry Rousso, *The Vichy Syndrome. History and Memory in France Since 1944* (Cambridge, Mass., 1991).

60 Walter Laqueur, *The Terrible Secret: An Investigation into the Suppression of Information about Hitler's 'Final Solution'* (London, 1980), pp. 3–4, 204–8.

61 Lawrence Stokes, 'The German people and the destruction of the European Jews', *Central European History*, 6 (1973), pp. 167–91.

62 Otto Dov Kulka, 'Public opinion in Nazi Germany and the "Jewish Question"' (Pt 2), *Jerusalem Quarterly*, 26 (1983), pp. 34–45.

63 Ian Kershaw, 'The persecution of the Jews and German popular opinion in the Third Reich', *Leo Baeck Institute Yearbook* 26 (1981), pp. 261–89, especially 280–9. See also idem, *Popular Opinion and Political Dissent in the Third Reich: Bavaria, 1933–1945* (Oxford, 1983), Chapter 9.

64 O. D. Kulka and Aron Rodrigue, 'The German population and the Jews in the

Third Reich: recent publications and trends in research on German society and the "Jewish Question" ', *Yad Vashem Studies*, 16 (1984), pp. 421–35.

65 Ian Kershaw, 'German popular opinion and the "Jewish Question", 1939–1943: some further reflections', in Arnold Paucker (ed.), *Die Juden im national-sozialistischen Deutschland* (Tübingen, 1986), pp. 354–86.

66 Hans Mommsen, 'Was haben die Deutschen vom Völkermord an den Juden gewusst?', in Walter H. Pehle (ed.) *Der Judenpogrom 1938. Von der 'Reich-kristallnacht' zum Völkermord* (Frankfurt am Main, 1988), pp. 160–75.

67 Arthur D. Morse, *While Six Million Died: A Chronicle of American Apathy* (New York, 1967); Saul S. Friedman, *No Haven for the Oppressed: United States Policy Toward Jewish Refugees, 1938–1945* (Detroit, Mich., 1973).

68 Henry Feingold, *The Politics of Rescue* (New Brunswick, NJ, 1970), especially pp. 308–33.

69 David S. Wyman, *The Abandonment of the Jews. America and the Holocaust 1941–1945* (New York, 1984), especially pp. 311–30.

70 Richard Breitman and Alan M. Kraut, *American Refugee Policy and European Jewry, 1933–1945* (Bloomington, Ind., 1987), pp. 3–10.

71 A. J. Sherman, *Island Refuge: Britain and Refugees from the Third Reich 1933–1939* (London, 1973); Bernard Wasserstein, *Britain and the Jews of Europe 1939–1945* (Oxford, 1979), pp. 349–57.

72 Martin Gilbert, *Auschwitz and the Allies* (London, 1981), p. 341.

73 John P. Fox, *European Studies Review*, 9 (1980), pp. 138–46; exchange between Fox and Wasserstein, *European Studies Review*, 10 (1980), pp. 487–92. See also John P. Fox, 'German and Jewish refugees, 1933–1945: reflections on the Jewish condition under Hitler and the western world's response to their expulsion and flight', in Anna C. Bramwell (ed.) *Refugees in the Age of Total War* (London, 1988), pp. 69–85.

74 John P. Fox, 'The Jewish factor in British war crimes policy in 1942', *English Historical Review* 92 (1977), pp. 82–106.

75 Wasserstein, *Britain and the Jews of Europe 1939–1945*, pp. 1–39, 271–95; Monty Noam Penkower, *The Jews Were Expendable. Free World Diplomacy and the Holocaust* (Urbana, Ill., 1981), pp. 1–30.

76 Dina Porat, *The Blue and the Yellow Stars of David. The Zionist Leadership in Palestine and the Holocaust, 1939–1945* (Cambridge, Mass., 1990; first published in Hebrew in 1986).

Part I

ANTECEDENTS, PRECONDITIONS AND LEGITIMATION

1

VOLKSGEMEINSCHAFT, 'ARYANIZATION' AND THE HOLOCAUST

Avraham Barkai

This chapter is an attempt to understand how the persecution of the German Jews, that started in 1933 and gradually escalated in the years preceding the war, conditioned the minds and behaviour of many Germans towards the eventual mass murder of the European Jews. This does not imply the existence of a blueprint or master plan, consistently put into action. Yet, no matter by which version of the 'intentionalist' or 'functionalist' accounts one prefers to approach this question, it soon becomes clear that without the prior deprivation, ostracism and institutionalized plunder of the German Jews – in full view and with the increasing approval and complicity of millions of Germans – the Final Solution would not have been possible. The cumulative radicalization of the Nazis' *Judenpolitik* was primarily a socio-psychological and behavioural process, motivated by ideological aims, and disseminated by an effective combination of propaganda and perceptible actions.[1] Only after these foundations were laid could it proceed, under the conditions of the war against the Soviet Union, towards the Final Solution.

In recent Holocaust research ideological aspects have lately gained more attention than was previously the case. In Germany a younger generation of historians appear to be freer to face, and grapple with, the evidence that the majority of Germans consented to the Nazis' political aims and the means of their realization. An effort to come to terms with this disturbing past is discernible in many local and regional studies on the histories of large or small Jewish communities. The persecution and expulsion of the Jews takes up a central part also in most general local studies.[2]

However, the importance of the *Volksgemeinschaft* concept in National-Socialist ideology still remains somewhat neglected, even by authors who acknowledge the centrality of racism and anti-Semitism. Though both of these elements are frequently found incorporated in *völkisch* thought, the three are by no means synonymous. This is not the place to retrace the origins of *völkisch* ideology from its beginnings in the philosophic and

33

literary school of German romanticism, through the aggressive nationalism of the '*Turnvater*' Jahn, Ernst Moritz Arndt and others.[3] Our present interest centres on *völkisch* political and social concepts as they evolved during and immediately after the First World War and their integration and deployment in the ideological stock-in-trade of Hitler and his party.

The term '*völkisch*' is as untranslatable from the German as the '*Volk*' to which it pertains. Through all its variations *völkisch* thought accorded a transcendental 'essence' to a group of people, which transformed it from a solely instrumental or contractual union of individuals into a mythical, self-perpetuating organism. Whereas nations or classes are compared with a heap of stones, the *Volk* appears as an indissoluble rock. In it every individual is bound by his or her inborn nature and emotions. It is the source of well-being and creativeness. Only in union with the other members of the *Volk* can the individual find full self-expression of his individuality.

Before 1914 *völkisch* ideology was mainly an intellectual affair of relatively small groups and circles. Nevertheless it was even then remarkably successful in penetrating the political and educational establishment. After the defeat in 1918 and the founding of the 'Undesired Republic' it acquired a broad political base. Hitler, in *Mein Kampf*, described at length how he succeeded in transforming a hodgepodge of rival *völkisch* sects, with more than a sprinkling of muddle-headed cranks, into a political party with considerable mass appeal. Then in the violent atmosphere of revolution and counter-revolution the National-Socialist German Workers' Party (NSDAP) set out to 'regain the millions of workers to the idea of the *Volk*'.[4]

The *Volksgemeinschaft* (*Volk*-community) was the answer of National or German Socialism to the Marxist challenge of the classless society. Even the term *Genossen* (comrade) was borrowed from the socialist parties to become *Volksgenossen*. Proletarians and capitalists, peasants and landowners, artisans, blue- or white-collar workers and intellectuals (*Arbeiter der Faust und der Stirn*) were to be united in the racially purified community of the German *Volk*, to toil together for the common weal of the fatherland.

Thanks to Hitler's obsessive Judeophobia, anti-Semitism, which had already become a part of later *völkisch* thought, now became the central issue. His programmatic speech 'Why are we anti-Semites?', opened as an attempt to explain 'the connection between the workers and the Jewish question'.[5] From then on the intertwining of the *Volksgemeinschaft* ideal with anti-Semitic diatribes became characteristic of most of Hitler's speeches during the formative years of his party.[6] Whether anti-Judaism or anti-Marxism took first place in Hitler's *Weltanschauung*,[7] what is essential in our present context is the interchangeability of anti-capitalism and anti-Bolshevism in assigning to 'the Jew' the role of the *Volksfeind*

(*Volk*-enemy). Jews were the primary target of *völkisch* aggression and invective, as the incarnation of everything opposed to the *Volksgemeinschaft*. This simplistic 'friend versus enemy' principle proved to be very effective. Nazi propaganda condemned the Jews as the eternal foe of peoples and races, the 'grasping' financial capitalists or the Marxist *Novemberverbrecher* (November criminals) of 1918. As conspiring plutocrats they were guilty of the Versailles Treaty, the reparations and the inflation. As the ringleaders of the Russian revolution they personified the Bolshevik menace to Germany and all Christian culture.

Anti-Semitic propaganda was probably not the most influential factor in the Nazis' rise to power, but there can be no doubt that the anti-Jewish invective during the hectic years of the short-lived republic poisoned the minds of many Germans. It may be that, even then, popular anti-Semitism in Germany was less brutally aggressive than in other, especially some east European, countries; but in no other country did anti-Semitism eventually become the main pillar of the officially proclaimed pseudo-religious ideology of a totalitarian state. With the Nazis in power, the notions of the *Volksgemeinschaft* versus the *Volksfeind* were effectively imparted by mass indoctrination. The following is a hypothetical attempt to trace the process by which these ideological tenets, and their propagandist and practical application, paved the way to the Final Solution.

Few historians will today deny the broad popular consensus behind the National-Socialist regime and its policies. Although coercion and terror always loomed in the wings, they were far from being decisive for most Germans. At first hesitant, the majority very soon identified enthusiastically with the new regime. In this process the government's early economic and political achievements were admittedly more important than any ideological factors. Nevertheless it resulted in what has been defined as the 'ecstasy of the ruled . . . a climate of mass-hysteria . . . generating constant and unconscious acclamation of the regime'.[8] Even if this climate was engineered and manipulated by propaganda, it nonetheless served to create at least the illusion of an all-embracing solidarity of the German people regardless of class or social background, standing united behind their 'Führer'.

Indeed, this was not entirely illusory. Many years ago Ralf Dahrendorf and David Schoenbaum turned our attention to the real social transformations which occurred in the Third Reich, in what they assumed to be an unintentional but nonetheless irreversible process of modernization.[9] Recently their argument was taken up by a group of young German historians who seek to replace *ex post facto* popular concurrence with Nazism with Hitler's vision as a farsighted social revolutionary.[10] Be that as it may, the central importance of *Volksgemeinschaft* ideology is stressed by all these authors. Today we know better than twenty or thirty years ago how this ideology functioned to achieve the consent of the German people.

Let us turn to some of the most outstanding examples. The Labour Front (*Deutsche Arbeitsfront*, or DAF), the largest mass organization in the Third Reich, gained influence and support not only by propaganda but by some real achievements which affected the social conditions of the workers at the factory as well as at home. The activities of its *Kraft durch Freude* (Strength by enjoyment) organization offered cheap recreation and travel abroad to lower-class Germans who had never before known their like.[11] The *Arbeitsdienst* (labour service) was also idealized as the 'school of the *Volksgemeinschaft*'. Besides providing re-employment and public works schemes it pursued paramilitary training in an atmosphere of egalitarian comradeship.[12] Even philanthropy, delegated to the party-affiliated *Nationalsozialistische Volkswohlfahrt* (NSV), became an effective tool of populist propaganda. Winter relief was staged as a demonstration of *Volks* solidarity in action, with ministers and party big-shots rattling collecting boxes on street corners.[13] Besides the yearly May Day mass rallies a chain of folklorist festivities, culminating in the grandiose cult of the annual party assemblies at Nuremberg, combined to convince many Germans that the ideal of the *Volksgemeinschaft* had come true.[14]

Needless to say, the Jews had no part in any of this. While the German economy recovered, Jewish businesses and employment declined. Jewish enterprises were progressively isolated as more and more Jews worked with and for other Jews. Barred from the Labour Front, Jewish workers and employees were not only excluded from its benefits but were soon dismissed from larger, even Jewish-owned enterprises. From 1935 on, welfare and winter relief for Jews in need was separately organized. Retail shop owners were the first and main targets of the anti-Jewish boycott. Those Jewish lawyers and physicians who, for some years, were exempted from the restrictive legislation of April 1933, lost most of their non-Jewish clients or patients. Gentile professionals were forbidden to share clinics or offices with Jewish colleagues. Jews were evicted from corporation boards and managements, from professional associations, savings banks and other cooperative credit or insurance companies.[15]

Economic persecution was only one side of a wide-ranging policy of social ostracism. The German Jews were gradually but consistently isolated from German society. While legislation was at first only partially and sporadically applied, the Nuremberg laws of September 1935 fulfilled the NSDAP's programme of 1920, reserving full citizen rights to 'pure-blooded' *Volksgenossen* only. At the same time the 'Laws for the purity of German blood' extended the isolation of the Jews to the intimate private sphere. What had already been largely accomplished by aggressive propaganda, organized boycott, personal harassment and central or local administration, now became the official legal status of an emotionally segregated minority. Any trust in the *Rechtsstaat* (rule of law) that German Jews might still have retained became pure self-deception in June 1936 at the latest, when the Supreme Court upheld the legality of the principle of 'civic death' on the grounds of 'lawfully acknowledged principles of racial policy'.[16]

The discussion about the influence of German public opinion on the decisions of the Nazi leadership, and specifically on their Jewish policy, has lately somewhat abated. Not many historians will agree that with regard 'to the visible anti-Jewish violence' of the Nazis during the pogroms of November 1938 the 'traditional German values retained the upper hand over Nazi propaganda'. Even fewer will subscribe to the opinion that 'Hitler and his henchmen murdered the Jews from Germany and other parts of Europe against the will of the German people.'[17] The evaluations made by scholars like Otto Dov Kulka and Ian Kershaw, which were at one time in conflict, have now to some extent converged. Remaining differences are largely semantic: whether the attitude of the German populace to the persecution and finally to the deportation of the Jews was one of 'indifference', 'acquiescence', 'passivity' or 'passive complicity'.[18] Most historians today will agree that all of these attitudes were in evidence but that almost no active, and very little passive opposition, can be positively identified. Still, to answer the most perplexing question, how so many Germans of every social and educational background could become murderers or accomplices to murder would require a profound socio-psychological exploration of day-to-day attitudes towards the Jews and their plight among ordinary men, women, adolescents and even children.[19]

To my knowledge no such project exists, but a host of local histories, amateur workshops and commemorative books for extinguished Jewish communities has in the last few years somewhat clarified the picture. This deluge of information is not without problems: at least some of these, by now over 2,000, titles have the disadvantage of being 'a history of the victims obscuring the perpetrators'.[20] And yet in almost all of them the evolution from pre-war persecution in home town or village to the Final Solution clearly emerges. Even if the local researchers are prevented by personal considerations or by the notorious 'data protection' rules of German archives from publishing the names of those who ordered the burning of the synagogues in November 1938 and of those who lit the fires, and of the 'Aryanizers' who profited from buying Jewish businesses and real estate at ridiculous prices, it becomes clear that such people did indeed exist. On the other hand only scarce evidence of active assistance to Jews, or even open expressions of sympathy with their fate, can be presented.

Some protests are, however, on record. Kulka's analysis of the popular reaction to the Nuremberg laws of 1935, according to which a sizeable portion of the population accepted them with indifference but condemned acts of violence,[21] is substantiated by most local studies. Interestingly, even more indignation is reported against the material destruction during the November pogroms than against earlier, less visible but no less violent outbursts. In any case these reactions were exceptional. I believe that an explanation of the different reactions of German Gentiles to diverse anti-Jewish actions is to be sought (beside, of course, purely personal differences) in the extent of their direct contact with Jewish acquaintances and neighbours. On another level we may find the motives for this variation in the degree of self-interested involvement in the anti-Jewish policies of the regime.

The less than half a million Jews living in Germany in 1933 constituted only 0.7 per cent of the total population. The majority of them lived in a small number of big cities and their economic activities were to a large extent concentrated in a few areas and occupations.[22] This means that millions of Germans had no, or only very limited and occasional, direct contact with Jews. On the other hand there were some occupational groups of Germans who felt particularly threatened by Jewish competition. This pertains mainly to some specific branches of the retail trade, and to physicians and lawyers in the professions. As is well known, anti-Semitic propaganda was most effective in these social groups before 1933.[23] Although pure economic interest should not be simplistically overrated as the sole explanation for ideological susceptibility, it certainly played quite an important role.

After the Nazis' rise to power, Jews in these occupations – the retail trade, medicine and law – were the first to be singled out as targets. The anti-Jewish boycott started officially on 1 April 1933, and from then on became a continuous, purposeful and organized affair with sporadic violent outbursts. In smaller provincial towns especially, SA men and Hitler Youth guards were time and again posted at Jewish shops to scare away prospective customers. Those who did not comply were photographed and appeared the following day in the *Stürmer* (the most virulently anti-Semitic newspaper) showcase and the local press, publicly denounced as *Volksverräter* (*Volk*-traitors). Respectable middle-aged Jewish shopkeepers were abused in vile language by frolicsome teenagers. Murderous slogans like *Juda verrecke* ('Jew, peg out') were smeared on walls and shop windows. Some of the bystanders protested, but apparently many more applauded these actions. The police, the press, teachers and clerics of both Catholic and Protestant confessions mostly remained silent.[24] In this way the brunt of the *Volksgemeinschaft-Volksfeind* ideology was brought to bear. The cumulative impact of these spectacles, combined with supportive propaganda, on both the juvenile perpetrators and the bystanders, must have been immense. Gradually the exceptional status of the Jews became fixed in their minds. Normal standards of propriety and civilized behaviour did evidently not apply to Jews.

The direct beneficiaries of these new behavioural norms were the 'Aryan' competitors and the prospective 'Aryanizers' of Jewish businesses. Elsewhere I have tried to prove that the liquidation and 'Aryanization' of Jewish firms started much earlier and progressed considerably faster than assumed.[25] These statistically derived results, as well as the methods and practices of the 'Aryanizers', are confirmed by most local studies. Single cases of decent negotiation and businesslike transactions are on record, but the evidence of contemporary sources like Gestapo files, as well as of post-war restitution litigation, prove their exceptional character. As a rule militant Nazis, middle-class businessmen and 'respectable' well-groomed industrial tycoons had no moral inhibitions against taking advantage of the desolate position in which Jewish proprietors found themselves. Staged boycotting, fabricated rumours of 'race defilement', denunciations and threats of arrest and concentration camp were very effective tools to convince hesitant sellers.[26]

Here, again, real or feigned ideological commitment was used to justify the violation of traditional norms. In *völkisch* thought the economy was conceived as the subordinated servant of the *Volk*'s political power. The term *Volkswirtschaft* (*Volk*-economy), describing in common German no more than the macro-economic entity, was here explicitly opposed to private economic interest, as well as to international economic cooperation. Property was declared to be *Volksvermögen* (*Volk*-property), granted as a kind of fief to individuals, who were closely controlled by the state, to be used for the common good under its dirigist control.[27] As Jews were not part of the *Volksgemeinschaft*, and were assumed to have gained their wealth by fraud, usury and profiteering, it was only right that their property should be restored to the common stock of the *Volksvermögen* or – in proxy – to the *Volksgenossen*. Established rules and attitudes of honest business practice could therefore self-righteously be abandoned when dealing with Jews.

To understand the relationship between, and the cumulative effect of, social ostracism, boycott riots and 'Aryanization', we have to distinguish between the real Jew next door and the mythical Jew of propaganda. Individual 'Aryanizers' had to deal with real people, in many cases with their former employer or neighbour. This explains the occasional cases of obliging accommodation and mutually favourable settlements. On the other hand the ever-present propaganda, of which the *Stürmer* was only the most extreme and venomous instrument, projected the image of a stereotyped mythical Jew. In the press, in films and on widely distributed posters he appeared in vicious caricature: with beard and sidelocks, in the traditional garb of the medieval or east European Jew, with repulsive physiognomy and gesticulation – a figure which no German had ever met on the street. Social segregation, economic boycott and popular abuse were aimed against this abstract Jew. In this distorted image he personified the world-wide Jewish conspiracy which endangered the German people. He, by his incorrigible racial quality, was the *Volksfeind*, no matter in what deceptive disguise he appeared. Through a progressive process of depersonalization, the majority of Germans, many of whom had never been well-acquainted with any Jew, were induced to internalize this abstract image and to identify the real Jew next door with the satanic mythical Jew of the propaganda.

Here traditional anti-Semitism comes in as an inseparable part of the process. The Nazis did not need to invent this imaginary mythical Jew.[28] Every single satanic quality or horrific crime ascribed to Jews on the pages of the *Stürmer* was copied from earlier Judeophobic invective. It was borrowed and adapted from the traditional stereotypes known from antiquity, through the Middle Ages, to the anti-Semitic press and literature of nineteenth-century France, Russia or Germany. Even the slogan *Die Juden sind unser Unglück* ('The Jews are our misfortune') on the front page of the *Stürmer* had been coined half a century before by a respected German historian.[29] Religious education and folklore had imprinted the mythological figure of the Christ-murdering, unrepentant and therefore eternally wandering, Jew on every Christian mind.[30] The racist, Social Darwinist variation of anti-Semitism was also adapted by the *völkisch* ideology from earlier but not solely German sources. If indeed anti-Semitism was initially not more popular in Germany than elsewhere in Europe, it was nonetheless sufficiently ingrained to serve as an absorptive fertile soil on which the Nazis' propaganda fell, leading to the gradual but consistent depersonalization of the real Jewish neighbour.[31]

This process developed gradually, as is clear from previous investigations of the reactions of Gentile Germans. The boycott riots of 1933 met with some open protests and demonstrated loyalty from Gentile customers and patients. Already, by 1935, such acts of defiance appear to have markedly declined. The evidence shows some, but far fewer, expressions of disapproval towards the violent boycott and harassment, but hardly any towards the Nuremberg laws and the ensuing 'lawful' actions. The impression of more negative popular reactions to the pogroms of November 1938 can be explained by their heightened visibility everywhere around the country. Again, most of these protests condemned the destruction of scarce merchandise, the devastation of buildings and the *Straßenbild* (street scenery), and the disturbance of public law and order, rather than the sacrilege of burnt-down synagogues or the maltreatment of Jewish individuals and their confinement in concentration camps. Apparently the process of depersonalization was at that time already quite advanced.

Parallel to the Jews' social isolation went the final elimination of all their remaining economic enterprises and the plunder of their property. After the pogrom of November 1938, the demolished stores and workshops were not allowed to reopen. Most Jewish businesses that were still active – at that time no more than 20 to 25 per cent of those extant in 1933 – were liquidated, while the more promising among them became lucrative objects of mandatory 'Aryanization' by state-installed trustees. Over one-half of the remaining Jewish property was directly confiscated by the state, to make up the billion-Mark *Sühneleistung* contribution or 'fine' and the so-called 'flight-tax' of the emigrants. The residue was closely controlled by the Gestapo through the frozen accounts of their original owners or in the fictitious capital funds of the *Reichsvereinigung der Juden in Deutschland*. The remaining members of the rapidly diminishing Jewish communities were literally fed and maintained for the little that was left of their lives by these funds. Finally, even the costs of their deportation were financed from this source. The principle that the Jews, being no part of the *Volk*, should be no burden on the *Volkswirtschaft* was consequently pursued to the very end.[32]

What was the Germans' attitude towards the Jews until their deportation, and towards the mass murder in the east? At the beginning of the war the isolation and social – partly also physical – ghettoization of the remaining Jewish community was almost complete. Years before, many Jews had left their homes in villages and small towns to seek anonymity, as well as Jewish companionship and assistance, in the larger cities. After the November pogroms and the subsequent persecutions hundreds of centuries-old small Jewish communities ceased to exist. The refugees from them clustered among other Jews even before the Gestapo forced them into overcrowded *Judenhäuser* or barrack-camps. Ever stricter limits on their movements and pursuits isolated them even more from Gentile society. Their forced labour had to be performed in segregated groups which were prohibited from using the same canteens or toilets as the 'Aryan' workers.[33] Consequently, when the wearing of the Jewish star was ordered in September 1941, SS situation reports recorded the surprise of the population 'that so many Jews were still around'.[34] The process of depersonalization had attained its goals.

In fact some contact or interaction of a very different character between Jews and Gentiles was still going on. On the one hand, the few thousand Jews who survived the war inside Germany depended on the assistance of Gentile acquaintances, friends or – in the case of those with non-Jewish spouses – non-Jewish relatives.[35] An unknown, though certainly not overwhelming, number of Germans took immense personal risks to help Jews in hiding, sometimes even total strangers. On the other hand, a far greater number of Jews living illegally were found and arrested by the Gestapo after being denounced by Gentile neighbours or former acquaintances who recognized them in the street.[36]

Only a short step led from the successful depersonalization of the Jew to the dehumanization of the Jewish *Volksfeind*. Though only a negligible number of totally isolated 'real' Jews still lived in Germany, the mythical phantom Jew remained the target of ever more vicious propaganda during the war years. In 1940–1 three anti-Jewish films were produced and shown in hundreds of cinemas in every German town and village, as well as in the occupied countries. They were *Jud-Süß*, *Die Rothschilds* and, the most murderously inciting of all, *Der Ewige Jude*. In no way did the distorted and malicious presentation of the Rothschild banking dynasty resemble the impoverished, frightened and unobtrusive remnants of German Jewry.[37] On the other hand, in spite of everything, they were not as down-at-heel and emaciated as the haggard, starved and ragged men, women and children in the east European ghettos who were cynically displayed on the screen. The German Jews were not the main targets of the film which put the Jews on a par with garbage-rummaging rats, and concluded with a quote from Hitler prophesying the radical solution of the Jewish question.

The German soldiers stationed in the occupied eastern countries arrived there after being exposed to this kind of propaganda for seven years. For those in their twenties, these were also their most formative years. Here, the external appearance of the real and the mythical Jews attained a closer resemblance. What had till then been impressed on the minds of young Germans as abstract enemy-figures now seemed to have come to life. In a special column in the *Stürmer* soldiers told of their encounters with Polish and Romanian Jews, admitting that they would not have believed that the paper's representations of the Jews 'were so alarmingly real'. A letter signed by two officers thanked the editors for not having 'exaggerated . . . as every German soldier can confirm'.[38] Even more explicit is a passage from a secret military report of October 1941: 'Should there still be people who have some compassion left for the Jews, they should be allowed to have a look at such a ghetto: the mass appearance of this rotten, corrupted and decayed race cures any sentimental humanism.'[39]

Today little doubt remains that the German population at home was more than just vaguely aware of what was going on in the east. The mass shootings by the *Einsatzgruppen* were widely reported by soldiers and civilians on leave, and even the more carefully concealed gassing at Auschwitz and other extermination camps seems to have leaked out to many people.[40] Among other evidence, this is convincingly borne out by the posthumously published diaries of Karl Dürkefelden, written between 1933 and 1945. This self-educated engineer from Lower Saxony was no Nazi Party member, but was careful not to defy the regime and public opinion openly. He had no personal contact with Jews and did not abstain from stereotypical remarks like 'the Jews are swindlers'. He refrained from buying in Jewish shops in his home town 'because I did not think it right to get into danger because of the Jews'. But Dürkefelden was obsessed with recording the truth 'as it really was'. Already in December 1941 he quoted a letter from Kiev where 'there are absolutely no Jews left, but I shall have to tell you myself how they were removed'. A later conversation with its writer confirmed that he was referring to the Babi-Yar massacre of 29–30 September. In February 1942 Dürkefelden recorded the first rumours of the gassings. He quoted verbatim Hitler's speech of 24 February in which his prophecy about the extermination of the Jews was repeated, noting the caption *Die Juden werden ausgerottet* ('The Jews are being exterminated') under which this part of the Führer's speech was printed in the regional Nazi paper. In January 1943 a former colleague, on leave from Vilna, told him about the almost total extermination of the city's Jewish community, as also of Jews sent to Poland from France and other west European countries, who 'were partly shot, partly gassed'.[41]

This writer was no highly placed functionary, had no special connections and lived in a small provincial town. There is no reason to believe that what he learned from his quoted sources remained secret to the majority of his contemporaries. The repression of this knowledge, or the public's retreat into the private sphere, may partly be ascribed to the personal hardship and worry of wartime. But essentially the German people's reactions – or indifference – cannot be explained without taking into account the cumulative influence of consistently indoctrinated anti-Semitism and *völkisch* ideology.

After half a century of research and scores of thousands of learned publications, most historians, sociologists and political scientists tend to give up, and to conclude that the Holocaust was a unique, totally inexplicable phenomenon, beyond the capabilities of historical research. This overlooks the fact that the perpetrators were not extraterrestrial monsters, but rather tens of thousands of perfectly ordinary people. After carrying out their abominable activities, they spent evenings with their families, played with their children or wrote them sentimental letters. They played cards at their regular tables in bars or canteens, or took delight in the music of Mozart or Beethoven. Because of this it is simply not possible to shirk the attempt to understand and explain what happened.

The account given here does not claim to supply a complete or final answer to these frightening questions. It simply seeks to show how seven or eight years of fanatical ideological indoctrination in racial discrimination, concretized by 'visual instruction' on the streets, could befog the consciences of millions of Germans and corrode their moral inhibitions. Without these prior developments, the Holocaust would not have been possible. From this perspective, the persecution of the German Jews seems the necessary although not sufficient precondition for the murder of the European Jews.

NOTES

1 The neglect of the ideological dimension is, in my opinion, the most objectionable point in the 'functionalist' theory. In it, the cumulative radicalization that led to the Final Solution is conceived as a chain of *ad hoc* decisions by competing high- and lower-ranking technocrats. Even where not explicitly stated, the picture that evolves is one of a highly organized, state-controlled mass murder where racism or anti-Semitism plays no, or at best only a secondary and dispensable, role. (See, for instance: M. Broszat, 'Hitler und die Genesis der Endlösung', *Vierteljahrshefte für Zeitgeschichte (VfZ)*, 25 (1977), pp. 739–75; H. Mommsen, 'Die Realisierung des Utopischen: Die "Endlösung der Judenfrage" im Dritten Reich', *Geschichte und Gesellschaft (GG)*, 3 (1983), pp. 381–420.) The role of scientists, technocrats and the intellectuals generally, in the practical implementation of the Final Solution is, of course, important in itself, but its investigation sometimes leads to questionable over-rationalization, as demonstrated lately by Susanne Heim and Götz Aly, 'Die Ökonomie der "Endlösung", Menschenvernichtung und wirtschaftliche Neuordnung' in idem, (eds) *Sozialpolitik und Judenvernichtung, Gibt es eine Ökonomie der Endlösung?* (Hamburg, 1987); idem, *Vordenker der Vernichtung. Auschwitz und die deutschen Pläne für eine neue europäische Ordnung* (Hamburg, 1991).

2 To mention only two typical publications: W. Frenz, J. Kammler and D. Krause-Vilmar (eds) *Volksgemeinschaft und Volksfeinde, Kassel 1933–1945* (Fuldabrück, 1987) (almost one-quarter of its over 400 pages deals with the persecution and economic deprivation of the city's Jewish population); J. Meynert, *Was vor der Endlösung geschah. Antisemitische Ausgrenzung und Verfolgung in Minden-Ravensberg 1933–1945* (Münster, 1988).

3 The most comprehensive analyses of the origins and developments of *völkisch* thought are still: Hans Kohn, *The Mind of Germany, The Education of a Nation* (New York, 1960), and George L. Mosse, *The Crisis of German Ideology. Intellectual Origins of the Third Reich* (New York, 1964).

4 *Mein Ziel ist, dem Volksgedanken die Millionen seiner Arbeiterschaft widerzugeben. Das geht nur mit ehrlicher Überzeugung von dem Ideal.*
(My aim is to regain the millions of workers to the idea of the *Volk*. Only with sincere conviction can this ideal be achieved.)
(Hitler's speech of December 1930 in Hamburg, quoted in W. Jochmann
   (ed.) *Nationalsozialismus und Revolution. Ursprung und Geschichte der NSADP in Hamburg 1922–1933* (Frankfurt a.M., 1963), p. 312 f.)

Die Eingliederung der heute im internationalen Lager stehenden breiten Masse unseres Volkes in eine nationale Volksgemeinschaft bedeutet keinen Verzicht auf die Vertretung berechtigter Standesinteressen. . . . Das schwerste Hindernis für die Annäherung des heutigen Arbeiters an die nationale Volksgemeinschaft liegt . . . in seiner internationalen volks- und vaterlandsfeindlichen Führung und Einstellung.
(The integration of the broad masses of our people who today still adhere to the internationalist camp, into a national *Volk*-community does not imply any renunciation of the representation of justified class interests. . . . The greatest obstacle to the rapprochement of the workers to the national *Volk*-community are his internationalist leaders and ideology.)
(Hitler, *Mein Kampf*, 59. Aufl., Munich, 1933, p. 372 f.)

5 *Ariertum bedeutet sittliche Auffassung der Arbeit und dadurch das, was wir heute so oft im Munde führen: Sozialismus, Gemeinsinn, Gemeinnutz*

vor Eigennutz. Judentum bedeutet egoistische Auffassung der Arbeit und dadurch Mammonismus und Materialismus, das konträre Gegenteil des Sozialismus.

(The 'Aryan' conception of work is an ethical and moral obligation, thereby everything that today we so often repeat: socialism, sense of community, common weal before personal weal. Judaism means the egoistic conception of work, and thereby mammonism and materialism, the contrary reverse of socialism.)

(Hitler's speech in Munich, 8 August 1920, quoted in R. H. Phelps, 'Hitlers "grundlegende" Rede über den Antisemitismus', VfZ, 7 (1968), p. 406)

6 For instance in a speech of 12 April 1922:

'national' und 'sozial' sind zwei identische Begriffe. Dem Juden erst ist es gelungen, durch die Umfälschung des sozialen Gedankens zum Marxismus diesen sozialen Gedanken . . . dem nationalen zu entfremden. . . . Sozial sein (heißt) den Staat und die Volksgemeinschaft so aufbauen, daß jeder einzelne für die Volksgemeinschaft handelt. . . . Die Schaffenden, ganz gleich ob Arbeiter des Kopfes oder der Faust, sind das Edelvolk unseres Staates, das ist das deutsche Volk.

('national' and 'social' are two identical concepts. Only the Jew has succeeded in . . . alienating this social idea from the national by its falsification to Marxism . . . so to be social means to build the state and the *Volksgemeinschaft* in such a manner that every individual works for the *Volksgemeinschaft.* . . . The working people, no matter if workers of the head or the fist, are the nobility of our state, this is the German people!)

(Eberhard Jäckel and Axel Kuhn (eds) *Hitler, Sämtliche Aufzeichnungen 1905–1924* (Stuttgart, 1980), p. 621.)

See also p. 664 ff. where Hitler explains his concept of 'socialism':

Ein Staatswesen kann nur aufgebaut sein auf einer sozialen Grundlage, und zweitens: Todfeind jedes wahren sozialen Gedankens ist der internationale Jude! Wer bereit ist für sein Volk so vollständig einzutreten, daß er wirklich kein anderes Ideal kennt, als nur das Wohlergehen dieses seines Volkes . . . wer in diesem Volke in jedem einzelnen das wertvolle Glied der Gemeinsamkeit erblickt, und wer erkennt, daß diese nur dann gedeihen kann, wenn nicht Herrschende und Unterdrückte sie bilden, sondern wenn alle, die gemäß ihrem Können ihre Pflicht dem Vaterland und der Volksgemeinschaft gegenüber erfüllen, demgemäß auch geschätzt werden . . . der ist ein Sozialist!

(Only on social foundations can a political system be built. . . . The mortal enemy of every genuine social idea is the international Jew! Only he who is prepared to stand up for his *Volk* until he really knows no other ideal than the common weal of his *Volk.* . . . He is a socialist, who regards every single member of this *Volk* as a valuable link of the community, and who recognizes that this [community] can prosper only if it does not consist of rulers and oppressed, only when everybody, who fulfils his duty to the fatherland as well as he can is accordingly estimated.)

7 Referring to the compilation mentioned in Note 6, where 'references to the Jews are approximately three times more numerous than those related to bolshevism, communism or Marxism', Saul Friedländer points out the 'obvious difference

between National Socialism and other types of fascism: in nazism, anti-Semitism occupies a central and particular place. And in fact the Jews, not the Marxists, were the targets of both Hitler's first, and last ideological statements' ('From anti-Semitism to extermination' in F. Furet, *Unanswered Questions, Nazi Germany and the Genocide of the Jews* (New York, 1989), p. 7). The most ardent protagonists of the 'primacy' of anti-Bolshevism in recent publications, although quite different in quality and outlook, are Arno J. Mayer, *Why Did the Heavens not Darken? The Final Solution in History* (New York, 1988), and Ernst Nolte, *Der europäische Bürgerkrieg 1917–1945, Nationalsozialismus und Bolschewismus* (Frankfurt/M and Berlin, 1987). The most outspokenly opposite view is presented by Lucy S. Dawidowicz, *The War against the Jews 1933–1945* (New York, 1975).

8 *Die nationalsozialistische Herrschaft gründete sich auf der Ekstase der Beherrschten. Zur Eroberung der Macht, zu ihrer Durchsetzung und Befestigung wurden . . . Institutionen ersonnen und Mechanismen installiert, die die Aufgabe hatten, das Volk in eine Art von permanentem Rauschzustand zu versetzen und ein Klima der Massenhysterie zu erzeugen und zu bewahren, ein Klima in dem ständige und bewußtlose Akklamation zum Regime gedieh.*
(The national-socialist rule was based on the ecstasy of the ruled. The institutions that were contrived and the mechanisms that were installed to conquer and establish [Nazi] power were aimed to permanently intoxicate the people, and to create a climate of mass hysteria which generated a consistent and unconscious acclamation of the regime.)
(Wolfgang Benz, *Herrschaft und Gesellschaft im nationalsozialistischen Staat* (Frankfurt/M., 1990), p. 9)

See also p. 27: '*Zur deutschen Schicksalsgemeinschaft fühlten sich auch die Regimegegner noch zugehörig. . . . Es war weitgehend gelungen, die "Volksgemeinschaft" als Realisierung eines der beliebtesten Schlagworte herzustellen.*'
(Even the opponents of the regime felt they belonged to the German 'community of fate'. . . . The concept of 'people's community' was highly successful as a popular slogan.)

9 Ralf Dahrendorf, *Gesellschaft und Demokratie in Deutschland* (Munich, 1965), p. 431 ff. and *passim*; David Schoenbaum, *Hitler's Social Revolution, Class and Status in Nazi Germany 1933–1939* (London, 1967), p. 117 and *passim*.

10 Rainer Zitelmann, *Hitler, Selbstverständnis eines Revolutionärs* (Stuttgart, 1989); U. Backes, E. Jesse and R. Zitelman (eds) *Die Schatten der Vergangenheit, Impulse zur Historisierung des Nationalsozialismus* (Frankfurt/M and Berlin, 1990).

11 See Timothy W. Mason, *Sozialpolitik im Dritten Reich, Arbeiterklasse und Volksgemeinschaft* (Opladen, 1977), p. 182 ff. on the 'Arbeitsfront als organisatorischer Träger der Volksgemeinschaft', and the KdF-activities.

12 R. Stommer, 'Da oben versinkt einem der Alltag . . . , Thingstätten im Dritten Reich als Demonstration der Volksgemeinschafts-ideologie', in: Detlev Peukert and Jürgen Reulecke (eds) *Die Reihen fast geschlossen: Beiträge zur Geschichte des Alltags unterm Nationalsozialismus* (Wuppertal, 1981), p. 158 ff.

13 A. zu Castell Rüdenhausen, ' "Nicht mitzuleiden, mitzukämpfen sind wir da!" Nationalsozialistische Volkswohlfahrt im Gau Westfalen-Nord', in Peukert and Reulecke, *Die Reihen*, p. 223 ff.

14 Stommer, 'Da oben versinkt', p. 154 f.; see also: D. Peukert, *Inside Nazi Germany, Conformity, Opposition, and Racism in Everyday Life* (New Haven and London, 1987), p. 187 ff.; Carola Sachse, *Siemens, der Nationalsozialismus*

und die moderne Familie (Hamburg, 1990). On the military aspects of the *Volksgemeinschaft* ideology, see J. Förster, 'Vom Führerheer der Republik zur nationalsozialistischen Volksarmee', in J. Dülffer, B. Martin and G. Wollstein (eds), *Deutschland und Europa, Kontinuität und Bruch* (Frankfurt/M and Berlin, 1990), pp. 311–28.

15 See A. Barkai, *From Boycott to Annihilation, The Economic Struggle of German Jews, 1933–1943* (Hanover and London, 1989).

16 In a judgement of 27 June 1936 concerning the claim of a Jewish film director. The court had to decide if Jewish descent justified the annulment of his contract, as in the case of severe illness or death (quoted in Ernst Fraenkel, *Der Doppelstaat* (Frankfurt/M, 1940), p. 126.

17 William S. Allen, 'Die deutsche Öffentlichkeit und die "Reichskristallnacht" – Konflikte zwischen Werthierarchie und Propaganda im Dritten Reich', in Peukert and Reulecke, *Die Reihen*, pp. 407 ff. Allen's argument leans heavily on Sara A. Gordon's dissertation of 1979 (published version: *Hitler, Germans, and the 'Jewish Question'* (Princeton, NJ, 1984)), a study that has become a real mine for apologists. For a critical assessment of her methods and conclusions, see R. Gellately, 'The Gestapo and German society: political denunciation in the Gestapo case files', *Journal of Modern History* (JMH), 60 (1988), pp. 669 f.

18 The convergence of opinions is evident from these authors' more recently published works, specially: Ian Kershaw, *The 'Hitler Myth', Image and Reality in the Third Reich* (Oxford, 1987; an updated translation of his German *Der Hitler Mythos, Volksmeinungund Propaganda im Dritten Reich* (Stuttgart, 1980) with an additional new chapter on the Jewish Question; idem, 'German popular opinion during the "Final Solution" ', in A. Cohen *et al.* (eds) *Comprehending the Holocaust* (Frankfurt/M, Berlin, New York and Paris, 1989), pp. 145–55; Otto Dov Kulka, ' "Public opinion" in Nazi Germany and the "Jewish Question" ', *The Jerusalem Quarterly*, 25 (1982), pp. 121–44; 26 (1982), pp. 34–45; idem, 'Die Nürnberger Rassengesetze und die deutsche Bevölkerung im Lichte geheimer NS-Lageberichte', VfZ, 32 (1984), pp. 582–624.

19 Many children and teenagers wrote enthusiastic letters to the editors of the *Stürmer*. For the youngest readers, the paper published a series of illustrated children's books and board games, some examples of which are held at the Yad Vashem Archives in Jerusalem and the Wiener Library at Tel-Aviv University. See Fred Hahn, *Lieber Stürmer, Leserbriefe an das NS-Kampfblatt 1924 bis 1945* (Stuttgart, 1978). On the children's books especially, see pp. 156 ff.

20 *An den Gemeindegeschichten fällt auf, daß die politisch motivierten Autoren letzendlich ihr Interesse von der Geschichte der Täter auf die der Opfer verlagert haben. Sie beschreiben die Geschichte der Judenverfolgung am Ort genau und versuchen, die Namen aller Deportierten ausfindig zu achen. Aber die Namen der örtlichen Täter erscheinen kaum. Es gab Verbrechen, aber niemand beging sie – eine Tat ohne Täter.*

(What strikes one in the communal histories is that politically motivated authors have ultimately shifted their interest from the history of the perpetrators to that of the victims. They describe the history of the local Jews' persecution very accurately, and try to discover the names of all deportees. But the names of the local perpetrators rarely appear. Crimes were performed, but nobody committed them – offences without culprits.)

(Monika Richarz, 'Luftaufnahme – oder die Schwierigkeiten der Heimatforscher mit der jüdischen Geschichte', *Babylon, Beiträge zur jüdischen Gegenwart*, 8 (1991), p. 30)

21 Kulka, 'Public opinion' p. 135 ff.
22 In 1933 one-third of all German Jews lived in Berlin, another third in six other big cities. Though almost 20 per cent of the Jews were still living in villages or small towns of less than 20,000 residents, they were quite concentrated in some 2,500, out of scores of thousands of locations, mainly in south and south-west Germany. See A. Barkai, 'Die Juden als sozio-ökonomische Minderheitsgruppe in der Weimarer Republik', in Walter Grab and Julius H. Schoeps (eds) *Juden in der Weimarer Republik* (Stuttgart and Bonn, 1986), pp. 330–46; see also Barkai, *From Boycott to Annihilation*, pp. 1–8.
23 See Michael H. Kater, 'Zur Soziographie der frühen NSDAP', VfZ, 19 (1971), p. 139 f.; Wolfgang Schieder (ed.) *Faschismus als soziale Bewegung* (Hamburg 1976), especially the contribution by Heinrich-August Winkler, pp. 97 ff.; Richard F. Hamilton, *Who Voted for Hitler?* (Princeton, NJ, 1982); Jürgen W. Falter, 'Wer verhalf Hitler zum Sieg?', *Aus Politik und Zeitgeschichte*, B28–29/1979; Thomas Childers, *The Nazi Voters: The Social Foundations of Fascism in Germany 1919–1933* (Chapel Hill and London, 1983).
24 A daring, certainly not typical, letter to the German Ministry of the Interior of December 1934 signed by Richard Schneider, who claimed to have been a party member since 1928, portrays this atmosphere. Some excerpts deserve to be quoted:

> *halbwüchsige Burschen im Alter von 16–17 Jahren (in Zivil) hielten die Eingänge zu Geschäften mit jüdischem Einschlag besetzt ... Flegel mit ekelhaften [sic], verbrecherischem Gesichtsaussdruck hatte man vor die Eingänge postiert, die unter dem Schutze der Polizei ihre Machtbefugnisse zum Trotze der gesamten zivilisierten Bevölkerung zur Geltung bringen sollten und auch unter der Mitwirkung der Polizei bringen konnten. Alte, aber feine, ergraute Herren, auch Männer, die unter schwersten Entbehrungen 4 Jahre im Kriege für das deutsche Vaterland gekämpft hatten, mussten sich von diesen Strolchen und Lausbuben, auf ihren Begehr nach Einlass, die Frage vorlegen lassen: 'Sind Sie Deutscher?' ... Und dies unter dem Schutze der Polizei, von einem ganz ordinären Pack von Menschen ... deren Einschluss in die Volksgemeinschaft unbedingt zu verweigern wäre.*

> (half-grown boys aged 16 or 17 years (clad in mufti) occupied the entrances of Jewish stores.... Louts with disgusting, criminal features were posted at the door, to impose their authority, under police guard, over the whole civilized population.... Old but distinguished gentlemen who, during four hard years, had fought for the German fatherland, had to suffer the questions of these rogues: 'Are you a German?' ... And all this under the protection of the police, by a vulgar bunch of people ... who should never be admitted to the *Volk*-community.)

(Bundesarchiv, Abtig. Potsdam, RMI, 15.01, 27079/29)

25 Barkai, *From Boycott to Annihilation*, pp. 69 ff., 109 f.
26 idem, 'German entrepreneurs and Jewish policy in the Third Reich', *Yad Vashem Studies* (YVS), 21 (1991), pp. 125–53; also Johannes Ludwig, *Boykott, Enteignung, Mord. Die 'Entjudung' der deutschen Wirtschaft* (Hamburg and Munich, 1989).
27 A. Barkai, *Nazi Economics, Ideology, Theory, and Policy* (New Haven and London, 1990), pp. 35 ff.; idem, 'Wirtschaftliche Grundanschauungen und Ziele der NSDAP', *Jahrbuch des Instituts für Deutsche Geschichte*, 7 (1978), pp. 355–85.

28 See Eva G. Reichmann, *Hostages of Civilisation: The Social Sources of National-Socialist Anti-Semitism* (London, 1950).

29 Heinrich von Treitschke, 'Unsere Aussichten', *Preußische Jahrbücher*, November 1879, p. 11.

30 The archbishop of Munich, Cardinal Michael von Faulhaber, is generally considered as an opponent of the Nazis' anti-religious and, to some extent also, racial policies. Before Christmas 1933 Faulhaber held a series of sermons, later published under the title *'Judentum, Christentum, Germanentum'* ('Judaism, Christianity, Germandom'). One paragraph is worth quoting:

> *Nach dem Tode Christi wurde Israel aus dem Dienst der Offenbarung entlassen. Sie hatten die Stunde der Heimsuchung nicht erkannt. Sie hatten den Gesalbten des Herrn verleugnet, verworfen, zur Stadt hinausgeworfen und ans Kreuz geschlagen. Damals zerriß der Vorhang im Tempel auf Sion und damit der Bund zwischen dem Herrn und seinem Volk. Die Tochter Sion erhielt den Scheidebrief, und seitdem wandert der ewige Ahasver ruhelos über die Erde.*
>
> (After the death of Christ Israel was dismissed from the offices of the revelation. They had failed to recognize the hour of the visitation. They had renounced the Lord's anointed, rejected him, driven him from the town, and crucified him. At that time tore the curtain in the temple of Zion, and with it the covenant of the Lord with His people. The daughter of Zion received her divorce, and from then on the eternal Ahasver walks restlessly over the earth.)
>
> (Quoted in Günther B. Ginzel, 'Mir geht es um die Bekämpfung des Antisemitismus', *Das Parlament*, 41/33 (August 1991), p. 8)

31 Michael H. Kater has convincingly contested the tendency to 'altogether discount preexisting notions of Judeophobia among the German people', naming specifically Thomas Nipperdey and William S. Allen. He also criticizes authors like Ian Kershaw and Detlev Peukert who, in his opinion, 'have overemphasized the degree of high-level Nazi management of anti-Jewish action, [and] conversely have down-played the spontaneity of such actions and its general popularity with the German public' ('Everyday anti-Semitism in prewar Nazi Germany: the popular basis', YVS, 16 (1984), pp. 129 f.

32 H. G. Adler, *Der verwaltete Mensch. Studien zur Deportation der Juden aus Deutschland* (Tübingen 1974), especially pp. 451 ff.; Barkai, *From Boycott to Annihilation*, pp. 167 ff.

33 Barkai, *From Boycott to Annihilation*, p. 159 ff.; recent local studies prove that many more forced-labour camps were installed in Germany than has so far been known. Meynert, *Was vor der Endlösung geschah*, p. 230 ff. brings evidence of two larger camps in Bielefeld, as well as smaller camps installed under the supervision of private firms who employed Jews in forced labour. Such camps are also mentioned in other local studies. The subject is at this time being investigated in a number of dissertations at German universities, under the guidance of the Wissenschaftliche Arbeitsgemeinschaft des Leo Baeck Instituts.

34 'Meldungen aus dem Reich', 9 October 1941, quoted in Marlis G. Steinert, *Hitlers Krieg und die Deutschen. Stimmung und Haltung der deutschen Bevölkerung im Zweiten Weltkrieg* (Düsseldorf and Vienna, 1970), p. 240.

35 Steinert (ibid.) also quotes reports of party functionaries expressing dissatisfaction with the fact that Jewish wives in mixed marriages were exempted from wearing the star. The fate of both the Jewish and the 'Aryan' partners in those families is excellently presented in Ursula Büttner, *Die Not der Juden teilen,*

Christlich-Jüdische Familien im Dritten Reich, Beispiel und Zeugnis des Schriftstellers Robert Brendel (Hamburg, 1988). According to her evidence many 'Aryan' relatives refused help, and severed connections with these families. See also Jochen Klepper, *Unter dem Schatten deiner Flügel. Aus den Tagebüchern der Jahre 1932–1942* (Stuttgart, 1968). Klepper, a well-known writer and devout Protestant, committed suicide in 1942, together with his Jewish wife and her daughter from her first marriage, who was to be deported to the east. The diaries leave no doubt about Klepper's knowledge of the fate that was awaiting his family after deportation.

36 From a scrutiny of Gestapo files, Robert Gellateley has recently derived evidence that most arrests of fugitive Jews or Gentile 'Jew-friends' resulted from denunciations from the general public, far more than from detection by the restricted staff of the Gestapo and its agents ('The Gestapo and German society: political denunciation in the Gestapo case files', JMH, 60, pp. 665–94). See also idem, *The Gestapo and German Society, Enforcing Racial Policy 1933–1945* (Oxford, 1990).

37 It is significant that in these films, produced after the Molotov-Ribbentrop agreement of 1939, and before June 1941, no reference to 'Judeo-Bolshevism' or the Soviet Union appears. The tactical reasons for this reticence are obvious, but it proves that Nazi anti-Semitism was indeed a primary and autonomous ideological tenet.

38 Hahn, *Lieber Stürmer*, p. 220 f.; see also the ghetto pictures, pp. 152 ff.

39   *Sollte es noch Leute geben, die irgendwie Mitleid mit den Juden haben, dann dürfte es sich empfehlen, sie einen Blick in ein solches Ghetto tun zu lassen: der Massenanblick dieser verrotteten, verderbten und bis in die Knochen verfaulten Rasse vertreibt jede Humanitätsduselei.*

                                          (Quoted in Steinert, *Hitlers Krieg*, p. 246).

40 Lawrence D. Stokes, 'The German people and the destruction of the European Jews', *Central European History*, 6 (1973), pp. 167–91, especially p. 190 f.: 'The German people saw and learned enough to be intimidated, but were sufficiently undisturbed in their own security to remain passive spectators.' Following Ernst Nolte, Stokes at the time attributed this passivity mainly to fear and the terrorizing effect of partly known atrocities, a viewpoint that, in the light of later research, can no longer be maintained.

41 Herbert and Sibylle Oberhausen (eds) *'Schreiben wie es wirklich war...', Aufzeichnungen Karl Dürkefäldens aus den Jahren 1933–1945* (Hanover, 1985), pp. 107 ff.

2

EUTHANASIA AND THE FINAL SOLUTION

Henry Friedlander

Nazi genocide, also known as the Final Solution or the Holocaust, can be defined as the mass murder of human beings because they belong to a biologically defined group. Heredity determined the selection of the victims.[1] This definition excludes members of groups murdered for their political affiliations (communists, socialists, Soviet POWs), their national origins (Poles, Russians, Ukrainians), their behaviour (criminals, homosexuals) or their activities (members of the resistance). The Nazi regime applied a consistent and inclusive policy of extermination only against three groups of human beings: the handicapped, Jews and Gypsies.[2]

Space and the thrust of this chapter do not permit me to document in detail how the Final Solution applied to Gypsies in the same way as to Jews. Those who deny the fact that the murder of Gypsies was genocide based on race argue either that there was no Nazi policy to exterminate all Gypsies or that they were only killed because the regime considered them anti-social elements.[3] Both arguments are fallacious. Already during the 1930s German bureaucrats described their anti-Gypsy programme as the 'total solution of the Gypsy problem' (*restlose Lösung des Zigeunerproblems*).[4] Nazi terminology classifying all Gypsies as 'asocials', in the same way that Jürgen Stroop described all Warsaw Jews as 'bandits', does not disprove the racial motivation of anti-Gypsy policies. Any system that categorizes all members of a group as anti-social is obviously establishing a racial definition based on heredity.[5] Finally, current research and documentary evidence indicate that all Gypsies were condemned to death and that the SS and police successfully carried out the death sentence.[6]

In the 1930s the regime moved to exclude members of the three designated groups – the handicapped, Jews and Gypsies – from the national community. The German government rapidly enacted laws that clearly isolated, excluded and penalized them. Against the handicapped, the regime enacted the Law to Prevent Offspring with Hereditary Diseases of July 1933 and the Marriage Health Law of October 1935.[7] Against Jews, it enacted the Law for the Restitution of the Professional Civil Service of April 1933 and in September 1935 the so-called Nuremberg racial laws:

the Reich Citizenship Law and the Law for the Protection of German Blood and German Honour.[8] Against Gypsies, it applied both the Nuremberg racial laws and the anti-Gypsy laws enacted prior to 1933, and also issued numerous directives to combat the so-called Gypsy plague.[9] Simultaneously, the regime excluded these groups by systematically reducing expenditures. For example, conditions imposed on the institutionalized handicapped deteriorated precipitously during the 1930s.[10] Similarly, the authorities did everything to exclude Jews and Gypsies from coverage under the German welfare system.[11] Moreover, members of all three groups faced the brutality of the state. During the 1930s the handicapped were sterilized against their will, Gypsies were incarcerated in so-called Gypsy camps, and Jews faced escalating harassment designed to force their emigration.[12]

The coming of war made more radical forms of exclusion possible. There had already been indications that the cover of war would be used to escalate persecution.[13] Consequently, after September 1939 the Nazi regime implemented killing operations – the most radical type of exclusion. The so-called euthanasia killing operation was the first to be implemented, and thus the handicapped became the first victims of Nazi genocide.[14]

The chronology of Nazi mass murder unambiguously shows that the killings of the handicapped, initiated in the winter of 1939–40, preceded those of Jews and Gypsies.[15] But this chronological sequence is not the only connection between these killing operations. A closer analysis shows us other links that bind these killing enterprises: decision making, personnel and technique. In short, euthanasia served as a model for the Final Solution.

The way Nazi leaders reached the decision to kill the handicapped tells us a great deal about how they decided on the Final Solution. Killing the handicapped had been advocated as early as 1920, and during the 1930s some party and government health care functionaries had championed that radical policy.[16] Nevertheless, no killing operations could commence until Adolf Hitler gave verbal instructions to implement the so-called euthanasia programme.[17] Hitler appointed both Dr Karl Brandt, his personal physician, and Philipp Bouhler, the chief of his personal chancellery (*Kanzlei des Führers* or KdF), as plenipotentiaries for euthanasia. Bouhler in turn appointed Viktor Brack to create and direct the organization, known as T4, that implemented the killing operation.[18] In the best tradition of CYA (Cover Your Ass), the bureaucrats of the KdF nevertheless needed a written authorization from their Führer for their own protection as well as to obtain the collaboration of physicians and government agencies. The KdF thus prepared the text of this authorization and, backdating it to the day war had started, Hitler signed it in October 1939.[19] Typed on the Führer's private stationery, with the German eagle and swastika as well as the name Adolf Hitler printed at the top left, one copy of this authorization has survived.[20] And thereafter Hitler continued to make all important decisions;

the plenipotentiaries consulted the Führer whenever they needed to initiate policy.[21]

I am convinced that the same process of decision making accompanied the implementation of the Final Solution. Although no testimony has survived to document this, it seems certain that Hitler commissioned Himmler and his SS and police to kill the Jews.[22] However, unlike euthanasia, there was no written authorization. The reasons for this seem to me self-evident. Too many persons had read the Führer's euthanasia authorization, and widespread knowledge about the killings could thus implicate Hitler. Obviously, he refused to sign another such document. In addition, the loyal SS could hardly attempt CYA by asking their Führer for an authorization. Still, Heydrich needed some form of written commission to compel the cooperation of other government agencies. As we know, it was provided by Hermann Gœring.[23] Like Hitler with euthanasia, Gœring did not initiate but only signed this authorization. Further, as with euthanasia, Hitler kept himself informed about the progress of the killing operations of the Final Solution, and major decisions needed his approval.[24]

Unlike the handicapped, whose relatives could and did cause problems, and the Jews, whose social contacts in Germany and abroad had to be considered, the Gypsies were deemed so marginal that their murder neither required written authorization nor produced intra-agency conflicts. Nevertheless, even here some policy decisions forced Hitler to serve as the final arbiter of their fate. For example, in 1942 Martin Bormann discovered that the Reich Leader SS had exempted certain pure Gypsies so that research on their 'valuable Teutonic practices' could be completed. On 3 December, Bormann complained about this arbitrary change in policy in a letter to Heinrich Himmler. On the front of this letter Himmler added a handwritten comment that he must prepare data concerning the Gypsies for Hitler.[25] It is probably no coincidence that thirteen days later Himmler issued his Auschwitz decree on Gypsies.[26]

Hitler's so-called stop order of August 1941 did not end the T4 killing programme. The story that his order ended euthanasia is a post-war myth. Indeed, the stop order applied only to the T4 killing centres. In fact, mass murder of the handicapped continued by other means, and more victims of euthanasia perished after the stop order than prior to August 1941.[27] Public knowledge and popular disquiet were the principal reasons for Hitler's decision. In 1940 public knowledge and discontent had led Himmler to suggest closing Grafeneck.[28] The same reasons led Hitler to issue his order in August 1941.[29] Those who directed killing operations had learned that such matters could not be kept secret within the borders of the Reich, and found that the creation of front organizations and the use of euphemisms did not prevent the public from assigning blame to the

Nazi movement and its formations.[30] Henceforth, further killing operations were moved to the east.

The euthanasia killings had been carried out by the KdF in collaboration with the health department of the Reich Ministry of the Interior, but the SS and police had also provided limited logistic support.[31] And just as the SS had assisted the KdF in managing euthanasia, the KdF later offered its expertise to the SS in executing the Final Solution. At first this happened only on the periphery. First, chemists previously associated with T4 (Albert Widmann and August Becker) aided the *Einsatzgruppen* leadership in testing the feasibility of killings with explosives and with gas.[32] Second, methods previously utilized to kill the handicapped in east Prussia were applied by the same SS unit (the Lange Kommando) in the first killing centre for Jews and Gypsies at Chelmno.[33] Third, as the Wetzel letter to Riga proposing 'Brack's remedy' and the services of T4 chemist Helmut Kallmeyer has shown, the KdF also offered its technical support for various other local killing operations.[34] We can thus see that the KdF served as 'godfather' to the emerging efforts to rationalize the Final Solution.

It is therefore not surprising that the KdF also served as a resource for the massive killing enterprise known as Operation Reinhard. When Himmler commissioned the Lublin SS and Police Leader Odilo Globocnik to kill the Polish Jews, Globocnik needed the experienced staff of T4 to carry out this assignment. In September 1941 Philipp Bouhler and Viktor Brack visited Globocnik in Lublin. Although at Nuremberg Brack denied that this visit had anything to do with the Final Solution, it seems likely that they discussed their future collaboration. And the KdF did delegate T4 staff members to operate killing centres at Belzec, Sobibor and Treblinka.[35]

First, experts were assigned during the period of construction. The T4 stonemason, Erwin Lambert, was assigned twice to Lublin as 'specialist for the construction of gas chambers'.[36] And after the assignment to introduce gassing in Riga had not materialized, T4 dispatched its chemist, Helmut Kallmeyer, to share his technical know-how about gas chambers with Lublin.[37]

Eventually, T4 men composed almost the entire personnel of the extermination camps of Operation Reinhard.[38] Christian Wirth, a commissar with the Stuttgart detective forces, was leader of this group.[39] Detached from the police for service with T4, he participated in the first experimental gassing in Brandenburg, served thereafter as non-medical director at Grafeneck and Hartheim, and apparently also served as a trouble-shooter in various other killing centres.[40] From T4 he moved to Operation Reinhard, bringing along to Lublin his Hartheim successors Franz Reichleitner and Franz Stangl.[41] In Lublin he first served as commandant of Sobibor, and then as Inspector of all three camps, advancing to the civil service rank of *Kriminalrat* and, through the intervention of Himmler, to the SS rank of first captain and then major.[42] Many witnesses have described him as the driving force behind the killings.[43]

At least ninety-two men, recruited from T4 headquarters and killing centres, were transferred to Lublin.[44] We do not know why these particular men were chosen. Physicians and nurses were not usually selected, and only one physician, Dr Irmfried Eberl, was assigned to Lublin as the first commandant of Treblinka. But because he could not exert sufficient administrative control over the killing operation, he was rapidly returned to his job as director of the much smaller killing centre at Bernburg.[45] The men transferred to Lublin thus belonged to the lower ranks of the T4 non-medical personnel. They had probably been selected because their superiors considered them capable of doing the killings expected in the east, because they had conscientiously fulfilled their tasks in T4, or simply because one of the T4 chiefs knew them. Anyhow, most were old party members, many were SA men, and some, like Josef Oberhauser (the T4 stoker who became Wirth's aide) and Kurt Franz (the T4 cook who became the last Treblinka commandant), came from the SS.[46] But not all had substantial party backgrounds. Some, as for example Franz Suchomel, were neither members of the Nazi Party nor of the SA nor the SS.[47]

Although the KdF had transferred these men to Globocnik, T4 continued to pay their wages and their supplemental allowances; T4 also delivered their mail, both letters and packages, which arrived in Lublin by courier.[48] Although Globocnik was their superior in the field, these men still worked for the KdF, which cared for their needs, providing, for example, liberal leave at the T4 rest home in Austria.[49]

The adoption of the euthanasia killing technique by the operators of the Final Solution illustrates even more than the use of T4 personnel the connection between the murder of the handicapped and the murder of Jews and Gypsies. The creation of the gas chamber was a unique invention of the Nazi criminals. But the method they developed to lure their victims to these chambers, to kill them on the assembly line, and to process their corpses, was an even more important discovery. If we were to apply the computer language of today, we would call the gas chambers 'killing hardware', and the method applied as 'killing software'. Hardware and software together comprised the killing technique that Nazi Germany bequeathed to the world.

During his post-war interrogation, a German perpetrator, who first helped to kill the handicapped at Hartheim and thereafter killed Jews in Belzec and Sobibor, provided an apt comparison between the techniques applied in both euthanasia and the Final Solution: 'The method employed in the camps [of Operation Reinhard] was the same as the one utilized in the castle in Hartheim, except that those killed there were all Jews.'[50] And when we compare the two procedures, using as representative examples

Hartheim for euthanasia and Sobibor for the Final Solution, we can see that they were almost identical.[51]

Of course, there were differences. For example, in the euthanasia killing centres located within the Reich, they used gas tanks from I. G. Farben with pure carbon monoxide, while in the Polish camps, where it was too expensive and time-consuming to obtain such tanks, they utilized impure exhaust fumes from diesel engines.[52] But the similarities are far more important. First, there is the subterfuge used to fool the victims upon arrival by giving the appearance of normality. In Hartheim physicians and nurses checking medical files made the killing centre look like a regular hospital, while in Sobibor the trappings of the reception area and the welcoming speech by a staff member made the killing centre look like a labour camp. The victims were told in both places that they had to take showers for hygienic reasons, and the gas chambers were disguised as shower rooms, while the belongings of the victims were carefully collected and registered to maintain the illusion of normality. (In both places, the practice of mass murder on the assembly line did, however, produce a callous barbarity that usually vitiated all attempts to deceive the victims.) Second, in both Hartheim and Sobibor the victims were crowded into the gas chamber, and their corpses were burned immediately after they had been killed. In Hartheim they used mobile crematoria; in Sobibor they utilized outdoor burning. In Hartheim the German staff had to remove and burn the corpses; in Sobibor they supervised while Jewish prisoners did the job. But in both places they robbed the corpses. The system of stealing gold teeth and gold bridge-work from the corpses of the murdered victims was first introduced in the euthanasia killing centres and then copied in the extermination camps of Operation Reinhard.[53]

In Auschwitz-Birkenau they improved upon this extermination technique first tried out in the euthanasia killings. They replaced carbon monoxide with hydrogen cyanide, known by the trade name Zyklon B, which acted faster.[54] There they also selected those still able to work, so that they could exploit their labour before killing them.[55] But even this had already been applied with euthanasia, where the killers deferred those handicapped institutionalized patients still able to work.[56]

In conclusion, I would like to offer the following summary for discussion. Racial ideology prepared the way for the killing operations by excluding entire groups on the basis of their heredity.[57] Civil servants from government and party implemented these killings with enthusiasm as soon as Hitler's authorization provided a protective shield for these crimes. There was no substantive difference between the killing operations directed against the handicapped, Jews and Gypsies. The murder of the handicapped came first, and in this so-called euthanasia the killers tried out their extermination technique. There the perpetrators also recognized the limits of the possible, and to avoid popular disapproval they transferred the killings from the Reich to the east. But the killing technique that had been developed and tested with euthanasia was used over and over again. And the instigators had learned that individuals selected at random would carry out terrible crimes 'without scruples'.[58]

NOTES

1 Limitations of space have made it impossible to analyse the euthanasia killing programme or the Final Solution in any detail. This chapter thus attempts only to sketch for further discussion the relationship between these two killing operations.

2 For a more detailed discussion, see my 'Das nationalsozialistische Euthanasie-programm', in Aurelius Freytag, Boris Marte and Thomas Stern (eds) *Geschichte und Verantwortung* (Vienna, 1988), pp. 277–97. See also Benno Müller-Hill, 'Selektion: Die Wissenschaft von der biologischen Auslese des Menschen durch Menschen', in Norbert Frei (ed.) *Medizin und Gesundheitspolitik in der NS-Zeit* (Munich, 1991), pp. 137–55.

3 See, for example, Yehuda Bauer, 'Jews, Gypsies, Slavs: policies of the Third Reich', *UNESCO Yearbook on Peace and Conflict Studies 1985* (Paris, 1987), pp. 73–100; idem, 'Gypsies', *Encyclopedia of the Holocaust*, 4 vols (New York and London, 1990), 2, pp. 634–8; idem, 'Literatur', *Vierteljahrshefte für Zeitge-schichte*, 37 (1989), pp. 524–8; idem, 'Holocaust and genocide: some comparisons', in Peter Hayes (ed.) *Lessons and Legacies: The Meaning of the Holocaust in a Changing World* (Evanston, 1991), pp. 36–46. For an extreme position, using Nazi stereotypes and Nazi language, see Bernhard Streck, 'Nationalsozial-istische Methoden zur Lösung der "Zigeunerfrage" ', *Politische Didaktik*, 1 (1981), pp. 26–37; and idem, 'Die nationalsozialistischen Methoden zur "Lösung des Zigeuner problems" ', *Tribüne: Zeitschrift zum Verständnis des Judentums*, 20, 78 (1981), pp. 54–77.

4 BAK (Koblenz), R18/5644: Oberregierungsrat Dr Zindel to Staatssekretär Pfundtner, 4 March 1936.

5 See Franz Calvelli-Adorno, 'Die rassische Verfolgung der Zigeuner vor dem 1. März 1943', *Rechtssprechung zum Widergutmachungsrecht*, 12, 12 (December 1961), pp. 529–37.

6 For an introduction, see Sybil Milton, 'The context of the Holocaust', *German Studies Review*, 13 (1990), pp. 269–83; idem, 'Gypsies and the Holocaust', *The History Teacher*, 24, 4 (August 1991), pp. 1–13.

7 For the eugenic legislation directed against the handicapped, see the Law to Prevent Offspring with Hereditary Diseases (*RGBl* 1933, 1:529) and the Mar-riage Health Law (*RGBl* 1935, 1:1246); for an English translation of these and similar laws, see Control Commission for Germany (British Element), Legal Division, British Special Legal Research Unit, 'Translations of Nazi health laws concerned with hereditary diseases, matrimonial health, sterilization, and castration (8 November 1945)' (available at the library of the National Institute of Health, Bethesda).

8 For the legislation against Jews, see the Law for the Restoration of the Pro-fessional Civil Service (*RGBl* 1933, 1:175) and the Nuremberg racial laws: the Reich Citizenship Law (*RGBl* 1935, 1:1146) and the Law for the Protection of German Blood and German Honour (*RGB1* 1935, 1:1146); for a listing and summation of all anti-Jewish laws and decrees, see Joseph Walk (ed.) *Das Sonderrecht für die Juden im NS-Staat: Eine Sammlung der gesetzlichen*

Massnahmen und Richtlinien – Inhalt und Bedeutung (Heidelberg and Karlsruhe, 1981).

9 For the legislation against Gypsies, see the collection of laws and decrees in StA Hamburg, Verfahren 2200 Js 2/84.

10 See BAK, R36/881: Verpflegungskosten in Heil- und Pflegeanstalten, 28 February 1939. See also Angelika Ebbinghaus, 'Kostensenkung, "Aktive Therapie" und Vernichtung', in Angelika Ebbinghaus, Heidrun Kaupen-Haas and Karl Heinz Roth (eds) *Heilen und Vernichten im Mustergau Hamburg: Bevölkerungs- und Gesundheitspolitik im Dritten Reich* (Hamburg, 1984), pp. 136–46.

11 See the documents in BAK, R36/1022 and 1023: Fürsorge für Juden und Zigeuner.

12 On sterilization, see Gisela Bock, *Zwangssterilisation im Nationalsozialismus: Studien zur Rassenpolitik und Frauenpolitik* (Opladen, 1986). On the Gypsy camps, see Ute Bruckner-Boroujerdi and Wolfgang Wippermann, 'Das Zigeunerlager Berlin-Marzahn, 1936–1945', *Pogrom*, 18, 130 (June 1987), pp. 527–32; Karola Fings and Frank Sparing, 'Das Zigeunerlager in Köln-Bickendorf, 1935–1958', *1999: Zeitschrift für Sozialgeschichte*, 6, 3 (July 1991), pp. 11–40; Eva von Hase-Mihalik and Doris Kreuzkamp, *Du kriegst auch einen schönen Wohnwagen: Zwangslager für Sinti und Roma während des Nationalsozialismus in Frankfurt am Main* (Frankfurt, 1990). On Jews, see Uwe Dietrich Adam, *Judenpolitik im Dritten Reich* (Düsseldorf, 1979).

13 See, for example, Hitler's 1935 statement to Gerhard Wagner that during a war he would implement euthanasia: United States Military Tribunal, Official Transcript of the Proceedings in Case 1, The United States of America vs. Karl Brandt *et al.* (Medical Case), p. 2482 (testimony Karl Brandt).

14 The regime applied the euphemism euthanasia to the killing of the handicapped, although these killings had nothing in common with the accepted meaning of the term. The victims of the eugenic-racial killings did not suffer from painful, terminal illnesses, but were selected – regardless of their life expectancy – because they were judged physically or mentally inferior. The concept of eugenic killings masquerading as euthanasia was first advanced in Karl Binding and Alfred Hoche, *Die Freigabe der Vernichtung lebensunwerten Lebens: Ihr Maß und Ihre Form* (Leipzig, 1920).

15 The handicapped were murdered in six killing centres: Grafeneck in Württemberg, Brandenburg on the Havel near Berlin, Hartheim near Linz, Sonnenstein in Pirna in Saxony, Bernburg on the Saale in the Prussian province of Saxony, and Hadamar in Hessen.

16 See Binding and Hoche, *Die Freigabe der Vernichtung lebensunwerten Lebens*. For statements during the 1930s that the handicapped should simply be killed, see, for example, GStA Frankfurt, Anklageschrift gg. Reinhold Vorberg und Dietrich Allers, Js 20/61 (GStA), 15 February 1966, p. 11 (testimony Otto Mauthe, 15 November 1961); NARA Washington, RG 238, Microfilm Publ. M-1019, Roll 46: interrogation Friedrich Mennecke, 11 January 1947, p. 23.

17 On children's euthanasia, see GStA Frankfurt, Anklageschrift gg. Werner Heyde, Gerhard Bohne, und Hans Hefelmann, Ks 2/63 (GStA), Js 17/59 (GStA), 22 May 1962, pp. 53–4 (testimony Hans Hefelmann). On adult euthanasia, see US Military Tribunal, Case 1 Transcript, pp. 2668–9 (testimony Hans-Heinrich Lammers), p. 2396 (testimony Karl Brandt).

18 See Ernst Klee, *'Euthanasie' im NS-Staat: Die 'Vernichtung lebensunwerten Lebens'* (Frankfurt, 1983).

19 US Military Tribunal, Case 1 Transcript, pp. 2369, 2402 (testimony Karl Brandt). The language of this authorization was prepared for the KdF by a

committee that included leading psychiatrists. GStA Frankfurt, Anklage Heyde, Bohne, und Hefelmann, Ks 2/63 (GStA), Js 17/59 (GStA), 22 May 1962, pp. 201ff.

20 Nuremberg Doc. PS–630. Also available in BAK, R22/4209.

21 ZStL, Heidelberg Docs 127, 398–127, 399: Richtlinien der beiden Euthanasiebeauftragten hinsichtlich der bei der Begutachtung anzulegenden Maßstäbe, unter Einbeziehung der Ergebnisse der Besprechungen in Berchtesgaden vom 10.3. 1941; US Military Tribunal, Case 1 Transcript, P. 2493 (testimony Karl Brandt). See also my 'Jüdische Anstaltspatienten im NS-Deutschland', in Götz Aly (ed.) *Aktion T4* (Berlin, 1987), pp. 34–44.

22 For the most recent analysis, see Richard Breitman, *The Architect of Genocide: Himmler and the Final Solution* (New York, 1991).

23 Nuremberg Doc. PS–710.

24 See also Gerald Fleming, *Hitler und die Endlösung* (Wiesbaden and Munich, 1982).

25 BAK, NS neu 19/180: Bormann to Himmler, 3 December 1942. The handwritten notation reads: 'Führer. Aufstellung. Wer sind Zigeuner'.

26 See StA Hamburg, Verfahren 2200 Js 2/84: RSHA Schnellbrief, 29 January 1943.

27 See, for example, StA Hamburg, Anklageschrift gg. Friedrich Lensch und Kurt Struve, 147 Js 58/67, 24 April 1973.

28 ZStL, Sammlung Schumacher, Bd. 121, Faszikel 401, and Nuremberg Doc. NO-018: Heinrich Himmler to Victor Brack, 19 December 1940.

29 On Hitler's stop order, see US Military Tribunal, Case 1 Transcript, pp. 2530–1 (testimony Karl Brandt), p. 7629 (testimony Viktor Brack).

30 On public opinion, see, for example, Nuremberg Docs NO-018, NO-665, NO-795, D-906.

31 On the support role of Reinhard Heydrich and the RSHA, see BAK, R22/5021: handwritten note by Dr Günther Joel transmitting to Franz Gürtner comments by Heydrich concerning his relationship to the euthanasia programme, 1 November [1940]; and BA-MA Freiburg, H20/463 and 465: Viktor Brack to Heinrich Müller, 5 July 1941; Viktor Brack to RSHA, Abteilung IVb2, 9 April 1942. On the activities of the SS as euthanasia killing units in border regions, see, for example, LG Hanover, Urteil gg. Kurt Eimann, 2 Ks 2/67, 20 December 1968; and Nuremberg Doc. NO-2275: Gruppenführer Richard Hildebrandt, Bericht über Aufstellung, Einsatz und Tätigkeit des SS-Wachsturmbann E.

32 ZStL: interrogation August Becker, 10 and 26 March 1960, 16 May 1961, 8 October 1963; StA Düsseldorf: interrogation Albert Widmann, 15 January 1960; StA Düsseldorf, Anklageschrift gg. Albert Widmann u.A., 8 Js 7212/59, 13 September 1960; LG Düsseldorf, Urteil gg. Albert Widmann, 8 Ks 1/61, 16 May 1961; StA Stuttgart, Anklageschrift gg. Albert Widmann, (19) 13 Js 328/60, 29 August 1962.

33 See Adelheid L. Rüter-Ehlermann and C. F. Rüter (eds) *Justiz und NS-Verbrechen: Sammlung deutscher Strafurteile wegen nationalsozialistischer Tötungsverbrechen*, 22 vols (Amsterdam, 1968–81) (hereafter *JuNSV*), vol. 21, no. 594 (1963 Kulmhof trial). On the Lange Kommando, see also Nuremberg Docs NO-2908, NO-2909, NO-2911, NO-1073 and NO-1076. See also BDC: dossiers Herbert Lange and Hans Bothmann.

34 Nuremberg Docs NO-365 and NO-997.

35 US Military Tribunal, Case 1 Transcript, pp. 7512, 7514 (testimony Viktor Brack). For the history of the camps of Operation Reinhard, see StA Düsseldorf,

Anklageschrift gg. Kurt Franz u.A., 8 Js 10904/59, 29 January 1963; LG Düsseldorf, Urteil gg. Kurt Franz u.A., 8 I KS 2/64, 3 September 1965; StA Düsseldorf, Anklageschrift gg. Franz Stangl, 8 Js 1045/69, 29 September 1969; LG Düsseldorf, Urteil gg. Franz Stangl, 8 Ks 1/69, 22 December 1970; LG Hagen, Urteil gg. Werner Dubois u.A., 11 Ks 1/64, 20 December 1966.

36 ZStL: interrogation Erwin Lambert, 26 April 1961, 4 May 1961, 3 April 1962. See also LG Düsseldorf, Urteil Franz, 8 I Ks 2/64, 3 September 1965, pp. 477f.

37 ZStL: interrogation Helmut Kallmeyer, 20 June 1961, 15 September 1961; interrogation Gertrud Kallmeyer née Froese, 31 May 1960, 27 February 1961, 17 August 1961, 5 September 1961, 20 September 1961, 7 December 1961, 10 February 1966.

38 Nuremberg Doc. NO-205: Brack to Himmler, 23 June 1942.

39 BDC: dossier Christian Wirth and file Operation Reinhard.

40 On Wirth's activities in Grafeneck, see US Military Tribunal, Case 1 Transcript, pp. 7704, 7733 (testimony Viktor Brack); on his activities in Hartheim, see DÖW Vienna, file E18370/1: LG Linz, interrogation Heinrich Barbl, 16 November 1964; Kreisgericht Wels, interrogation Stefan Schachermeyer, 11 March 1964; file E18370/2: Bezirksgericht Ybbs, interrogation Franz Sitter, 20 March 1947; file E18370/3: Anstalt Ybbs to Anstalt Niedernhart, 21 May 1946; Gendarmeriepostenkommando Gmunden, interrogation Gertraud Dirnberger, 13 August 1946. On Wirth's appearance in other killing centres, see, for example, GStA Frankfurt, Eberl Akten, II/151, 7:58–62: Aktenvermerk by Dr Heinrich Bunke, 9 July 1941, concerning Wirth's behaviour in Bernburg on 8 July 1941.

41 See DÖW, E18370/2: Polizeidirektion Linz, Schlußbericht betr. Hartheim, 29 July 1946; StA Düsseldorf, Anklage Stangl, 8 Js 1045/69, 29 September 1969.

42 BDC, file Operation Reinhard: Beförderungsliste and correspondence.

43 See, for example, Adalbert Rückerl, NS-Vernichtungslager im Spiegel deutscher Strafprozesse (Munich, 1977), p. 72.

44 ibid., pp. 117–18.

45 GStA Frankfurt, Eberl Akten, III/683/4–5, 7:144–8: Irmfried to Ruth Eberl, 19 April 1942, 29 June 1942. See also ZStL: interrogation Josef Oberhauser, 18 November 1968; interrogation Franz Suchomel, 14 September 1967.

46 Rückerl, NS-Vernichtungslager, pp. 295ff. See also ZStL: interrogation Josef Oberhauser, 2 March 1961, 18 November 1968, and interrogation Kurt Franz, 9 May 1962, 5 December 1962.

47 ZStL: interrogation Franz Suchomel, 24 October 1960, 25 October 1960, 5 February 1963, 24 April 1964, 14 September 1967, 18 September 1967. See also LG Düsseldorf, Urteil Franz, 8 I Ks 2/64, 3 September 1965, pp. 395–8.

48 ZStL: interrogation of T4 courier Erich Fettke, 2 September 1965.

49 See above, Notes 45–7, interrogations Oberhauser, Franz and Suchomel.

50 DÖW, E18370/1: LG Linz, interrogation Heinrich Barbl, 5 October 1964.

51 My Hartheim account is based on the 1945 interrogation of the stoker Vinzenz Nohel (DÖW, E18370/3: Kriminalpolizei Linz, interrogation Vinzenz Nohel, 4 September 1945), and my Sobibor example is based on the findings of the Hagen district court in the Sobibor trial (LG Hagen, Urteil gg. Karl Frenzel, 11 Ks 1/64, 4 October 1985, pp. 98–104).

52 On the giant chemical concern I. G. Farben, see Joseph Borkin, The Crime and Punishment of I. G. Farben (New York, 1978).

53 On the collection of gold teeth in the T4 killing centres, see HHStA Wiesbaden, 461/32061/7: LG Frankfurt, Protokoll der öffentlichen Sitzung im Hadamar Prozeß, 4a KLs 7/47, 3 March 1947, p. 32 (testimony Ingeborg Seidel); DÖW, 11440: StA Linz, Anklageschrift gg. Franz Stangl, Karl Harrer, Leopold Lang

und Franz Mayrhuber, 3 St 466/46, 24 April 1948, p. 5; StA Stuttgart, Verfahren Albert Widmann, Ks 19/62 (19 Js 328/60): testimony Klara Mattmüller, 17 February 1966; StA Düsseldorf, Verfahren Albert Widmann, 8 Ks 1/61 (8 Js 7212/59): interrogation Albert Widmann, 15 January 1960, p. 5.

54 See Müller-Hill, 'Selektion', p. 150.
55 See *JuNSV*, vol. 21, no. 595 (1965 Auschwitz trial). See also Hermann Langbein, *Menschen in Auschwitz* (Frankfurt, Berlin and Vienna, 1980).
56 See, for example, US Military Tribunal, Case 1 Transcript, pp. 2506, 2510, 2515–16 (testimony Karl Brandt), pp. 7571–2 (testimony Viktor Brack), p. 1906 (testimony Friedrich Mennecke); StA Hamburg, Verfahren 147 Js 58/67, Gesundheitsbehörde Bd 1: reporting form for institutions, August 1940.
57 See Benno Müller-Hill, *Tödliche Wissenschaft: Die Aussonderung von Juden, Zigeunern und Geisteskranken, 1933–1945* (Reinbek bei Hamburg, 1984).
58 StA Düsseldorf, Anklage Franz, 8 Js 10904/59, 29 January 1963, p. 98.

3

THE IDEA OF THE FINAL SOLUTION AND THE ROLE OF EXPERTS

Benno Müller-Hill

When I read the protocol of the Wannsee Conference for the first time ten years ago, two details aroused my curiosity: first, the fact that seven of the fourteen participants (not counting Heydrich) held doctoral degrees.[1] Most of them were top civil servants. In Germany civil servants are traditionally trained in law. But that so many of them had bothered to get a real or honorary doctoral degree seemed both strange and ominous. Second, that this was the only one of thirty copies to have survived the fall of Nazism. Those legal experts and their helpers had been most efficient in their attempt to destroy almost every trace of their planning of the big crime.

At that time I began to collect material to document the involvement of German human geneticists, anthropologists and psychiatrists in the various racial programmes and crimes.[2] The role of those experts seemed to be vastly underestimated. Germany was one of the most highly developed countries in the world when the Nazis took power. The terror the Nazis directed against their racial and political enemies was directed specifically against carefully selected individuals and minorities. Mistakes happened of course but were not encouraged. Thus the majority of the Germans felt protected from the terror and so on the whole remained loyal until the end. To achieve this the Nazis made intensive use of the university-trained intelligentsia. Two groups were particularly involved in executing the racial programmes: medical doctors trained in genetics and anthropology; and the law profession.

I will give only a few examples: the sterilization programme of 1933–9 needed and produced medical doctors and judges educated in genetics. A research institute headed by a psychiatrist was set up as part of the Reichsgesundheitsamt (National Health Institute) to select the few true Gypsies worthy to survive and be permitted to reproduce. Thirty-nine medical doctors and nine professors of psychiatry made the life-and-death decisions in the euthanasia programme of 1939–41. An MD had to open the carbon monoxide valve in the extermination centres. Only MDs had the right to select for the gas chambers of Auschwitz. From these examples, it can be seen that the work of the specialists was in part technical and in part symbolic. It was just this amalgam of technique and symbol which became highly characteristic of the Nazi system. Ample documentation for the facts mentioned above can be found in the recent literature.[2]

In this chapter I discuss a special example of this amalgam. Not only judges, prosecutors and lawyers but also public servants traditionally had a university education in law in Germany. The more ambitious public servants even held doctoral degrees in law. As I said before, seven of the fourteen participants (excluding Heydrich) at the Wannsee Conference held doctoral degrees in law. This might be expected among top German civil servants. But it is startling that six of the fifteen *Einsatzgruppenführer* (Achramer-Pifrader, Fuchs, Rasch, Schumacher, Stahlecker and Thomas) held doctoral degrees.[3] At least three others (H. Böhme, Ehrlinger, Panziger) had studied law. Furthermore sixteen of the sixty-nine *Einsatzkommandoführer* also held doctoral degrees. This is a highly important fact which I will analyse further, specifying, first, in which field these mass murderers obtained their degree, then, what qualities their theses had. And finally, I discuss what conclusions can be drawn from this amalgam of university education and mass murder.

Let me recall that the *Einsatzgruppenführer* were the commanders of the four *Einsatzgruppen* and that each *Einsatzgruppe* was divided into four or five *Kommandos*. Each *Kommando* consisted of 100 to 200 men and was headed by a *Kommandoführer*. They were instructed, in the Soviet Union, to kill all Jews, including their children, on the spot, also communists active as partisans. They also killed all the Gypsies and patients of mental asylums they could find. The exact number of their victims is unknown but 1.25 million seems to be a reliable estimate.[4]

The *Einsatzgruppenführer* and *Kommandoführer* had one thing in common: most of them entered the SS, the SA or the NSDAP as very young men at the earliest moment they could. This reflects the popularity of the Nazis among students in the Weimar Republic. Later most of them entered offices of the Ministry of the Interior to become public servants. From there they were selected in a fairly random manner to be sent to the east.

The personal files available in the Berlin Document Centre often indicate the university and the place and year of a dissertation but they never give the title. To find the dissertations I consulted the annual volumes of the *Jahresverzeichnis der an den Deutschen Unversitäten und technischen Hochschulen erschienenen Hochschulschriften* listing all German dissertations (the Austrian dissertations cannot be spotted easily). Then I tried to get copies of the dissertations. They often, but not always, contain a short curriculum vitae which confirms authorship.

THE DISSERTATIONS

1 *Humbert Achramer-Pifrader*: according to his curriculum vitae, Dr iur. (doctoral degree in law) 1934 in an Austrian university, but this could not be verified.

2 *Josef Auinger*: an Austrian, who studied law in Austria; presumably Dr iur. A dissertation could not be identified.

3 *Gerhard Bast*: he received his doctoral degree in law on 10 December 1935 at the University of Graz. This was confirmed by the Universitäts-archiv of Graz. I was informed that a written dissertation was not required at the time in Graz.

4 *Walter Blume*: title of dissertation, 'Prozessuale Probleme bei der Been-digung des gesetzlichen Güterstandes während eines Prozesses des Ehemanns über eingebrachtes Gut der Frau'; Friedrich-Alexander Univ-ersität zu Erlangen, juristische Fakultät (Law School), 27 February 1933; a short but concise discussion about a special problem in the law of divorce.

5 *Otto Bradfisch*: title of dissertation, 'Ausgewählte Volkskrankheiten im Lichte quantitativer und qualitativer Bevölkerungspolitik'; Leopold-Franzens Universität zu Innsbruck, Fakultät der Staatswissenschaften (Department of Social Sciences), November 1926; 136 pages on tubercu-losis, sexual diseases and alcoholism and the possible strategies against these diseases.

6 *Werner Braune*: title of dissertation, 'Gibt es eine Zwangsvollstreckung aus Verurteilungen zur Abgabe einer Willenserklärung'; Universität Tübingen, juristische Fakultät (Law School), 15 October 1934; a short but concise dissertation about a special problem of bankruptcy.

7 *Friedrich Burchardt*: title of dissertation, 'Das Recht der nationalen Minderheiten in Lettland' (on the legal status of minorities in Latvia), Universität zu Jena, juristische Fakultät (Law School), 23 January 1933.

8 *Alfred Filbert*: title of dissertation, 'Kann das Ablehnungsrecht des Konkursverwalters des Vorbehaltskäufers mit der Anwartschaft des Käufers auf den Eigentumserwerb ausgeräumt werden?'; Hessische Ludwigs-Universität zu Giessen, juristische Fakultät (Law School), 19 December 1934; a short discussion of a special aspect of bankruptcy law.

9 *Wilhelm Fuchs*: title of dissertation, 'Eine neue Methode zur künstlichen Infektion der Gerste mit Helminthosporium gramineum Rbh. und ihre Anwendung zur Prüfung von Beiz- und Immunitätsfragen'; Universität Leipzig, Philosophische Fakultät (Faculty of Arts and Sciences), 3 March 1930; also published in *Phytopathologische Zeitschrift* 2, Heft 3; experimental work on a practical problem of botany or agriculture. Dr Fuchs worked first for Darré (Secretary for Agriculture in the first National Socialist government) on organizing agriculture.

10 *Walter Haensch*: title of dissertation, 'Der organisatorische Weg zur einheitlichen Reichspolizei'; Universität Leipzig, juristische Fakultät (Law School), 12 September 1939; 60 pages on the legal framework of centralization of the police under the Nazis.

11 *Erich Isselhorst*: title of dissertation, 'Die Schlichtungsnotverordnung'; Universität zu Köln, juristische Fakultät (Law School), 12 June 1931; 50 pages on the emergency law of the Weimar republic allowing arbitration in union–industry conflicts.

12 *Erhard Kroeger*: title of dissertation, 'Die rechtliche Stellung des Ausländers in Lettland'; Albertus-Universität zu Königsberg, juristische Fakultät (Law Faculty), 12 November 1929; 76 pages outlining the rights of foreigners in Latvia.

13 *Rudolf Lange*: title of dissertation, 'Das Direktionsrecht des Arbeitgebers'; Universität Jena, juristische Fakultät (Law School), 12 December 1933; 118 pages discussing employers' rights.

14 *Erich Müller*: presumably Dr iur.; dissertation could not be identified – the name was too common.

15 *Manfred Pechau*: title of dissertation, 'Nationalsozialismus und deutsche Sprache'; Ernst-Moritz-Arndt-Universität zu Greifswald, philosophische Fakultät (Faculty of Arts and Sciences), department of German literature, 10 August 1934; 106 pages discussing the new words coined by the Nazis.

16 *Otto Rasch*: Rasch produced two dissertations: (1) 'Wohnungsmarkt und Wohnungspolitik in England in der Kriegs- und Nachkriegszeit'; Universität Leipzig, philosophische Fakultät (Faculty of Arts and Sciences), 19 July 1922; 123 pages advocating a free market as opposed to planning and market controls; (2) 'Die verfassungsrechtliche Stellung des Preußischen Landtagspräsidenten'; this dissertation was not available to me.

17 *Martin Sandberger*: title of dissertation, 'Die Sozialversicherung im nationalsozialistischen Staat'; Eberhard-Karls-Universität zu Tübingen, juristische Fakultät (Law School), 3 February 1934; 91-page apology for the social security system in Nazi Germany.

18 *Hans Karl Schumacher*: title of dissertation, 'Die Sicherungsübereignung unter besonderer Berücksichtigung des Treunehmers im Konkurs des Treugebers und bei der Zwangsvollstreckung gegen denselben'; Universität Erlangen, juristische Fakultät (Law School), 27 December 1932; 30 pages on a special aspect of bankruptcy law.

19 *Franz Alfred Six*: title of dissertation, 'Die politische Propaganda der NSDAP im Kampf um die Macht'; Ruprecht-Karl-Universität Heidelberg, philosophische Fakultät (Faculty of Arts and Sciences), 6 May 1934; 75 pages in praise of Goebbels's language.

20 *Walter Stahlecker*: title of dissertation, 'Die Voraussetzungen der Anordnungen der Fürsorgeerziehung nach dem Rechte des

Bürgerlichen Gesetzbuches und des Reichsjugendwohlfahrtsgesetzes unter der Berücksichtigung des württembergischen Landesrechtes'; Eberhard-Karls-Universität zu Tübingen, juristische Fakultät (Law School), 7 November 1926; 166-page discussion about German social security legislation.

21 *Max Thomas*: studied science, medicine and law. According to his curriculum vitae he got his doctoral degree in 1923. Possible title of his dissertation in (bio-)chemistry 'Über neue Salicylsäurederivate' (on new derivatives of salicylic acid), philosophische Fakultät (Faculty of Arts and Sciences), der Universität zu Jena, 1 August 1923; identity not verified. A medical dissertation could not be identified.

22 *Erwin Weimann*: presumably Dr med. Title of dissertation 'Ein Fall von Lipodystrophia progressiva', Universität zu Tübingen, medizinische Fakultät (Medical School), 3 January 1935.

What can be said in general about these doctoral theses? Nine of them (including Thomas's PhD) were obtained before the Nazis came to power in Germany, the rest during or after the *Machtübernahme* (legal takeover). Twelve are dissertations in law, three in political science, two in science, and one each in medicine and in German literature. They are of differing quality, as one would expect, and typical for their time, no worse and no better. I just note that they were all freely available as if they were written by normal authors of normal dissertations.

Before drawing any general conclusions, I would like to comment on the case of one of the aforementioned authors: Dr Alfred Six. He wrote fast and spoke well. He published extensively between 1937 and 1944.[5] In 1937 he was asked to teach political science (*Lehrauftrag*) at the University of Königsberg. In 1940 he became Professor of Political Science at the department of foreign politics at the University of Berlin. During those years he was also active in the SD as *the* top anti-Jewish expert. As such, in 1937 he wrote for the SD (Sicherheitsdienst or secret police) a report full of praise of his subordinate, Adolf Eichmann.[6] In 1941 he became head of the *Vorkommando Moskau* of the *Einsatzgruppe* B. After a short time he arranged, apparently without any damage to his career, to leave this murderous business and go back to Berlin.[7] 'The only disadvantage which resulted was personal conflict between me and Heydrich till his death' (*Ich hatte keine Nachteile außer dem, daß ich mit Heydrich bis zu seinem Tode in einem persönlichen Zerwürfnis lebte*), he said later.[8] He was then promoted to a high office in the Foreign Office. As such he opened the conference of experts on Jews from German embassies (*Arbeitstagung der Judenreferenten der deutschen Missionen*, 3 and 4 April 1944) in the Hotel Sanssouci, Krummhübel.[9] There he gave a talk on 'Die politische Struktur des Weltjudentums' ('The political structure of world Jewry'). As a true expert he could, according to the protocol, state: 'Jewry in Europe has ended its biological and also political roles . . . the physical elimination of the Jewry of the East deprives Jewry of its biological reserves' (*Das Judentum in Europa habe seine biologische und gleichzeitig politische Rolle ausgespielt. . . . Die physische Beseitigung des Ostjudentums entziehe dem Judentum seine biologische Reserve*).[10] Directly after Six, Leg. Rat. v. Thadden spoke. The protocol notes: 'Since the details the speaker gave about the present state of the executive measures in the various countries are to be kept secret they have not been included in protocol' (*Da die von dem Referenten vorgetragenen Einzelheiten über den Stand der Exekutivmaßnahmen in den einzelnen Ländern geheim zu halten sind, ist von der Aufnahme ins Protokoll abgesehen worden*).[11] This is not the place to analyse the Sanssouci-Krummhübel Conference. I merely note that twelve out of its twenty-four participants had doctoral degrees presumably in law, and I go on to emphasize the easy mingling of the rather different spheres: university – *Einsatzgruppen* – Foreign Office. Six was condemned in Nuremberg in 1948 to twenty years in jail. In 1952 he was a free man. He made a second career in business administration and finally became head of Porsche advertising.[12]

I have studied the curricula vitae of only some of the *Einsatzkommandoführer*. Among them I noted twelve former students of law (Batz, H. J. Böhme, Breder, Matschke, Mohr, Panziger, Poche, Rapp, Richter, Schäfer, Schindhelm, Suhr), two teachers (Loos, Steimle), one Protestant priest (Biberstein) and one former student of sociology (Otto Ohlendorf). Ohlendorf joined the SS very early. He never got around to writing his thesis, but in 1933 he became *Assistent* (research fellow) in Kiel University at the Institut für Weltwirtschaft. In 1935 he became head of a department at the Institut für Angewandte Wirtschaft at Berlin University where he had the title of professor. He rose high in the SD and became Führer of the *Einsatzgruppe* D. When he returned to Berlin in July 1942 he got a top position in the Reichswirtschaftsministerium. His collaborators wrote a book which was published under his name, Otto Ohlendorf, *Der deutsche Binnenhandel* (Berlin, Elsner, 1942). He was put on trial in Nuremberg. I would just like to mention how this authority in sociology quoted and believed medical authority. In Nuremberg he explained that according to Himmler's orders the *Gaswagen* were for women and children only: 'women and children should not be put under the mental stress of the execution act' (*Frauen und Kinder sollten der seelischen Belastung der Exekutionshandlung nicht ausgesetzt werden*).[13] When asked about their possible suffering he answered that a medical doctor had checked and had reported that death in the *Gaswagen* was fast and the victims were not aware of it. Maybe he did not believe it, but he believed the judge might believe it. He was hanged in 1951.

When those leading troops who shoot innocent children, women and old people have law degrees, their academic record is bound to impress their subordinates. In the case of Thomas, a medical doctor with special training (*Facharzt*) in psychiatry, a similar argument could certainly be made. When a medical doctor and psychiatrist orders shootings it can't be wrong. That the authority of law and medical science can be used in this way is certainly one of the most disquieting discoveries and achievements of the Nazis. The infamous role that some members of the medical profession played under Nazism has recently been discussed quite openly in Germany.[14] A true avalanche of books has opened the discussion. But I am not aware that the legal training of the *Einsatzgruppenführer* has ever been explicitly mentioned as a question or as a reproach to the legal profession. When discussing the phenomenon of the involvement of geneticists in the crimes of Nazi Germany I have often heard American colleagues argue that this just proves that scientists are human too. True, but when the medical or the legal profession directs mass murder, it is worse than when ordinary men do it. They should know better.

The code name of the proposed murder of all Jews, *Endlösung* or *Gesamtlösung*, suggested that a scientific or technological problem was being attacked scientifically. Equations have solutions, and to (dis)solve something means to make it disappear. The successful solution of this particular problem was the disappearance of those who supposedly created it: the Jews. To attack it (note the military term!) a vast effort of interdepartmental cooperation was needed. This is what the Wannsee Conference was all about: to coordinate the efforts of the various agencies of the German government. Interdepartmental cooperation implies that everybody is very busy but nobody feels responsible for the project as a whole. Specialists have no knowledge outside their field. They need this reassurance to make progress in their own sphere. Specialists who investigate the matter subsequently have to understand and believe this.

The gigantic, murderous operation which needed the help of all German embassies and several governmental departments, of the SS and the army, can also be seen as the void out of which a new order would emerge, a void which was to be filled by economic planning.[15] So we witness legal experts executing, medical experts killing by gas, and with them political scientists, sociologists and economists analysing, and planners restructuring the robbed properties and the ruins on paper.

Is this true genetics, true medicine, true economics, true sociology and true law? Superficially yes. The details of these fields are kept intact by logic, the papers published are not outstanding but they are not completely wrong either. There is just one fundamental defect in this construction of a unified world of science and planning: nobody is allowed to question the final goals and values. The final goals and values have become – as taboos – part of the whole technological construction itself. The authority of the Führer merges with the authority of science and technology. Science has then been successfully amalgamated with the terrible religion of the Nazis.

When science is strongly supported by a government because its leaders believe in it as if it were a religion, it has a great appeal for young people. They like science and they need something to believe in. And they take the exciting new jobs created by the government. In Germany the message was: we are the higher race, we shall therefore remain and the others shall disappear from this earth. This particular religion failed. Millions of people had to die to defeat it. Its history should be remembered for ever as an eternal warning to anyone who tries to resurrect a similar religion.

NOTES

I thank Alfred Streim for providing the birth dates necessary to prove authorship of the dissertations, and Heinrich Herbertz for help in locating some of them.

1 Besprechungsprotokoll. National Archives NG 2586.
2 B. Müller-Hill, *Murderous Science. Elimination by Scientific Selection of Jews, Gypsies and Others, Germany 1933–1945* (Oxford University Press, Oxford, 1988); R. J. Lifton, *The Nazi Doctors. Medical Killing and the Psychology of Genocide* (Basic Books, New York, 1986); R. N. Proctor, *Racial Hygiene. Medicine under the Nazis* (Harvard University Press, Cambridge, Mass., 1988); P. Weindling, *Health, Race and German Politics between National Unification and Nazism 1870–1945* (Cambridge University Press, 1989); M. H. Kater, *Doctors under Hitler* (University of North Carolina Press, Chapel Hill, NC, 1989).
3 H. Krausnick, *Hitlers Einsatzgruppen. Die Truppen des Weltanschauungskrieges 1938–1942* (Fischer, Frankfurt a.M., 1985), pp. 360–4; and H. Krausnick and H. H. Wilhelm, *Die Truppe des Weltanschauungskrieges* (Deutsche Verlagsgesellschaft, Stuttgart, 1981). Krausnick's list (pp. 360–4) contains some inevitable minor mistakes. It omits the Führer of *Einsatzgruppe* C (October or November 1941 to June 1942) Dr Hans Karl Schumacher. He mistakenly claimed doctoral degrees in law for four *Kommandoführer* (Ehrlinger, Hubig, Körting and Strauch). All four indeed studied law.
4 S. Spector in *Encyclopedia of the Holocaust*, 2, (Macmillan, New York, 1990), p. 438.
5 F. A. Six, *Pressefreiheit und internationale Zusammenarbeit* (Hanseat. Verl. Anst., Hamburg, 1937); *Freimaurerei und Judenemanzipation* (Hanseat. Verl. Anst., Hamburg, 1938); *Freimaurerei und Christentum. Ein Beitr. zur polit. Geistesgeschichte* (Hanseat. Verl. Anst., Hamburg, 1940); *Reich und Westen* Junker u. Dünnhaupt, Berlin, 1940); *Die Bürgerkriege Europas und der Einigungskrieg der Gegenwart* (Steiniger, Berlin, 1942); *Studien zur Geistesgeschichte der Freimaurerei* (Hanseat. Verl. Anst., Hamburg, 1942); *Das Reich und Europa* Eher, Berlin, 1943); *Europa, Tradition u. Zukunft* (Hanseat. Verl. Anst., Hamburg, 1944).
6 In Personal-Bericht, Adolf Eichmann. Berlin Document Centre, 1937.
7 ibid.
8 In E. Klee, W. Dressen and V. Riess, *'Schöne Zeiten'. Judenmord aus der Sicht der Täter und Gaffer* (Fischer, Frankfurt a.M., 1988), p. 83.
9 Arbeitstagung der Judenreferenten der deutschen Missionen in Europa am 3.

und 4. April 1944 in Krummhübel/Rsgb., Hotel Sanssouci, Tagungsfolge und Protokolle. Berlin Document Centre.

10 ibid.

11 ibid.

12 *Braunbuch Kriegs- und Naziverbrecher in der Bundesrepublik. Staatsverlag der DDR* (Berlin, 1965), p. 78.

13 *Der Prozeß gegen die Hauptkriegsverbrecher vor dem internationalen Militärgerichtshof, Nürnberg, 14.11.1945 – 1.10.1946* (Nuremberg, 1947), vol. 4, p. 368.

14 It is impossible to list all the important books here, so I am just mentioning a very few: *Beiträge zur Nationalsozialistischen Gesundheits- und Sozialpolitik*, vols 1–6 (Rotbuch Verlag, Berlin, 1985–8); A. Götz and K. H. Roth, *Die Restlose Erfassung. Volkszählen, Identifizieren, Aussondern im Nationalsozialismus* (Rotbuch Verlag, Berlin, 1984); E. Klee, *Euthanasie im NS-Staat. Die Vernichtung lebensunwerten Lebens* (S. Fischer Verlag, Frankfurt a.M., 1983); W. Wuttke-Groneberg, *Medizin im Nationalsozialismus. Ein Arbeitsbuch* (Schwäbische Verlagsgesellschaft, Tübingen, 1980); P. Weingart, J. Kroll and K. Bayertz, *Rasse, Blut und Gene. Geschichte der Eugenik und Rassenhygiene in Deutschland* (Suhrkamp Verlag, Frankfurt a.M., 1988); N. Frei (ed.) *Medizin und Gesundheitspolitik in der NS-Zeit* (Oldenbourg, Munich, 1991). They all go back to A. Mitscherlich and F. Mielke, *Das Diktat der Menschenverachtung. Eine Dokumentation* (Lambert Schneider, Heidelberg, 1947).

15 A. Götz and S. Heim, *Vordenker der Vernichtung. Auschwitz und die deutschen Pläne für eine neue europäische Ordnung* (Hoffmann und Campe Verlag, Hamburg, 1991).

Part II

OPERATION BARBAROSSA, THE *WEHRMACHT* AND THE QUESTION OF TIMING

4

HIMMLER, THE ARCHITECT OF GENOCIDE

Richard Breitman

In my recent book, *The Architect of Genocide: Himmler and the Final Solution* (1991),[1] I sought to describe the range of high-level planning on resolving the so-called Jewish question and to illuminate general relationships among Hitler, Heinrich Himmler, Reinhard Heydrich, Oswald Pohl, Hermann Goering, Hans Frank, Alfred Rosenberg, Joachim von Ribbentrop and others. The historian's attribution of responsibility for plans and decisions that are poorly (if at all) documented is bound to be somewhat speculative, depending partly on one's assessment of personalities and the personal and political relationships among individuals and agencies. So I do not expect we will ever have full agreement on just who initiated, planned, improvised or ordered the Final Solution, let alone when.

In my view Hitler, Himmler and Heydrich all played major, if somewhat different, roles in developing the *plans* for the Final Solution. (One would need at least Raul Hilberg's three volumes to cover the range of key people and agencies involved in implementation.[2]) Lest any doubt be raised by my book's focus on Himmler, I regard *Hitler* as the originator of the idea of the Final Solution and as the single most important influence. It is not necessary for me to repeat here all the arguments already developed by Eberhard Jäckel, to which I generally subscribe.[3] I would simply add that outside foreign policy and military affairs, Hitler was not a man to control all the details, a tendency all the more likely in this case because there were political grounds for him to maintain some apparent distance from the vast crimes. Hitler gave the commission for genocide, but he needed people who would do his bidding without insisting on formal laws or written authorization, without showing or giving in to moral qualms or doubts, without shirking from the task of persuading or compelling large organizations to participate or cooperate. He had a number of people who possessed those qualifications, but the most important ones were Heydrich and Himmler.

Heydrich was a major force in the radicalization of Jewish policy in November 1938 when he filled in during Himmler's absence. In 1940 Heydrich asserted that the Führer had entrusted him with the planning of a territorial solution to the Jewish question, and the Madagascar Plan emerged. And when Himmler finally initiated implementation of the Final Solution outside the Soviet territories, he appears to have referred to it as Heydrich's plan.[4] The designation of the extermination programme for Polish Jews, *Aktion Reinhard*, was an apparently posthumous honour given to Heydrich.[5] This by no means exhaustive list of Heydrich's accomplishments raises a question: what was left for Himmler to do?

Most of his contemporaries underestimated Himmler, and it would not be difficult for historians to lose him in the umbra of Hitler and Heydrich. Yet Himmler not only hired Heydrich in the first place, but trained him ideologically.[6] As Heydrich rose to prominence and accumulated greater powers, Himmler kept restraints on him by reserving separate spheres for personal and organizational rivals such as Theodor Eicke, Kurt Daluege and Oswald Pohl. It worked, at least to some extent, because all were jealous of Heydrich.[7] Although there were undoubtedly some personal strains between Himmler and Heydrich produced partly by Himmler's management technique, partly by Heydrich's ambition, and partly by friction from close contact between two very different personalities, I have found no evidence of political or policy disagreements between the two. Charles W. Sydnor, who has been working on a biography of Heydrich for some years, concurs with this judgement.

If Heydrich sometimes claimed responsibility for, and control of, the Final Solution, we know today that in the east Daluege's Order Police were heavily involved in its implementation, as of course were the Higher SS and Police Leaders, the *Kommandostab Reichsführer SS*, and to a lesser extent the Waffen-SS generally – all directly subordinate to Himmler.[8] Himmler paid personal attention to the performance of his key subordinates in the east by frequent inspections and correspondence. He did not turn them over to Heydrich.

Most people associate the Final Solution with the extermination camps. There is a reasonable case for making this connection in spite of the fact that older methods of mass murder preceded the gas chambers and claimed perhaps more than 1.3 million victims.[9] Mass shootings were more likely to cause problems and information leaks; they were politically dangerous in Germany and the west. They were less efficient, consuming more time and manpower, and also bringing some adverse psychological repercussions for the executioners, a problem to which Himmler was particularly sensitive and Heydrich was not.[10]

In December 1941 Himmler even issued orders to his commanders in the east to take personal responsibility for ensuring that men who carried out executions did not suffer damage to their spirits or character. Himmler suggested social gatherings in the evening as a way of reinforcing camaraderie, but warned against the abuse of alcohol on such occasions. A good meal, good beverages and music would take the men 'to the beautiful realm of German spirit and inner life.'[11]

It is hard to conceive of a serious attempt to physically eliminate the Jewish people across the continent without Auschwitz-Birkenau, Chelmno, Maidanek, Belzec, Sobibor and Treblinka. Here Himmler's stamp is far stronger, especially in the planning stages. Of course, Hitler had raised the idea of gassing Jews in *Mein Kampf*; Himmler did not have to show great originality, but only loyalty, faith and persistence to pursue its feasibility on a vast scale. It was Himmler, not Heydrich, who in December 1939 plotted out a scheme for 'crematorium-delousing' units in concentration camps, and it was Himmler who viewed the gas van operations of Sonderkommando Lange in the Wartheland during 1940 as particularly important.[12] Himmler selected Globocnik over the head of his nominal superior Friedrich-Wilhelm Krüger to run Jewish policy in the Lublin region, and then *Aktion Reinhard*. In July 1941 Himmler called in Rudolf Höss to turn Auschwitz into an extermination camp. Himmler's much-touted weakness at the scene of mass shootings seems to have had a direct bearing on his decision to rely on gas chambers in extermination camps. As Erich von dem Bach-Zelewski once described, Auschwitz (meant as a generic term) was the creation of bureaucrats,[13] a term that fits Himmler far better than Heydrich, the man with the heart of iron. Himmler therefore was the architect of genocide because he devised or selected the preferred, even essential, means by which it was carried out: the extermination factory, where death came or was supposed to come deceptively, smoothly and efficiently.

The so-called intentionalist-functionalist controversy has focused much scholarly attention on the issue of the timing of genocide. We may be able, through determination of when key decisions were made, to establish the immediate climate surrounding those decisions, and perhaps even the motives of the decision-makers. Timing, therefore, is important, but the timing of exactly what?

Approval and implementation of a continent-wide programme for the 'extermination' of European Jewry are landmark events, but they should not completely overshadow earlier, less comprehensive Nazi objectives for the mass murder of Jews. If our concern is to determine under what circumstances and why Nazi officials promoted policies of mass murder, then the SS's plans before the Second World War to murder German Jews who could not leave the country and killings by the *Einsatzgruppen* in Poland during and after the autumn 1939 campaign are more than adequate indicators of lethal ideological motives behind the regime's Jewish policy.[14] Nor should we overlook the racial hostility that contributed to plans and early killings of Poles and Gypsies. As Michael Burleigh and Wolfgang

Wippermann have recently formulated it, Nazi Germany was from its inception a racial state.[15] The cover of war simply provided appropriate opportunities for Hitler and other Nazi leaders to pursue their racial paranoia to extreme limits. So whatever the exact timing of the Final Solution, Nazi ideology is an important part of the explanation.

In the historiographical debates over the timing of the Final Solution historians have sometimes ignored the planning (and authorization) which had to precede operational decisions. Much of the time but particularly with serious matters in normal life, most people develop some idea of what they intend to do before they do it.[16] There is a natural time-lag between the original idea and any decision based on it, and often another one between a decision and its realization. So it strains credibility to argue that the SS had no general conception of what it was going to do with the Jews until just before – or even after – the construction of the first extermination camps.

Then there is the matter of what constitutes adequate evidence of planning and of decisions. If some historians reject anything but absolutely explicit, unambiguous evidence of Nazi plans for genocide, they may be able to retain their view that the Final Solution was improvised, but at the cost of losing touch with linguistic and political behaviour in the corridors of power in Nazi Germany. Few Nazi officials wanted to talk about mass murder explicitly on paper: where such matters were discussed, they were not written down – or the minutes were sanitized. This discretion was quite in keeping with Hitler's fundamental command on secrecy and with Himmler's normal methods as well. I might cite but two famous examples of sanitizing documents directly connected with the Final Solution (which is itself a euphemism). Eichmann testified that the famous Wannsee Protocol was revised several times, partly to remove references to specific methods of killing. And we know from a contemporary document that Himmler instructed SS statistician Richard Korherr, who was supposed to carefully tot up the casualties of the Final Solution in early 1943, not even to use the term 'special treatment' in his report: Korherr was supposed to write that the Jews were passed through the camps.[17] These examples are not exceptional; they illustrate a general pattern.

The evidence of Nazi plans for the Final Solution comprises an array of Nazi euphemisms for mass murder in contemporary documents, with fragments of evidence from a multitude of sources that together, if properly reconstructed, form a recognizable mosaic. I can present only some of those fragments here, but they lead to the conclusion that the general framework of the Final Solution was conceived not later than January 1941, in connection with Hitler's plans for the invasion of the Soviet Union.

To create an eastern empire that was both pure and secure, Hitler wanted to purge racial and political enemies and eliminate sources of racial impurity. So it was not coincidental that shortly after Hitler signed War Directive Number 21, Case Barbarossa, Heydrich began negotiations with Army Commander-in-Chief Walther von Brauchitsch regarding the use of *Einsatzgruppen* in the campaign against the Soviets. By early February 1941 Heydrich was willing to tell outsiders that the negotiations had gone well, and that a formal agreement was expected soon.[18] Heydrich would have been reticent about revealing the exact functions of the *Einsatzgruppen* to Brauchitsch, but there is credible testimony that by March or April high officials from the Reich Security Main Office (RSHA) discussed among themselves the mass murder of enemies in the Soviet Union, particularly Jews.[19]

It is quite plausible that by early 1941, Hitler would also have sanctioned the goal of killing all European Jews, and that Himmler and Heydrich would have begun to plot out the means. For it was, within their mental horizon, the appropriate time to think in terms of the entire continent. The attack on the Soviet Union was designed not only to create a vast empire in the east, but also to end the last British hope of successful resistance in the west, to secure Nazi dominance of the continent and beyond, and to establish the prerequisites for the New Order.[20]

Practices of mass murder considered appropriate for the USSR, however, were not necessarily viable elsewhere. In any case, we cannot simply assume that when Nazi leaders made decisions about their enemies in the USSR, they also charted out a course for the continent, logical as that deduction may appear. We need to look first at the rise and fall of the Madagascar Plan in order to understand the timing of the plan that replaced it.

The Madagascar Plan was born in May 1940 and died, at the latest, by December 1940. As a result of the successful military campaign in the west, by late May Hitler was thinking of demanding the return of German colonies in Africa as part of a peace settlement with the British, and there was talk of taking Madagascar from the French. At the same time, Himmler was frustrated over his inability to dump massive numbers of Jews into Poland, with Hans Frank, Goering and military authorities having effectively impeded his far-reaching resettlement schemes there.[21]

In a memorandum for the Führer on the treatment of eastern peoples, Himmler took advantage of the prevailing political wind to insert a brief reference to the possibility of a great emigration of Jews into a German colony in Africa or elsewhere. This initially vague option – Himmler did not specify Madagascar – became a substitute for the former Jewish reservation in Poland. Hitler approved the memorandum as a whole on 25 May and gave Himmler authorization to notify a select group of officials, including Hans Frank, the eastern *Gauleiter*, and Himmler's own key subordinates. This move helped to advance the SS's control of Jewish policy and of racial policy in the east generally.[22]

There was something of a competition over the rights to Madagascar. The Foreign Office was clearly interested and involved, and there are credible signs and testimony that the Führer Chancellery wanted a role.[23] But Heydrich took control, and it was the RSHA that eventually worked out a detailed plan.

This institutional rivalry, taken in conjunction with SS efforts to develop a colonial police force and the detailed (if unrealistic) proposals in the long RSHA description of the Madagascar Plan,[24] provides good reason for historians to take it seriously, since some Nazi officials took it seriously. Yet the adoption of the Madagascar Plan also served a convenient political purpose for Himmler, placating Hans Frank and (to a lesser extent) Goering. Whether or not it was realistic to think of shipping millions of Jews to Madagascar could be settled later.

Fragmentary evidence also suggests that Himmler viewed the Madagascar project as a possible solution for the west European Jews who could be held hostage there, but not for the *Ostjuden*. Himmler probably gave instructions in late June 1940 to leave the *Ostjuden* in place, which helps to explain the fact that during the second half of 1940 the SS was establishing new concentration and labour camps designed to exploit Jewish labour under brutal conditions for some years.[25]

The expulsion of thousands of Jews from Alsace, Lorraine, Baden and the Saar-Palatinate into the unoccupied zone of France during the latter half of 1940 is not evidence against either the Madagascar Plan or an early conception of the Final Solution. Some Nazi officials, such as *Gauleiter* Robert Wagner of Baden and Joseph Bürckel of Saar-Palatinate, were eager to rid themselves of Jews immediately and were looking for convenient dumping grounds. I presented some evidence in *The Architect of Genocide* that SS and police authorities did not initiate the expulsions of Jews in the west into areas outside German control and that transference of these Jews to Vichy did not fit in with Himmler's plans.[26] Since then, Konrad Kwiet has generously sent me a very interesting document which strengthens that conclusion.

On 30 October 1940, in an instruction to Security Police representatives in all the occupied western countries regarding policies and preparations for the treatment of foreigners, the RSHA distinguished between immediate measures against Jews and the continuing basic objective of regulating the Jewish question for all of Europe under German influence. Jews in western Europe who were subjects of Germany (including Austria, Czechoslovakia and Poland) had to be prevented from returning to areas of German sovereignty, but whatever measures were adopted, they had to be consistent with the overall plan for a continental solution.[27] So the RSHA wanted Jews in occupied western European countries interned in camps, so that they would be immediately accessible as soon as the time came for the entire evacuation of Jews from the continent. In fact, they would be the first to be shipped off, and it was suggested that officials select locations for the camps that would be convenient for evacuation overseas.

This document from RSHA section IV D 6, which went out under Heydrich's signature to SS and police authorities in Paris, Brussels, Strassburg, Metz, the Hague, Oslo, Luxemburg and Copenhagen, very much suggests that there was serious consideration of how western European Jews could be rounded up and shipped to Madagascar. Yet it is not a sign of clear and definite commitment to the Madagascar project on the part of higher authorities. In September 1940, in a revealing memo concerning the resettlement of Czechs from Bohemia, Heydrich explicitly stated that he was willing to draw up schemes to push unwanted people to a currently *imaginary* destination simply to advance the prospect of German settlement of Bohemia.[28] The same consideration could easily apply to the Jews.

This new document does highlight the priority given to the early incarceration of these Jews by the RSHA, as well as its clear objective of entirely removing all Jews from Europe.[29] At almost the same time as this instruction appeared, the RSHA was banning the emigration of Jews from Poland, partly on the spurious grounds that Polish Jews would crowd out German Jews in the competition for havens in the US, but partly also on the accurate grounds that the escape of eastern Jews was too dangerous to Germany.[30] So Heydrich was not interested in getting rid of Jews by letting them escape. Finally, the principle that short-term measures must not conflict with the broader objective of removing all Jews from Europe, but must actually advance it, helps to explain the significance of new moves in December 1940 and January 1941.

In December Hitler told Hans Frank that the General Government would have to accept an influx of Poles and Jews soon, for if the Nazi regime waited until after the war, there would be international difficulties. This comment followed and helped to resolve a longstanding battle between Himmler and Frank over the 're-Germanization' of Germany's eastern provinces, with Himmler having been eager to expel all Jews and many Poles into the General Government.[31] Once Hitler stepped in, Frank could no longer effectively contest this policy. But any short-term measure to deal with Jews was supposed to advance and be consistent with the overall goal of ridding the continent of Jews, and Poland was not on the way to Madagascar. The obvious implication is that now Poland had replaced Madagascar as the destination for the Jews.

Viktor Brack of the Führer Chancellery testified after the war that after the end of 1940 Madagascar was no longer a conceivable option. Claiming that he and his co-workers had earlier pushed the idea of Madagascar as an alternative to the mass extermination of the Jews, Brack said that his superior, Philipp Bouhler, had passed the proposal on to Hitler or Himmler, but that it was not approved. Brack's testimony also came after he was trapped in a lie by a crafty American interrogator, after he broke down and sobbed that he would now tell the truth.[32]

Interrogator Fred Rodell pressed Brack on the significance of his efforts to advance Madagascar.

'You know, your statement implies that the destruction of the Jews was already decided in 1940.'
'May I say on that that I in no case heard anything officially.'
'What does it mean to hear nothing officially? It was an open secret in high party circles.'
'Yes, that is the right designation.'[33]

One might quarrel with use of the term 'decision' to describe the period before there was a geographical strategy for the mass extermination of European Jews and while Madagascar was still a fading option, but Brack's awareness in 1940 of the likelihood of the Final Solution was certainly well-founded.

In January 1941 Adolf Eichmann's colleague Theo Dannecker disclosed that the Führer wanted a final solution (*endgültige Lösung*) of the Jewish question after the war in all parts of Europe ruled or controlled by Germany. Hitler, through Himmler and Goering, had given Reinhard Heydrich the task of developing a Final Solution project (*Endlösungsprojekt*). On the grounds of its extensive experience in Jewish matters and thanks to longstanding preparatory work, Heydrich's office had then worked out the essential features of this project, which now lay before the Führer and Goering.[34] We know from Brack's aforementioned testimony as well as a contemporary statement by Adolf Eichmann that this project was not the Madagascar Plan.

In mid-March 1941, during a meeting at the Propaganda Ministry regarding the evacuation of Jews from Berlin, Eichmann gave a similar account of the authorization: the Führer had already entrusted Heydrich with the 'final evacuation' of the Jews (*endgültigen Judenevakuierung*). In early to mid-January Heydrich had then presented a proposal to the Führer, Eichmann said, which remained unfulfilled only because the General Government of Poland was not yet in a position to receive one Jew or Pole from the Old Reich.[35] So Heydrich's 'final evacuation' of the Jews clearly involved the General Government, and Hitler had apparently accepted it. The Jews from the Reich had been destined for Madagascar, like others in the west. Now that the Madagascar Plan was gone, they were due for 'final evacuation' to Poland. And there is credible, independent testimony of Hitler's formal authorization, in January 1941, of a plan said to be to make Germany free of Jews (*judenfrei*) before the end of 1942.[36]

As Gerald Fleming argued some years ago,[37] the term 'evacuation' was often used as a convenient cover for physical elimination. But 'evacuation' was not used exclusively to veil mass murder, so this suggestive point is not absolutely conclusive. Taken together, however, Dannecker's and Eichmann's comments nonetheless reveal a great deal. Dannecker specified a continent-wide programme which was based on past experience but had to be carefully planned: the SS had long since planned to separate Jews from the surrounding population, make use of adult Jewish males for hard labour, and to kill some Jews. Eichmann spoke of a 'final evacuation'; Poland was not to be a transit point. Yet a Jewish 'reservation' in Poland would, in Nazi eyes, threaten the security of German occupation forces and settlements in the east. There was only one logical conclusion – Europe's Jews were to be made to disappear in the east.

Hitler's own pledge to Hans Frank on 17 March 1941 that the General Government would become the first territory to be made free of Jews underlined the significance of Eichmann's 'final evacuation'.[38] It was not possible to have a 'final evacuation' of Jews to Poland and simultaneously to make Poland free of Jews unless the Jews were to be murdered in Poland. Himmler hinted at this goal when in April 1941 he responded to Friedrich-Wilhelm Krüger, who had passed along Odilo Globocnik's ideas about the use of Jewish labour in concentration camps. Himmler agreed to discuss these proposals when he visited Krüger, but said he had a new task in mind for Globocnik.[39]

This sequence of events and the evidence from which they are reconstructed are admittedly incomplete and imperfect. Taken in conjunction with the nearly simultaneous planning of mass murder of Jews and other groups in the Soviet territories, however, this evidence is, I believe, convincing that the general scheme for the elimination of the Jewish 'race' was not produced after the early Nazi victories in the summer of 1941, let alone after the military difficulties in the winter of 1941–2, but in the period from December 1940 to March 1941. Of course, in this case like many others, there was a time-lag between the planning at the highest levels and implementation, during which uninformed parties and agencies could and did raise ideas and proposals of their own. Lower-level initiatives were symptomatic of the general climate and sometimes influential on matters of methods and timing, but they were not decisive in the general course of events. In the summer and autumn of 1941 Hitler was undoubtedly influenced by German military successes,[40] but whatever 'euphoria' he experienced only facilitated or accelerated the realization of pre-existing plans.

The contemporary evidence of planning for genocide in January 1941 is so persuasive that I cannot absolutely rule out testimony, admittedly from a dubious source, that Hitler made the key decision at a meeting in Berlin in December 1940. On 16 August 1945 American Third Army counter-intelligence officers captured Hans Georg Mayer near his home in Obersalzburg. Mayer had held a series of high positions in the Order Police, in Lodz, Pabianice and in Norway. Once a member of the SA, he had switched to the SS in mid-1940 and held the rank of *Sturmbannführer*. There was no apparent reason why he would have been privy to extremely sensitive information, except that he resided in Obersalzberg and would have been acquainted with Hitler's own entourage.[41]

In the presence of a newspaper reporter from United Press at a Third Army interrogation centre, Mayer testified on 27 August 1945 that the December 1940 conferees – Hitler, Himmler, Goebbels, Heydrich and Kaltenbrunner – decided that all Jews unfit for heavy work would be gassed to death. All those able to work would be worked until they were so weak that they could not continue. Then they too would be sent to the gas chambers.[42]

It must be said that Goebbels did not fit in with the rest of Hitler's guests, and that Goebbels's diary entries contain nothing about such a meeting. Goering was a far more likely participant than Goebbels; either Mayer or the reporter could have confused the two. A private gathering in which Hitler voiced a firm goal and the others began to figure out how to achieve it would have been enough to set events in motion.

Mayer's reported testimony is at best a highly speculative hearsay account of key events, and I am far from convinced that it is correct. There is at present a remote possibility that it is partly accurate. But because of several important pieces of contemporary evidence dating Heydrich's plan to early January 1941, we need to investigate carefully all sources regarding the activities of Hitler, Himmler, Gœring and Heydrich in December 1940 and early January 1941. This part of the mosaic is of crucial significance.

NOTES

1 Richard Breitman, *The Architect of Genocide: Himmler and the Final Solution* (New York, 1991).
2 Raul Hilberg, *The Destruction of the European Jews*, revised edn (New York, 1984).
3 Eberhard Jäckel, 'Hitler orders the Holocaust', in Eberhard Jäckel, *Hitler in History* (Hanover, NH, 1984), pp. 44–65.
4 Breitman, *Architect of Genocide*, pp. 55–9, 124–5, 198.
5 Yitzhak Arad, *Belzec, Sobibor, Treblinka: The Operation Reinhard Death Camps* (Bloomington, Ind. 1987), p. 13. Challenged by Uwe Dietrich Adam, 'The gas chambers', in François Furet (ed.) *Unanswered Questions: Nazi Germany and the Genocide of the Jews* (New York, 1989), pp. 144, 352 note 70, but reaffirmed by Richard Breitman and Shlomo Aronson, 'Gaps in the Himmler papers', in George Kent (ed.) *Historians and Archivists: Essays in Modern German History and Archival Policy* (Fairfax, Va, 1991).
6 See Richard Breitman and Shlomo Aronson, 'Eine unbekannte Himmler-Rede vom January 1943', *Vierteljahrshefte für Zeitgeschichte*, 37 (1990), pp. 341, 345.
7 On Eicke, see Charles W. Sydnor, *Soldiers of Destruction: The SS Death's Head Division, 1933–1945* (Princeton, NJ, 1990), pp. 21–2. On Heydrich and Daluege, see Heydrich's letter to Daluege of 30 October 1941 responding to Daluege's

letter to Heydrich of 1 October 1941, United States National Archives (hereafter NA), Record Group 242, Microfilm Series T-175/Roll 123/frames 2648601-15.

8 Ruth Bettina Birn, *Die Höheren SS-und Polizeiführer: Himmlers Vertreter im Reich und in den besetzten Gebieten* (Düsseldorf, 1986); Yehoshua Büchler, 'Kommandostab Reichsführer SS: Himmler's Personal Murder Brigades in 1941', *Holocaust and Genocide Studies*, I (1986), pp. 1–15; George H. Stein, *The Waffen-SS: Hitler's Elite Guard at War* (Ithaca, 1966); Bernd Wegner, *Hitlers politische Soldaten: Die Waffen-SS, 1933–1945* (Paderborn, 1982).

9 Hilberg, *Destruction of the European Jews*, III, p. 1,219.

10 When in December 1941 Friedrich Jeckeln reported to Himmler on the success of killing operations in the Ostland, Himmler said that shooting caused too many problems, that it was better to use gas trucks (Helmut Krausnick and Hans-Heinrich Wilhelm, *Die Truppe des Weltanschauungskrieges: Die Einsatzgruppen der Sicherheitspolizei und des SD 1938–1942* (Stuttgart, 1981), p. 548).

11 Richard Breitman, 'Himmler and the "Terrible Secret" among the executioners', *Journal of Contemporary History*, 26 (1991), p. 444.

12 Breitman, *Architect of Genocide*, pp. 87–9, 103.

13 ibid., pp. 188–90, 204.

14 ibid., pp. 64–5. On the *Einsatzgruppen*, see Krausnick and Wilhelm, *Die Truppe des Weltanschauungskrieges: Die Einsatzgruppen der Sicherheitspolizei und des SD 1938–1942*, pp. 52–83.

15 Michael Burleigh and Wolfgang Wippermann, *The Racial State: Germany 1933–1945* (Cambridge, 1991).

16 I am indebted to Gerhart M. Riegner, who made these remarks in the course of discussions at the Wiener Library conference.

17 On the array of Nazi euphemisms, see Henry Friedlander, 'The manipulation of language', in Henry Friedlander and Sybil Milton (eds) *The Holocaust: Ideology, Bureaucracy, and Genocide: the San José Papers* (New York, 1980), pp. 103–13. For Himmler on secrecy, Breitman, *Architect of Genocide*, p. 73. On the Wannsee Protocol, Adolf Eichmann's testimony, reprinted in Raul Hilberg (ed.) *Documents of Destruction: Germany and Jewry, 1933–1945* (London, 1972), pp. 101–4. On Himmler and Korherr, see Rudolf Brandt to Korherr, 20 April 1943, NA RG 238, Nuremberg Series NO–5196.

18 Künsberg Aufzeichnungen, 4 and 10 February 1941, NA RG 238, M–946/R 1/ 1100–01, NG–5225; Picot to Künsberg, 10 February 1941, NA RG 238, M–946/ R 1/109–13.

19 Breitman, *Architect of Genocide*, p. 151.

20 Gerhard L. Weinberg, 'Der deutsche Entschluss zum Angriff auf die Sowjetunion', *Vierteljahrsheft für Zeitgeschichte*, 1 (1953), pp. 301–18; Klaus Hildebrand, *Vom Reich bis Weltreich: Hitler, NSDAP, und koloniale Frage 1919–1945* (Munich, 1969), p. 719; Jürgen Förster in Militärgeschichtliches Forchungsamt (ed.) *Das Deutsche Reich und der Zweite Weltkrieg*, vol. 4, *Der Angriff auf die Sowjetunion*, ed. Horst Boog et al. (Stuttgart, 1983), especially pp. 3–18.

21 On Madagascar, see especially Leni Yahil, 'Phantom of a solution for the Jewish question', in Bela Vago and George L. Mosse (eds) *Jews and Non-Jews in Eastern Europe 1918–1945* (New York, 1974), pp. 315–34. On Himmler's frustrations with Frank and Goering, see Breitman, *Architect of Genocide*, pp. 95–101.

22 Breitman, *Architect of Genocide*, pp. 117–22.

23 Christopher R. Browning, *The Final Solution and the German Foreign Office: A Study of Referat III D of Abteilung Deutschland* (New York, 1978), pp. 38–43. On 23 June 1940 Hitler rejected Bouhler's request for a colonial

mission. Bormann's notes on Hitler's schedule, NA RG 242, T–84/R 387/497. Brack later testified that Bouhler wanted to become police governor of Madagascar (Brack testimony in Nuremberg Military Tribunal, Case 1, Medical Case Trials, cited by Philip Friedman, *Roads to Extinction: Essays on the Holocaust* (New York, 1980), p. 49). See also pp. 79–80, this volume.

24 Yahil, 'Phantom of a solution', p. 326. Text of RSHA plan in NA RG 242, T–120/R 780/372056–71. See the analysis in Browning, *Final Solution*, pp. 40–1.

25 Breitman, *Architect of Genocide*, p. 125.

26 ibid., pp. 131–5.

27 Special State Archives, Moscow, 500.5.3, pp. 15–23.

28 Breitman, *Architect of Genocide*, p. 138.

29 Special State Archives, Moscow, 500.5.3, p. 20.

30 Breitman, *Architect of Genocide*, p. 142.

31 See ibid., pp. 95–104, 118–20, 126–7, 142–3.

32 Interrogation of Viktor Brack, 13 September 1946, NA RG 238, M–1019/R 8/975–7, 981–2. Brack also testified that he made a second effort to prevent the extermination of European Jewry, which was a proposal for the sterilization of some millions of Jews capable of labour. This proposal survives in written form and came in March 1941 (Brack to Himmler, 28 March 1941, NA RG 238, NO–203).

33 Interrogation of Victor Brack, 13 September 1946, NA RG 238, M–1019/R 8/988.

34 Dannecker's memo, 'Zentrales Judenamt', in Paris, 21 January 1941, reprinted in Serge Klarsfeld, *Vichy-Auschwitz: die Zusammenarbeit der deutschen und französischen Behörden bei der 'Endlösung der Judenfrage' in Frankreich* (Nordlingen, 1989), pp. 361–3. I am very grateful to John P. Fox for calling my attention to this document.

35 Notiz. Betrifft: Evakuierung der Juden aus Berlin, 21 March 1941, NA RG 242, T–81/R 676/5485604–5.

36 Gerald Fleming, *Hitler and the Final Solution* (Berkeley, Calif., 1984), pp. 20–1.

37 Paul C. Squire interview with Dr Carl J. Burckhardt, 7 November 1942, NA RG 84, American Consulate Geneva, Confidential File 1942, 800. Harrison to Undersecretary of State, Personal, 23 November 1942, NA, RG 59, 740.00116 E. W. 1939/653. Burckhardt was told independently by two high German officials, whom he trusted implicitly, that they had both seen this order. One was said to be a high official in the Foreign Ministry, the other in the War Ministry.

38 Werner Präg und Wolfgang Jacobmeyer (eds) *Das Diensttagebuch des deutschen Generalgouverneurs in Polen 1939–1945* (Stuttgart, 1975), pp. 332–3, 336–7.

39 Himmler to Krüger, 19 April 1941, Berlin Document Center, Odilo Globocnik SS File.

40 Christopher R. Browning, *Fateful Months: Essays on the Emergence of the Final Solution* (New York, 1985), pp. 37–8, gives Hitler an authorizing role at this time; in Chapter 8 of this volume Browning stresses Hitler's euphoria over military successes. Browning has consistently deprecated evidence of planning of the Final Solution before the summer of 1941.

41 Preliminary Interrogation Report on Dr Hans Georg Mayer, 27 August 1945, NA RG 238, M–1270/R 25/868. Berlin Document Centre, Hans Georg Mayer SS File.

42 Robert Musel, 'SS man tells how Jews slaughter was planned', *P.M.*, 27 August 1945.

5

THE RELATION BETWEEN OPERATION BARBAROSSA AS AN IDEOLOGICAL WAR OF EXTERMINATION AND THE FINAL SOLUTION

Jürgen Förster

In 1942, Reinhard Heydrich assembled a number of senior officials and SS officers in Berlin and told them that he had been appointed to prepare and implement 'the final solution of the Jewish question'. The *Wehrmacht* was not invited. Most historians agree that the Wannsee Conference of 20 January 1942 does not mark the starting point of the Holocaust. The systematic murder of the Jews was already under way by then. Since the beginning of the 1960s, there has been a wealth of serious scholarship on both the destruction process and the Hitler era. Although it was Andreas Hillgruber who in 1969 stressed the close connection between the Nazi racial policy and the course of the war, historians have not yet closely linked the history of the Holocaust with that of the Second World War, as Michael R. Marrus observed twenty years later. I agree with his observation. An analysis of the broad pattern of racism in the Nazi ideology, not only anti-Semitism, and its transformation during the war, of the linkage between the concepts of *Volksgemeinschaft* (national community) and *Lebensraum* with that of racial purification, of the interaction between the euphoria over Barbarossa and the Europe-wide mass murder of Jews, and of the *Wehrmacht* as an instrument of destruction, is still on the historical agenda. Only when we give as much attention to the war years as to the period before 1939 can we arrive at both an adequate interpretation of the Third Reich and a deeper understanding of what happened to European Jewry.

For far too long the memoirs of German generals, quickly translated into English during the Cold War, shaped the public's image of the *Wehrmacht's* record in the Second World War. Many a historian relied on such accounts as *Lost Victories* by Erich von Manstein (1958) or Heinz Guderian's *Panzer Leader* (1952). Moreover, with his book *On the Other*

Side of the Hill (1951), B. H. Liddell Hart had already provided them with a large audience to whom they could talk about the campaigns in Europe and Africa and their purely professional part in them. From Nuremberg onwards, the notion has existed of separating the Führer from his followers, the generals from their supreme commander, and the *Wehrmacht* from the crimes of the SS. Many a veteran still doggedly perpetuates the myth that the soldiers had nothing to do with the ideological side of Barbarossa. Yet the war which Hitler unleashed in September 1939 had been an ideological one from the very start.

Hitler was a revolutionary and a racist. He saw history as a conflict between races and believed that conflict 'in all its forms' was inevitable and the 'father of all things'. It determined the life of individuals and nations. He thought that the races could be graded on a scale of merit and that the struggle for survival was to be a permanent one until the 'more worthy' German people had proved their claim to world mastery.

As a social revolutionary, Hitler's concrete dream envisaged a biologically homogeneous German people led by a new civilian and military elite. 'Racial principles' would govern the necessary selection process which would be accompanied by the ruthless elimination of all ideological and biological enemies and 'asocials' in order to purify the new *Volksgemeinschaft* of blood and destiny. Peace was desirable only as an opportunity to prepare it for war. In this ideological context, war took on a very special meaning for Hitler. It was not only the 'highest expression of the life force' of a people, but also the legitimate and inevitable tool in the hands of German statesmen for acquiring sufficient *Lebensraum* to secure the nation's future racially, economically and militarily. War was not a moral issue, a question of right or wrong, but the physical means to a social end: the survival of the superior Germans. With survival of the German race being contingent on military victory, politics and strategy became indistinguishable. In this new kind of war there would be no distinction between the home front and the combat zone. The full force of the fighting German people would strike at all national and racial enemies within and without the Reich. There would be no legal restraints. Hitler's programme was no detailed blueprint for action. Yet *Lebensraum*, in itself an amalgam of race, autarky, living space, and world politics, did mean something concrete, even if the road there was 'twisted'. It meant war, conquest, annihilation, and reshaping German and European society.

In January and February 1939, Hitler addressed selected military audiences and the public via the Reichstag. His purpose in all these speeches was to explain to his listeners the basic National Socialist principles behind his policies since 1933. The speeches were intended to inspire them with particular devotion, and to motivate them to follow these principles with renewed purpose. These speeches did not present the audiences with new ideas. Every listener must have been certain who the racial and political enemies were, Jewry and Bolshevism. Only the open threat to the Jews before the Reichstag in the Kroll opera house on 30 January 1939 and, ten days later, the clear-cut demand from the officer corps to acknowledge him as their supreme ideological leader in the coming racial war stand out as specific pieces of rhetoric. The latter did not fall on barren ground within the *Wehrmacht*. On 18 December 1938, the army leadership had already instructed the officer corps to master National Socialism, to be its standard-bearer, and to act according to these ideas in every situation, both as the political and tactical leader of their soldiers.[1] If the Nazi *Weltanschauung* was seen by the officer corps as their compass, there would be no need for a replica of the Soviet commissar system within the *Wehrmacht*.[2] True to his conviction, Hitler declared before his military leaders on 23 November 1939 that 'a racial war has broken out and this war shall determine who shall govern Europe and with it, the world'.[3]

Hitler ordered the *Wehrmacht* in the spring of 1939 to prepare for an offensive war against Poland. In two addresses to senior military commanders, on 23 May and 22 August 1939, Hitler outlined his view that Germany only had the alternative of a risky attack now or certain annihilation sooner or later. It was not Danzig that was at stake but the expansion of German living space to the east. The goal was the destruction of Poland and its human potential in order to gain the necessary territories for the resettlement of Germans. Only victory mattered, not pity.[4] The *Wehrmacht* planned, however, for a normal war. The 'elimination of all active and passive resistance' was not yet determined on ideological terms. Hitler relied on the SS to fight the racial struggle and purify the acquired living space from all that could infect the German people. Heinrich Himmler deployed six and a half *Einsatzgruppen*, formed from the Security Police, Security Service, Order Police and the Waffen-SS. His loyal lieutenant Heydrich officially defined the role of these mobile killing squads, which were subordinated to the armies they were attached to, as 'combating all Reich and state enemies behind the front-line troops'. Significantly, this task paralleled that of the SS within Germany.

Seen with the eyes of 1941, the occupation of Poland looks like a test case of the Nazi racial policy. Such a view diminishes the significance which can be assigned to the conditions created by the war itself and overlooks the role the Soviet Union had in Hitler's race and war policy. Though Poland clearly marks an escalation in the persecution of the Jews, the Final Solution was not a concrete aim in 1939–40. The foremost target of the *Einsatzgruppen* was the Polish intelligentsia. Tens of thousands of them were killed, especially in those territories which were to be annexed. Many Jews were murdered too, yet at that time the Final Solution meant deportation and ghettoization. Together with Poles and Gypsies, they were shipped to the Generalgouvernement, the 'dumping ground' of the master race. This was only a first step in the wider scheme of the racial cleansing of German living space for which Himmler had just gained overall powers (7 October 1939).

The attitude of the *Wehrmacht* to the indigenous population in Poland was a mixture of racial arrogance, insecurity and naive trust in the methods of force. 'The life of a non-Aryan was worth very little.'[5] The army acted ruthlessly against insurgents and was responsible for mass executions of prisoners-of-war and indiscriminate shootings of civilians, among them many Jews. What it did forbid were 'wild' requisitions, unauthorized, spontaneous measures against Jews, and the participation of soldiers in executions carried out by the SS. The 'barbarization of warfare', to use a phrase from Omer Bartov, began in Poland, not in the Soviet Union. The commanders reacted to the threat to military discipline with the means of courts martial. On 4 October 1939, however, Hitler pardoned all military and police personnel who had stepped beyond the military law, and justified this by saying that such crimes had been the natural result of bitterness unleashed by Polish behaviour towards Germans. This amnesty was itself an encouragement to further acts of SS terror.

Since 17 October 1939, the army leadership had had a clear knowledge of the Nazi destruction programme in Poland. It neither objected on principle nor shared its information with the officer corps at large, because it was content to wash its hands of responsibility for the administration of Poland. Yet local commanders protested against the slaughter of Poles and Jews by the SS forces. A man like Colonel-General Johannes Blaskowitz, who himself defined Jews and Poles as 'our arch-enemies in the eastern sphere', became increasingly concerned about the spread of 'brutalization and moral debasement' among valuable German manpower.[6] The commander-in-chief of the army, however, took the edge off such protests when he made himself an advocate of Hitler's programme against Poland rather than a defender of law and order. What Field-Marshal Walther von Brauchitsch did stress was the maintenance of the army's spirit and discipline by restraining the troops from acts of violence against the indigenous population.[7] The army leadership had accepted the 'severity' of the SS in carrying out the necessary German expansion but feared the brutalization of the soldiers. When Himmler made it perfectly clear to the army's top commanders in Koblenz on 11 March 1940 that the SS action had been ordered by Hitler, the discontent of many and the criticism of a few concerning German policy in Poland was brought to an end. The Führer's triumph in the west acted as an additional pacemaker for the acceptance of the SS's 'unparalleled radical measures' for the 'final ethnic solution of the *Volkstumskampf* [racial struggle] which has been raging for centuries along the eastern frontier'.[8] Significantly, this directive was issued by Colonel-General Georg von Küchler, Commander of the 18th Army, who, ten months earlier, had infuriated Himmler by acting against crimes. This had cost him a field-marshal's baton. A few weeks later, the same army instructed its troops about the 'attitude of the German soldier towards the non-German population in the east'. One army corps informed its superiors about experiences with this instruction. Although a final assessment would depend on the approach of German politicians to the organization of the Generalgouvernement in the near and distant future,

> the attitude of the German soldier towards the Jews is not under any discussion. Down to the last man, the standpoint has been taken that it is impossible to mix with this race and that it must be completely removed from the German living space one day.[9]

On 22 June 1941, Hitler began his war against the Soviet Union. It was undoubtedly planned and prepared as a *Vernichtungskrieg* (war of destruction), not as a conventional war. This singular character resulted from Hitler's determination to realize his *Lebensraum* concept. The difference between Operation Barbarossa and the campaign against Poland was that in 1941 the line between military and ideological warfare was erased before the first shot was fired. In Poland, Hitler had pardoned soldiers and SS men after the campaign. For the war against the Soviet Union, a pre-emptive amnesty for crimes was decreed. The concept of destruction was a component of the tactical planning, rear area security and economic exploitation. Military strategy and racial politics had achieved a symbiosis. The idea of acquiring living space through the conquest of Russia was inextricably intertwined with the extermination of Bolshevism and Jewry, with the doctrine of economic self-sufficiency, and with the strategic necessity of thereby winning the war against Great Britain.

When the military preparations for Operation Barbarossa were already far advanced, Hitler defined – first within the small circle of his military advisers and then before a large gathering of senior commanders and their chiefs-of-staff – the campaign as more than a mere conflict between two enemy nation-states and their armies. It would also be a clash of antagonistic ideologies and races. Hitler stated openly that he wished to see Barbarossa conducted not according to military principles but as a *Vernichtungskrieg* against an ideology and its adherents, whether as functionaries within the Red Army or in civilian positions.[10] There was to be a division of responsibility between the army and the SS to bring about the liquidation of enemy cadres, the 'Jewish-Bolshevik intelligentsia'; this would also lead to the quick break-up of the Soviet regime and the speedy pacification of the conquered territory. While the SS was charged with the elimination of the civilian cadres of the inimical *Weltanschauung*, the army was to eliminate the 'Jewish-Bolshevik intelligentsia' within the Red Army, the commissars, and the real or potential carriers of resistance. This was to be done directly by the troops, and not by courts martial. Hitler declared the *Vernichtungskrieg* against the enemy *per se* in the east a military necessity. The officers had to understand what was involved in this kind of war.

Such guidelines from the supreme ideological leader for the warfare in Russia neither came as a surprise to the army nor fell on barren ground. When Colonel-General Franz Halder, the Chief of the Army General Staff, noted in his diary the essence of Hitler's address of 30 March 1941, he made a telling side-note: 'In the east, severity is mildness for the future.'[11] This echoes Hitler's remark of 17 October 1939, when he had outlined his maxims in the government of Poland: 'Shrewdness and severity . . . in this racial struggle [would] spare us from having to go into battle again.'[12] Three days before the large gathering in the Reich Chancellery on 30 March 1941, Brauchitsch had told his commanders that the troops should see the German–Russian war as a 'struggle between two different races and act with the necessary severity'.[13]

Although it was Hitler who wanted to transform a military campaign into a war of destruction against Bolshevism and Jewry, he played no visible role in implementing his ideological intentions. This was left to his own military staff, the army and the SS. Here we have another typical example of what Raul Hilberg has defined as the 'mechanism of destruction'. The directives which were to give the war in the east its singular character, the 'criminal orders', emerged out of a routine bureaucratic process within the relevant departments of the *Reichssicherheitshauptamt* (Reich Security Main Office) and both the High Commands of the *Wehrmacht* and the army. Despite their knowledge of the murders in Poland, the *Wehrmacht* accepted that the SS was entrusted with 'special tasks' within the army's zone of operation and was entitled to take 'executive measures' against the civilian population on its own responsibility, this time even without being subordinated to military command staffs. It was an officer in the Naval Staff who wrote in the margin of the Wehrmacht High Command (OKW) guidelines of 13 March 1941: 'That will have consequences!'[14]

The relationship between Hitler and the *Wehrmacht* with regard to the Soviet Union was determined in large measure by a considerable consensus both on Germany's role in Europe and the world and on ideological matters. German expansion to the east had long been justified not only in economic and political terms, but also in the Social Darwinist sense of the right of the stronger in the struggle for survival. The military leaders did not merely comply with Hitler's dogmatic views, they were not mere victims of an all-absolving principle of obedience. The military leaders, too, believed that the dangers of Russia and Bolshevism should be eliminated for ever. The Soviet Union and Germany were seen as being divided by a yawning chasm, both in ideology and race. Had it not been Jewry and Bolshevism that had stabbed the armed forces in the back and had caused the downfall of Imperial Germany? 'Domestic and foreign Bolshevism' (Werner von Fritsch) and the influence of Jewry were both seen by the military as a threat to the German national state. Thus, Operation

Barbarossa assumed an even higher justification than the war against the 'hereditary enemy', France. The triumph in the west, however, had strengthened the bond between the military and their leader.

At the centre of the army's preparation for the war of destruction against the Soviet Union stood Halder, not Brauchitsch or his often-mentioned 'General Officer for Special Duties' Lieutenant-General Eugen Müller. From October 1940, Müller was subject to Halder's directives 'regarding the military jurisdiction and against the population of occupied territories'. Halder was convinced that the troops should participate in the ideological war as well. Thus, the army not only drafted its own instruction to restrict military jurisdiction and to allow for the shooting of those merely suspected of being guerrillas, but also took the bureaucratic initiative for the execution of the commissars. The army's leadership saw an inherent connection between the two illegal measures which it justified with the need for ensuring absolute security for the German soldier and with its own version of post-1918 German history. Courts martial were to be confined to the maintenance of discipline. The troops were expected to deal themselves with 'criminal elements' of the indigenous population. In cases where they could not be shot 'while fighting or escaping', an officer was to decide whether they were to be executed. The commissars, the 'bearers of the Jewish-Bolshevik worldview' within the Red Army and the 'initiators of barbaric, Asiatic methods of combat', were to be shot after being taken prisoner on the order of an officer who had to identify the commissars in consultation with two other officers or NCOs. The fear that if taken prisoner, such hardliners might continue to disseminate Bolshevik propaganda in the Reich was another factor dictating the shooting of political commissars. It was assumed that Jewish commissars would be more convinced of communist ideology than others. In the minds of the military also was so-called 'military necessity': the hope for a speedier and less costly advance by driving a wedge between the apparently decent Russian soldier and his criminal political leadership cadre.

Such evidence on the origin of the commissar order makes it highly unlikely that the decision to murder the Jews can be based on this directive, as Hans Mommsen claims.[15] It was also not intended to move the army 'toward acceptance of the general killing of Jews', as Richard Breitman asserts.[16] The final decrees of 13 May and 6 June were issued by the OKW. They had to go through the Army High Command (OKH). Brauchitsch made amendments to both before he passed them on to the troop commanders. On the one hand, he laid the burden for segregating and executing the commissars 'inconspicuously' on the shoulders of any officer. On the other hand, he stressed the duty of all superiors to prevent arbitrary, unauthorized actions against the Soviet population. Concern for the discipline of the troops was obviously more important than scruples about illegal shooting of captive commissars or of civilians who were mere suspects. After the experience in Poland, this concern was well founded. Yet in the *Vernichtungskrieg* against the Soviet Union, the army's attempt to preserve the institutional control of violence and prevent the brutalization of the soldiers while calling for ideologically motivated measures must be seen as 'riding the tiger'. The troops themselves were instructed to see Bolshevism as the 'deadly enemy of the National Socialist German Nation. It is against this destructive ideology and its adherents that Germany is waging war.' The battle demanded 'ruthless and vigorous measures against Bolshevik inciters, guerillas, saboteurs, *Jews*, and the complete elimination of all active and passive resistance.'[17] These OKW guidelines and Halder's amendment of the draft agreement between the SS and the army of 26 March 1941 for the Balkan campaign make it clear that Jews were singled out by the *Wehrmacht* as Germany's enemies before 22 June 1941 and before it allowed the *Einsatzkommandos* to select and execute Jews in the prisoner-of-war camps.[18]

The concept of the war of destruction against 'Jewish Bolshevism' was strengthened by the OKW's directive on the use of propaganda during Barbarossa. It was not the peoples of the Soviet Union who were the enemies of Nazi Germany but their Jewish-Bolshevik leadership. The centrepiece of the German propaganda against the Red Army comprised attacks against the commissars who were literally 'Enemy Number One'. They were described as Jews, liars, slave-drivers and murderers. The German soldiers, too, were to be indoctrinated with this Nazi dogma. Propaganda was to back the execution of the commissar order. The June issue of the OKW's 'Information for the Troops' stated that 'anyone who has once looked into the face of a Red Commissar, knows what Bolsheviks are. . . . It would be insulting animals if you described these mostly Jewish features as animal-like.'[19] Hitler's order of the day also justified the attack on the Soviet Union in ideological terms, and held the conspiracy of the Jewish Bolsheviks together with the Anglo-Saxon warmongers responsible for the war.

As the *Wehrmacht* was sent to carry out the decisive strike against the external enemy, international Jewry and Bolshevism, the inner enemies of the *Volksgemeinschaft* were handled differently. While the Gestapo preventively arrested communists on behalf of the OKW, the army slowed down the process of its inner purification of Jewish influence.[20] At the beginning of June 1941, the field commanders were instructed by the Chief of the Army Personnel Office, General Bodewin Keitel, to look upon the 'Aryan paragraph' of 1935 with 'great favour', if a soldier had proved his worth in the face of the enemy. This instruction is another instance of the interaction between the course of the war and Nazi racial policy. Blood and merit in battle formed the basis of the selection process of the new German national community.[21] About the decision-making process for Barbarossa within the SS, we know much less than about the military side.

In reference to the 'special commission' given to him by the Führer, Himmler deployed four *Höhere SS- und Polizeiführer* (Higher SS and Police Leaders). They were his representatives both in the army's rear area and in the territories under civil administration, the later *Reichskommissariate*.[22] These leaders were given the task of directing the different SS formations deployed in the east: the *Einsatzgruppen* of the Security Police and Security Service that followed the attacking armies and Panzer groups, the three Waffen-SS brigades under their own command staff *Kommandostab Reichsführer-SS* and the three police regiments of the Order Police that were deployed in the Army Groups' rear area.

All these formations were given guidelines, directives and oral instructions which specified their mission and their chain of command. It was clear from the outset that the demands of the *Wehrmacht* had precedence over their 'special measures'. There is now sufficient evidence to demonstrate that, before 22 June 1941, the SS formations were only entrusted with a more general authorization to eliminate both the biological and political manifestations of Bolshevism. Heydrich's communication to the Higher SS and Police Leaders of 2 July 1941 to liquidate all civilian communist officials and Jews in the service of the party or the state, and 'other extremist elements (saboteurs, propagandists, snipers, assassins, agitators, etc.)'[23] corresponds more with Hitler's first aim of liquidating the 'Jewish-Bolshevik intelligentsia' than with the Final Solution. The SS and police commanders, however, were granted a discretion which permitted individual initiatives. The first formal order, to kill immediately 'all male Jews of 17–45 years of age' was issued by the Commander of Police Regiment Centre, Lieutenant-Colonel Max Montua, on 11 July 1941. He himself acted on the orders of the Higher SS and Police Leader Centre, *Gruppenführer* Erich von dem Bach-Zelewski.[24] The necessity of killing male Jews was not justified by Montua with any reference to partisan activities but 'resulted from the political situation'. Since the SS was still liquidating selected target groups, the Intelligence Officer of the *Kommandostab Reichsführer-SS* informed his superiors in his after-action report of 28 July 1941 that 'all persons involved are in doubt whether the Jewish problem can be brought to a fundamental solution by the multitude of executions of male Jews alone.'[25] While the *Einsatzkommando* 3 under Karl Jäger began to include Jewish women and children on 15 August 1941, the Police Regiment Centre only increased the age band for men to be killed to 16–65. Its 3rd Battalion, however, executed sixty-four Jewish women, too, in Minsk on 1 September 1941. The evidence on the practice of liquidating after 22 June 1941 suggests that a second, principal decision was made in the summer of 1941, this time to cleanse the conquered living space more thoroughly from any manifestations of Jewry and Bolshevism, to make it 'free' of Jews and communists.

German security policy in the occupied territories in the east was a highly complex matter from the very outset of the campaign. Military security and administration either overlapped or were jointly conducted by the army and the SS. Both tools of German rule were committed to the 'closest cooperation'. The army's own plans for military security were determined by the vast expanse of Russian territory and the shortage of security forces. Therefore it had welcomed the deployment of police and Waffen-SS formations in the rear area. At the beginning of the operations, especially in those territories which the Soviets had occupied after autumn 1939, the army consciously aimed at freeing the population from the yoke of Bolshevism and at avoiding measures that would make it hostile to the German invader. In fact, the Germans were actually welcomed in traditional fashion in some villages. The still small number of sabotage incidents made it feasible to strike a 'bargain' between the interests of the *Wehrmacht* and the peaceful population. Let the latter only be still, work and obey orders, and the suffering would be minimized by combating resistance activities with reprisal executions chiefly of Jews, Russians and communists. Thus, the *Wehrmacht* appropriated minorities for its own use as scapegoats in the western parts of the Soviet Union.

Yet by the end of July 1941, the army leadership ruled differently. It had learned of detailed Soviet directives which instructed political functionaries to form partisan units, and believed that the German troops had not dealt energetically enough with partisan activities. These grounds were reason enough for Brauchitsch to supplement the earlier directives with a special order for the 'treatment of enemy civilians and of Russian prisoners of war' in the army group rear areas. Within this order the C-in-C of the army mixed military and ideological, punitive and preventive measures. He accused the supporters of the 'Jewish-Bolshevik system' of being responsible for the renewal of resistance in already pacified areas, and justified reprisals and collective punishments instead of taking hostages. The mass shooting of suspected civilians and the destruction of villages were seen as appropriate reactions to any unidentified instances of sabotage. The guiding principles were to be the 'absolute security of the German soldier' and the spread of terror 'so as to crush every will to resist among the population'.[26] Some military commanders and officers in the east still tried to avoid arbitrary reprisal measures and to draw a line between ideological warfare and military necessity. it was in reaction to their not fully compliant attitude that Field-Marshal Wilhelm Keitel issued his order of 12 September 1941. In reminding them of his guidelines of 19 May 1941, Keitel declared again that 'the struggle against Bolshevism demands ruthless and energetic action especially against the Jews, the main carriers of Bolshevism.'[27] Four days later, Keitel informed the military commanders in the occupied areas, not just in the Soviet Union, that the Führer had given orders to use 'everywhere the harshest methods to crush the [communist insurrectionary] movement within the shortest possible time'. In this context, Keitel gave guidelines which demanded from the military occupation forces 'unusual severity' to prevent any further spread of rebellion, in which in any case, 'no matter what the individual circumstances may be, Communist origins must be assumed to be present'. He considered the summary execution of 50–100 'communists' as an 'appropriate atonement for the life of a German soldier'.[28]

There were other military commanders and officers in the east, however, who saw a causal connection between 'Jewish Bolshevism' and the partisan movement. For them, professionalism and ideology went together well. On 25 September 1941, Lieutenant-General Walter Braemer, *Wehrmacht-befehlshaber Ostland*, issued his 'Guidelines for military security and maintenance of quiet and order' in his province. Reacting to Keitel's above-mentioned orders of 12 and 16 September, Braemer stated that the security of the fighting troops, of the country, and its economic situation would demand 'imperatively to eliminate all factors threatening quiet and order'. As such factors, he specified 'a) Bolshevik soldiers and agents (partisans) dispersed or purposely dropped or left behind in the forests, b) communist and other radical elements, c) Jews and pro-Semitic (*judenfreundliche*) circles'. All German organizations and individuals should cooperate with *Wehrmacht* and police to eliminate these elements. The guideline for combating partisans must be 'speedy and ruthless, brutal action'.[29] Against the background of this order, the radical measures of the 707th Infantry Division in *Weißruthenien* now appear in a different light. Being assigned to Braemer, it acted according to his guidelines although its situation reports themselves represent an example of self-fulfilling prophecy in the extermination of 'Jewish Bolshevism'.[30] In its area in White Russia, the 707th Infantry Division shot 10,431 'captives' in one month, out of a total of 10,940, while in combat with partisans the division suffered only seven casualties, two dead and five wounded.[31] Among those 'captives' were former Soviet soldiers, escaped prisoners-of-war and civilians arrested by mopping-up operations.

Another example of 'abnormal' warfare in the east is General Max von Schenckendorff's 'Course for combating the partisans', held in Mogilev between 24 and 26 September 1941. It also shows the close cooperation between the army and the SS. Schenckendorff had charged the SS-Cavalry Brigade under *Standartenführer* (Colonel) Hermann Fegelein with mopping up the Prypiat Marshes. This operation had begun on 29 July 1941, after Himmler had instructed his men to act harshly against 'a racially and humanly inferior' population. All male Jews were to be shot, women to be driven into the marshes. Suffering 17 dead, 3 missing-in-action, and 36 wounded, Fegelein could proudly report to his leader that the brigade had shot 699 Soviet soldiers, 1,001 partisans and 14,178 Jews.[32] In an earlier, differently worded communication of 3 September 1941, Fegelein had informed the Commander of the Rear Area of Army Group Centre of the 'pacification of the Prypiat Marshes,' asserting that contact between the partisan units was maintained 'above all by Jews' and that villages 'free from Jews' had in no instance served as partisan bases.[33] This rather dubious assertion did not fall on barren ground, as Schenckendorff's report of 10 August 1941 to the OKH shows.[34] The practice of the SS was not only recommended to his own security divisions; combating partisans was also defined as a soldierly activity in which commanders could prove their receptiveness and creativity.[35] In addition, Schenckendorff initiated the above-mentioned course. The sought-after 'exchange of experience' between the army and the SS was led by Lieutenant-Colonel Montua. After lectures by Bach-Zelewski on 'the apprehension of commissars and partisans' and by Arthur Nebe, leader of *Einsatzgruppe* B, on 'the Jewish question with special reference to the partisan movement', the 'right' screening of the population was demonstrated on the closing day of the course by a live exercise of the 7th Company of Police Battalion 322 in Knjashizy, 14 kilometres north-west of Mogilev. We read in its war diary:

> The action, first scheduled as a training exercise, was genuinely (*ernstfallmäßig*) executed in the village itself. Strangers, especially partisans could not be found. The screening of the population, however, revealed 13 Jews, 27 Jewish women, and 11 Jewish children of whom 13 Jews and 19 Jewish women were shot in cooperation with the Security Service.[36]

The same police company had been part of the guard of honour when Schenckendorff had handed over parts of his territory to *Gauleiter* Wilhelm Kube in Minsk on 1 September 1941. On the same day outside that town, the 9th Company of Police Battalion 322 shot, in cooperation with the SD and *Nationalsozialistische Kraftfahrkorps* (NSKK), 914 Jews, among them 64 women.[37] It was not surprising that participants in such a course, which was repeated in May 1942, returned to their units with the doctrine: 'Where the partisan is, there is the Jew, and where the Jew is there is the partisan.'[38]

It was not in the Soviet Union alone that military commanders and officers saw the Jews as being specially hostile to the German occupation and acted accordingly. It happened in Serbia too. In Sabač 'central European Jewish refugees, mostly Austrians, were shot by troops predominantly of Austrian origin in retaliation for casualties inflicted by Serbian partisans on the German Army!'[39] This was not merely done in compliance with the guidelines issued by Keitel on 16 September 1941. But the military commanders in Serbia had already carried out reprisal executions against Jews and communists prior to the OKW's instruction, which did not mention Jews explicitly. As long as anti-Jewish measures were 'perceived and construed as military measures against Germany's enemies, it did not require nazified zealots (though surely such were not lacking), merely conscientious and politically obtuse soldiers to carry them out'.[40]

The deliberate intermingling of ideological warfare with military necessities took on a new form in the east in autumn 1941. The blitzkrieg illusion was gone but not the belief in victory. The *Wehrmacht*, however, knew that it had to fight a fierce and stubborn enemy at the front. Moreover, the *Wehrmacht* was now facing a better organized and trained partisan movement under the leadership of party functionaries or officials and was short of troops in the vast rear areas. The solution was ever more ruthless action against actual and suspected 'supporters of the hostile attitude', that is Jews and communists. This becomes especially clear in the well-known orders of the commanders of the 6th, 11th and 17th Armies – Field-Marshals Walther von Reichenau and Erich von Manstein[41] and Colonel-General Hermann Hoth. They all called for the complete extermination of the Soviet war machine as well as the annihilation of the 'Jewish-Bolshevik system'. Even more explicit than Reichenau and Manstein, Hoth turned his soldiers' thoughts to German history, to the guilt (as he saw it) of the Jews for the domestic conditions after the First World War: 'The destruction of those same Jews who support Bolshevism and its organization for murder, the partisans, is a measure of self-preservation.'[42] Hoth, who had been present in the Reich Chancellery on 30 March 1941, followed his supreme ideological leader and strove to render Hitler's unequivocal maxims into guidelines for his soldiers. In contrast to the campaign against France, he saw two irreconcilable worldviews in conflict in the east: 'German feelings of honour and race, and a centuries-old German soldierly tradition against Asiatic thought and its primitive instincts stirred up by a few, mostly Jewish, intellectuals.' This fight could only be ended by the destruction of one or the other. There was no room for compromise. Manstein concluded his order with an appeal to maintain discipline and to preserve military honour. It seems as if in their struggle for survival against 'Jewish Bolshevism', the German people, 'because of their superiority of race and deeds' (Hoth), could reconcile the two ideas of destruction and honour.

It is not sufficient to justify the arbitrary and ruthless reprisal policy of the German Army in Russia, Serbia and Greece by stressing the need for the security of the soldier against partisan warfare. Nor can it be explained by the fact that German military doctrine since 1871 had advocated policies of indiscriminate retaliation and of preventive repression as the best means of checking partisan activity.[43] Total exoneration of the army is no more of an aid towards the understanding of this chapter in German history than is total condemnation. There were, of course, commanders who tried to draw a distinct line between military and police measures, who warned the troops not to consider every one as their enemy just because he looked like a Bolshevik – in rags, unhygienic, unkempt.[44] But it was a futile fight.

The considerable discrepancy between the number of 'partisans' killed and the German casualties on the one hand, and the minor difference between the numbers arrested and those later executed, point to the dialectical dimension of the *Wehrmacht*'s reprisal policy. The destruction was inspired by ideology, but rational in its implementation. Military necessity provided the bridge. A few examples will make this context clear. After a mopping-up operation near Mirgorod in the rear area of Army Group South, the 62nd Infantry Division shot the 'entire Jewish population (168 souls) for associating with partisans', in addition to executing forty-five partisans. After a similar operation near Novomoskovsk in the same area, the 444th Security Division reported '305 bandits, 6 women with rifles (*Flintenwei-ber*), 39 prisoners-of-war, 136 Jews' shot. The 2nd Army informed the Army Group Centre that in 'combating partisans', it had arrested 1,836 persons and shot 1,179 between August and October 1941.[45] The 285th Security Division reported that it had shot nearly 1,500 'partisans, civilians, Soviet soldiers' in combat or after between 22 June and 31 December but it had suffered only 18 casualties, 7 dead and 11 wounded. The disproportion in the *Wehrmacht* reprisal policy is most strikingly demonstrated by the report of the 707th Infantry Division (see p. 95). This practice took on more the aspect of an extension of Nazi racial policies according to Hitler's formula of 16 July 1941 than of military operations against partisans.

The orders of Reichenau, Manstein and Hoth had also taught their soldiers to show understanding of the 'necessity of harsh punishment of Jewry'. This could only be understood by the troops as justification of the mass executions carried out by the *Einsatzgruppe* C. Thus, these commanders went further along with the programme of extermination than Field-Marshal Wilhelm von Leeb and Colonel-General Ernst Busch who had favoured a policy of 'turning a blind eye' to the savage public pogroms in Kaunas.[46] In mid-August 1941, the 2nd Army had pointed out that the troops would refrain from excessive collective punishments if they were given a guarantee that the 'experienced specialists', that is *Sonderkommando* 7 b, would deal with the 'dangerous elements' in their rear.[47] Time and again, commanders and staff officers at the front and in the rear areas identified Jews with Bolsheviks and partisans, construed a connection between the reprisal policy and the mass murder of the Jews in the occupied territories in the east or recorded pitilessly the extermination measures of the SS.[48] In regard to the relationship between the army and the SS, a distinction should be made between the Soviet Union and Serbia. While in the latter, 'the mass murder of the male Jews was accomplished primarily by the German Wehrmacht, though it certainly received willing help from the Ordnungs- and Sicherheitspolizei of the SS',[49] in the former it was the other way round. Babi Yar, the name of a gorge near Kiev, has become the symbol not only of the mass executions of Jews in the Soviet Union, but also of the support the *Einsatzgruppen* received from the *Wehrmacht*.[50] Army commanders restricted themselves to issuing orders to prevent individual soldiers from taking an 'unauthorized' part in the executions of Jews by the SS or taking pictures of the massacres. Their concern was the maintenance of discipline. If we agree with Gordon A. Craig that 'the extermination of the Jews is the most dreadful chapter in German history',[51] then we have to accept that the *Wehrmacht* wrote some pages of this chapter, either by participating in or by allowing the wholesale murder of Jews in their zone of operation, by turning away and knowingly disregarding the enforcement of racial policies. The majority rationalized that the war of destruction against the Soviet Union permitted such harshness. Even opponents of National Socialism, such as Erich Hoepner, Carl-Heinrich von Stülpnagel and Claus Schenk von Stauffenberg, were able to combine this attitude with a militant anti-Bolshevism.

How does this documentation fit into the wider historiographical debate on the Holocaust and the Second World War? I would side with Christopher Browning.[52] The development of the broad pattern of racism can be viewed both as programmatic and evolutionary, dogmatic and flexible. The transformation and fusion of long-range concepts like *Lebensraum* (living space), *Volksgemeinschaft* (folk community), *Entfernung der Juden* (removal of the Jews) and *Vernichtungskrieg* (war of extermination) must not be seen in post-Barbarossa perspective. 'Nazi racial policy was radicalized in quantum jumps'[53] between 1939 and 1941, with war shaping those objectives by its own momentum. The war not only opened up favourable conditions for ideologically fixed aims, but they themselves were the reason for going to war. The racial end justified the radical means. Between 1939 and 1941, the military followed its supreme ideological and military commander in both fields and moved from 'abdication of responsibility to outright complicity'.[54] Hitler must be credited with making the key decisions in the summer of 1940, and in the spring and summer of 1941. What the *Wehrmacht* and the SS did is what Hitler thought, not the other way round. The symbiosis between ideology and strategy, end and means, was realized with the *Vernichtungskrieg* against the Soviet Union. The concept of destruction was defined as a military necessity and became a component of the warfare in the east. The deliberate mixing together of ideological goals with military needs, of preventive with punitive measures, paved the way for the army's joining the SS in striking a fatal blow against the phantom of Jewish Bolshevism. Jews and communists were in fact and *a priori* classified as suspected partisans and shot. In the west it had not been obvious to the military that Jews would be among Germany's enemies. The murder of the cadres of the 'Jewish-Bolshevik' system, either by the SS or the army, was decided in connection with the military preparations for Operation Barbarossa. Backed by the euphoria of victory over 'Jewish Bolshevism' in the summer of 1941, Hitler's two most cherished objectives could be fused: the acquisition of *Lebensraum* and the elimination of Jewry. The vision of a purified Germanic empire, stretching from the Atlantic to the Ural Mountains, led to the decisions first to extend the target group in the Soviet Union by age and sex, and second to prepare for the Final Solution of the Jewish question by Europe-wide mass murder of all Jews. It is in the context of victory over the Red Army that one can claim a connection between Barbarossa and the Final Solution, the essence of the latter emerging as the Europe-wide mass murder of all Jews. The fundamental decision for this Final Solution was made in the summer of 1941. The later actions were only operational ones to accomplish the destruction of the Jews. The Final Solution was not decided in autumn 1941 because the blitzkrieg had failed or the feared opposition of the army to that programme had not materialized. It should not be overlooked that Hitler and the military considered the twin battle of Bryansk and Vyazma as the most decisive one and compared it to that of Königgrätz. Thus, victory looked imminent in the autumn of 1941. It was in the context of a second euphoria that the organizational problems arising from the fundamental decision were being tackled and that the Wannsee Conference became reality. If we look at the Holocaust and the war we shall see that the long way to Auschwitz is both a straight path and a twisted road.

NOTES

1 Extracts of both the address of 10 February 1939 and Walther von Brauchitsch's directive on education are cited in Jürgen Förster, 'New wine in old skins? The Wehrmacht and the war of "Weltanschauungen", 1941', in *The German Military in the Age of Total War*, ed. W. Deist (Leamington Spa, 1985), pp. 304–5.
2 See Major-General Hermann Reinecke's lecture on 'Officers and politics' before the officers of the OKW (High Command of the Armed Forces), in *Bundesarchiv-Militärarchiv Freiburg*, RW 6/v. 156 (hereafter: BA-MA).
3 Helmuth Groscurth, *Tagebücher eines Abwehroffiziers 1938–1940*, ed. H. Krausnick and H. C. Deutsch (Stuttgart, 1970), p. 414.
4 Both addresses can be found in *Nazism 1919–1945*, ed. J. Noakes and G. Pridham, vol. 3, *Foreign Policy, War and Racial Extermination* (Exeter, 1988), pp. 736–43.
5 *Das Deutsche Reich und der Zweite Weltkrieg*, ed. Militärgeschichtliches Forschungsamt, vol. 5/1 (Stuttgart, 1988), p. 48.
6 Noakes and Pridham, *Nazism*, vol. 3, pp. 938–9 (6 February 1940).
7 See H. Krausnick and H.-H. Wilhelm, *Die Truppe des Weltanschauungskrieges. Die Einsatzgruppen der Sicherheitspolizei und des SD 1938–1942* (Stuttgart, 1981), pp. 103–4 (7 February 1940).
8 ibid., p. 112 (22 July 1940). Küchler's directive can also be found, with a wrong date and slightly different wording, in Noakes and Pridham, *Nazism*, vol. 3, p. 941.
9 Communication of 20 September 1940, signed by the Chief of Staff, Colonel (GS) Faeckenstedt, in BA-MA RH 24–3/36.
10 Quoted in Noakes and Pridham, *Nazism*, vol. 3, pp. 1086–1088 (30 March 1941).

11 Generaloberst Halder, *Kriegstagebuch*, ed. H.-A. Jacobsen, vol. 2 (Stuttgart, 1962), p. 337.
12 Noakes and Pridham, *Nazism*, vol. 3, p. 928.
13 Notes of the 1st General Staff Officer of the 18th Army, in BA-MA RH 20–18/71.
14 See the copy that was sent to the Navy High Command, in ibid., RM 7/985.
15 Hans Mommsen, 'The realization of the unthinkable: The "Final Solution of the Jewish Question" in the Third Reich', in *The Policies of Genocide. Jews and Soviet Prisoners of War in Nazi Germany*, ed. G. Hirschfeld (London, 1986), p. 121.
16 Richard Breitman, *The Architect of Genocide. Himmler and the Final Solution* (New York, 1991), pp. 149–50.
17 'Guidelines for the conduct of the troops' of 19 May 1941, quoted in Noakes and Pridham, *Nazism*, vol. 3, p. 1090 (my italics).
18 Halder's order of 2 April 1941, in BA-MA RH 31–l/v. 23. The draft agreement between the SS and the Wehrmacht of 28 June 1941 is quoted by Christian Streit, *Keine Kameraden. Die Wehrmacht und die sowjetischen Kriegsgefangenen 1941–1945* (Stuttgart, 1978), pp. 91–2.
19 See *Das Deutsche Reich und der Zweite Weltkrieg*, vol. 4 (Stuttgart, 1983), p. 442.
20 Directive of Abwehr III of 22 June 1941, in BA-MA RW 4/v. 300.
21 See the notes of the Chiefs of Staff of 3rd Panzer Group, Army Group North, 17th and 18th Army on their meeting with the army leadership in Zossen on 4 June 1941, in BA-MA RH 21–3/v.46, RH 20–18/71 and 14499/5 (17th Army). The relevant directive on *Mischlinge* of 16 July 1941 can be found, in ibid., RH 22/271.
22 See Ruth Bettina Birn, *Die Höheren SS- und Polizeiführer. Himmlers Vertreter im Reich und in den besetzten Gebieten* (Düsseldorf, 1986).
23 Noakes and Pridham, *Nazism*, vol. 3, pp. 1092–3.
24 Military Archives Prague, Pol Rgt.
25 ibid., KdoS RF SS, box 5, folder 27.
26 Order of 25 July 1941, signed for Brauchitsch by General Müller, in BA-MA RH 22/271.
27 ibid., 99th Infantry Division, 21 400/17.
28 Documents on German Foreign Policy, Series D, vol. 12, p. 542.
29 This order was recently found in the State Archives in Riga and has been cited by H.-H. Wilhelm, 'Motivation und "Kriegsbild" deutscher Generale und Offiziere im Krieg gegen die Sowjetunion', in *Erobern und Vernichten*, ed. P. Jahn and R. Rürup (Berlin, 1991), p. 172.
30 See Förster, 'New wine in old skins?', p. 317.
31 Monthly report of 10 October – 10 November 1941, in BA-MA RH 26–707/v. 1.
32 Report of 18 September 1941, in Military Archives Prague, KdoS RF SS, box 24, folder 154.
33 BA-MA RH 22/224.
34 ibid., RH 22/227. Schenckendorff had explicitly drawn a causal connection between the 'oppression of the Jews' and the successful pacification of the area.
35 Order of 14 September 1941, in ibid., RH 22–221/13.
36 Entry of 25 September 1941, in Military Archives Prague, Pol Rgt, folder 251. Cf. Konrad Kwiet, 'From the diary of a killing unit', in *Why Germany?*, ed. J. Milfull (Oxford, 1992).

37 Entries of 31 August and 1 September 1941, in Military Archives Prague, ibid. cf. Christopher R. Browning, *Ordinary Men* (New York, 1992), pp. 15–25.
38 Testimony in court after the war. See Krausnick and Wilhelm, *Die Truppe*, p. 248.
39 Christopher Browning, 'Wehrmacht reprisal policy and the mass murder of Jews in Serbia', in *Militärgeschichtliche Mitteilungen*, 33 (1983), p. 39.
40 ibid., p. 39.
41 Orders of 6 October and 20 November 1941 in *The Trial of Major War Criminals*, International Military Tribunal, Nuremberg 1947–59, vol. 35, pp. 84–6, and vol. 34, pp. 129–32.
42 Order of 17 November 1941, in BA-MA RH 20–17/44.
43 See Geoffrey Best, *Humanity in Warfare. The Modern History of the International Law of Armed Conflicts* (London, 1980).
44 See the communication of the commander of the III (motorised) Army Corps, General Eberhard von Mackensen, of 24 November 1941, in BA-MA RH 24–3/136. Cf. the 'Personal reflections on the Ukrainian question', by 1st Lieutenant Dr Pauls, of 20 September 1941, ibid., RH 26–22/67.
45 For this and the following, see *Das Deutsche Reich und der Zweite Weltkrieg*, vol 4, p. 1055.
46 See Krausnick and Wilhelm, *Die Truppe*, pp. 205–9.
47 Communication of 11 August 1941, in BA-MA RH 20–2/1091.
48 See *Das Deutsche Reich und der Zweite Weltkrieg*, vol. 4, pp. 1045–6: action reports of the intelligence officers of the 281st Security Division of 15 August 1941 (BA-MA, RH 26–281/13) and the 221st Security Division of 14 December 1941 (RH 26–221/70) and those already-mentioned reports of 707th Infantry Division.
49 Browning, 'Wehrmacht reprisal policy', p. 42.
50 See Krausnick and Wilhelm, *Die Truppe*, pp. 235, 237–8. Kovno may become the symbol of the participation of the Soviet population in the murder of the Soviet and Reich Jews. Cf. Dina Porat, 'The legend of the struggle of Jews from the Third Reich in the Ninth Fort near Kovno, 1941–1942', in *Tel Aviver Jahrbuch für Deutsche Geschichte* (Tel Aviv, 1991), pp. 363–92.
51 *Germany 1866–1945* (Oxford, 1978), p. 749.
52 See his article, 'Nazi resettlement policy and the search for a solution to the Jewish question, 1939–1941', in *German Studies Review*, IX (1986), pp. 497–519.
53 ibid., p. 519.
54 ibid.

6

WEHRMACHT, EINSATZGRUPPEN, SOVIET POWS AND ANTI-BOLSHEVISM IN THE EMERGENCE OF THE FINAL SOLUTION

Christian Streit

There are two main questions about the emergence of the Final Solution which have not yet been satisfactorily answered: did a definite order to murder *all* Jews exist when the *Wehrmacht* invaded the Soviet Union on 22 June 1941? And what made it possible to turn cultured and well-educated people into the organizers and perpetrators of crimes of a magnitude and barbarity which had seemed inconceivable before?

In this chapter I want to show that a definite order to kill *all* Soviet Jews cannot have existed before the attack on the Soviet Union, and that extreme anti-Bolshevism played a decisive role both in removing the inhibiting factors *and* in producing the conditions under which, somewhere around the turn of 1941–2, the hazy notion of destroying the European Jews turned into a practicable aim. To avoid any misunderstandings I want to stress that if I underscore anti-Bolshevism as an important factor I do not mean to question the significance of anti-Semitism as the primary causal factor. It does not mean, either, that I accept Ernst Nolte's interpretation that the *Endlösung* resulted from anxiety-induced reactions to extermination processes during the Russian revolution.[1]

A large number of the scholars focusing on the Final Solution would contend that the first question has been answered convincingly and that there is sufficient proof to show that the Final Solution was set in motion by a Führer order in the spring of 1941. This specific order, they say, was passed on by Heydrich to the *Einsatzgruppen*. The massacres committed by these units in the occupied Soviet territories were, according to this reasoning, the first part of the implementation of a master plan which had been decided on during the spring of 1941. The transition to a factory-style extermination of the Jews in occupied Poland did, in this view, not signify a qualitative change.[2]

103

This is admittedly a tempting interpretation because it offers, in many respects, a plausible explanation of what seems to be a linear and logical development. It means, however, deducing the genesis from the result, and I think that there are a number of facts and circumstances which make this interpretation appear doubtful.[3] If we ask what expectations the Nazi leaders had and could reasonably have had in the spring of 1941 the assumption that they *expected* that, one year later, the *Einsatzgruppen* would have killed more than half a million Soviet Jews, and that the destruction of the whole Jewish people would be well under way in the extermination camps in occupied Poland, seems highly questionable.

In the spring of 1941 the Nazi leaders could not take it for granted that they would be able to carry out large-scale mass murders. The massacres which some SS units had committed in Poland in 1939–40 – and which cannot be compared in size with those the *Einsatzgruppen* were to perpetrate in the Soviet Union – had caused considerable unrest in the army. Hitler could therefore not rely on the willingness of the army to tolerate mass murders of a quite different scale.[4] In addition, it must have been more than doubtful how the elites in the armed forces, bureaucracy and industry, which were in large part conservative, would react to the destruction of the entire European Jewry, and whether it would be possible to win their cooperation to the degree necessary for the realization of full-scale genocide.

The claim that the decision to destroy *all* Jews was taken during the spring of 1941 and that the *Einsatzgruppen* were given the order before 22 June rests mainly on the post-war affidavits of *some* leaders of the *Einsatzgruppen* and *Einsatzkommandos*. Alfred Streim has shown convincingly that the relevant statements cannot possibly be correct, particularly if we keep in mind that the *Einsatzgruppen* members tried to save their necks by pleading binding orders.[5]

The wording of the agreement between Reinhard Heydrich and the Army Quartermaster General, General Eduard Wagner, of 26 March 1941, which laid down the rules for the activities of the *Einsatzgruppen* in the rear army group and army areas, did not permit them to execute all Jews summarily.[6] The directives which Heydrich issued to the *Einsatzgruppen* in the weeks following 22 June reveal that he, too, was not at all certain about what could be achieved.[7] He put his units under the obligation to 'cooperate most loyally' with the army under 'strict observance' of the agreement with Wagner.[8] Repeatedly he urged the leaders of the killing squads to 'trigger' pogroms by the local population against communists and Jews, 'to intensify them if necessary and to channel them properly' – 'without leaving any trace', however, and without giving the perpetrators any opportunity to plead orders later.[9] A report of the leader of *Einsatzgruppe* A, Dr Walter Stahlecker, of October 1941 tells us why. It was 'unwelcome', he wrote:[10]

that the *Sicherheitspolizei* was in evidence in connection with the measures which were really uncommonly harsh and which were bound to cause a sensation in German circles. It had to be demonstrated to the public that the indigenous population had taken the first measures on its own initiative as a natural reaction to decades of Jewish oppression and to communist terror.

Apart from the fact that Heydrich, like the commanders of the *Einsatzgruppen*, obviously placed exaggerated hopes in the anti-Semitism of the Soviet population, this statement shows that they aimed at securing a possible retreat in case the murders met with opposition from the *Wehrmacht*. That possible opposition from the *Wehrmacht* was a point of concern is underscored by the close attention which the *Einsatzgruppen* reports devoted to the attitude of the *Wehrmacht* towards the massacres. Repeatedly the *Einsatzgruppen* leaders emphasized how much they had succeeded in bringing about a positive attitude of the army to their activities.[11] The wording of their reports shows that this had not been taken for granted.

One document survives in which Heydrich defined the groups of victims more precisely. On 2 July 1941, he sent instructions to the four Higher SS and Police Leaders who had been appointed for the occupied Soviet territories.[12] Because of an organizational blunder he had not been able to give them his orders personally. His instructions called for the execution of all functionaries of the Communist Party, including the 'radical lower ones', of all 'other radical elements' and of 'all Jews in state and party positions'. The significance of this document has been questioned,[13] but I do not see any reason why Heydrich would have issued these instructions if he was not serious about them. They describe, as it were, the minimum programme Heydrich had at that time. The instructions also corresponded to what had been agreed upon with the army. The Commissar Order and the Barbarossa Directive as well as the implementing regulations which had been issued by the High Commands of the *Wehrmacht* and the army describe the same group of victims with the exception of the 'Jews in state and party positions'.[14]

There is another argument which has not yet been taken into account and which, in my opinion, is crucial. In June 1941 both Hitler and the military leaders took it for granted that the Red Army would be defeated in less than ten weeks.[15] In early July Leningrad, Kiev and Moscow were expected to fall within days. On 4 July Heydrich requested *Einsatzgruppe* B to name all members of the *Einsatzkommando* which would enter Moscow with the advance troops.[16] According to the original plans the army was expected to have conquered, by autumn, all Soviet territories west of the line connecting Arkhangelsk in the north and Astrakhan on the Caspian Sea, a line some 300 miles east of Moscow. All that means that the *Einsatzgruppen*, with about 3,000 men, would have had to 'purge' an area three times as large as that which was actually conquered by the *Wehrmacht* in 1941. Under these circumstances they could quite obviously *not* be expected to kill *all* Jews living in the conquered territories. The groups defined by Heydrich's instructions to the Higher SS and Police Leaders are, therefore, not only those agreed on with the army, but also those whose murder seemed most 'urgent' and could be accomplished with the personnel available at that time. It is not improbable, on the other hand, that Heydrich, in his briefing of the *Einsatzgruppen* leaders, had made clear that he expected more than just the realization of the minimum objective. An indication for this might be that in his Operations Order No. 3 of 1 July 1941 he demanded that the leaders of the killer units 'show exemplary initiative'.[17] Stahlecker wrote in his report of October 1941[18] that 'according to the basic orders' his *Einsatzgruppe* 'had had the aim of eliminating the Jews *as far as possible*' (*hatte eine moeglichst umfassende Beseitigung der Juden zum Ziel*).

It might be argued[19] that there is only a marginal difference between an order to *kill all Jews* and to *eliminate as many Jews as possible. Ex post*, this may seem so. I want to stress again, however, that Heydrich was not sure what his men would be able to achieve. In the tradition of German *Auftragstaktik* he gave them a problem and told them to try hard to find a solution. It was up to the leaders of the *Einsatzgruppen* and *kommandos* how far they were prepared to go.

Yet another document shows that the solution of the 'Jewish question' was not the only task the *Einsatzgruppen* had been given, and that as late as September 1941 *Einsatzgruppe* C did not even think it was the main task. It reported to the *Reichssicherheitshauptamt* that its men had found out that Bolshevism was supported not only by the Jews but by all ethnic groups. The aim of achieving political security would not be reached 'if the *main task of destroying the communist apparatus* was put to second or third rank in favour of the task of eliminating the Jews, a task which was easier to accomplish' (*wuerde man die Hauptaufgabe der Vernichtung des kommunistischen Apparates zugunsten der arbeitsmaeßig leichteren Aufgabe, die Juden auszuschalten, in die zweite oder dritte Reihe stellen*).[20]

This interpretation does not mean that I want to question whether there was a general intention to destroy the Jewish people. But even the Nazi leaders approached the idea of the physical extermination of a whole people only hesitantly. In May 1940 Himmler himself had clearly rejected this, as he put it, 'Bolshevist method' as 'un-Teutonic and impossible'.[21] There is much to be said for Martin Broszat's assumption that in 1941 the basic intention of destroying the Jews had taken shape in the aim of 'deporting the Jews to the East' (*nach Osten abschieben*). This phrase is usually understood to have been a code word for the outright murder of the Jews, and indeed it was later generally used this way. In my opinion there is ample evidence to show that in documents written in the summer and autumn of 1941 it was usually used in its most literal sense: it meant the enforcement of the migration of all Jews to Siberia, where they, like the other millions of 'unwanted' Soviet people who were to be driven there, would not have the remotest chance of survival. This was what seemed possible after the Blitz victory in the east. Once the *Einsatzgruppen* had liquidated the Jewish leaders it would be an easy task to push the Jewish masses east simply by showing what was in store for them if they chose to stay. *Einsatzgruppe* C found out, when it penetrated beyond the Dnieper river in September 1941 that rumours about the mass murders had caused a large-scale exodus. The majority of the Jews were said to be fleeing behind the Urals. This, *Einsatzgruppe* C pointed out, was a remarkable contribution to the solution of the Jewish question in Europe.[22]

In 1941 this *Abschieben nach Osten* was considered an ingenious solution for all the 'unwanted' ethnic groups the Nazi planners wanted to get rid of.[23] Many millions of Soviet citizens were intended to share the fate of the Jews. This concept even appears in army plans concerning the removal of the survivors of Leningrad and Moscow.[24]

When Himmler, on 18 September 1941, wrote to *Gauleiter* Arthur Greiser[25] that the German Jews who were sent to the Lodz ghetto would be deported 'further east' in the following spring, this was not yet a cover name for liquidation but should be understood quite literally. The fact that they *were* murdered later does not prove anything about the intentions pursued in September. Victory over the Soviet Union seemed, at that time, imminent. Accordingly, the possibility of sending the Jews to their doom in the swamps of Siberia still seemed real. In one of his table talks Hitler remarked, on 25 October 1941: 'Nobody should tell me we could not send them [the Jews] to the swamps.' Alfred Rosenberg declared, in a secret speech on 18 November 1941, that the 'Jewish question' could only be solved by a 'biological destruction' (*biologische Ausmerzung*) of Jewry in Europe; to achieve this it was necessary, he added, to 'shove the Jews across the Urals or to bring them to destruction by some other means' (*sonst irgendwie zur Ausmerzung zu bringen*). Governor-General Hans Frank knew about the general aim of destroying the Jewish people, but as late as December 1941 he had no idea how it could be accomplished technically: 'We can't shoot millions of Jews,' he said, 'we can't poison them, but we will be able to perform operations that will somehow lead to successful destruction'.[26] The deportation of millions of Jews to Siberia seemed practicable as far as the manpower requirement was concerned. The planners of genocide were, on the other hand, not at all certain about the feasibility of immediate destruction, and not only because they did not yet know how to effect it technically. The idea that his SS would have to slaughter men, women and children by the millions was something which seems to have worried Himmler considerably.[27]

The fact that hundreds of Jews were shot in the first few days following the German invasion does not disprove my thesis. From the first day the murder squads interpreted the definition of victims very broadly. I want to show this later in connection with the mass executions of Soviet prisoners-of-war. It can be maintained, however, that during the first eight weeks the *Einsatzgruppen* proceeded 'cautiously' compared with what was to come. Their reports reveal, as far as they provide enough details, that the numbers of those executed jumped in mid-August. *Einsatzkommando* 3, about whose murders we have fairly detailed statistics, began to include women and children indiscriminately on 15 August.[28] Before then, less than one-tenth of the victims had been women; children had apparently been spared. Up to 15 August that unit had counted 9,188 killed; within just two more weeks its members murdered another 33,000. *Einsatzgruppe* D reported a similar escalation: its executioners shot 4,425 people before 19 August, and close to 36,000 before the end of September.[29] There is enough evidence to show that other *Einsatzkommandos* also killed predominantly men during the first weeks. This seems to confirm statements of several leaders of *Einsatzkommandos* that the order to liquidate *all* Soviet Jews was issued *after* the attack on the Soviet Union, in August 1941.[30]

Two prerequisites were necessary to permit this fundamental change from organized mass murder to full-scale genocide. First, the thrust of the German armies into the Soviet Union was slowed down considerably by the dogged resistance of the Red Army. The killer squads gained, as a report of *Einsatzgruppe* C of mid-September 1941 states, 'time for a more thorough treatment of the territory'.[31] The second, more decisive factor was that the *Einsatzgruppen* had realized by then that the *Wehrmacht* was now, in marked contrast to what had happened in Poland two years earlier, willing to tolerate massacres of an unprecedented magnitude.

This altered attitude of the *Wehrmacht* must be seen in connection with a process in which, beginning in February 1941, it had been conditioned to wage a merciless war of extermination. During this process the number of potential victims had been increased at an exponential rate. When Hermann Gœring, on 26 February 1941, brought up the topic for the first time – as far as we know – he mentioned 'only' the necessity to liquidate the 'Bolshevist leaders'.[32] The Commissar Order, however, included all subordinate functionaries among the victims, and the Barbarossa Directive legitimized the killing of any Soviet citizen who was suspected of offering active or passive resistance.[33]

The circle of potential victims was again expanded when the High Command of the *Wehrmacht* and Heydrich agreed, on 17 July 1941, that additional *Einsatzkommandos* should select and shoot all 'politically intolerable elements' among the Soviet prisoners of war.[34] The definition of such 'intolerable elements' covered, among others, 'all important state and party functionaries', 'the members of the Soviet intelligentsia', 'all persons who can be established as being agitators or fanatical communists' and –

'all Jews'. Here we find the intention to exterminate *all* Jews put down in writing for the first time. Nevertheless it would be hasty to infer from this order that Hitler himself had ordered the destruction of *all* Jews by that time. The decision had been taken in negotiations between Heydrich and the Prisoner-of-War Department in the High Command of the *Wehrmacht* (OKW), which was subordinate to General Hermann Reinecke, a fanatical Nazi. The selections were limited to the areas under the jurisdiction of the High Command of the *Wehrmacht*. General Wagner, the Army Quartermaster General, issued instructions for those areas under the jurisdiction of the High Command of the Army – i.e. the rear army group and army areas behind the front – one week later. In these instructions we find again the victim groups defined in the Commissar Order and the Barbarossa Directive: 'politically intolerable and suspicious elements, commissars and agitators'. The Jews, however, although subjected to discriminatory treatment, were excepted from execution, and Wagner expressly prohibited any involvement of *Einsatzkommandos* in the measures. This would have been quite impossible if the Heydrich-Reinecke agreement had been based on a definite decision by Hitler.

In October 1941, the Army High Command (OKH), too, permitted the selection of Jews among the Soviet POWs. This, however, was again not the result of any direct intervention of Hitler. It was apparently Reinecke, who put pressure on the OKH. Wagner for his part could not but realize that a large part of those responsible in the front areas had flatly disregarded his orders and left the selection and execution of the 'intolerable' prisoners – including the Jews – to the *Einsatzkommandos*.[35]

These selections of Soviet POWs show the efforts of the murder squads to give the most inclusive interpretation of the definitions of victims issued by Heydrich. Some *Einsatzkommandos* were not satisfied with shooting higher-ranking or 'radical lower' party functionaries, but killed any functionary they could lay hands on. At least for some time units of both *Einsatzgruppen* A and C killed simple party members as well. A number of *Einsatzkommandos* shot skilled workers and engineers as 'members of the intelligentsia'. Moreover, on their own initiative they began to include groups of Soviet POWs who had not even been mentioned in the orders, but were, however, considered 'inferior' or 'unworthy to live' (*lebensunwert*) in Nazi ideology. *Einsatzgruppe* B shot hundreds of Asiatic POWs. The same happened to prisoners and civilians who were said to be incurably ill, disabled or insane.[36] At least 140,000 Soviet POWs fell victim to the *Aussonderungen* (selections) of the *Einsatzkommandos*.[37]

In this process of radicalization which, as already pointed out (p. 108), expanded the number of victims at an exponential rate, the direct influence of Hitler can be identified only in the initial stage. In various conferences with the head of the *Wehrmachtführungsstab* in the OKW, General Alfred Jodl, and with the Chief of Staff of the Army, General Franz Halder, and then again in an address to some 250 generals of units deployed in the east, Hitler mentioned only a sweeping and vague aim: liquidation of the 'Jewish-Bolshevist intelligentsia'.[38] Everything beyond that was organized by the operations staffs in the OKW and the OKH, partly in cooperation with Heydrich.

It was, then, not Hitler who was the driving force behind the dynamism which had developed, but the general agreement of those involved as to the true objective: the liquidation of the Bolshevist system. It is remarkable that, judging by the surviving documents, the term 'Jew' did not have any real significance in the ensuing developments. This is also true for the agreement concerning the activities of the *Einsatzgruppen*. When Jodl first mentioned them, on 3 March 1941, he stated that 'the necessity of liquidating all Bolshevist chiefs (*alle Bolschewistenhaeuptlinge*) and commissars' called for the deployment of *SS-Einsatzgruppen*.[39] Reinecke, in his order of 17 July 1941, justified the executions of the 'intolerable' POWs, including the Jews, by saying that the *Wehrmacht* had 'immediately [to] rid itself of all those elements among the POWs which must be considered Bolshevist instigators'.[40]

Anti-Bolshevism was a factor of crucial importance not only in the genesis and expansion of the policies of extermination during the planning of Operation Barbarossa. It also contributed decisively to the fact that the German troops on the Eastern Front did – apart from some individuals – not only fail to offer resistance to these policies but, on the contrary, rendered valuable assistance in many cases.

The identification of Bolshevism and Jewry was generally accepted. Dozens of documents could be quoted to demonstrate the extent to which that occurred.[41] We find the classical phrasing in the notorious orders of Field-Marshal Walter von Reichenau and Generals Erich von Manstein and Hermann Hoth, who, in October and November 1941, demanded that the soldiers of their armies must have a 'full understanding of the necessity' for the extermination of the Jews, who were the 'intellectual supporters of the Bolshevist terror'.[42]

It was this identification which caused even a good many of those soldiers who held conservative views and rejected Nazi ideology to put up with the murders of the *Einsatzgruppen*. General Hoth's predecessor as the commander of the 17th Army, General Carl-Heinrich von Stuelpnagel, may be cited as a prominent example. His opposition to Hitler is well-documented, but his army cooperated very closely with *Sonderkommando* 4b, and Stuelpnagel himself, in a memorandum of August 1941, called for 'an increased [propaganda] fight against Bolshevism and above all against . . . Jewry, which works for its objectives'.[43]

Including those soldiers who were not really anti-Semites in the policies of destruction became easier to the extent that the Jews were identified not only with Bolshevism but also with the partisan movement. This movement was insignificant at first. The merciless policies of extermination, oppression and exploitation, however, which the *Wehrmacht* helped to implement, led to its rapid growth. The armies were glad to leave much of the fight against this movement, which was considered dirty work, to the *Einsatzgruppen*, which were thus in a position to define who was a partisan and who was not.[44] This enabled them to manipulate the soldiers, who, for their part, were able to silence their consciences by telling themselves that the thousands who were shot were, after all, partisans: 'bandits and criminals carrying arms when they were seized', as Field-Marshal Fedor von Bock jotted in his diary referring to mass executions by *Einsatzgruppe* B.[45] This fiction also offered the members of the *Einsatzgruppen* a 'positive' aim for their ghastly activities, because they allegedly helped to secure the troops against insidious partisan attacks and to destroy Bolshevism once and for all.

From the very beginning, the commanders of the killer squads had taken pains to stage the shootings accordingly. They talked about 'punitive actions' and 'reprisals' because of 'the atrocities of the Bolshevists'; of 'military executions' of 'criminals' or 'partisans' or 'communist agitators' or 'accomplices of partisans'; of executions because of 'Bolshevist activities' or 'sedition' or 'sabotage'.[46] However flimsy and weak this fiction was, its significance for the removal of the inhibitions which were still there should not be underestimated.

In the war against the Soviet Union these inhibiting factors had been eliminated to a very large degree anyway. The intention behind the basic orders like the Barbarossa Directive and the Commissar Order had been to make every last soldier understand that this was an absolutely different kind of war and that the life of a Soviet citizen was held to be of no particular value. The execution of many thousands of hostages, partisan suspects and prisoners of war by *Wehrmacht* and SS units, the starvation of hundreds of thousands of POWs and civilians, which resulted from the basic decision to pay no heed whatsoever to the rules of international law, and the unheard-of brutality of the fighting, which had been set in motion by the German policies, led to an unprecedented brutalization of the German troops[47] and to the erosion of inhibiting factors from the very beginning.

It is more than a mere coincidence that the discovery of the technical means to implement the Holocaust with a minimum of material and personal expense and the preparation of the infrastructure at two of the most important death factories, Auschwitz and Maidanek, are also connected with the dynamic described above. In this case, it was particularly the treatment of the Soviet POWs which speeded up developments.

Two large groups of Soviet prisoners were involved. The first comprised those prisoners who were selected and executed as 'politically intolerable'. Before the end of December 1941 at least 33,000 such prisoners had been executed in the concentration camps of the Reich and the General Government.[48] The second group consisted of those Soviet POWs who had been allotted to Himmler as slave labourers in the SS enterprises. The decision to turn these POWs into Himmler's slaves also resulted from the basic decision to brush aside international law in the war against the Soviet Union. Of the 100,000 originally intended for that purpose some 30,000 to 40,000 were actually sent to improvised *SS-Kriegsgefangenenlager* inside the concentration camps in October/November 1941.[49]

Repeatedly during the summer of 1941, and starting with a convoy of several hundred in July, groups of Soviet prisoners of war, who had been selected as 'intolerable', had been taken to the Auschwitz concentration camp to be executed there.[50] To ease the mental strain of the shooting squads and to save costs and energies the executors soon started looking for a simpler method. It was probably deputy commander Karl Fritzsch who experimented in early September 1941 with a pesticide, Zyklon B, to murder some 600 such prisoners and another 250 camp inmates who had been selected as 'unfit for work'. After more such 'test gassings' – there were at least two more convoys of Soviet prisoners among the victims, one numbering 900 men – the gassings of Jewish victims were started in January or February 1942.

It is remarkable that two main lines of development in the emergence of the Final Solution met in the first mass gassing in September: the 'euthanasia action' (its file reference in the concentration camp system was '14 f 13') and the murder of the 'politically intolerable' Soviet prisoners of war (file reference '14 f 14').

Even the infrastructure used in the Final Solution, the Birkenau camp with its rail connection,[51] had originally been intended for 100,000 Soviet prisoners of war who were to be Himmler's allocation of slave labourers for the giant industrial complex at Auschwitz which I. G. Farben and the SS were planning as a joint venture. Soviet prisoners numbering 10,000, who were to build the huge Birkenau camp for 100,000 POWs, had been brought to Auschwitz in October 1941. By the end of November half of them were dead, by February 1942 about 8,000. Only 186 were still alive on 1 May 1942. Those prisoners who had not starved had been tortured to death. The *Kapos* – most of them German criminals from Sachsenhausen – had boasted to fellow inmates upon their arrival at the camp that, in a briefing by Commandant Rudolf Höss, they had pledged themselves 'to do in 1,000 Bolshevists each', and that Höss had advised them to get special cudgels for that purpose.[52]

Even under the inhumane conditions which existed at Auschwitz before it was turned into the extermination camp which was to become the symbol of the Holocaust, mass murders of that dimension were something new. I think it says a great deal for this conclusion that even at Auschwitz the preparation of, and the habituation to, genocide was advanced decisively by the fact that a 'Bolshevist' was conceded even less right to live than – up to then – other inmates, even, I think, Jews.

This process was not limited to Auschwitz, though. 'Intolerable' prisoners were executed in almost all concentration camps, ranging from groups of a few hundred at Flossenbürg and several thousand at Buchenwald and Dachau to at least 10,000 at Sachsenhausen.[53] The prisoners of the second group mentioned shared the fate of those 10,000 who had been sent to Auschwitz. Most of the concentration camps received detachments of between 1,000 and 5,000 Soviet prisoners in October-November 1941. Although the camp commanders were ordered to prevent any confusion[54] of the two groups the numbers of slave worker POWs were rapidly decimated. A large part fell victim to additional 'selections', another to murder and maltreatment from the hands of SS guards and *Kapos*, the rest starved to death. By February 1942, only a few hundred Soviet prisoners survived in the *SS-Kriegsgefangenenlager*.

Quite obviously here, as in the case of the *Einsatzgruppen*, the preparedness to kill produced its own dynamic. The fact that the second group of prisoners was supposed to serve as workers in the SS industries did not increase their chances of survival. The situation created by overcrowding the concentration camps, the appalling physical condition of most prisoners when they arrived – which made them *lebensunwert* by SS standards – but most of all the desire to get rid of the 'Bolsheviks' led to a complete disregard of the economic aims. Evidently Himmer did not mind the way things developed. He shared the view that the east would provide an unlimited supply of slave labourers. Only when the Soviet POWs died by the hundreds of thousands and when the German attack failed a few miles west of Moscow, did Himmler realize that he would not be able to replace those POWs who had died off from the millions in the *Wehrmacht* prison camps, which had seemed inexhaustible. On 26 January 1942, one week after the Wannsee Conference, he announced to Richard Glücks, the head of the concentration camps, that he would dispatch 150,000 German Jews to the concentration camps within the following four weeks[55] – another crucial step towards the Final Solution, but not yet the decision to kill the Jews concerned.

*

In retrospect, the summer and autumn of 1941 prove to be the crucial time in which the *Einsatzgruppen*, the SS in the concentration camps, but also many *Wehrmacht* units became gradually habituated to murders of unparalleled dimensions. The dynamism which speeded up that process to a crucial degree resulted from the methods which had been chosen and accepted for the destruction of Bolshevism. In that decisive test phase Hitler and Himmler explored gropingly not only ways towards a 'solution of the Jewish question', but also the limits to which the SS and the *Wehrmacht* were willing to follow. There can be little doubt that at many twists and turns in that development they found things easier than they had expected. By August 1941 it was clear that the *Wehrmacht* had neutralized itself as a power factor and that it would cooperate in the destruction of the Soviet Jews rather than oppose it. In the late autumn of 1941 the Nazi leaders were able to conclude that, if they wanted to destroy the Jews, they did not have to wait for the opportunity to drive them into the swamps of Siberia, but that now a situation had come about in which even full-scale genocide could be put into effect. Anti-Bolshevism thus proves to be a crucial factor which paved the way to the Final Solution. This does not apply to the formulation of the aim, which can be traced back to the *völkisch* anti-Semitism of before 1918, but it applies to the *implementation* of that aim.

NOTES

An earlier version of this chapter was presented to the conference 'The Shoah and the war' at the University of Haifa in January 1989. A revised version appeared in *Geschichte und Gesellschaft*, 17 (1991), pp. 242–55. Translations from German publications and sources are mine.

1 Cf. Ernst Nolte, 'Zwischen Geschichtslegende und Revisionismus?' and 'Vergangenheit, die nicht vergehen will', in *Historikerstreit. Die Dokumentation um die Einzigartigkeit der nationalsozialistischen Judenvernichtung* (Munich, 1987), pp. 13–35, 39–47; idem, *Der europäische Bürgerkrieg 1917–1945. Nationalsozialismus und Bolschewismus* (Berlin, 1987). For a convincing refutation of Nolte's thesis see the contributions of Eberhard Jäckel, Hans Mommsen and Heinrich August Winkler in *Historikerstreit*.

2 See e.g. Helmut Krausnick and Hans-Heinrich Wilhelm, *Die Truppe des Weltanschauungskrieges. Die Einsatzgruppen der Sicherheitspolizei und des SD 1938–1942* (Stuttgart, 1981), pp. 150–72; Andreas Hillgruber, 'Der Ostkrieg und die Judenvernichtung', in Gerd R. Ueberschär and Wolfram Wette (eds) *'Unternehmen Barbarossa'. Der deutsche Überfall auf die Sowjetunion 1941* (Paderborn, 1984), pp. 219–36.

3 In the following I want to carry on the approaches of Martin Broszat and Hans Mommsen (Martin Broszat, 'Hitler und die Genesis der "Endlösung" ', *Vierteljahrshefte für Zeitgeschichte* (VfZ), 25 (1977), pp. 739–75; Hans Mommsen, 'The realization of the unthinkable: the "Final Solution of the Jewish Question" in the Third Reich', in Gerhard Hirschfeld (ed.) *The Policies of Genocide. Jews and Soviet Prisoners of War in Nazi Germany* (London, 1986), pp. 97–144).

4 Cf. Klaus-Jürgen Müller, *Das Heer und Hitler. Armee und nationalsozialistisches Regime 1933–1940* (Stuttgart, 1969); Christian Streit, *Keine Kameraden. Die Wehrmacht und die sowjetischen Kriegsgefangenen 1941–1945* (Stuttgart, 1978), pp. 50–9. (A new edition under the same title has just appeared (Bonn, Dietz, 1991).)

5 Cf. Alfred Streim, *Die Behandlung sowjetischer Kriegsgefangener im 'Fall Barbarossa'* (Heidelberg, 1981), pp. 74–93; idem, 'The tasks of the Einsatzgruppen', in *Simon Wiesenthal Center Annual*, 4 (1987), pp. 309–28; idem, Reply to Helmut Krausnick, in *SWC Annual*, 6 (1989), pp. 331–47.

6 Cf. the text of the agreement in Hans-Adolf Jacobsen, 'Kommissarbefehl und Massenexekutionen sowjetischer Kriegsgefangener', in *Anatomie des SS-Staates* (Munich, 1967), p. 170f.

7 Cf. his orders to the *Einsatzgruppen, Bundesarchiv* R 70 SU/32.

8 'Merkblatt für die Führer der Einsatzgruppen und Einsatzkommandos', BA R 70 SU/15. This, by the way, would have enabled the armies to take action against mass shootings in their rear areas, as the agreement provided only for the 'seizure (*Sicherstellung*) of *especially important individuals* (leading emigrants, saboteurs, terrorists, etc.)' (my italics).

9 Cf. Heydrich's operation orders of 29 June, 1 July and 2 July 1941: BA R 70 SU/32.

10 Nuremberg Doc. (ND) 180-L, IMG, vol. 37, p. 672.

11 Cf. *Ereignismeldungen UdSSR* (EM) nos 8, 12, 27, 28, 32, 43, 58, 90, 97, 128, 132 (30 June – 11 November 1941), BA R 58/214–18; cf. Streit, *Keine Kameraden*, pp. 110–14.

12 BA R 70 SU/32.

13 Cf. Helmut Krausnick, 'Judenverfolgung', in *Anatomie des SS-Staates*, p. 300 f.; Hillgruber, 'Der Ostkrieg', p. 226; Ronald Headland, 'The Einsatzgruppen: the question of their initial operations', *Holocaust and Genocide Studies*, 4 (1989), p. 405. Headland, p. 402, says that *Wehrmacht* orders like the Commissar Order and the Barbarossa Directive were to be passed on only orally and that no written records were to be kept. He concludes that the SS was 'operating on a similar fashion', and that really important orders – like the alleged Führer order to kill *all* Jews – were passed on orally. It is true that the orders mentioned were to be passed on in writing only down to army level. There are, however, scores of documents with excerpts from these orders, reports, etc. in the files not only of army groups and armies, but of units down to divisions. The *Einsatzgruppen* and -*kommandos* had no qualms either about producing lots of written records, the most prominent examples being the so-called Jäger report and the *Ereignismeldungen UdSSR* – which Headland himself uses. The order to implement the joint RSHA/OKW decision to kill *all* Jews among the Soviet POWs (see p. 108) was distributed widely under the same security classification –'*Geheim*', not even '*Geheime Kommandosache*' – as Heydrich's order to the Higher SS and Police Leaders. So Headland's argument does not seem to be valid.

14 This complex of ideological orders is discussed in detail in Streit, *Keine Kameraden*, pp. 28–61; Jürgen Förster, 'Das Unternehmen "Barbarossa" als Eroberungs – und Vernichtungskrieg', in *Das Deutsche Reich und der Zweite Weltkrieg*, vol. 4 (Stuttgart, 1983), pp. 413–47. Texts of the orders in Ueberschär and Wette, '*Unternehmen Barbarossa*', pp. 305–8, 313f., 337f.

15 Cf. Streit, *Keine Kameraden*, pp. 80–2.

16 Operations order no. 6, BA R 70 SU/32.

17 BA R 70 SU/32.

18 ND 180-L, p. 687, my italics.

19 As does Headland, 'The Einsatzgruppen', p. 404.

20 EM 86 of 17 September 1941, quoted by Raul Hilberg, *Die Vernichtung der europäischen Juden* (Berlin, 1982), p. 244 (my italics).

21 Cf. Himmler's 'Gedanken über die Behandlung der Fremdvoelkischen im Osten', VfZ, 5 (1957), p. 197.

22 EM 81 of 12 September 1941: Hilberg, *Die Vernichtung*, p. 243.

23 Cf. ND EC-126, IMG, vol. 36, pp. 144 f., 155. Czeslaw Madajczyk, 'General-

plan Ost', *Polish Western Affairs*, 3 (1963), pp. 391–442; Helmut Heiber, 'Der Generalplan Ost', VfZ, 6 (1958), pp. 281–325.

24 Cf. OKW/Wehrmachtführungsstab, 'Vortragsnotiz Leningrad' of 21 September and Jodl's directive of 7 October 1941: Ueberschär and Wette, *'Unternehmen Barbarossa'*, pp. 333–5. Even the lower echelons were familiar with this concept. The (*Wehrmacht*) Propaganda Abteilung Ostland demanded in a report in early 1942 to give 'the Russian' more positive aims than 'the perspective of being driven behind the Urals' (*Bundesarchiv/Militärarchiv* RH 22/v. 234).

25 Broszat, 'Hitler und die Genesis', p. 750.

26 Werner Jochmann (ed.) *Adolf Hitler. Monologe im Führerhauptquartier 1941–1944* (Hamburg, 1980), p. 106; Rosenberg's speech: Politisches Archiv des Auswaertigen Amtes, Pol. XIII, 25, 198 817; Frank's statement: Werner Praeg and Wolfgang Jacobmeyer (eds) *Das Diensttagebuch des deutschen Generalgouverneurs in Polen 1939–1945* (Stuttgart, 1975), p. 457.

27 This aspect has not yet been looked into sufficiently, but there are enough indications for Himmler's concern. When he ordered the destruction of the Jews in the Prypiat marshes on 28 July 1941, he told the SS Cavalry Brigade to 'drive the women and children into the swamps', see n. 28 below. Himmler had reason to worry, too. By November 1941 there was at least one mental hospital 'where SS men are cared for who have broken down while executing women and children' (letter from Helmuth von Moltke to his wife, quoted in Michael Balfour and Julian Frisby, *Helmuth von Moltke. A Leader against Hitler* (London, 1972), p. 175). For Himmler's grotesque attempts at controlling the negative repercussions of the mass executions on his men, see his order of 12 December 1941. In it Himmler stresses the 'holy duty' of each SS leader to take care that the executioners did not become brutalized or suffer psychically. The best way of making them forget their 'difficult tasks' was to organize 'comradely get-togethers' with dinners 'in the best German family fashion' (*in bester deutscher häuslicher Form*) in which 'our men are led into the beautiful fields of German culture and the German mind' (*in die schönsten Gebiete deutschen Geistes und Gemütslebens*). For the text of this order from the Latvian State Archive, Riga, I am indebted to Hans-Heinrich Wilhelm.

28 See the so-called 'Jäger report' of 1 December 1941: Adalbert Rückerl (ed.) *NS-Prozesse. Nach 25 Jahren Strafverfolgung: Möglichkeiten – Grenzen – Ergebnisse* (Karlsruhe, 1971), appendix. The SS Cavalry Brigade, which was under the immediate command of Himmler's *Kommandostab RFSS*, received orders, during its 'pacification' of the Prypiat marshes, on 28 July 1941, to kill all male Jews and 'to drive the women and children into the swamps': see Yehoshua Büchler, 'Kommandostab Reichsführer SS: Himmler's Personal Murder Brigades in 1941', *Holocaust and Genocide Studies*, 1 (1986), p. 15. This, again, does not disprove my thesis that there was *no* general order to kill *all* Jews at that time. It shows, on the contrary, that, even if Himmler stepped up the destruction process with that order – only for a small segment of the SS killer units – he did hesitate to order even the most reliable SS units under his immediate command to murder women and children with their own hands.

29 See Krausnick and Wilhelm, *Die Truppe*, p. 201.

30 See the publications by Streim (as in Note 5).

31 EM 88 of 19 September 1941, BA R 58/217.

32 Streit, *Keine Kameraden*, p. 28.

33 For a more detailed analysis of that process see ibid., pp. 28–61, and Förster, 'Das Unternehmen "Barbarossa" '.

34 ND NO-3414. For the background and the following, see Streit, *Keine Kameraden*, pp. 87–100.
35 Streit, *Keine Kameraden*, pp. 100–4.
36 ibid., pp. 96–100.
37 Streim, *Behandlung*, p. 244; Streim emphasizes that this is an absolute minimum figure. Cf. Streit, *Keine Kameraden*, pp. 105, 344 (1991 edn).
38 Streit, *Keine Kameraden*, p. 34.
39 *Kriegstagebuch des Oberkommandos der Wehrmacht (Wehrmachtführungsstab) 1940–1945*, ed. Percy Ernst Schramm, vol. 1 (Frankfurt, 1961), p. 341.
40 The order is only preserved as part of NO-3414; Reinecke repeated it, however, on 8 September 1941: ND 1519-PS.
41 Cf. Streit, *Keine Kameraden*, pp. 109–25; Krausnick and Wilhelm, *Die Truppe*, p. 205 ff.; Theo J. Schulte, *The German Army and Nazi Policies in Occupied Russia* (Oxford, 1989), pp. 211–39.
42 Their orders: Ueberschär and Wette, '*Unternehmen Barbarossa*', pp. 339–44.
43 BA/MA AOK 17/14499/52.
44 In September 1941 the leader of *Einsatzgruppe* B, Nebe, the *HSSPF Russland Mitte*, von dem Bach-Zelewski, and the Commanding General of Rear Army Group Area Centre, General von Schenckendorff, jointly organized a course of instruction on anti-partisan warfare. Special emphasis was put on 'the Jewish question'. Participants learned that 'wherever there is the Jew there is the partisan, and wherever there is the partisan there is the Jew'. During the exercise the Jews of one village were rounded up and shot (Streit, *Keine Kameraden*, p. 122; Krausnick and Wilhelm, *Die Truppe*, p. 248; *Der Spiegel*, no. 44, 27 October 1986, p. 96).
45 Streit, *Keine Kameraden*, p. 121.
46 Cf. the *Ereignismeldungen UdSSR*, BA R 58/214–19.
47 Cf. Omer Bartov, *The Eastern Front, 1941–45, German Troops and the Barbarisation of Warfare* (Basingstoke, 1985).
48 Cf. Streit, *Keine Kameraden*, pp. 93 f., 343 f. The *minimum* number for the Reich area is 16,000, for the General Government 17,000 (for 1941); cf. also Streim, *Behandlung*, pp. 224–33.
49 Streit, *Keine Kameraden*, pp. 218–23.
50 For the following cf. Streit, *Keine Kameraden*, pp. 217–23; Martin Broszat (ed.) *Kommandant in Auschwitz. Autobiographische Aufzeichnungen des Rudolf Höss* (Munich, 1963), pp. 125–7; Stanislaw Klodzinski, 'Die erste Vergasung von Häftlingen und Kriegsgefangenen im Konzentrationslager Auschwitz', *Die Auschwitz-Hefte. Texte der polnischen Zeitschrift 'Przeglad Lekarski' über historische, psychische und medizinische Aspekte des Lebens und Sterbens in Auschwitz*, vol. 1 (Weinheim, 1987), pp. 261–75.
51 The same is true for the Maidanek concentration camp. It developed from an *SS-Kriegsgefangenenlager*, whose construction had been begun by 5,000 Soviet POWs, who were as rapidly decimated as those at Auschwitz (Streit, *Keine Kameraden*, p. 221).
52 Jerzy Brandhuber, 'Die sowjetischen Kriegsgefangenen im Konzentrationslager Auschwitz', *Hefte von Auschwitz*, 4 (1961), pp. 5–62.
53 See the *Ereignismeldungen UdSSR*, BA R 58/214–19.
54 Even experts like Streim find it difficult to distinguish one group from the other, see *Behandlung*, pp. 226–33.
55 Martin Broszat, 'Nationalsozialistische Konzentrationslager 1933–1945', *Anatomie des SS-Staates*, vol. 2 (Munich, 1967), p. 108 f. We should hesitate to draw the conclusion that this was in fact Himmler's order to kill *all* Jews. The

institution in charge was not Heydrich's RSHA but the *SS-Wirtschafts- und Verwaltungshauptamt*. Himmler announced big economic orders for the concentration camps. The Jews were to replace the Soviet POWs, who had died off too fast, in the I. G. Farben project. It seems to me that at that point the destruction of the Jews taken to Auschwitz was not the primary objective, but that the difficulties in sheltering them – the POW camp was not yet finished – accelerated the decision to kill the larger part of those who arrived.

7

OPERATION BARBAROSSA AND THE ORIGINS OF THE FINAL SOLUTION

Omer Bartov

In recent years, scholars have increasingly focused on the relationship between the German Army's campaign in the Soviet Union and the murder of the Jews. At the same time, however, efforts to clear the *Wehrmacht* of involvement in Nazi crimes, indeed to present it as having pursued a fundamentally just cause and as having become merely one more of Hitler's victims, have also intensified. The historical debates in Germany during the last decade, ranging from the Bitburg controversy, through the *Historikerstreit* to the continuing polemics in the wake of German reunification, have thus all been concerned with the extent of the army's role in the implementation of Nazi policies and its significance for our understanding of both the Third Reich and post-war German society.

It should be pointed out, however, that both the revisionists and their opponents have by and large concentrated on the higher levels of decision making, bureaucratic organization, administration and logistics. Where personalities were discussed, they have tended to be those of the political and military leaders; where ideology was mentioned, one similarly confined oneself to its influence (or lack of it) on those in positions of authority. Consequently, almost by default, both schools have created the impression that whatever the connection between the war in the east and the Holocaust may have been, the individuals involved in executing the regime's policies remained untouched by these larger concerns. In other words, even if the army's war in Russia did indeed make genocide possible, the simple soldier at the front had little to do with all this, preoccupied as he was with military duties and sheer physical survival.[1]

In this chapter I would like to argue that this was not the case. Quite the contrary, the war in the east profoundly transformed the German soldier's view of reality, and thereby contributed both to his brutalization and to his acceptance of and support for the regime's murderous policies, whether he actually participated in their implementation or merely passively observed them. Thus I would claim that the connection between

Barbarossa and the Final Solution was not only one of creating the technical preconditions for genocide, but also of moulding the mentality of the individual and creating a psychologically favourable attitude towards actions which under different circumstances would have been impossible to contemplate and might well have given cause for opposition. It was by fighting a barbarous war in the east that the German soldier came to view the industrial murder of millions of men, women and children as a logical and unavoidable by-product of his own battle for survival rather than as a horrendous crime. And it was these soldiers' tenacity and motivation at the front which made for the continued implementation of these policies. That the troops' own perception of the war in the east and the criminal policies of the *Wehrmacht* and the regime has recently been revived as reflecting an actual historical reality is only an indication of the extent to which the Nazi presentation of its actions has been perpetuated long after the collapse of the Third Reich.[2]

I

The most obvious connection between the war in the Soviet Union and the Final Solution is the complex of what has been called the criminal orders issued to the German Army in the east as part of the Barbarossa decree on 22 June 1941. These orders stipulated that military jurisdiction concerning the prospective occupied population would be curtailed, that ruthless measures should be employed against such political and biological enemies of the Reich as communist functionaries, partisans, people of Mongol origin and Jews, that the political commissars of the Red Army should be shot without trial, and that the army should closely collaborate with the *Einsatzgruppen*, the extermination squads of the SS and SD.[3]

It was by issuing and implementing these orders that the *Wehrmacht* became deeply involved in the criminal policies of the regime. Although most generals, and quite a few historians, have claimed after the war that the army resisted, on various levels, the actual execution of these orders, and that some commanders even refused to issue them, the evidence as found in the archives and analysed in a number of important works, provides a very different picture. The *Wehrmacht* became a crucial part of the elaborate genocidal machinery of the Nazi regime on a number of levels and in a complex relationship. First, it made possible the murder of millions of people by occupying huge tracts of land in the east and protecting the killers – initially the *Einsatzgruppen* and later the death camp administrators – from enemy attacks; second, it provided logistical support, and at times also personnel, for the actual killing operations; third, it participated itself in wide-ranging murder campaigns ostensibly described as 'anti-partisan' and 'purging' operations in which very large numbers of civilians, mostly Jews, were killed; fourth, it murdered over half a million

Soviet prisoners of war described as political and biological enemies of the Reich, and was directly or indirectly responsible for the death of an overall number of more than three million prisoners by starvation, exposure, overexertion, epidemics and all other forms of maltreatment; fifth, it actively participated in the economic exploitation of the occupied territories of the Soviet Union, which led to the death of millions of civilians; sixth, it conducted large-scale scorched earth policies which caused the devastation of huge areas, the destruction of thousands of villages and towns, and the subsequent death of large numbers of men, women and children; all this quite apart from such well-known instances as the siege of Leningrad which cost the lives of about a million inhabitants.[4]

The fact that until recently the clear connection between the *Wehrmacht*'s policies in the east and the Final Solution has been ignored has little to do with the lack of empirical evidence, but rather with the political implications of this assertion. To admit that Hitler and Himmler would not have been able to carry out their genocidal plans without the active collaboration of the *Wehrmacht*'s command and the acquiescence and active participation of the junior officer corps and the rank and file, would have meant that a much larger portion of the German population shared the responsibility for the regime's crimes than one would have liked to admit after the collapse of the Third Reich. What is more, the soldiers of the *Wehrmacht* formed the future generation of both parts of post-war Germany. And while the GDR presented itself as continuing the heritage of 'anti-fascism' and completely dissociated itself from the 'capitalist' Germany which had committed these crimes, the FRG, which presented itself as the bearer of German identity, was compelled to limit to the greatest extent possible the scope of collaboration with the regime in the darkest epoch of Germany's history. It is precisely for this reason too that recently some German scholars have once more argued for the patriotic and thereby legitimate role played by the *Wehrmacht* in the Third Reich which allegedly merely sought to protect the territorial integrity of Germany.[5]

Even when it was demonstrated that the *Wehrmacht*'s leadership was deeply involved in Nazi policies, many historians, not all of them German, conservative or revisionist, continued to assert that the man at the front had remained aloof from such political/ideological matters.[6] Yet glancing through the files of combat formations on the Eastern Front one finds a very different picture. Indeed, it soon becomes clear not only that the German soldier carried out the criminal orders issued to him by his commanders, he also committed a wide array of unauthorized brutalities against enemy soldiers and the civilian population. These actions, described by the officers as constituting a case of the troops running wild (*Verwilderung*), included indiscriminate shooting, rape, robbery, plunder, destruction of property and livestock, and all other acts associated with a ruthless army of occupation. And although warned repeatedly by their commanders, the troops kept on with these actions till they were finally pushed back into German territory. The officers, it should be noted, did not oppose such actions through any moral compunction; after all, they ordered far more destructive policies themselves. What they objected to was the soldiers' acting on their own initiative, and what they feared was a decline in military discipline as a consequence. Yet this did not happen, even though soldiers were in fact rarely punished for such breaches of discipline. Indeed, it appears that it was precisely due to the acquiescence of officers with unauthorized acts of brutality by their troops that they were able to enforce extremely harsh combat discipline, with the result that some 15,000 soldiers were executed for such offences as desertion, cowardice and self-inflicted wounds. To be sure, such brutal disciplinary measures did contribute to the army's battle performance at a time when the traditional social organization which had hitherto sustained its cohesion was in the process of disintegration under the pressure of huge casualties and a constant and increasingly severe manpower shortage; but they in turn further brutalized the troops and made them ever more aware of the cheapness of human life in the east.[7]

Under such circumstances, it is no wonder that soldiers who were themselves liable to act with extreme brutality towards the occupied population did not react with particular alarm when exposed to, or ordered to assist in, the murder operations of the SS. Nor should one be astonished to find that soldiers who later on saw the death camps functioning at full steam during their travels back and forth from the front did not perceive them as anything too extraordinary. As far as they were concerned, this was only one more aspect of a brutal, ruthless war. Murder was the norm at the front, and there was no reason why the regime's enemies should be treated differently anywhere else.

II

War is always a brutalizing affair, for not only is it mainly concerned with violence, it also allows, indeed demands, actions deemed criminal in peacetime. This is particularly the case in conscript armies, where the soldiers no longer belong to a special category, a so-called military society, but are recruited from, and ultimately return to, civilian society. But the fighting on the Eastern Front in the Second World War had a more brutalizing effect on the troops of the *Wehrmacht* than any other modern armed conflict.

When speaking of the war in the Soviet Union, we can point to three main circumstantial causes for the brutalization of German troops. First, the scale of the fighting and the horrendous losses it entailed; second, the peculiar geographical and climatic conditions at the front; third, the cultural differences between the invaders and the occupied.

The *Ostheer* (Eastern Army) marched into the Soviet Union with more than three million men, and by the end of the war had sustained about six million casualties on that front alone. Such massive losses created among the troops a sense of taking part in an apocalyptic event whose very nature made all previous codes of behaviour and moral assumptions wholly irrelevant. The scale of human destruction thus encouraged the development among the troops of a nihilistic, Social Darwinist approach to their reality, according to which everything was allowed which enabled them to survive, and anything perceived as endangering their existence had to be eradicated. Along with their growing contempt for or indifference to death and suffering, the *Ostheer*'s troops came to accept the reality of the war, which they had done so much to create, as unavoidable and unchangeable, and they therefore behaved according to what they perceived as the rules of that horrific reality without any serious misgivings or pangs of conscience. The nature of the war legitimized actions which ensured its continuation. This was, indeed, a vicious circle which could only be smashed by total victory or total defeat, just as the regime had claimed all along.

The fighting in the east was different from that on other fronts due also to the geographical and climatic conditions which characterize Russia. The troops were struck time and again by the endless spaces they had to conquer, by the extreme temperatures, the vast forests, the impenetrable swamps, the boundless steppe, the impassable mud and the huge expanses of snow. These natural conditions were felt all the more keenly due to the backward transportation infrastructure in the Soviet Union, on the one hand, and the rapid demodernization of the German front, on the other. By the first winter in Russia, most German soldiers found themselves living in the most primitive conditions conceivable, often lacking proper shelter, food and clothing, spending long weeks and months in the mud and snow, dependent on horse-drawn carts for transportation, constantly lice-ridden and suffering from an innumerable array of diseases. These conditions also enhanced the sense that this war constituted a return to some kind of primeval confrontation in which the legal and moral traditions of human civilization no longer mattered. Thus the unthinkable came to be perceived as natural, indeed as necessary and inevitable.[8]

This image of war which emerged on the Eastern Front was closely tied to the image of the enemy. Here German troops confronted a civilization which seemed to them so alien, so primitive, so completely different from anything they had seen or expected, that they tended to perceive it as composed of a different species altogether, or simply of *Untermenschen*. Accounts of the occupied population and of Soviet POWs by German soldiers are replete with a sense of astonishment at their physical appearance, living conditions and savagery. This was very different from the impression gained by Germans occupying the west, which could at best be described as a degenerate civilization, and often aroused also some sense of affinity. Many German officers, for instance, could speak French, and were at pains to show that they were capable of conducting themselves as well as the occupied. But very few of them spoke Russian, and even fewer had any sense of affinity with the population, but at best expressed some pity, more often disgust and derision and, as civil resistance increased, hatred and fear. Hence in this sense too, the war in the east created or at least enhanced among German troops the feeling that they were up against people who could hardly be seen or treated as human beings. And, once this division of humanity into higher and lower categories shifted from a theoretical ideological plane to the concrete practice of daily conduct, there was little reason to object to mass killings and all other forms of maltreatment, exploitation and enslavement.[9]

III

The manner in which German troops perceived the reality of the front, and the impact of that perception on their conduct and their acceptance of the regime's criminal policies, were of course not merely the result of the actual conditions at the front, nor of the 'criminal orders' *per se*, but also of the massive indoctrination to which they were exposed before and during their military service. Indeed, these issues were closely connected. On the one hand, it is doubtful whether the troops would have reacted to their experiences in the same manner, and would have followed their orders so obediently, had they not been thoroughly prepared before actually confronting the enemy. On the other hand, the conditions of fighting and surviving in the east greatly enhanced the soldiers' ideological convictions and their willingness to implement the regime's criminal policies.

Any attempt to analyse the ties between the Final Solution and popular opinion in Germany, and especially the opinions and actions of the *Wehrmacht*'s troops, must take into account the fact that in the Third Reich it was almost impossible to avoid being influenced by the ideology of the regime. This was all the more the case with those youngsters and teenagers who were soon to make up the bulk of the army's combat soldiers. German youth in the 1930s went through an increasingly Nazified educational system, and, even more importantly, spent much of their time in the Hitler Youth and *Arbeitsdienst* (labour service), where the ideological tenets of the regime featured not merely as theoretical issues, but were practised as constituting a fundamentally new way of living. By the time they were conscripted, the vast majority of German youths had internalized a view of life as a constant struggle for survival between competing ideological systems and races, in which Germany was bound to win due to its innate racial superiority and the leadership provided by Hitler, while its foes, identified especially with the 'Judeo-Bolsheviks' and 'Mongol hordes' of the east had to be eradicated as a lethal threat to German culture and western civilization.[10]

This outlook was naturally an essential precondition for the success of the army's own indoctrination. As a number of studies have shown, the *Wehrmacht* leadership did indeed make a concerted effort further to stiffen the ideological resolve of the troops, reaching even the most remote units on its far-flung fronts. Moreover, there are numerous indications that this indoctrination was welcomed both by the junior officers and the rank and file as a necessary element in the battle motivation of front-line units.[11] Even more striking is the extent to which soldiers integrated the view of the enemy and the perception of their mission in the war provided them by the regime into their own portrayals of reality in letters, diaries, post-war memoirs and oral testimonies. The soldiers repeatedly reported that what they actually found upon encountering the enemy was precisely what they had been told to anticipate, and in some cases even asserted that reality was worse than their expectations: the Russians were more vicious and primitive, the Jews more depraved, the atrocities committed by the enemy more horrible than even such pornographic sheets as the *Stürmer* had claimed. Thus the notion that the reality of the front had a sobering effect on the troops is wholly false; rather, the soldiers experienced it as a powerful confirmation of their worst expectations and fears and thereby also of the ideological claims of the regime. It is no wonder that this made it all the easier to carry out the policies advocated by the Nazis with little reluctance, indeed, in many cases with a great deal of enthusiasm. Nor should we be surprised to find the troops expressing understanding for the mass killings by the SS, witnessed by, and not infrequently carried out with the active assistance of, the army.[12]

The profound racist sentiments among the *Wehrmacht*'s troops can be illustrated by examining some of their letters. We should keep in mind that although the *Wehrmacht*'s censorship made critical remarks about the regime a dangerous undertaking, soldiers were under no obligation to express sympathy with its views and policies, and could, if they so chose, limit themselves to personal matters. Thus it seems that their comments about the nature of the enemy they were confronting and the manner in which he was treated indeed reflected their own feelings.

As early as 5 July 1941 the Panzer Sergeant Karl Fuchs wrote home: 'Russia is nothing but misery, poverty and depravity!'[13] Two weeks later he promised: 'When I go back I will tell you endless horror stories about Russia. Yesterday, for instance, we saw our first women soldiers. . . . And these pigs fired on our decent German soldiers from ambush positions'.[14] Another soldier expressed his conviction that 'this time an end will cer-tainly be put to this God-hating power'. He was especially moved by finding 'evidence of Jewish, Bolshevik atrocities, the likes of which I have hardly believed possible. . . . You can well imagine', he concluded, 'that this cries for revenge, which we certainly also take'.[15] An NCO wrote at the time:

> The German people owes a great debt to our Führer, for had these beasts, who are our enemies here, come to Germany, such murders would have taken place that the world has never seen before.... What we have seen, no newspaper can describe. It borders on the unbelievable, even the Middle Ages do not compare with what has occurred here. And when one reads the *Stürmer* and looks at the pictures, that is only a weak illustration of what we see here and the crimes committed here by the Jews. Believe me, even the most sensational newspaper reports are only a fraction of what is happening here.[16]

Lance-Corporal Paul Lenz maintained early on in the campaign:

> Only a Jew can be a Bolshevik, for this blood-sucker there can be nothing nicer than to be a Bolshevik.... Wherever one spits one finds a Jew.... As far as I know ... not one single Jew has worked in the workers' paradise, everyone, even the smallest blood-sucker, has a post where he naturally enjoys great privileges.[17]

Private Reinhold Mahnke described his impressions of Russia: 'Only in Poland have I seen so much filth, mire, and rabble, especially Jews. I think that even there it was not half as bad as here.'[18] He also furnished a detailed account of Bolshevik-Jewish atrocities against the Lithuanians. Not only did they eject them from their houses and then burn them down, they also 'cut off their feet and hands, tore out their tongues.... They even nailed men and children to walls. Had these criminals come to our country', Mahnke now realized, 'they would have torn us to pieces and mangled us, that's clear. But the Lithuanians have taken revenge', he concluded, referring to the anti-Jewish pogroms conducted by the local population with the encouragement of the *Einsatzgruppen* and under the observing eye of the *Wehrmacht*.[19] Lance-Corporal Heinrich Sachs similarly noted 'how the Jewish question was solved with impressive thoroughness under the enthusiastic applause of the local population'. He then went on to quote Hitler's speech before the Reichstag threatening the Jews with destruction if they caused a war against Germany, and added that the 'Jews should have known that the Führer was serious and must now bear the appropriate consequences'.[20]

Captain Hans Kondruss, writing from Lvov (Lemberg) in mid-July, also discovered ample evidence to show that 'here clearly a whole people has systematically been reared into subhumanity. This is clearly the most Satanic educational plan of all times, which only Jewish sadism could have constructed and carried through.' The fact that the municipal library contained the Talmud, and that among the massacred civilians there were allegedly no Jews, was to his mind 'indicative of the real originators'. He too was satisfied to note that the 'wrath of the people has however been turned upon this people of criminals'. Indeed, he asserted: 'It will be necessary radically to scorch out this boil of plague, because these "animals" will always constitute a danger.' The Jews had turned the population away 'from everything which to us human beings has been eternally holy', for their goal was 'the brutalization (*Vertierung*) of a whole people, in order to make use of it as an instrument in the war for Judas' world domination'.[21] Lance-Corporal Paul Rubelt agreed that the 'Jews were for the most part the evil doers' in the Lvov massacres, and noted that now the 'culprits are shot'.[22] Indeed, Corporal K. Suffner, who maintained that the 'Bolsheviks and the Jews have murdered 12,000 Germans and Ukrainians in a beastly manner', reported that 'the surviving Ukrainians arrested 2,000 Jews and exercised frightful revenge'. He concluded: 'We swear that this plague will be eradicated root and branch.'[23] Lance-Corporal Hans Fleischauer expressed similar sentiments: 'The Jew is a real master in murdering, burning and massacring. . . . These bandits deserve the worst and toughest punishment conceivable.' The consequences he drew from his experience with Jewish atrocities were far from untypical: 'We all cannot be thankful enough to our Führer, who had protected us from such brutalities, and only for that we must follow him through thick and thin, wherever that might be.'[24] Private von Kaull believed that 'international Jewry', already in control of the capitalist world, had taken 'as a counterweight this proletarian insanity' as well: 'Now these two powers of destruction have been sent to the field, now they are incited against Europe, against the heart of the west, in order to destroy Germany.' He was impressed with the scale and significance of the conflict:

> Such a huge battle has never before taken place on earth. It is the greatest battle of the spirits ever experienced by humanity, it is waged for the existence or downfall of western man and the highest values which a people consciously carries on its shield.

Consequently: 'We must give our all to withstand this battle.'[25] Private Gregor Lisch asked his family in the rear to 'be happy that the Bolsheviks and the Jews had not come to us', for 'the Jews have destroyed these poor people'.[26] And Private Fallnbigl, while stressing that 'we should be happy that we have not had this scourge of humanity in our own country', was convinced that 'the German world would not be prepared for such heinous deeds even after years of preparation'.[27]

In early August 1941 one soldier wrote that 'the brutality which constantly characterizes the Russian can be explained only by incitement'. Indeed, he believed that the Russians were 'a people which needs long and good schooling in order to become human'.[28] Karl Fuchs reported at the time that the

> pitiful hordes on the other side are nothing but felons who are driven
> by alcohol and the threat of pistols pointed at their heads. . . . There
> is no troop morale and they are at best cannon fodder. . . . They are
> nothing but a bunch of assholes!

He was impressed by the obvious inferiority of Russian POWs: 'Hardly
ever do you see the face of a person who seems rational and intelligent.
They all look emaciated and the wild, half-crazy look in their eyes makes
them look like imbeciles.' He simply could not understand how 'these
scoundrels, led by Jews and criminals, wanted to imprint their stamp on
Europe'.[29] But he had no doubt that the 'war against these subhuman
beings' was nearly over, and found it 'almost insulting when you consider
that drunken Russian criminals have been set loose against us. They are
scoundrels, the scum of the earth! Naturally', he was happy to point out,
'they are not a match for us German soldiers'.[30] He thus concluded:

> Everyone, even the last doubter, knows today that the battle against
> these subhumans, who've been whipped into a frenzy by the Jews,
> was not only necessary but came in the nick of time. Our Führer
> has saved Europe from certain chaos.[31]

Later that month another soldier wrote from Russia:

> Precisely now one recognizes perfectly what would have happened
> to our wives and children had these Russian hordes . . . succeeded in
> penetrating into our Fatherland. I have had the opportunity here
> to . . . observe these uncultivated, multi-raced men. Thank God they
> have been thwarted from plundering and pillaging our homeland.[32]

And his words were echoed by those of a comrade, who himself spoke
the language of the *Wehrmacht*'s propaganda brochures:

> What would have happened to cultural Europe, had these sons of the
> steppe, poisoned and drunk with a destructive poison, these incited
> subhumans, invaded our beautiful Germany? Endlessly we thank our
> Führer, with love and loyalty, the saviour and the historical figure.[33]

By September 1941, Fuchs was firmly convinced that 'Russia is like a
pigsty',[34] and added in another letter that 'no matter where you look, there
is nothing but dirty, filthy block houses. You can't find a trace of culture
anywhere. Now we realize what our great German Fatherland has given
its children. There exists only one Germany in the entire world.'[35] This
was also the opinion of an NCO who claimed that 'our propaganda has
certainly not exaggerated, perhaps understated' what he called the 'pre-
flood conditions' reigning in the Soviet Union.[36] Private Walter Sperath
expressed indignation at discovering that even 'animals are treated better

back home than the manner in which these people are housed and fed', and he too swore that he and his comrades 'will not end this battle before this rabble is eradicated root and branch with the blessing of European culture and humanity'.[37] And Lance-Corporal G. S. had similar sentiments, noting that among 'this mixture of races the devil would feel at home. It is, I believe, the most depraved and filthiest [people] living on God's earth.'[38] On 22 September Fuchs asked his wife: 'Can you imagine that human beings grow up like animals? That seems to be the case here. . . . I suppose it's just impossible to ask a Russian to think of something beautiful and noble', he concluded.[39] In another letter he described the 'distorted, grimacing faces' of the Russians, 'driven by a political insanity', and the rage which they awakened in him. 'In my opinion, these Bolsheviks are murderers of all culture!'[40] Fuchs was quite sure he had come face to face with reality: 'We have seen the true face of Bolshevism', composed, to his mind, of 'communist scoundrels, Jews and criminals', and, he assured his mother, he and his comrades 'will know how to deal with it in the future'.[41]

A *Wehrmacht* major who happened to pass through Warsaw on his way to the front in the autumn of 1941 ascribed the horrors of the ghetto not to Nazi barbarism, but rather to the Jews' own inhumanity:

> The conditions in the ghetto can hardly be described. . . . The Jew does business here with the others also on the street. In the morning, as I drove through in my car, I saw numerous corpses, among them those of children, covered anyhow with paper weighed down with stones. The other Jews pass by them indifferently, the primitive 'corpse-carts' come and take away these 'remainders' with which no more business can be done. The ghetto is blocked by walls, barbed-wire, and so forth. . . . Dirt, stench and noise are the main signs of the ghetto.[42]

Similarly, another man reported from Minsk in October that

> Following [partisan] attacks a number of people, especially Jews, are summarily taken and shot on the spot, their houses set on fire. Recently . . . POWs were simply shot down in a pile by the guards. The lads quarrelled over bread and old pieces of clothing which had been thrown to them. Three lay dead and were instantly buried on the spot by the Jews like mad dogs.[43]

That same month an NCO described the Soviet POWs as 'dull, animal-like and ragged – and yet often treacherous',[44] and another maintained that the Russians were 'no longer human beings, but wild hordes and beasts, who have been bred by Bolshevism during the last twenty years'. Therefore, he explained: 'One may not allow oneself to feel any compassion for these people, because they are all very cowardly and perfidious.'[45]

These views regarding the Germans' real and perceived enemies persisted throughout the war. Thus one lance-corporal exclaimed in April 1942 in reference to the Jews: 'These swine of human creatures. They have clearly brought us this outrage of a war.'[46] Typical of the inversion process common among the troops and the sense that the murderous treatment of the Jews merely confirmed their inhumanity was the following letter sent in July 1942:

> About events in the east concerning the Jews one could write a book. But it would be a waste of paper. You can be sure that they come to the right place, where they will no longer oppress any peoples.[47]

And another NCO wrote at the time that

> the great task given us in the struggle against Bolshevism lies in the destruction of eternal Jewry. Once one sees what the Jew has done in Russia, one can well understand why the Führer began the struggle against Jewry. What sorrows would have come to our homeland, had this beast of a man had the upper hand? . . . Recently a comrade of ours was murdered in the night. He was stabbed in the back. That can only have been the Jew, who stands behind these crimes. The revenge taken for that act brought indeed a nice success. The population itself hates the Jews as never before. It realizes now, that he is guilty of everything.[48]

And in the same vein, one corporal wrote:

> although in the course of this war a little more light will have been cast on the Jewish question even for the most pigheaded philistine (*Spieser*), it is nevertheless still of the utmost importance that this question be further put in the necessary light, and here the *Stürmer* has, thank God, still remained true to its old positions. Just as the eastern Jew now reveals himself in all his brutality, so have all this vicious lot, no matter whether in the west or in the east.[49]

Indeed, Streicher's yellow sheet seems to have maintained its popularity at the front, or even enhanced it, following more than a year of fighting in the east. One NCO reported in August 1942 that

> I have received the *Stürmer* now for the third time. It makes me happy with all my heart. . . . You could not have made me happier. . . . I recognized the Jewish poison in our people long ago; how far it might have gone with us, this we see only now in this campaign. What the Jewish regime has done in Russia, we see every day, and even the last doubters are cured here in view of the facts. We must and we will liberate the world from this plague, this is why the German soldier protects the Eastern Front, and we shall not

return before we have uprooted all evil and destroyed the centre of the Jewish-Bolshevik 'world-do-gooders'.[50]

Thus we can conclude that for a large number of soldiers fighting in the east, the war was not only a military affair in which they were preoccupied with fighting the enemy and attempting to survive. Rather, they accepted the regime's perception and image of the war as an ideological struggle in which they were duty-bound to destroy the 'enemies of humanity', Bolshevism, 'Asiatic barbarism' and the Jews. Such men cannot have found the mass killings performed by the SS and defended by the *Wehrmacht* as abhorrent, but rather as a service to the German cause as they understood it. Not many of them were willing to admit this after the war. But from some conversations with veterans conducted many years after the event one does occasionally glean the manner in which they perceived reality during those years in the Soviet Union. As one man who had been a junior officer in Poland and Russia said to hs interviewer in the early 1980s:

Well, of course, what they [the Nazis, rather than 'us', the *Wehrmacht*] did to the Jews was revolting. But we were told over and over again that it was a necessary evil. . . . No, I must admit, at the time I had no idea we had fallen into the hands of criminals. I didn't realize that until much later, after it was all over.[51]

IV

When speaking of Operation Barbarossa and the origins of the Final Solution we can thus say that in stark contradiction to assertions made after the war and revived recently by some revisionist historians, the two events cannot be seen in isolation from each other. To be sure, it is impossible to know whether the Third Reich would have sooner or later pursued a similar genocidal policy had it not invaded the Soviet Union; but the actual timing of the Final Solution, as well as the logistical, geographical and psychological context within which the war in Russia was conducted, leave little doubt as to the close ties between Barbarossa and the regime's extermination policies. Indeed, the nature of the campaign in the east, its definition as an ideological struggle, its practice as a war of annihilation and enslavement, and the images it conjured in the minds of the German troops who fought it, all served as an essential background for the realization of the Nazi utopia of racial domination and a universal biological purge.

It is for this reason that one is repeatedly struck by the attempts to dissociate these two events. Such attempts have tackled the issue from a number of angles. The most common has been the argument that the army was strictly occupied with its professional duties, and while carrying out a legitimate patriotic task had no time for, and no interest in, the more criminal activities of the regime's murder agencies. The generals claimed that they had refused to issue the 'criminal orders', let alone execute them, the rank and file argued that they had no knowledge of what was taking place in the rear.[52] This has been shown to be false, for the generals were deeply involved in the phrasing, distribution and implementation of these orders, while the troops were frequently exposed to, and not rarely took part in, murder operations.[53] Some western historians, who preferred to take at face value the German generals' assertions rather than examine their veracity in the archives, and constructed an image of an honourable, *korrekt Wehrmacht*,[54] had to be corrected in turn by a younger generation of German scholars who refused to believe the *Wehrmacht*'s former commanders and investigated the evidence of widespread indoctrination promoted by the army's leadership and close collaboration with the SS.[55]

More recently, some old apologetic arguments have been rehashed and streamlined, claiming to offer a new approach to the study of German history. Ernst Nolte and some of his supporters have asserted that both the war in the east, and the extermination policies of the regime, must be seen as a reaction to a real or perceived threat by communism. That these were old arguments can be gauged from the fact that they had already been employed by the Nazis themselves, who always liked to present the murder of the Jews and the struggle against Bolshevism as a preventive measure, a notion readily accepted by the soldiers, much of the German public and, indeed, not a few other Europeans as well.[56] Quite apart from the fact that this argument is rooted in a recognition of the tie between Barbarossa and the Final Solution (an assertion also commonly made by the Nazis), in order to give their thesis a more modern appearance Nolte and his followers went on to argue that Nazi policies must be 'contextualized' in an era of extermination or, more specifically, that it was the Soviet Gulags which 'originated' Auschwitz. In this sense, if everyone is guilty of the same type of crimes, then no one is guilty; and if anyone must bear the blame, then it surely is the originators rather than those who merely emulated them. Thus, while recognizing the ties between Auschwitz and the invasion of the Soviet Union, Nolte dismisses the whole issue as part of a wider context for whose creation others are responsible. Uninterested as they are in empirical facts, Nolte and his colleagues do not bother to compare in detail, and fail to note the essential difference both between the Gulag and Hitler's death camps, and between the conduct of war by the Red Army and the *Wehrmacht*.[57] Suffice it to say that while the Red Army did often behave brutally, and Stalin did establish dictatorial regimes in eastern Europe, the Soviet Union did not pursue a policy of wholesale extermination comparable to that of the Third Reich. Indeed, had it done so, it is doubtful whether we would now be faced with a reunified Germany including a GDR which, though a corrupt dictatorship, did continue to survive as a state. Nor would a Nazi victory have allowed a similar development in Russia merely fifty years after the event.

A third set of arguments makes the plea for a 'historicization' of the period not so much on the international level, but rather with a strong domestic orientation. Thus the historian Andreas Hillgruber has accepted Nolte's argument that the Third Reich's policies can be understood only in the context of a general European drive towards wholesale destruction of social, racial and political enemies, and claims that in essence the policies of Britain, Soviet Russia and the Third Reich had the same ends in mind. But he is more concerned with the mentality and motivation of the individual German soldier. Here he wishes to compartmentalize the troops' experience in two ways: first, to dissociate their actions at the front from their consequences, that is to ignore, quite consciously, the fact that by holding the front the soldiers made possible the continued industrial murder of millions of people in the death camps; second, to dissociate the troops who were fighting to defend German territory in the last phase of the war from those who had done their best to conquer vast territories beyond Germany's frontiers and had done so within the context of an unprecedented murderous campaign. Limiting his gaze to the winter battles of 1944–5 in east Prussia, Hillgruber is thus able to claim that the historian 'must' identify with these soldiers who were conducting a patriotic, defensive and therefore legitimate, indeed heroic fight against the so-called '*Racheorgie*' (orgy of revenge) of the Red Army. He thus returns to the old argument of the *Wehrmacht* as a patriotic tool, though he both employs allegedly new methods of 'historicization' and, quite strikingly, asserts that the Nazi propaganda claim, according to which there was no alternative to Hitler except Stalin, had in fact become a reality.[58]

A last and very different attempt to deal with the connection between Barbarossa and the Final Solution was made by the American historian Arno Mayer, who has argued that the main focus of Hitler's regime was a crusade against Bolshevism, and that it was only due to the failure of the campaign that the Nazis turned against the Jews. In other words, he asserts that Auschwitz was the outcome of the failed blitzkrieg in Russia, and might not have taken place had the campaign ended with the same swiftness as that in the west.[59] Yet not only does his argument raise numerous questions of timing, due to the fact that the decision regarding the murder of the Jews appears to have been made before the campaign began to falter, it also ignores the fact that the Nazis always claimed that Bolshevism and the Jews were identical. Indeed, Mayer's argument brings us back to the main assertion of this chapter. As we have seen from some of the soldiers' letters cited here, and as can be demonstrated by any number of propaganda brochures, orders of the day, policy papers and so forth, the war in the east was always presented as a struggle against 'Judeo-Bolshevism', as a campaign for the eradication of the Jews, the Bolsheviks and the Slavs, with the former two categories openly and clearly slated for physical destruction. It is precisely here that one sees the direct connection between Barbarossa and the Final Solution, not only in the administrative and circumstantial sense, but also in the ideological one, as well as in the manner that the war was understood and perceived by those who actually fought it, the *Wehrmacht*'s soldiers.

NOTES

1 See, e.g., Hans Mommsen, 'Kriegserfahrungen', in *Über Leben im Krieg*, ed. Ulrich Borsdorf and Mathilde Jamin (Reinbeck bei Hamburg, 1989), p. 13.
2 See, e.g., Andreas Hillgruber, *Zweierlei Untergang. Die Zerschlagung des Deutschen Reiches und das Ende des europäischen Judentums* (Berlin, 1986).
3 Christian Streit, *Keine Kameraden* (Stuttgart, 1978), pp. 28–61.
4 Omer Bartov, *The Eastern Front 1941–45. German Troops and the Barbarisation of Warfare* (London and New York, 1985/6), pp. 106–41; Helmut Krausnick and Hans-Heinrich Wilhelm, *Die Truppe des Weltanschauungskrieges* (Stuttgart, 1981); Rolf-Dieter Müller, 'Von der Wirtschaftsallianz zum kolonialen Ausbeutungskrieg', and 'Das Scheitern der wirtschaftlichen "Blitzkriegstrategie" ', both in *Der Angriff auf die Sowjetunion* (Stuttgart, 1983), vol. 4 of *Das Deutsche Reich und der Zweite Weltkrieg*, ed. Militärgeschichtliches Forschungsamt; Streit, *Keine Kameraden*.
5 On this, see, e.g., Peter Baldwin (ed.) *Reworking the Past. Hitler, the Holocaust, and the Historians' Debate* (Boston, 1990); Charles S. Maier, *The Unmasterable Past* (Cambridge, Mass., 1988).
6 See, e.g., Alexander Dallin, *German Rule in Russia 1941–45*, 2nd edn (London, 1981), pp. 416, 440–2, 454–5, 461–2, 500–1, 505–10, 515–19, and so forth.
7 Manfred Messerschmidt, 'German military law in the Second World War', in *The German Military in the Age of Total War*, ed. Wilhelm Deist (Leamington Spa/New Hampshire, 1985); Omer Bartov, *Hitler's Army. Soldiers, Nazis, and War in the Third Reich* (New York and Oxford, 1991), pp. 29–58, on the destruction of the 'primary group', and pp. 59–105 on the perversion of discipline.
8 See Bartov, *Eastern Front*, pp. 7–39; and idem, *Hitler's Army*, pp. 12–28.
9 On the higher ranks of the *Wehrmacht*, see especially Jürgen Förster, 'The German Army and the ideological war against the Soviet Union', in *The Policies of Genocide*, ed. Gerhard Hirschfeld (London, 1986); and idem, 'New wine in old skins? The Wehrmacht and the war of "Weltanschauungen", 1941', in *The German Military in the Age of Total War*, ed. Wilhelm Deist (Leamington Spa/New Hampshire, 1985).
10 On schools see, e.g., Harald Scholtz, *Erziehung und Unterricht unterm Hakenkreuz* (Göttingen, 1985); Geert Planter (ed.) *Schule im Dritten Reich – Erziehung zum Tod?* 2nd edn (Munich, 1984). On the Hitler youth, see H. W. Koch, *The Hitler Youth* (London, 1975); Arno Klönne, *Jugend im Dritten Reich*, 2nd edn (Cologne, 1984). On the youth experience, see Rolf Schörken, 'Jugendalltag im Dritten Reich', in *Geschichte im Alltag – Alltag in der Geschichte*, ed. Klaus Bergmann and Rolf Schörken (Düsseldorf, 1982). On students, see R. G. S. Weber, *The German Student Corps in the Third Reich* (London, 1986); G. J. Giles, *Students and National Socialism in Germany* (Princeton, NJ, 1985). Also see Omer Bartov, 'The missing years: German workers, German soldiers', *German History*, 8 (1990), pp. 46–65.

11 Bartov, *Eastern Front*, pp. 68–105; Volker R. Berghahn, 'NSDAP und "Geistige Führung" der Wehrmacht', *Vierteljahrshefte für Zeitgeschichte*, 17 (1969), pp. 17–71; Manfred Messerschmidt, *Die Wehrmacht im NS-Staat. Zeit der Indoktrination* (Hamburg, 1969).

12 In much greater detail, see Bartov, *Hitler's Army*, pp. 106–78. Also see the documentary collection in Ernst Klee *et al.* (eds) *'Schöne Zeiten', Judenmord aus der Sicht der Täter und Gaffer* (Frankfurt/M, 1988).

13 H. F. Richardson (ed.) *Sieg Heil! War Letters of Tank Gunner Karl Fuchs 1937–1941* (Hamden, Conn., 1987), p. 116.

14 ibid., p. 119.

15 Ortwin Buchbender and Reinhold Stertz (eds) *Das andere Gesicht des Krieges* (Munich, 1982), pp. 72–3, letter 101.

16 ibid., p. 71, letter 96.

17 *Deutsche Soldaten sehen die Sowjetunion* (Berlin, 1941), p. 36.

18 ibid., p. 16.

19 ibid., p. 38. See also Klee, *Schöne Zeiten*, pp. 31–51, for eye-witness accounts and photographs of the pogroms in Lithuania; and Krausnick and Wilhelm, *Die Truppe*, for Army-*Einsatzgruppe* collaboration in the Kovno pogroms.

20 *Deutsche Soldaten*, p. 38.

21 ibid., pp. 41–3.

22 ibid., p. 44.

23 ibid., pp. 44–5.

24 ibid., p. 45.

25 ibid., pp. 59–60.

26 ibid., p. 43.

27 ibid., pp. 43–4.

28 Buchbender and Sterz, *Das andere Gesicht*, p. 76, letter 108.

29 Richardson, *Sieg Heil!*, p. 122.

30 ibid., p. 123.

31 ibid., p. 124.

32 Buchbender and Sterz, *Das andere Gesicht*, p. 78, letter 166.

33 *Deutsche Soldaten*, p. 60.

34 Richardson, *Sieg Heil!*, p. 132.

35 ibid., pp. 125–6.

36 Buchbender and Sterz, *Das andere Gesicht*, p. 79, letter 188.

37 *Deutsche Soldaten*, p. 49.

38 ibid., pp. 52–3.

39 Richardson, *Sieg Heil!*, p. 138.

40 ibid., p. 135.

41 ibid., p. 147.

42 Buchbender and Sterz, *Das andere Gesicht*, p. 170, letter 345.

43 ibid., p. 170, letter 346.

44 ibid., p. 84, letter 135.

45 ibid., p. 85, letter 139.

46 ibid., p. 171, letter 349.

47 ibid., letter 350.

48 ibid., letter 351.

49 ibid., p. 172, letter 352.

50 ibid., pp. 172–3, letter 353.

51 Bernt Engelmann, *In Hitler's Germany. Daily Life in the Third Reich* (New York, 1986), p. 115.

52 See, e.g., Heinz Guderian, *Panzer Leader*, 3rd edn (London, 1977), p. 152.

53 See, e.g., Bartov, *Eastern Front*, pp. 106–41; Klee, *Schöne Zeiten*; Streit, *Keine Kameraden*.
54 See, e.g., B. H. Liddell Hart, *The Other Side of the Hill* (London, 1948), p. 29.
55 Krausnick and Wilhelm, *Die Truppe*; Messerschmidt, *Die Wehrmacht*; Streit, *Keine Kameraden*.
56 Jürgen Förster and G. R. Überschär, 'Freiwillige für den "Kreuzzug Europas gegen den Bolschewismus" ', in *Der Angriff auf die Sowjetunion* (Stuttgart, 1983), vol. 4 of *Das Deutsche Reich und der Zweite Weltkrieg*, ed. Militärgeschichtliches Forschungsamt.
57 The contributions of Ernst Nolte, Klaus Hildebrand and Joachim Fest to the 'Historians' Controversy' are all to be found now in *'Historikerstreit'. Die Dokumentation der Kontroverse um die Einzigartigkeit der nationalsozialistischen Judenvernichtung*, ed. Serie Piper, 3rd edn (Munich, 1987).
58 Hillgruber, *Zweierlei Untergang*. See also Omer Bartov, 'Historians on the Eastern Front; Andreas Hillgruber and Germany's tragedy', *Tel Aviver Jahrbuch für deutsche Geschichte*, 16 (1987), pp. 325–45.
59 Arno J. Mayer, *Why Did the Heavens Not Darken?* (New York, 1988).

8

HITLER AND THE EUPHORIA OF VICTORY

The path to the Final Solution

Christopher R. Browning

One issue in particular remains at the centre of the ongoing debate over the origins of the Final Solution. Quite simply, did Hitler and the Nazi regime take the last steps along the path to genocide in an atmosphere of victory euphoria or of frustration and rage over military setback? I have long argued for the former interpretation,[1] while quite recently Philippe Burrin[2] and Arno Mayer[3] – albeit in quite different ways – have joined the late Uwe Adam, the late Martin Broszat and Hans Mommsen in arguing the latter. Where do matters stand now? I will argue that both new evidence and a new look at old evidence strengthen the case for euphoria of victory.

First let us review the emerging pattern of decision making before the decisive year of 1941.[4] In mid-September 1939, with quick victory over Poland assured, Heinrich Himmler submitted to Hitler his plans for a racial reorganization of the newly conquered regions – Germanization of the incorporated territories, the dumping of expelled Poles into the General Government, and the concentration of Jews and Gypsies in the Lublin Reservation at the furthest extremity of the German empire. Hitler approved, but the plan nonetheless eventually succumbed to logistical realities.

In late May 1940, when German Panzers had broken through to the English Channel and quick victory over France was imminent, Himmler submitted to Hitler his memorandum on 'the treatment of alien populations in the east'. Himmler argued that the General Government should be a labour reservoir of denationalized Poles, while he hoped 'completely to erase the concept of Jews through the possibility of a great emigration of all Jews to a colony in Africa or elsewhere'. Hitler considered these ideas 'very good and correct'.[5] Within weeks Hitler was touting the Madagascar Plan to Mussolini and others, and Hans Frank was halting ghetto building in the General Government as 'illusory' in view of the Führer's plan to send the Jews to Madagascar. The Battle of Britain brought this plan to nought. In short, both the Lublin Plan and the Madagascar Plan as

137

solutions to the Jewish question were broached to Hitler in a period of victory euphoria. While he approved both, neither could in fact be realized.

But does this pattern of coincidence between Hitler's approval of radically new solutions to the Jewish question and German military success hold true for 1941? First let us consider the assault on Soviet Jewry. The debate between the late Helmut Krausnick and Alfred Streim focused on when the *Einsatzgruppen* had been ordered to carry out the systematic mass murder of Soviet Jews. Krausnick argued that clear orders had been given before the invasion, while Streim argued that the circle of victims was gradually expanded after the invasion, with total murder as the explicit goal only in August. For the most part that debate remained focused on post-war testimony, and each protagonist lauded the credibility of his own favourite witnesses while debunking that of his rival.[6] In a situation in which some of the witnesses lied all the time, and virtually all of the witnesses lied some of the time, a new methodological approach was desperately needed.

It was the pioneering work of the Israeli historian, Yehoshua Büchler, on Himmler's *Kommandostab* that in my opinion opened the most promising approach.[7] By shifting the focus from the *Einsatzgruppen* to other formations that became involved in the killing campaign, he widened the field of investigation and hence of potential documentation. His research established a far greater personal involvement on Himmler's part in the operations of one of the *Kommandostab* SS brigades than can be documented for any of the *Einsatzgruppen*. More importantly, he opened the new dimension – hitherto neglected – of manpower.

Accepting the evidence of Streim, Burrin and others that a systematic mass murder of Soviet Jews, particularly women and children, is not revealed in the *Einsatzgruppen* documentation until August, and building on Büchler's approach of including the manpower dimension and the experience of other than *Einsatzgruppen* units, I would suggest the following scenario.[8] Before the invasion the *Einsatzgruppen* were not given explicit orders for the total extermination of the Jews on Soviet territory. Along with the general incitement to an ideological and racial war, however, they were given the general task of liquidating 'potential' enemies. Heydrich's directive of 2 July 1941 was a minimal list of all those who had to be liquidated *immediately*, including all Jews in state and party positions. A mere force of 3,000 men, assigned to move as quickly as possible into the vast Russian interior behind the advancing German Army, was clearly not expected to murder all of Soviet Jewry at that time. They were, however, to incite pogroms and eliminate select categories of Jews. The overwhelming majority of *Einsatzgruppen* victims in the first five weeks were in fact the Jewish male leadership and intelligentsia.

It is very likely, however, that at least the highest *Einsatzgruppen* leaders were told of the future goal of a *judenfrei* Russia through systematic mass murder. In documents written later, several *Einsatzgruppen* commanders implied early awareness of such a future task. In January 1942, Rudolf Lange wrote: 'The goal that Einsatzkommando 2 had in mind *from the beginning* [italics mine] was a radical solution to the Jewish problem through the execution of all Jews.'[9] More frequently cited, of course, is the Stahlecker report of 15 October 1941.[10] Because 'it was expected *from the start* [italics mine] that the Jewish problem would not be solved solely through pogroms' and 'the security police cleansing work had *according to basic orders* [italics mine] the goal of the most complete removal possible of the Jews', Stahlecker had carried out 'extensive executions'. Mayer has suggested that the Stahlecker report was a self-promoting document written with hindsight.[11] Burrin argues that historians have failed to read this document in the perspective of the then prevailing expectation of a very short war, after which large-scale executions would no longer be possible. The 'most complete removal possible of the Jews' does not, he therefore argues, imply total extermination.[12]

One piece of old evidence that in my opinion must be reconsidered in evaluating the awareness of top *Einsatzgruppen* commanders at the beginning of Barbarossa is the comment of Artur Nebe reproduced in Report No. 31 of 23 July 1941 (and hence presumably initially written and sent to Berlin many days earlier).[13] Nebe reported that one and a half million Jews resided in the Byelorussian area. 'A solution of the Jewish question during the war seems impossible in this area because of the tremendous number of Jews. It could only be achieved through deportations.' If expulsion of the Jews was still being considered as the long-term solution, as Burrin and Mayer argue, and the *Einsatzgruppen* leaders had not yet received any indication of the final goal of extermination, Nebe's comment is puzzling. What was the intended solution made impossible by the large number of Byelorussian Jews? Why and to what was deportation posed as the only possible alternative? The comment makes perfect sense, however, if Nebe knew he was ultimately responsible for killing these one and a half million Jews but despaired of achieving that goal with a meagre force of 600–700 men scattered all over White Russia and including a *Vorkommando* that was expected to go all the way to Moscow.

The issue of manpower, I would argue, is as salient for the historian as it was for Nebe. If the historian wants to know when the Nazi leadership decided that the mass murder of Russian Jewry was no longer a future task but rather a goal to be achieved immediately, he must ascertain when the decision was taken to commit the necessary manpower. On 16 July Hitler spoke with Goering, Lammers, Rosenberg and Keitel in a way that showed his clear conviction that victory was at hand.[14] Intensified pacification – through exterminating 'anyone who is hostile to us' and 'shooting anyone who even looks askance at us' – would create 'a Garden of Eden' from which Germany would never withdraw. Himmler did not attend this meeting but was in close proximity to Hitler from 15 to 20 July.[15] What Hitler confided to him personally, we do not know, but we do know what he did in the following weeks. On 19 July Himmler assigned the SS Cavalry Brigade to Higher SS and Police Leader (HSSPF) Centre, Erich von dem Bach-Zelewski. On 22 July he attached the 1st SS brigade to the HSSPF South, Friedrich Jeckeln. Within a week of Hitler's 16 July 'victory speech', Himmler had increased the number of SS men operating behind the advancing German Army by 11,000 men.[16]

But that was only the beginning of the build-up. At least eleven battalions of Order Police (each of approximately 500 men) were part of the invasion force. These battalions had initially been assigned to various military commanders in the rear areas. On 23 July Himmler reassigned them to the three HSSPF in north, central and southern Russia. As the war diary of Police Battalion 322 stated: 'For the impending tasks of the batalion, it is placed directly under the HSSPF von dem Bach'.[17] The minimum of eleven police battalions constituted a reinforcement of another 5,500–6,000 men. By the end of the year the number of police battalions on Soviet territory had risen to twenty-six.[18] Himmler was still not finished, however. Just a few days later he was in Riga, where he 'mentioned that he intends to set up police formations consisting of Lithuanians, Latvians, Estonians, Ukrainians, etc., employing them outside of their own home areas. This is possible right away.'[19] Units of native collaborators had already played a significant role in the killing process. By the end of 1941, the strength of these units had reached 33,000.[20] As Nebe rightly indicated, the task of killing Russian Jewry with 3,000 men of the *Einsatzgruppen* was 'impossible'. By the end of July 1941, Himmler had taken the steps for a massive build-up of manpower to begin killing on just such a scale.

What instructions were these units given? Himmler was much involved with the Pripet Marsh sweep of his SS Cavalry Brigade, ordering cryptically that 'All Jews must be shot. Drive the female Jews into the swamp'.[21] The intent of Himmler's order was clear, as *Sturmbannführer* Franz Magill reported back: 'Driving women and children into the swamp was not successful, because the swamp was not so deep that sinking under could occur'.[22] A different method for killing women and children would have to be found.

Further south in the Ukraine, Himmler did not express himself so ambiguously. When Reserve Police Battalion 45 reached the town of Schepetowka, its commander Major Franz was summoned by the commander of Police Regiment South, Colonel Besser. Franz remembered the conversation vividly. According to Besser, Himmler had ordered that the Jews in Russia were to be destroyed and that Reserve Police Battalion 45 was to participate in carrying out this order. Several days later Besser instructed Franz to shoot the Jews – women and children included – in Schepetowka.

When did this occur? The diary of one policeman reliably placed the battalion in Schepetowka between 24 July and 1 August 1941.[23]

Further east the commander of *Einsatzkommando* 5, Erwin Schulz, was summoned to Zhitomir by his superior, Dr Dr Otto Rasch of *Einsatzgruppe* C. Schulz dated this meeting rather precisely to either 10 or 12 August. Rasch let his officers know that he had been reproached for not treating the Jews harshly enough. HSSPF Jeckeln had now ordered that all non-working Jews, women and children included, be shot. Some of the officers replied that it was *already* known that Jeckeln's units were doing this. They noted that this practice had severe psychological effects on the men and led to increased support for the partisans. Rasch then invoked a binding order of Himmler. Schulz claimed that his commando continued to drag its feet in implementing this order. When Schulz returned to Berlin on 24 August, Heydrich's chief of personnel, Bruno Streckenbach, confirmed to him that the order to kill women and children came from the highest authorities. Already considered 'too weak', Schulz was able to procure a transfer.[24]

In the south it would appear that the murder order came from Himmler via HSSPF Jeckeln and worked its way forward. *Einsatzgruppe* C, rather than being at the cutting edge of the murder campaign, was in fact the last initiated into the total murder policy. Thus I would argue that the dominant focus on the *Einsatzgruppen*, characteristic of previous scholarship, has in fact confused the issue, because different units of the *Einsatzgruppen* learned of the new turn at different times and in some cases rather belatedly.[25]

In the Baltic, the leader of *Einsatzgruppe* A, Stahlecker, seems to have been completely initiated no later than Himmler's end-of-July visit to Riga. On 27 July 1941, the Reichskommissar for the Ostland, Hinrich Lohse, had issued 'guidelines' for the treatment of Jews that dealt with such issues as foreign Jews, *Mischlinge*, marking, ghettoization, property and forced labour. He neither consulted Stahlecker first nor delineated any sphere of responsibility for the Jewish question to the Security Police. The HSSPF North, Hans Adolf Prützmann, provided Stahlecker with a copy of the offending guidelines and offered the *Einsatzgruppe* commander the use of a plane to fly to Kovno for a meeting with Lohse, which he considered imperative.[26] Stahlecker had already received a copy of the guidelines from *Einsatzkommando* 3 commander Karl Jäger in Kovno. Stahlecker sent Jäger a three-page position paper on the guidelines, which the latter was to transmit to Lohse orally.[27]

Stahlecker's position paper – a recent 'find' in the Soviet archives[28] – indicated that much more than a mere jurisdictional issue was at stake. 'The new possibilities in the east for a cleaning up of the Jewish question had not been taken into consideration', Stahlecker noted. Lohse wanted to create conditions similar to those in the General Government.

He thereby did not consider on the one hand the altogether different situation created through the impact of the eastern campaign and refrained on the other hand from keeping in mind the radical treatment of the Jewish question now possible for the first time.

Lohse's measures indicated long-term ghettoization rather than 'immediate measures' for the 'resettlement of the Jews'. Because of their Bolshevik connections, these Jews were much more dangerous than those in the General Government. The situation required 'an almost 100 per cent immediate cleansing of the entire Ostland of Jews'.

Stahlecker then provided Jäger with alternative measures to Lohse's guidelines, which were in effect a cover story. Jewish reservations were to be created in the wide expanses of the Ostland, and Jewish reproduction was to be prevented by separating the sexes. The reason for the cover story was hinted at. In a handwritten note at the end of his position paper, Stahlecker noted that the Lohse draft 'to a great extent touches on general orders from higher authority to the Security Police that cannot be discussed in writing'. An indication of the content of those 'general orders' that could not be put in writing can be found subsequently in the carefully collected statistics of Jäger himself. Beginning on 15 August 1941, the number of victims claimed daily by *Einsatzkommando* 3 jumped sharply and henceforth regularly included large numbers of women and children.[29]

Also on 15 August, Himmler was concluding yet another of his visits to the killing units in the east and witnesssed an *Einsatzgruppe* execution in Minsk. Though shaken by what he had seen, Himmler assured the men that he and Hitler alone bore the responsibility for their difficult but necessary task. Following his visit, Jewish women and children in that region as well were regularly included in the executions.[30] Faced with the complaints of Nebe and von dem Bach-Zelewski about the psychological burden on the men of killing women and children, Himmler ordered the search for alternative killing methods that led to the development of the gas van.[31]

Let me briefly summarize. In mid-July, convinced that the military campaign was nearly over and victory was at hand, an elated Hitler gave the signal to carry out accelerated pacification and racial 'cleansing' of Germany's new 'Garden of Eden'. What had hitherto been seen as a future task was now to be implemented immediately. Himmler promptly responded with a massive build-up of killing forces behind the lines. Moreover, he travelled through much of the eastern territory, personally contacting such people as von dem Bach-Zelewski, Stahlecker and Nebe, and exhorting many of his killing units to carry out their difficult but historic task of eliminating Soviet Jewry – men, women and children. For other units and leaders not graced with a visit from the Reichsführer-SS, the orders filtered eastward more slowly and less systematically. For example,

Reserve Police Battalion 45 learned before the end of the month; *Einsatz-gruppe* C officers were initiated only on 10 or 12 August, though they had already heard of the new turn of events informally before that. The complete extermination of Russian Jewry that Hitler had at least roughly envisioned in the spring was set in motion in mid-July – at a time when no historian I know of has suggested that Hitler was anything but confident of victory. By mid-August the extermination programme was in full swing. It did not originate in any downturn in German military fortunes.

If the systematic mass murder of Soviet Jewry was unleashed in an atmosphere of victory euphoria, what about the extension of the mass murder to European Jewry in autumn 1941? I have already argued that the crucial turning point came in late September and early October, and Philippe Burrin has presented additional evidence to support that contention. Here we do not differ over the end-date, though I think this phase of the decision-making process began two months earlier than Burrin's mid-September. Even more decisively, however, Burrin and I differ over how Hitler perceived the military situation at this time and how this influenced his decision making.

In Burrin's view Hitler's mood was one of steady degeneration from mid-July confidence of early victory to a grim awareness by mid-September that the blitzkrieg against Russia had failed, the US was about to enter the war, and Germany was doomed to a prolonged struggle on all fronts. This, for Burrin, was precisely the 'condition' under which Hitler had long 'intended' to kill all the European Jews. In my view, Hitler's mood did not steadily degenerate. Rather it fluctuated. Furthermore, one can once again chart a striking coincidence between the peaks of German military success and Hitler's key decisions.

When Hitler gave his 'victory' speech in mid-July and instigated the systematic mass murder of Soviet Jewry, he also in my opinion conveyed to Himmler and Heydrich his desire for a 'feasibility study' for the mass murder of European Jewry. This is what lay behind Heydrich's subsequent visit with Goering on 31 July to have the latter sign his authorization to draw up and submit a plan for a 'total solution' of the Jewish question in Europe.

Hitler then attempted to persuade his generals to consolidate the Central Front, while the bulk of the Panzers there were to be turned to the north and south. The generals resisted stubbornly until Hitler unequivocally imposed his will on 18 August, insisting that there would be no resumption of an offensive against Moscow until all his goals in the south and north had been achieved.[32] It was during this period of strategic stalemate with his generals that Hitler also resisted the pressures of Goebbels and Heydrich to begin immediate deportations from the Reich. They were not to begin 'during the war'.[33]

The Ukrainian campaign that Hitler imposed upon his reluctant generals was a tremendous success. On 12 September Ewald von Kleist's Panzers broke through the Russian lines behind Kiev. On the same day German forces cracked the Russian perimeter around Leningrad. In the words of Alan Clark, this day could be 'reckoned the low point in the fortunes of the Red Army for the whole war'. By 16 September Kleist had joined up with Heinz Guderian to complete the vast Kiev encirclement.[34] By 26 September the last pockets of resistance around Kiev had been crushed, and 665,000 Russian prisoners had been taken.[35] On 29–30 September, the victors of Kiev carried out the great Babi Yar massacre of some 33,000 Jews.

As Hitler experienced triumph in the Ukraine, he became increasingly amenable to proposals for immediate deportation of Jews that a month earlier he had deferred till after the war. On 18 September Himmler informed Greiser, 'The Führer wishes that the Old Reich and Protectorate be emptied and freed of Jews from west to east as soon as possible'.[36] On 23–24 September, Hitler met with Himmler, Heydrich and Goebbels. The Propaganda Minister learned: 'The Führer is of the opinion that the Jews are to be removed from Germany step by step. The first cities that have to be cleared of Jews are Berlin, Vienna and Prague.' But there was one catch. 'This could occur as soon as we arrive at a clarification of the military situation in the east.'[37]

That clarification was not long in coming. Already on 6 September Hitler had ordered Army Group Centre to prepare for a decisive campaign to destroy the Russian forces facing it.[38] On 30 September, just four days after the end of resistance around Kiev, Guderian's Panzers began the offensive, and on 2 October the rest of the forces of Operation Typhoon struck along the Russian Central Front.

Still Hitler hesitated. On 6 October he again spoke of deportations. 'All Jews have to be removed from the Protectorate, not only to the General Government but straight on to the east. . . . Together with the Jews of the Protectorate all the Jews of Vienna and Berlin must disappear.' But once again there was a problem. 'Only the great shortage of transport prevents this being done at once.'[39] By 7 October the Germans had completed the double encirclement of Vyazma and Bryansk that ultimately led to the capture of another 673,000 Russian troops. According to Ernst Klink, 'Unanimity over the favourableness of the situation reigned everywhere.'[40] According to the late Andreas Hillgruber, Hitler exuded a 'spirit of total victory' (*voller Siegestimmung*) reminiscent of mid-July.[41] In this atmosphere of euphoria, the last hesitations were overcome. In Prague on 10 October, Heydrich announced 'the Führer wishes that by the end of the year as many Jews as possible are removed from the German sphere'.[42] On 15 October resistance died in the Vyazma pocket, and panic began to spread through Moscow. On that same day the first deportation train left Vienna for Lodz. By the time the Bryansk pocket was liquidated on 18

October three more Jewish transports had departed from Prague, Luxemburg and Berlin.[43] That same day Himmler informed Heydrich that further Jewish emigration from the German sphere was banned.[44] As late as 23 October 1941, the High Command of the Armed Forces (OKW) reconfirmed the plan of 14 July (cited by Burrin as evidence of Hitler's initial confidence in early victory) to demobilize the equivalent of forty-nine divisions for the benefit of the armaments industry, airforce and navy.[45] At the same time Germans in Belzec and Chelmno were already preparing to construct the first extermination camps.[46]

In short, between 16 September, when the Germans completed the encirclement of Kiev, and 18 October, when the last resistance ended in Bryansk, the following had occurred: Hitler approved the deportation of Jews to the east, the first practical steps for the construction of death camps at Belzec and Chelmno were taken, the first four Jewish transports departed for Lodz, and Jewish emigration from the continent was banned. As in mid-summer, this second great intensification of the Nazi murder programme coincided with the second peak of German military success.

German expectations of imminent victory, so prevalent in mid-October, in fact vanished with almost bewildering suddenness by the end of the month. The bad weather, terrible roads, shortage of supplies, exhaustion of German troops, and stubborn retreat of the remnants of the Red Army all combined to bring the *Wehrmacht* to a halt. The road to Moscow was not open after all. But just as Hitler later could not contemplate a strategic withdrawal from any of the territories his armies had conquered, so he could not now contemplate retreating from his latest decisions on Jewish policy. The trains continued to roll, the extermination camps continued to be built. The Soviet Union was saved, but the Jews of Europe were not. While the plan to exterminate the Jews of Europe had been conceived and approved in the euphoria of victory, it was tenaciously and fanatically carried out in the years of looming defeat.

NOTES

1 Christopher R. Browning, 'Zur Genesis der "Endlösung". Eine Antwort an Martin Broszat', *Vierteljahrshefte für Zeitgeschichte* (hereafter VfZ), 29/1 (1981), pp. 97–109; and idem, *Fateful Months: Essays on the Emergence of the Final Solution* (New York, 1985; revised and expanded edition, 1991), pp. 8–38.
2 Philippe Burrin, *Hitler et les Juifs: Genèse d'un génocide* (Paris, 1989).
3 Arno Mayer, *Why Did the Heavens Not Darken? The Final Solution in History* (New York, 1989).
4 Christopher R. Browning, 'Nazi resettlement policy and the search for a solution to the Jewish question, 1939–1941', *German Studies Review*, 9/3 (1986), pp. 497–519.
5 Helmut Krausnick (ed.) 'Einige Gedanken über die Behandlung der fremdvölkischen im Osten', VfZ, 5/2 (1957), pp. 194–8.
6 Most recently, see: Alfred Streim, 'The tasks of the Einsatzgruppen', *Simon*

CHRISTOPHER R. BROWNING

Wiesenthal Center Annual (hereafter SWCA), IV (1987), pp. 309–28; and the exchange between Krausnick and Streim, SWCA, VI (1989), pp. 311–47.

7 Yehoshua Büchler, 'Kommandostab Reichsführer-SS: Himmler's Personal Murder Brigades in 1941', *Holocaust and Genocide Studies*, I/1 (1986), pp. 11–26.

8 At the moment I have seen only a few of the documents from the increasingly accessible Soviet and Czech archives. A large increase in documentation may substantially alter the historian's understanding of the course of the Final Solution on Soviet territory.

9 Cited in Helmut Krausnick and Hans-Heinrich Wilhelm, *Die Truppe des Weltanschauungskrieges: Die Einsatzgruppen der Sicherheitspolizei und des SD 1938–1942* (Stuttgart, 1981), p. 534.

10 *Trials of the Major War Criminals before the International Military Tribunal* (hereafter cited as IMT) (Nuremberg, 1947–9), vol. 27, p. 687 (180-L).

11 Mayer, *Why Did the Heavens not Darken?*, p. 259.

12 Burrin, *Hitler et les Juifs*, p. 123.

13 *The Einsatzgruppen Reports*, ed. Yitzhak Arad, Shmuel Krakowski and Shmuel Spector (New York, 1989), p. 43. See also the remarks in Report No. 33 of 27 July 1941 on pp. 47–50.

14 IMT, vol. 38, pp. 86–94 (221-L).

15 Richard Breitman, *The Architect of Genocide: Himmler and the Final Solution* (New York, 1991), pp. 184, 295.

16 Büchler, 'Kommandostab', p. 15.

17 Yad Vashem Archives (hereafter YVA), 0-53/127/53 (war diary of Police Battalion 322, entry of 23 July 1941).

18 Berlin Document Centre, 0 464, Osteinsatz, 'Die im Osten eingesetzten Stäbe'.

19 *The Einsatzgruppen Reports*, p. 83 (Report No. 48, 10 August 1941).

20 NO-286 (Daluege report on the Order Police, January 1943).

21 *Justiz und NS-Verbrechen: Sammlung Deutschen Strafurteile wegen Nationalsozialistischen Tötungsverbrechen 1945–1966* (hereafter cited as JNSV) (Amsterdam), vol. 20, p. 44 (No. 570, LG Braunschweig 2 Ks 1/63).

22 *Unsere Ehre Heisst Treue* (Vienna, 1984), pp. 229–30 (Magill report of 12 August 1941).

23 Zentrale Stelle der Landesjustizverwaltungen, II 204 AR-Z 1251/65 (LG Regensburg Ks 6/70, judgement against Engelbert Kreuzer), pp. 11–15.

24 Landgericht Köln, 24 Ks 1/52, vol. 3, pp. 747–55 (testimony of Erwin Schulz, 3 February 1953).

25 The dates offered in most of the testimony of witnesses cited by Streim cluster in the late July/early August period. Alfred Streim, *Die Behandlung sowjetischer Kriegsgefangener im 'Fall Barbarossa'* (Heidelberg, 1981), pp. 85–6.

26 YVA, 0-53/144/409–10 (Riga to Stahlecker, 5 August 1941).

27 YVA, 0-53/144/412 (Stahlecker to Heydrich, 10 August 1941).

28 Historical State Archives, Riga: 'Betrifft: Entwurf über die Aufstellung vorläufiger Richtlinien für die Behandlung der Juden im Gebiet des Reichskommissariates Ostland, August 6, 1941, Nowoselje', signed by Stahlecker. I am grateful to Professor Gerald Fleming for a copy of this document. It is now printed in *Herrschaftsalltag im Dritten Reich*, ed. Hans Mommsen (Schwann, 1988), pp. 467–71.

29 YVA, 0-53/141/30–38 (Jäger report, 1 December 1941).

30 JNSV, XIX, pp. 795–6 (No. 567, LG Kiel 2 Ks 1/64).

31 Browning, *Fateful Months*, p. 59.

32 *Kriegstagebuch des Oberkommandos der Wehrmacht 1940–41*, ed. Percy

146

Schramm (Munich, 1982), pp. 1029–68. See also Ernst Klink, 'Die Krieg gegen die Sowjetunion bis zur Jahreswende 1941/42', *Das Deutsche Reich und der Zweite Weltkrieg*, IV, *Der Angriff auf die Sowjetunion* (Stuttgart, 1983), pp. 489–507.

33 Bernhard Lösener, 'Als Rassereferent im Reichsministerium des Innern', VfZ, 9/3 (1961), p. 303; Goebbels's diary entries of 19 and 20 August 1941, cited in Martin Broszat, 'Hitler und die Genesis der "Endlösung". Aus Anlass der Thesen von David Irving', VfZ, 25/4 (1977), pp. 749–50.

34 Alan Clark, *Barbarossa: The Russian–German Conflict 1941–45* (New York, Signet Edition, 1966), p. 166.

35 *Kriegstagebuch des OKW*, p. 661.

36 National Archives Microfilm, T-175/54/256695 (Himmler to Greiser, 18 September 1941).

37 Goebbels's diary excerpts of 23 and 24 September 1941, cited in Broszat, 'Genesis der "Endlösung" ', p. 751.

38 Klink, 'Die Krieg', p. 569.

39 Koeppens's note of 7 October 1941, cited in Broszat, 'Genesis der "Endlösung" ', p. 751.

40 Klink, 'Die Krieg', pp. 576–7.

41 *Staatsmänner bei Hitler: Vertrauliche Aufzeichnungen über Unterredungen mit Vertretern des Auslandes 1939–41*, ed. Andreas Hillgruber (Frankfurt/M, 1967), p. 626.

42 H. G. Adler, *Theresienstadt 1941–45* (Tübingen, 1960, 2nd edn), pp. 720–2 (protocol of conference in Prague, 10 October 1941).

43 *Kriegstagebuch des OKW*, 702 and 708, for the end of resistance at Vyazma and Bryansk.

44 Burrin, *Hitler et les Juifs*, p. 146.

45 Rolf-Dieter Müller, 'Die Entwicklung der militärischen Personalsteuerung', *Das Dritte Reich und der Zweite Weltkrieg*, V, *Organisation und Mobilisierung des Deutschen Machtbereichs*, Erster Halbband, *Kriegsverwaltung, Wirtschaft und Personelle Ressourcen 1939–1941* (Stuttgart, 1988), p. 868.

46 Browning, *Fateful Months*, pp. 29–31.

Part III

THE IMPLEMENTATION OF THE FINAL SOLUTION AND RESPONSES

9

THE RESPONSE OF POLISH JEWRY TO THE FINAL SOLUTION

Yisrael Gutman

I am well aware of the shortcoming of the term 'response' when we attempt to express the complete lack of options of the Jews in general and east European Jews in particular in the face of the fanatical anti-Jewish obsession and the determination of the Nazis to implement the Final Solution with all their power. Nor can we discuss the subject without first briefly dealing with the structure and trends of development, of Polish Jewish society during the period between the two world wars and their attitudes, activity and behaviour during the period of the Second World War and the Holocaust.

In this short chapter it will only be possible to present a few crucial considerations and, even then, only to touch on matters and events in general terms, without going into detailed analysis.

Raul Hilberg, in the first edition of his standard work *Destruction of the European Jews*,[1] said nothing about the Polish Jews as a people, while giving a most detailed description and evaluation of the anti-Jewish German plans and actions involved in the operation of the Final Solution. In so doing he established a trend, almost a model, in scholarship, that was perpetuated by many other eminent historians. Such an approach obscures the reality that the Polish Jews had developed a rich cultural, social, economic and political life. As a consequence, studies of the history and problems of the Holocaust become the stories of perpetrators and executors, wherein the Jews are marginalized, being characterized as mute victims of extraordinary historical circumstances.

During the last decades of the nineteenth century and especially between the First and Second World Wars, Polish Jewry had undergone a dynamic process of transformation. The most significant evidence of a growth in national self-awareness among Polish Jews was the growing political and cultural activities of the Zionist, socialist and religious parties and youth movements. In other words, on the eve of the Second World War the Jews of Poland can be seen to have constituted a socio-political and religious

151

entity with a strong consciousness of national identity and national aspirations. The Jews in Poland during the interwar period were organized into their own political parties and their own religious, cultural and professional bodies and institutions. They were represented by a separate faction in the Polish Parliament, published a wide spectrum of daily and periodical publications in Yiddish and Hebrew as well as Polish, demonstrated remarkable creativity in the fields of literature, theatre and the arts, and had established educational networks around the country. Polish Jewish society in this last stage of its free existence combined traditional elements with contemporary European cultural and political virtues.

In October 1938 the Polish Ambassador to Berlin, Józef Lipski, was granted an audience by Hitler. In the course of their meeting Hitler mentioned that he was considering a solution to the Jewish question through emigration to colonies in cooperation with Poland, Hungary and perhaps also Romania.[2] In January 1939 Hitler declared that

> if the international Jewish financiers in and outside Europe again succeed in plunging the nations into a world war, the result will be not the Bolshevisation of the globe and therefore the victory of Jewry, but the annihilation of the Jewish race in Europe.[3]

German documentation sheds no light on concrete plans or outlines relating to Polish Jews at the time of the 'Polish crisis' and the preparation of 'Fall Weiss', the aggression against Poland in September 1939. But soon enough it became obvious that the Nazi concept of racism was not limited to the goal of making great Germany 'Judenrein' (free of Jews). Hitler's grave prediction of January 1939, repeated many times during the war, and especially after the beginning of the Barbarossa campaign in June 1941, was not just an outburst of rage or political propaganda, but a significant component of German war policy. The anti-Jewish legislation and persecution (and subsequent deportations, mass killing and the Final Solution) were by no means a necessity, nor did they aid the German war effort. On the contrary, the annihilation of the Jews was visibly counterproductive. The loss of Jewish forced labour was only one of the losses Germany sustained through the murder of the Jews.

The Polish Jews were immediately trapped, without the benefit of even a brief period of preparation such as that which enabled Jews in Germany, Austria and the Protectorate to try to confront the Nazi challenge or to escape. Furthermore, the Nazi administrative power in occupied Poland was from the very beginning composed of veteran Nazis who were free to conduct radical and unrestrained policies of persecution at the local level.

The initial stage of the Jewish experience during the occupation of Poland (often somewhat inaccurately described as that of 'concentration') lasted from September 1939 until the implementation of the Final Solution. It was characterized by ghettoization, confiscation of public and private property, elimination from economic life and forced labour, and culminated in starvation and disease. Through all this, Polish Jews struggled to the utmost for bare existence: as one of the ghetto underground activists put it, 'we told ourselves that no other people would be able to survive under such circumstances, but still we would survive in spite of everything'.[4]

The Jews disregarded many Nazi orders and regulations, especially when the directives of the oppressors were, as written in one of the ghetto diaries, 'an absolute evil'. In some ghettos the Jews maintained some of their former economic ties with the outside world through illegal channels, while within the ghettos Jews set in motion clandestine workshops. Eighty per cent of all the food consumed in the Warsaw Ghetto was obtained by smuggling through ingenious, illegal means. Chaim Aharon Kaplan noted in his Warsaw Ghetto diary, under the entry for 30 October 1939, that

> after the prohibition forbidding a Jew to keep more than 2000 zloty in his home, the Jews of Germany would probably have been standing in line for the banks the next day. . . . But the Polish Jews emphatically said: No! They didn't deposit a single penny, and you won't find a single Jew whose strongbox contains more than 2000 zloty.[5]

The Polish Jews never recognized the German occupation as a legitimate regime which deserved obedience and a measure of loyalty. It was quite natural that under these circumstances the majority of the Jews created a structure of mutual solidarity and self-help and developed networks of underground activity. Moreover, for quite a long time the German administration in occupied Poland was ignorant of and seemingly indifferent to the inner life and cultural and political clandestine work in the ghettos. The Jews took advantage of this relative indifference by undertaking a whole range of activities: an underground press in Warsaw, an illegal education system, the ghetto archives and secret religious observances are only the best known of these. Besides the Judenräte (Jewish councils appointed by the Germans to run the ghettos), which were established as a link between the Jewish population and the Nazi administration (and were often guided by the desire to serve Jewish interests in so far as it was in their power so to do), there were individual and small groups of collaborators. But by and large Jewish society under the occupation remained under the influence of the so-called alternative leadership, represented by persons with a record of service in Jewish social and political life, and by the organized political underground.

Despite all attempts to mitigate their own condition during this first phase, we can state that the Jews suffered agony and losses which were historically almost unprecedented. The main victims were the refugees in the ghetto, the old, children and the weak: between 6 and 8 per cent of the Jewish population in the occupied territories of Poland died before the implementation of the Final Solution. However, when we examine the situation during the last months before the deportations to the death camps, we see some hints of stabilization and relief in a number of ghettos, including the Warsaw Ghetto. The death rate decreased, the epidemics almost ceased and more people were employed and managed to survive one way or another.

Hence I disagree with the assumption that it was the living conditions in the ghettos or the health conditions that stimulated the local bureaucracy to the idea of physical liquidation and that their impact was crucial to the decision to initiate the policy of physical destruction. I cannot enter here into the complicated discussion of the character and competence of the bureaucracy in totalitarian regimes, but in any case there is no solid evidence supporting the above conjecture. On the contrary, various ties of cooperation and mutual interest gradually developed between the local administration and the *Wehrmacht* on the one hand and the Jews in the ghettos on the other. So the Final Solution was without doubt solely an invention and initiative of Hitler and the highest-ranking members of the Nazi Party and the SS. Above all, it was a product of the ideological dynamic and the development of war operations which reached a point of fusion in the Barbarossa campaign.

Scholars and writers are constantly preoccupied with discussions and speculations regarding unanswered questions about the decision-making process that led to the Final Solution: whether the process towards total physical liquidation was set in motion during the action of the *Einsatzgruppen* in the first phase of Barbarossa or a few months later; the real role and extent of personal involvement of Hitler; whether Himmler was the chief executor; if the physical destruction was a last consistent stage in the master plan or an improvisation elicited in the atmosphere of expected victory and resultant war euphoria. All these problematic areas are of clear importance and thus justifiable subjects for research. However, it can seem that concentration upon such secondary issues obscures the enormity of the fact that a decision was taken and implemented, a decision to murder *en masse* a people who were not a party to the war. The substantive issue is that with the killing operations of the *Einsatzgruppen* taking part in the Barbarossa campaign, the Nazi state crossed the Rubicon and transformed extreme oppression into direct, planned and systematic murder of a people, executed with enormous barbaric brutality; this made the Holocaust unique and unprecedented.

Mass extermination of the Jews started in the Soviet conquered territories, switched to the Warthegau by the end of 1941, later to the Lublin area and whole General Government through Operation Reinhard. Finally it encompassed all the occupied countries in the course of 1942, expanding to cover allied and dependent countries as the opportunity arose, such as Slovakia in 1942 and Hungary in 1944. The Jewish historian and chronicler of the Warsaw Ghetto, Emmanuel Ringelblum, wrote towards the end of 1942, 'Hitler will use every means in his power to "free" Europe of all the Jews. Our life or death depends on the scope of time. If they have enough time at their disposal, we are lost. Only a speedy and sudden downfall can bring us salvation'.[6]

We shall now try to analyse briefly the Jewish reactions to and interpretations of the mass deportations from the ghettos. First, there is the issue of how much was known or understood about the fatal nature of the deportations. Some scholars suggest that neither Jews nor Jewish leadership really knew what happened to those who were deported from the ghettos. Other writers speak of a gap between knowledge of facts on the one hand and lack of the psychological ability to absorb and comprehend such awful facts on the other.

In fact, the Jewish communities in western and central Europe did not know – at least they had only partial knowledge of – the true destination of the transports 'to the east'. But do we have sufficient proof to state that most Jews in Lithuania, Ukraine and Poland did not know about the disappearances and mass murder in the transports? In any case they knew the truth during the later stages of the deportations. To the best of our knowledge at present, there was no substantial difference in the behaviour and reaction of these two categories, those who knew and those who did not. I believe that the main source of frustration and confusion was difficulty in absorbing and grasping the meaning of the Final Solution. In other words, many Jews knew of the mass killings and of the existence of the concentration and death camps where the act of mass murder was taking place. However, this knowledge was not identical with the awareness that a decision to undertake complete annihilation had been made. The Nazi methods of 'gradual' execution, the temporary exclusion from deportation of people employed in the war industry and finally the system of deceit that was set in motion by the apparatus in charge of the operation – all this contributed to the inability to absorb fully and accept the dimensions of the catastrophe.

The lack of full knowledge and comprehensive understanding was not the only reason for passivity and confusion. Some leaders of the Judenrats tended to accept the argument that productive work, organized in the ghettos, would preserve its inhabitants, or at least a major part of them, from deportation and annihilation. This policy was adopted by the leaders in the ghettos of Vilna, Bialystok, Lodz and others. This was not simply a response to German pressure and an act of submission – it stemmed from a strong belief that under the circumstances this was the only viable option remaining to the ghetto communities. On the other hand, the assumption that 'work will save life' and that productive efforts could bring to a stop or at least minimize the annihilation process was not accepted by all.

Hence, another point of view and line of activity developed in the ghettos, a network opposing the Judenrats which eventually became a fighting organization. The initiators of this movement were mostly members of Zionist and socialist youth movements, which comprised the radical sector of the political underground in the ghettos. The movement began at the end of 1941 in Vilna, a town which was, until the Barbarossa campaign, under Soviet rule, and in which there were some 55,000 Jews of whom only about 18,000 remained after the first wave of killing by the *Einsatzgruppen*. A declaration was made on 1 January 1942 by Abba Kovner, a young poet and leader of a Zionist youth movement, on behalf of this group. It is as follows:

> Do not trust those who deceive you! ... All ways from Vilna lead to Ponar and Ponar is death! ... Hitler decided to destroy all European Jews, and the Jews of Lithuania are fated to be the first in line.... It is true that we are weak and defenceless, but the only answer to the murderer is armed rebellion![7]

We see, therefore, that from a very early stage the youth movement in Vilna read the situation correctly and understood the true meaning of the mass executions.

Of course, we raise an interesting question when we ask how the young members of the underground reached this fateful conclusion. Did they have access to secret information or documents? No such proof was in their hands, so their opinion and proclamation was a pure expression of intuition or inner conviction. No less surprising was the adoption of this opinion by the branches of the youth movements in the ghettos of central Poland, places like Warsaw and Cracow, where German Nazi rule had existed for years without the advent of mass murder.

Political groups that had always been in conflict – the Zionist and the socialist – now established a common fighting organization in many ghettos. Their aim was to make all the necessary preparations for revolt and open resistance to the Nazis at such time as full and final deportation took place. The fighters chose the ghetto as the arena for the uprising. The reason for this was that since the Jewish communities were being uprooted from those locations which had been their home for generations, it was appropriate that they should manifest their resistance and reaction there.

The determination to resist physically faced many obstacles. The Jews in general and the youth movements in particular had no trained soldiers among them, no arms, no knowledge of how to conduct combat in an urban area. They received no serious help or support from the resistance movement in the Polish and Soviet underground. Moreover, the Jewish leadership and parts of the elite of the older generation were against them. They often even accused them of being irresponsible, jeopardizing the chance of some Jews being rescued. The most severe clash occurred between the underground and the Judenrats. In the eyes of the leaders of the Judenrats, the fighters were obstructing their concept of rescue and were a source of danger. In a number of ghettos, like Vilna and Warsaw, this conflict developed into open physical clashes. At the same time, both the Judenrats and the fighting organizations attempted to communicate their respective views to the masses in the ghetto, seeking to mobilize members, supporters and followers.

The idea of fighting could not offer the possibility or chance of rescue, or even an illusion of salvation. It is no wonder, then, that until the end the majority in the ghetto preferred to hope for some chance of survival and to stay with their families in those days of ordeal. Further, the fighters could not be sure which of the many deportations would represent the final move to remove all Jews and empty the ghetto, but it was this final action which was, as already stated, selected by the fighters as the signal for the beginning of the revolt. Thus the idea of resistance and uprising in the ghettos could only attract small groups of devoted believers, and was not a programme for the majority. Nevertheless, at one point in time – during the uprising of the Warsaw Ghetto in April–May 1943 – the remnants of the Jewish population (around 50,000 souls) became followers of and participants in the efforts of the fighters and, in the final stage, active partners in the Warsaw Ghetto revolt.

I would like to deal, albeit briefly, with one final aspect: the issue of help and rescue attempts made by the local non-Jewish population and organizations. In my opinion, we cannot look at this particular historical chapter without some prior knowledge of the anti-Jewish atmosphere that prevailed in all European countries during the last decade before the Second World War. Questions regarding the potential scope for rescue versus its actual dimensions and achievements can be considered and answered only in the light of this background of indifference and enmity. Only at the beginning of 1943 did the Polish underground, influenced by compassion on one side and the thought of future political responsibility on the other, bring under its auspices the organization for the rescue of Jews named Zegota, provide it with some facilities and give recognition to its activity. But even then the rescue of Jews remained mostly the province of dedicated brave individual men and women. Yet there were also groups of people in the Polish population who specialized in recognizing, discovering and informing on Jews in hiding.

I have not had the opportunity in the course of this short chapter to raise many other relevant points, such as the subject of Jewish membership of Polish partisan units, the place of Jews in the Polish armies outside Poland, the policy of the Polish government-in-exile in France and Great Britain. I have focused only on an analysis and exploration of the stages of the destruction process, and the response of the Jewish masses and their leadership.

NOTES

1 The first edition of Hilberg's important book *The Destruction of the European Jews* appeared in Chicago and London in 1961. The second revised, enlarged and corrected edition in three volumes was published in New York in 1985. With regard to the issue under consideration there is no substantial change in the second edition of the monumental work done by Hilberg.

2 *Dokumenty, Materialy & przedcdnia Drugiej Wojny Jwiatowej* Vol. 1 (Warsaw, 1949), p. 173, report of the Polish Ambassador to Berlin, Józef Sipski, to the Polish Foreign Minister, 20 September 1938. It is worth mentioning that in response to Hitler's remark, Lipski declared that if Hitler would help Poland solve the Jewish question, a beautiful monument would be erected in Warsaw to his honour (ibid.).

3 See N. H. Baynes (ed.) *Speeches of Adolf Hitler* Vol. 1 (London, 1942, pp. 737–41.

4 Nathan Eck, *Wandering on the Roads of Death (Life and Thoughts in the Days of Destruction)* (Jerusalem, 1960), p. 37 (Hebrew).

5 *The Warsaw Diary of Chaim A. Kaplan*, trans. and ed. Abraham I. Katsh (New York, 1973), p. 61.

6 Emmanuel Ringelblum, 'The Warsaw Ghetto Diary' (Yiddish), in *The Ghetto Writings*, Vol. 1 (Warsaw, 1961), pp. 379–80.

7 See *Documents on the Holocaust, Selected Sources on the Destruction of the Jews of Germany and Austria, Poland and the Soviet Union*, ed. Y. Arad, I. Gutman and A. Margaliot (Jerusalem, 1981), p. 433.

10

THE HOLOCAUST IN LITHUANIA

Some unique aspects

Dina Porat

Historians and writers of chronicles have already related the sequence of events in Lithuania during the Holocaust.[1] In this chapter an attempt will be made to define the particular combination of circumstances which made the fate of Lithuanian Jewry unique. Such an attempt should, of course, take into consideration the general background of the time and place, Lithuanian Jewry being one Jewish community among many under the same Nazi occupation. Our main question here is whether this uniqueness had implications for further developments and whether it supplied lessons to be applied elsewhere, for the German authorities as well as for the Jewish communities.

THE STARTING POINT OF THE FINAL SOLUTION

The Final Solution – the systematic overall physical extermination of Jewish communities one after the other – began in Lithuania. This was not the only country which German forces and their allies invaded on 22 June 1941, later continuing their way southward, eastward and northward, but it was in Lithuania that the German killing squads, the *Einsatzgruppen*, following in the footsteps of the army units, began organizing the murder of the Jews. A report sent to Berlin by the *Einsatzgruppe* A commander, SS General Walter Franz Stahlecker, identifies as the 'first pogrom' the violence that took place in Kovno on the night of 25–26 June 1941, only four days after the invasion started, when 1,500 Jews were killed.[2] Also, the appeal to the Jewish pioneering youth to practise self-defence, written and read out at their meeting in Vilna on 1 January 1942 by Abba Kovner, then leader of the Hashomer Hatza'ir movement, predicted: 'The Jews of Lithuania are fated to be the first in line.'[3] And so they were.

Other countries had been invaded by Nazi Germany before June 1941, but the attack on the Lithuanian Jewish community was the first to occur after the German invasion into the areas of Soviet domain, an invasion that initiated a ruthless general lethal assault. The short time that elapsed between the invasion and the beginning of the implementation of the Final Solution, along with 'Lithuania's common border with Germany, doomed the fate of its Jews', as the Jewish Lithuanian historian Ya'acov Robinson put it.[4]

LITHUANIAN JEWS: THE FIRST IN LINE

No other Jewish community was so extensively and comprehensively affected. About 95 per cent or 96 per cent of this Jewish group was murdered following Germany's invasion of the Soviet Union.

A comparison of the different Jewish sources that try to estimate losses in Lithuania leads to the same result. According to the *Holocaust Encyclopedia* (a joint effort of historians, coordinated by Yad Vashem, to present most of the available data), there were 168,000 Jews in Lithuania, excluding the Vilna area and city. On the eve of the invasion the Soviet authorities expelled some 7,000 to Siberia, and another 14,000–15,000 fled eastward when the invasion started. Out of the remaining 145,000 (plus 3,000 refugees from the Reich), 140,000–143,000, or about 94.5 per cent to 96 per cent, were killed. The Vilna area and city, which were annexed to Poland for about twenty years, between the two world wars, were returned to Lithuanian sovereignty in October 1939, as part of the Ribbentrop–Molotov pact. Including the Vilna Jews, as well as the 13,000–15,000 Polish Jewish refugees who arrived in Lithuania during the last months of 1939, there were 265,000 Jews in Lithuania, out of whom 254,000 were killed – again, about 95 per cent.[5]

The book *Lithuanian Jewry*, the most comprehensive effort of Lithuanian Jews to record their own history, estimates their number at the beginning of the German invasion at 225,000–235,000 people. The same source estimates the number of survivors in July 1944, when the Red Army liberated the Baltic countries, as being 2,000–3,000, including partisans in the forests, plus a few thousand more who had previously been evacuated to forced labour camps in Germany.[6] If the number of survivors was indeed about 8,000–9,000 altogether,[7] then the losses are again about 96 per cent.

It seems, then, that two Jewish sources, though slightly differing in detail, reach the identical conclusion that only a few thousand Lithuanian Jews survived the Holocaust. The *Lithuanian Encyclopedia*, under the entry 'Jews' (Zydai), simply makes a factual statement: a quarter of a million Jews were murdered in Lithuania. The first committee of the Jewish Historical Institute established in Vilna after the war wrote in an appeal to the Soviet authorities: 'The common estimation is that only one or one and a half per cent of the Jewish population survived, including partisans.'[8] 'One might say', recalled Yitzhak (Antek) Zukerman, one of the Warsaw

Ghetto revolt commanders, 'that from Vilna we got word [in 1942] that the disaster is total.'[9]

THE TIMING AND SCOPE OF THE MURDERS

Most of the Lithuanian Jews were murdered immediately, during the months following the invasion, between the end of June and December 1941. The *Einsatzgruppen* reports, written at that time and sent to Berlin as a record of their activities, show that about 80,000, a quarter of the Jewish population, were killed by October.[10] This figure includes the Vilna area. A later report, written towards the end of the year, reports that 136,400 Jews were already 'out of the way'.[11] This means that by the end of the year 80 per cent of Lithuanian Jews were dead, whether the Vilna area is included or not.[12] Both Jewish and German sources agree that about 175,000 out of about a quarter of a million had already been killed in all areas of Lithuania by the end of the year, again 80 per cent.[13]

Yet German and Jewish sources do not agree on the number of Jews left in the ghettos: according to the latter about 45,000 Jews were concentrated in the ghettos of Vilna (about 20,000), Kovno (17,500), Shavli (5,000), Swieciany and a number of small labour camps. All Jewish sources agree on a number of ghetto inmates that is considerably higher than estimated by the Germans. The Germans estimated the number mainly by the cards they issued, whereas the Jews hid about 8,000 more in the three main ghettos, subsisting on the same cards and food rations.[14] This discrepancy between Jewish sources and German ones, which occurs time and again regarding the number of Jews in various ghettos, as well as other issues, is a warning to historians. They should not rely too heavily for figures, at least, on German sources although these are famous for being meticulous. It was the Jewish council who had the correct figure in most cases. It seems that a full picture of the events of the Holocaust in each country arises only from the integration of the three main types of sources: Jewish, German and local. In any case, the ghettos of Lithuania ceased to exist in the summer of 1943 (Vilna and most of the small camps) and in the summer of 1944 (Kovno, Shavli and the remaining small places).

The decisive majority of Lithuanian Jews, about 80 per cent, did not undergo the preliminary stages that characterized German policy against the Jews in western, southern and central Europe. They did not experience the two or two and a half years of ghetto life before the deportations to the death camps started, as the Jews in the Polish ghettos of the General Government did. They were not even killed in the two waves of extermination practised by the Germans in most of the areas they occupied in the Soviet Union, the first until the end of 1941 and the second beginning in the spring of 1942.[15]

The wave that hit most of the Lithuanian Jews not only diminished the major communities to half (Kovno) or even a third (Vilna) of their former size. It erased the small towns, the famous Jewish Lithuanian *Shtetles*, almost to the last person, in a few months. Like the rest of the Jews in the German-occupied areas in the Soviet Union they were shot near pits and in woods close to their former places of residence, and were not sent to death camps.

Not only Lithuanian Jews were killed there. About 5,000 Jews from Germany, Austria and Czechoslovakia were murdered in the pits of the Ninth Fort, one of a chain of fortresses around Kovno, at the end of 1941. At the same time, tens of thousands of Jews were deported from the Reich to the ghettos of Minsk, Riga and Lodz. Some were immediately killed, but most of them were interned in these ghettos, or in separate nearby ones. The question is, then, whether the German policy makers regarded Lithuania as an experimental killing site, both for the local Jews and for those deported from the Reich, even before the Wannsee Conference participants decided to implement the Final Solution all over Europe. A few more thousand Jews from Belgium, Holland and especially from the transit camp of Drancy, France, were executed in the Ninth Fort during 1942–4. It is also possible, though, that the Ninth Fort served as a killing site because it best suited the task, not due to its location in Lithuania. And one more possibility that cannot be ignored when considering German operations is the constant struggles for prestige and power among German authorities, which could have brought about a decision to send Jews to Lithuania only to be killed there and not to join, even temporarily, one of its ghettos.[16]

THE LOCAL POPULATION

Such an almost total annihilation, carried out with such speed, was possible not only because the implementation of the Final Solution began in Lithuania immediately following the German invasion. The intense involvement of the local population, in large numbers, in the murder of the Jews, entailed a fatal combination of Lithuanian motivation and German organization and thoroughness.

The reports of *Einsatzgruppe* A testify to the eagerness the Lithuanians demonstrated. This is a significant testimony because the purpose of these reports was to display German, not Lithuanian, determination and devotion to their so-called mission, despite the many 'difficulties' which the Nazi authors emphasized. The reports indicate clearly that groups of 'partisans', civil units of nationalist-rightist anti-Soviet affiliation, initiated contact with the Germans upon their entry into Kovno. The German authorities used these 'partisans' to establish a new unit, formally called the Labour National Guard, that operated all over Lithuania.[17] A German report praises this new unit as having fulfilled its mission 'very well', especially in the planning and execution of 'the largest Aktionen'.[18]

Indeed, this unit, assisted by many other locals, performed the first massive killings of thousands of Jews in a few weeks in Kovno,[19] later in Vilna,[20] and especially in smaller towns and rural settlements. According to German reports groups with no more than one German in charge of Lithuanians numbering from eight to forty-five killed most of the Jews outside the major cities by December 1941, 'in all of Lithuania, systematically, region by region'.[21] A table annexed to the Stahlecker report lists dozens of small towns, where the Jews were murdered by Germans 'and Lithuanian Partisans', mostly during the summer of 1941, through the same means.[22]

Yet, according to Jewish sources, there was hardly any need for the presence of Germans in the small places. A declaration issued after the war by the Lithuanian Jews in the American zone in Germany regarding 'the guilt of the Lithuanian people in the extermination of Lithuanian Jewry' concludes: 'The small places in the Lithuanian provinces, without any exception, were erased by the Lithuanians.'[23] This declaration actually sums up the events detailed in *Lithuanian Jewry*, the volume on the Holocaust: the handful of survivors of 220 *Shtetles* and small towns describe how the Jews in those places were killed. Their descriptions, in which the Germans are hardly mentioned, make it quite clear that Lithuanians perpetrated most of the torture and killing, generally without any German officials on the spot. Recent research confirms Jewish sources to a large extent. The German historian Hans-Heinrich Wilhelm, in his research on the *Einsatzgruppen*, assumes that 'possibly half or two-thirds' of Lithuanian Jews were killed by local units. It seems, then, that the part played by the Lithuanians was greater than the Germans could afford to admit in their reports to their headquarters.[24]

The Ninth Fort, the killing site and burial place of about 40,000 people, mostly Jews, was organized and supervised by Lithuanian police volunteers. Some of them lived in the vicinity with their families, some came to assist when needed. The German command of the *Einsatzgruppen* came to the Fort only when the great *Aktionen* of thousands at a time were taking place and left immediately after the *Aktionen* were over. (The ghettos' civil German command killed smaller numbers from time to time until 1944.) The Lithuanians in charge killed those alive, wounded or intact, in the pits or otherwise on the spot, and prepared the Fort for forthcoming activities.[25] It should be noted that this description was given after the war by the Lithuanian commanders of the Fort, in the Soviet courts that declared them war criminals who practised the killing of 'Soviet citizens'. Since it is clear that the Lithuanians were out to defend themselves and diminish their crimes, the above may be considered an accurate, if not even minimized, description of their deeds.

The activities of the Lithuanian 'partisans' were so much in line with German plans that by the end of July 1941 the German command began the establishment of twenty police battalions. About 8,400 men, all volunteers, were charged with the murder of the local Jews, under the supervision of Franz Lechthaler, commander of the 11th Battalion of the German reserve police. By the end of the year, after most of the Lithuanian Jews had been killed, some of the battalions were sent to Byelorussia and to Poland, where they perpetrated killings in a string of towns, camps and ghettos, including Treblinka and Maidanek, and took part in the annihilation of the Warsaw Ghetto with General Stroop's troops.[26] German reports include references to the cruelty manifested by the members of these battalions, both in Lithuania and outside. It seems that their deeds even surpassed the capacity of some Germans and Byelorussians. When the Germans entered Kovno, they filmed the massacre of the Jews by the Lithuanians so as to 'make clear that it was the local population that spontaneously took the first steps against the Jews'. This was done because 'it was preferable that at least at the beginning the cruel and unusual means, which might upset even German circles, would not be too conspicuous'.[27] In other words, it seems that upon commencing the mass murder, the German troops did not know what it would look like physically. They were perhaps surprised and even taken aback by the extremity of Lithuanian conduct, and worried about the reaction of German circles once they found out that these deeds were enacted in an area under German occupation. The films could also serve as evidence of the enthusiasm which the Final Solution met with in the German occupied areas, thereby legitimizing Nazi propaganda and the Germans' own cruelty.

Carl, the German Gebietskommissar in Sluzk, Byelorussia, who witnessed an *Aktion* brutally carried out in his area by the infamous 12th Lithuanian Police Battalion, under the supervision of the German reserve police battalion, had one request: to get rid of the Lithuanian battalion.[28] His argument was not an objection to the murder of Jews *per se* – this was out of the question – but rather the Lithuanians' use of methods that provoked anti-German feelings among the local population. And Wilhelm Kube, Generalkommissar of Byelorussia, sent word to Heinrich Lohse, Reichskommissar for Ostland, to find out whether

> the slaughter [of the Reich Jews sent to the east is] to be carried out by the Lithuanians and Letts, who are themselves rejected by the [Byelorussian] population here? I couldn't do it. I beg you to give clear directives [in this matter], with due consideration for the good name of our Reich and our Party, in order that the necessary action be taken in the most humane manner.[29]

These words are more than clear.

It seems that the Lithuanians were aware of these facts. 'Do we have to be the Arch-hangmen of Europe?' asked an anti-Nazi underground Lithuanian publication in 1943. 'The Germans who shoot Jews now will shoot us later, and the world will support them because Lithuanians are hangmen and sworn sadists.'[30]

A number of questions are worth mentioning in this context. First, the possibility that Germans who served on the civil administration, and especially in reserve battalions, were more reluctant to back the Lithuanians than were other German units such as the *Einsatzgruppen*, who had quite a record for their own brutality. It seems that at least some of the civil German commanders thought that the zeal of the Lithuanian police battalions surpassed their own by far.

The question at stake is whether German civil and reserve units, who did not receive the training for murder given to the *Einsatzgruppen*, accepted, at least during the first months following the invasion, the Nazi regime's presentation of the killing of the Jews as a necessity – but not as a task which civilized people would indulge in with pleasure.

Second, even the *Einsatzgruppen*, after being trained for murder, were still murderers only in theory. Once the killings started, they became practical murderers, and the Lithuanians were the first ones to provide them with this transition from theory to practice. The Lithuanians showed them how to murder women and children, and perhaps made them accustomed to it.

Lithuanian conduct must have encouraged the German command to make further use of local units. It seems that when the German units became familiar with a place and situation, and when problems arose due to brutality and disorder (see Note 29), the lower echelons of the German command which were on the spot, such as Carl in Sluzk, became more reluctant to use local units. But the higher command exercised pressure to continue the practice.

Third, the question of the timetable: the above-mentioned chronology in Lithuania supports the view expressed by the Israeli historian, Yehoshua Büchler, that an order to kill Jewish men in the Soviet areas, as, or along with, communist activists, saboteurs, etc., was issued before the invasion. Indeed, at the onset of the invasion the German units killed mostly men, while the Lithuanians killed unselectively. A second order, to kill all Jews in the Soviet Union, was perhaps issued around 17 July 1941, when Himmler was appointed head of police security forces in the former Soviet areas, and issued instructions for the enrolment of locals into collaborationist units (see Note 17). Indeed this is when the Germans started organizing the Lithuanians in battalions, and progressed with the help of these units to wholesale murder of the Jews. Even if an oral, somewhat vague, order to kill everyone was issued before the invasion, it was convenient to have the Lithuanians fulfil it, and for the German units to join in when they grew more accustomed to murder, and when a clearer order was issued.

So it seems that the conduct of the Lithuanians, though anticipated in principle, encouraged the German command to press on. The scope, thoroughness and methods used by the Lithuanians made the Germans expect such support in other areas as well. Therefore this was an additional milestone towards the decision to kill all Jews in Europe.

Finally, Auschwitz became the symbol of the Holocaust due to the massive systematic murder perpetrated there. Perhaps the mass shootings by the killing pits in the Soviet Union should have become such a symbol. Auschwitz was the embodiment of a death factory, devised to avoid eye-to-eye and face-to-face contact with the children, women and elderly killed there, thus sparing the murderers all possible inconvenience. But the killing by the pits was done by direct contact, a sight that provoked drunkenness and nightmares. Nevertheless, the murders went on, and the murderers grew used to performing the horror.

One issue that lies outside the scope of this chapter concerns the explanations for the Lithuanians' extreme conduct. In short, it was a combination of a complex of factors such as national traditions and values, religion (Orthodox Catholic, in this case), severe economic problems and tragically opposed political orientations. Lithuanian Jews supported the Soviet regime in Lithuania during 1940–1, being partly of socialist inclination, and in the full knowledge that 'life imprisonment [Soviet regime] is better than life sentence [Nazi rule]', as in the Yiddish saying. By contrast, the Lithuanians fostered hopes of regaining, with German support, the national independence that the Soviets extinguished, as a reward for anti-Jewish and anti-Bolshevik stances. During the Soviet rule of Lithuania these feelings heightened and burst out following the German invasion. One might say that the Germans provided the framework and the legitimation for the killing of Lithuania's Jews, while the national aspirations and the hatred for communism provided the fuel. Still, this is not a full explanation for such brutality, especially as there was no tradition of pogroms in Lithuania. Not all Lithuanians took part in the killings, and one cannot depict all of them as murderers. At least one thousand Lithuanians sheltered Jews, thereby risking their own and their families' lives. A few tens of thousands took active part in the mass murders while the rest were either apathetic or aggravated the misery of the Jews in lesser ways than actual killing.

After the first stage of indiscriminate murder by the Lithuanians in July 1941, the Germans established the police battalions and planned a second stage. During August and September the remainder of Lithuanian Jewry was enclosed in four ghettos. During October and November, large Aktionen were initiated by the Germans with the active participation of the Lithuanians, in order to spare only the 'productive elements'. In December, Lohse ordered a halt to the killings of Jews because their manifold professional skills were indispensable.[31] The year 1942, and the first part of 1943, until the German defeat at Stalingrad, were relatively quiet in the ghettos and camps of Lithuania, where about 40,000–45,000 Jews still survived.

Summing up the uniqueness of the Holocaust in Lithuania from an external point of view, that is Jews vis-à-vis Lithuanians and Germans, one might say that the combination of its position as the first place to be hit by the Final Solution and the deep involvement of many among the local population, of all classes and circles, enabled the immediate killing of Lithuanian Jews with unsurpassed speed, scope and means.

*

Lithuania served as a starting point from an internal Jewish point of view as well. It was said there by Jews, for the first time, three weeks before the Wannsee Conference, that 'Hitler aims to destroy all the Jews of Europe'.[32] This was the location where Jews first understood the essence of the Final Solution as a comprehensive, systematic plan that concerned all the Jews of Europe.

It seems that the reason why they grasped this unprecedented plan first in Lithuania lies with a unique background and in a unique chain of circumstances that occurred there, directly affecting the Jewish public. The chain began with Vilna, the Jerusalem of Lithuania, being returned to Lithuania under the Ribbentrop–Molotov pact in October 1939. This meant the reunion of the 60,000 Jews of Vilna, and the countless treasures of Jewish culture accumulated there, with the rest of Lithuanian Jewry. Moreover, Vilna was then located in an independent state, though it was quite obvious that the independence of a small country such as Lithuania between Nazi Germany and Soviet Russia was bound to be shortlived. Nevertheless, about 14,000–15,000 Jews from German-occupied Poland made their way to Vilna, and then dispersed to Kovno and several smaller towns as well. They were the cream of Polish Jewry, leaders, intellectuals, activists of all parties in the political spectrum, 2,000 Talmudic students with their rabbis and another 2,000 youth movement members, mostly Zionist, with their leaders. They, too, like the Jews of Vilna, reinforced Jewish public life and thinking. These Polish refugees maintained contact with the rest of the Jewish world, especially with American Jewry and the *Yishuv* in Palestine. These contacts produced financial resources, documents and encouragement, at a time when most of European Jewry was under the Nazi or Soviet yoke.[33]

Lithuanian independence ended not long afterwards, in June 1940, when it was annexed to the Soviet Union. During the year that elapsed until June 1941, the Soviets dismantled all Jewish organizations, forbade all forms of public life, especially education and journalism, arrested leaders and deported them to Siberia, and terrorized the country. Jewish youth movements and political parties went underground, and tried to maintain contacts and activity at least on a limited scale. Contacts were especially strong among the youth movement members who had formed an umbrella organization in 1940. So it happened that this small, active and well-organized Jewry had a year to practise underground life, facing a hostile regime.[34] True, the other two Baltic countries, as well as western Byelorussia and Ukraine, all experienced the same year of Soviet rule. But Lithuanian Jewry had Vilna, the Polish refugees and contacts with the outside world.

The process continued after the German invasion. The strong ties among members inside each of the youth movements, as well as between them, enabled the creation of an information network. It was, of course, an amateur non-professional network based on personal ties. Young people, mostly girls, serving as couriers, reached the places devastated by the Final Solution in Lithuania and even beyond its former borders. They returned to tell what they had heard and sometimes seen. Since Jews were confined to their designated places by a series of unequivocal regulations, the couriers moved slowly and weeks elapsed before their reappearance. The information was collected by the youth movement leaders, who tried to analyse it in a series of meetings and consultations. These leaders gradually concluded that the Germans, assisted by the local population, were operating the same method of killing in a succession of areas – gathering the communities and herding them to pits and woods outside towns – and that the use of this method was spreading not only in Lithuania but in other areas of German occupation as well.[35]

This conclusion was crystallized in a proclamation, read out to a meeting of the pioneering youth in Vilna on 1 January 1942, warning that 'Hitler aims to destroy all the Jews of Europe' – not only Lithuanian Jews. This warning was perhaps phrased with some exaggeration, in order to focus attention and to dispel any illusions regarding the scope of the disaster. It certainly contained quite a measure of prophecy and insight. First, the idea of total murder was then unprecedented, reached far beyond the facts in hand and was beyond all experience, even Jewish, until then. Second, the Lithuanians did most of the killings, demonstrating initiative and clear policies. This was an obstacle to understanding the fact that the overall murder plan actually originated in Berlin. Third, for many weeks after the invasion the ghettos in Lithuania were cut off from each other. In Vilna there was no information about events in Kovno or in small rural locations. Later it became known in Vilna that in Bialystok a ghetto of 40,000 people lived in relative calm, and that in Warsaw half a million were alive and active, if starving. This could have indicated that Vilna in particular, and Lithuania in general, were exceptionally unfortunate to have more murderous than usual local German commanders. Fourth, the facts gathered about the murders in Lithuania and neighbouring areas could have been seen as linked to the German anti-Bolshevik campaign and hence limited to the former Soviet areas only, not necessarily to overall German policies in Europe in general.

It should also be taken into consideration that the massive deportation of Polish Jews from their ghettos, and of Jews from other European countries, to the death camps, only started in the spring of 1942 (though Chelmno started operating as early as the end of 1941).

The announcement of such a prediction to a doomed public was the result both of the afore-described circumstances and of the personal courage of the youth movements' leaders, particularly Abba Kovner, who formulated the proclamation and read it out.[36] The proclamation was then sent by courier to Warsaw, the largest ghetto and the centre of Jewish organizations. Also, word was spread from Warsaw to a number of other ghettos.[37]

It so happened, then, that the existence of the Final Solution embracing all Europe was grasped by a Jewish public on 1 January 1942, three weeks before the Wannsee Conference. This was no coincidence, but rather the parallel results of, on the German side, the invasion of Soviet Russia and the beginning of the murder there;[38] and, for the Jews, the circumstances that enabled at least some of the Lithuanian Jews, especially its Zionist youth movements, to see events correctly as the implementation of the first stage in a comprehensive plan.

Did this conclusion, first reached in Vilna, convince the other Jewish communities in Lithuania? Did the fact that the Lithuanian community was the first to be hit by the Final Solution affect other Jewish communities? Long painful deliberations took place even among the Vilna youth movement members, before and after 1 January 1942. Once most of these members accepted the idea that total annihilation awaited each and every Jew, their way was clear. Youth movement members in other places such as Warsaw were deeply shocked by the news from Vilna, yet each ghetto needed its own experience to reach the same conclusions. And most of the older Jewish public, who could not join the underground or leave for the forest, because they were responsible for children and parents, still hoped to survive through work and hold on till German defeat.

Comprehension of the situation led to the next stage. The proclamation called upon Jewish youth to defend itself and its community. Indeed, an underground movement was established in each of the four ghettos of Lithuania. The largest one was in Vilna, a coalition of all the forces in the Jewish population, including the Bund and the communists. The latter were instrumental in maintaining contacts with the communist underground outside the ghettos, in the Lithuanian cities of Vilna and Kovno and later in the forests. A small amount of arms and ammunition was smuggled in with great risk and served to train the members, mainly during the year that elapsed beween mid-1942 and mid-1943.

These four undergrounds began organizing and building in 1942. This fact demands attention, because 1942 was a relatively quiet year. No more large *Aktionen* took place after Lohse's order to stop the killing until the ghettos were transferred, in the summer of 1943, from the civil administration to the SS. It seemed that Jewish labour was indeed necessary, because workshops and factories were put up in the ghettos, and Jewish labourers worked there as well as in German enterprises outside the ghetto. The *Wehrmacht* needed various products and services that Lithuanians could not supply, and there was at least some room for hope that Jewish labour would help spare the rest of Lithuanian Jewry. The remnant of the Jewish communities, being given a short breathing space, developed cultural, religious and social activities, even a theatre (in Vilna) and a court of justice (in Kovno). The Jewish councils tried to maintain at least a semblance of normality. Indeed, there were no epidemics in the Lithuanian ghettos. The essence of daily life was the struggle for food but there was no famine or death by hunger; the streets were clean, and violation of public regulations was punished. These achievements were perhaps another result of the cohesiveness and inner organization that developed in the small Jewish community in Lithuania long before the war started.

Yet it was during 1942 despite the fact that it was a year of relative calm and hope that the youth movements were transformed into active underground organizations. Contact with the outside world, including with Palestine, was cut off a few months before the invasion. The couriers' route to the General Government and back became increasingly difficult as the pace of extermination accelerated in Poland and more than a quarter of a million people were deported from Warsaw to Treblinka in the summer of 1942. The Jewish local hinterland ceased to exist, once the Jews in the small towns were almost all dead. The Jewish underground in Lithuania had to cope with isolation, lack of information and, more important, with the illusion that naturally took hold of people when the killings stopped. Under these circumstances it was a lot more difficult to adhere to the basic conclusion that the Final Solution would not spare anyone in the long run, and that the halt was only temporary.[39] Perhaps the fact that the realization of German intentions first emerged in Lithuania gave the underground strength to insist on the stance they formulated.

The severe conflicts within the Vilna underground, between the public in the ghetto and the Jewish council, or the good relations that existed between these three elements in the ghettos of Kovno and Shavli, cannot be discussed here. Suffice it to say that the German authorities were aware of the unrest in Vilna and of the determination of its underground and feared another variation of the Warsaw Ghetto revolt. They were worried about the increase of Soviet or Soviet-oriented partisans in eastern Lithuania and in Byelorussia in the summer of 1943 and their ties with the ghetto underground. With a few acts of deception the Germans ended the existence of the ghetto before the underground could act.[40] The calmer ghettos in Shavli and Kovno were turned into concentration camps that resumed work until the German retreat in the summer of 1944.

One may conclude that Jewish organized resistance in the ghettos of eastern Europe began, at least as an idea, with an analysis of the situation in Lithuania, an analysis of German plans and the transmission of the conclusions to other ghettos in 1941–2. The conditions which made this analysis and these conclusions possible came into being much earlier. They formed, in fact, about 300 years before the Holocaust, when the 'Litvak' type appeared on the Jewish stage, and his special blend of logic and knowledge of the Halacha created a school of rabbinical thought. This school, still in existence today, made Lithuanian Yeshivas (Talmudic academics) the acknowledged powerhouse of Jewish Talmudic studies for about two centuries, and the centre of *Mismagdim* – opponents – of the Hassidic movement. The Haskala (Enlightenment), the socialist and the Zionist movements that strengthened in Lithuania in the nineteenth century, fostered an active public life with parties and youth movements spanning right and left, a fine system of education that encompassed 90 per cent of Jewish children between the wars, an extensive press and prolific literature, in both Yiddish and living Hebrew, let alone the largest library in the east European Jewish world, the Strashun library, the Yivo, the first and only institute for Jewish research and studies, the first Jewish press, music institute, pen club, technicum, high school that taught in Yiddish, and the second in the world to teach in Hebrew (the first was in Jerusalem). All this occurred in Vilna, the city nicknamed the Jerusalem of Lithuania.

It seems logical to assume that this specific background influenced the way Lithuanian Jews handled their affairs during the Holocaust in the ghettos. The best proof is the fact the survivors of ghettos and camps, gathered after the liberation in the American Zone in Germany, elected the few surviving leaders of the Kovno ghetto as their representatives, press editors and chairmen of committees. Leib Garfunkel for instance, vice-chairman of the Jewish council in the Kovno ghetto, became one of the leading figures in the camps in Germany, and later in Italy. The Vilna partisans, headed by Abba Kovner and joined by the Kovno fighters of the Lithuanian Division, led the surviving partisans. This expression of respect which other Jews had for Lithuanian Jewry seemed confirmation that it was a unique population in its life and in its death.

NOTES

1 See the list of publications in: Yitzhak Arad, *The Struggle and Destruction of the Jews of Vilna* (Tel Aviv, 1976), pp. 409–14 (Hebrew); Dov Levin, 'Jews of the Baltic countries in ripeness and in destruction', *Masua*, 12 (April 1984), pp. 40–1 (Hebrew); Abraham Tory, *Ghetto Everyday, Diary and Documents*

from the Kovno Ghetto, ed. with introduction and notes Dina Porat (Tel Aviv, 1988), pp. 589–90 (Hebrew). On Lithuania in general, see *Lithuanian Jewry*, vol. IV *The Holocaust, 1941–1945* (Tel Aviv, 1984) (Hebrew).

2 See the 31 January 1942 Stahlecker report in *The Final Solution, Documents on the Destruction of European Jewry by Nazi Germany* (Tel Aviv, 1960), pp. 22–5 (Hebrew). See also Yosef Gar, 'Details on the destruction of Lithuania as reflected in the Einsatzgruppen reports in "The Walter Stahlecker Report" and in Karl Jaeger's Conclusive List', *Lithuanian Jewry*, IV, pp. 21–6.

3 *Documents on the Holocaust*, ed. Yitzhak Arad, Yisrael Gutman and Avraham Margaliot (Yad Vashem, Jerusalem, 1981), p. 433.

4 Ya'acov Robinson, 'The destruction of Lithuanian Jewry as part of the Holocaust in general', *Lithuanian Jewry*, IV, p. 19.

5 *Encyclopedia of the Holocaust*, ed. Y. Gutman (Tel Aviv, 1990), vol. V, pp. 1282, 1284 (Hebrew).

6 Yitzhak Arad, 'Policies and implementation of the "Final Solution" in Lithuania', *Lithuanian Jewry*, IV, p. 47.

7 *Encyclopedia of the Holocaust*, 'Lithuania', by Dov Levin, vol. III, p. 638. The figure of 8,000 given here is not quite clear. See Dov Levin, 'On the relations between Jews and Lithuanians during World War II', *Kivunim*, 2 (February 1979), p. 30: 92 per cent (Hebrew).

8 Zydai, *Lietuviu Enciklopedija*, vol. 35 (Boston, Mass., 1966), p. 293. See the appeal, written at the beginning of November 1944, in Abba Kovner, 'The beginning of the "Bricha" [escape] as a mass movement', *Yalkut Moreshet*, 37 (June 1984), pp. 17–18.

9 Itzchak Zuckerman (Antek), *Those Seven Years, 1939–1946, The Ghetto Fighters' House* (1990), p. 137 (Hebrew).

10 Stahlecker report, *The Final Solution*, p. 25, a balance sheet.

11 Jaeger report, *The Final Solution*, p. 29. SS Standarten-führer (between colonel and brigadier-general) Karl Jaeger, commander of the *Einsatzkommando* 3 of *Einsatzgruppe* A, wrote his report on 1 December 1941.

12 The second report, reproduced in *Lithuanian Jewry*, IV, p. 26, contains a map which excludes the Vilna area. The figure 136,400, out of 148,000, seems too high. Perhaps different boundaries of regions could account for that.

13 *Lithuanian Jewry*, IV, p. 56 and Levin, 'Jews and Lithuanians', 85 per cent. Cf. Levin and Arad, *Lithuanian Jewry*, IV, pp. 31, 39 respectively: 80 per cent.

14 The Jaeger report estimates the number of Jews in the ghettos at 15,000 each in Vilna and Kovno, and 4,500 in Shavli. There are a number of other errors in this report. See Dina Porat, 'The legend of the struggle of Jews from the Third Reich in the Ninth Fort near Kovno, 1941–1942', *Tel-Aviver Jahrbuch für Deutsche Geschichte*, 1991, pp. 363–92. (See English full text of the report in *Documents Accuse*, compiled and with annotations by B. Baranaukas and K. Ruksenas (Vilnius, 1970), pp. 230–8.)

15 The small Estonian community, that numbered 1,000 Jews when the German occupation started, was also killed by the end of 1941.

16 Porat, 'Jews from the Third Reich'.

17 In Lithuanian: Tautinio Darbo Apsauga; in fact it was a national security service. See Sara Nishmit, 'Between collaboration and uprising – to the history of German occupation in Lithuania', *Dapim Leheker Ha'Shoa Vehameri*, second series, vol. I, *The Ghetto Fighters' House* (1970), pp. 152–79 (Hebrew). As to the stages in the formation of local units in the Soviet-occupied territories, see Yehoshua Büchler, 'Local police units – Schutzmannschaften – in the murder campaign in the Soviet Union' (to be published).

18 Stahlecker report, *Lithuanian Jewry*, IV, p. 25.
19 See the *Einsatzgruppe* A (EK 1b) report no. 8, of 30 June 1941, in *The Einsatz-gruppen Reports*, ed. Y. Arad, Shmuel Krakowski and Shmuel Spector (New York, 1989), p. 1; 'During the last three days Lithuanian partisan groups have already killed several thousand Jews.'
20 ibid., pp. 3, 5, 13–15, 22–3.
21 Jaeger report, *The Final Solution*, p. 29. About forty-five Lithuanians headed by one German, see Levin, 'Jews and Lithuanians', p. 39.
22 'The Jaeger conclusive list', *Lithuanian Jewry*, IV, p. 24; Yosef Gar, *The Destruction of Jewish Kovno* (Munich, 1948), pp. 268–9 (Yiddish).
23 *Unzer veg*, Munich, 22 July 1947 (Yiddish).
24 *Lithuanian Jewry*, IV, pp. 237–373; Helmut Krausnick and Hans-Heinrich Wilhelm, *Die Truppe des Weltanschauungkrieges* (Stuttgart, 1981), pp. 596–7.
25 Porat, 'Jews from the Third Reich'. Regarding the killing of small numbers of Jews from Kovno until 1944, see Tory, *Ghetto Everyday*.
26 See *Masinēs Zudynēs Lietuvojé, 1941–1944* (Mass Murder in Lithuania) (Vilnius, 1965), part I, Document 29 (Lithuanian). This is a collection of proceedings of Soviet trials against Lithuanian war criminals. These details are often mentioned. See, for example, *Lithuanian Jewry*, IV, pp. 19, 25, 52–3, 451. Hereafter: 'Mass murder'. According to Alexei Michailovitch Litvin, 'The Jewish question in Byelorussia during the fascist occupation' (paper presented at the Historical Institute of the Ukraine conference on 'The Holocaust in the Soviet Union' in Kiev in October 1991), the Lithuanian battalions killed 40,000 Jews in Byelorussia. According to Krausnick and Wilhelm, *Die Truppe*, p. 169, by the end of 1942 there were eight Ukrainian, four Lithuanian, two Latvian and only one Byelorussian battalions in Byelorussia.
27 Stahlecker report, *Lithuanian Jewry*, p. 25.
28 'Mass murder', Document 235; *'Schöne Zeiten', Judenmord aus der Sicht der Tater und Gaffer*, ed. Ernst Klee, Willi Dressen and Volker Riess (Frankfurt, 1988), pp. 164–7, the full Carl report.
29 *Documents on the Holocaust*, pp. 408–9. On German reserve units, and their reactions to brutality demonstrated by local units, see Jean Ancel, 'The solution of the "Jewish problem" in Bessarabia', *Yad Vashem Studies*, XIX (1988), pp. 187–232, especially p. 19. Ancel's article is based on *Documents Concerning the Fate of Rumanian Jewry*, selected and edited by Jean Ancel (New York, 1985), vol. VI, pp. 546–75, where the full report of the German reserve unit is given.
30 Levin, 'Jews and Lithuanians', p. 41.
31 Arad, *Lithuanian Jewry*, IV, pp. 42–3.
32 *Documents on the Holocaust*, p. 433.
33 Dina Porat, 'The concentration of Jewish refugees from Poland in Vilna, 1939–1941', MA thesis, Tel Aviv University, 1974 (Hebrew).
34 Dov Levin, *The Jews in the Soviet-Annexed Territories, 1939–1941* (Tel Aviv, 1989).
35 For a first-hand description, see Reizl Korchak (Ruzke), *Flames in Ash* (Merchavia, 1965), pp. 46–53 (Hebrew).
36 ibid., p. 53. Abba Kovner's part in the formulation of the proclamation is well established. Still, in his testimony, given to me on 5 January 1989, in Tel Aviv University, Nissan Reznik, also a member of the underground command, emphasized the consultations and the team work prior to the formulation of the proclamation.
37 Zuckerman, *Those Seven Years*, pp. 130–49.

38 The historians' dispute regarding the Germans' motivation to start the mass murder of the Jews because of their victories in the Soviet Union, or because of their failure to go on as planned, is outside our scope.

39 The Vilna underground proclamation of April 1942 warned that the economic interest would not bring salvation. First published in Reizl Korchak, *Flames in Ash* (Merchavia, 1946), p. 288.

40 Arad, *Lithuanian Jewry*, IV, pp. 46–7.

11

TYPES OF GENOCIDE?

Croatians, Serbs and Jews, 1941–5

Jonathan Steinberg

Nobody can say precisely how many Serbs, Jews and Gypsies died during the short but bloody existence of the Independent State of Croatia. The Institut für Zeitgeschichte has recently made a very thorough investigation and concluded that the number of Jews who died under Croatian rule between 1941 and 1945 must have been just over 30,000: 20,000 to 25,000 in the Ustasha death camps and another 7,000 deported from Croatian territory to the gas chambers.[1] In a paper given in early 1992, Damir Mirković reckoned that in addition to the Jews there were roughly 27,000 Gypsy and 487,000 Serb victims of Ante Pavelić's regime.[2]

It may seem that the horrors of wartime Croatia have little, if anything, to do with the cold, bureaucratic deliberations recorded on 20 January 1942 in the villa at 56/58 Am Grossen Wannsee. People have massacred their neighbours for millennia; Croatians and Serbs continue to do so today. Communal slaughters, committed in hate and hot frenzy, seem almost 'normal' in comparison to the icy calm of Wannsee or the brutal detachment of an *Einsatzkommando* report. Yet Heydrich and the SS were perfectly prepared to use primitive, ancient hatreds as long as they resulted in more dead Jews. In a telegram to all the *Einsatzkommandos* sent on 29 June 1941, a week after the invasion of Russia, Heydrich instructed them

> to place no obstacles in the way of autonomous cleansing efforts
> (*Selbstreinigungsbestrebungen*) by anti-communist or anti-Jewish cir-
> cles in the newly occupied territories. On the contrary they are to
> be intensified if necessary and directed into the right channels, to be
> sure, without leaving traces so that later these 'self-protection circles'
> [in inverted commas in the original as '*Selbstschutzkreise*'] cannot
> claim that they acted on orders or were given political assurances.[3]

Estonians, Latvians, Lithuanians, Ukrainians, Romanians and Poles joined lustily in pogroms and massacres, in 'Jew hunts' and attacks on property. In this litany of human bestiality, Croatian genocide stands out because, unlike the '*Selbstschutz*' practised by ethnic groups on the Eastern Front, the Croatian crimes were state-authorized and directed from the beginning.

The Ustasha wore the uniform of the Croatian national movement. They acted as representatives of the 'new Croatia', reborn from the ashes of the old Yugoslavia. The Croatian state set up its own concentration camps. It adopted its own anti-Semitic legislation. It needed little encouragement from the Germans to kill Jews and none to kill Serbs.

Croatia was unique in another sense; it was the only Axis satellite to have murdered more non-Jewish than Jewish civilians. Even the Axis leadership were shocked and revolted by the sheer scale of Ustasha bloodshed. At a summit conference of the Axis military leadership in Rome on 18 November 1942, Generaloberst Löhr reported that

> in Croatia conditions were very unsatisfactory. The authority of the government very tenuous. The Croatian army can only be used with support from German troops and the Ustasha have become more undisciplined and are hated in large sections of the population. (The Duce intervened at this point, it was madness of the Poglavnik to think that he could exterminate two million Serbs.)[4]

A third peculiarity of the Croatian crimes is the role of religion. Let me take one example: Vladko Maček had been leader of the Croatian Peasants Party before 1941. In October of that year he was arrested and sent to Jasenovac, the Auschwitz of the Croatian death camps. In his memoirs he recalled:

> The camp had previously been a brick-yard and was situated on the embankment of the Sava river. In the middle of the camp stood a two-story house, originally erected for the offices of the enterprise. . . . The screams and wails of despair and extreme suffering, the tortured outcries of the victims, broken by intermittent shooting, accompanied all my waking hours and followed me into sleep at night.[5]

Maček was too important to be hacked to death but he was too dangerous to be left. One of those who guarded him night and day was an Ustasha officer who used to make the sign of the cross each night before going to sleep. Maček pointed out

> the monstrosity of his actions. I asked if he were not afraid of the punishment of God. 'Don't talk to me about that', he said, 'for I am perfectly aware of what is in store for me. For my past, present and future deeds I shall burn in hell but at least I shall burn for Croatia.'[6]

This combination of Catholic piety, Croatian nationalism and human bestiality raises uncomfortable questions about what happened fifty years ago in Europe and why. The standard image of fascism has been sketched for us by secular historians and sociologists. For most of them religion is an opiate of the elderly, a childhood complaint or, perhaps, the source of an occasional pang of guilt. As a result, recent explanatory approaches to the Holocaust and genocide in the Second World War, with the notable exception of Arno Mayer's *Why Did the Heavens not Darken?*, confront the questions with resolutely secular assumptions. At best Nazism and fascism have been seen as surrogate religions, taking the place of traditional Christianity, in a world in which God had long since died and been interred.

Yet Croatia was by no means the only avowedly Catholic state in Hitler's new order. Father Tiso's Slovakia bore the cross as prominently and deported its Jews as thoroughly as did Ante Pavelić's Croatia. Much of the legitimacy of Pétain's Vichy regime came from those traditions of reactionary Catholicism which had never accepted the republic, the separation of church and state, civil marriage, divorce or Jewish emancipation. The story of German Protestantism's enthusiastic reception of the Nazi renewal of morality has been traced by a small industry of scholars and was recognized by the German Protestant churches in a collective act of expiation in 1945.[7]

In all these studies, religion and churches react; they do not act. Even those who criticize the silence of Pius XII never suggest that the Vatican caused the massacres; the issue is whether the Pope and the clergy did enough to stop them. The Croatian case will not fit such comfortable secular categories. Croatian fascism, the Ustasha movement (the word means 'to stand up' or 'rebel'), combined Catholic piety, Croatian nationalism and extreme violence. The terrible evidence of those years and the terrible revenge claimed in ours reminds us of the religious wars of the sixteenth century. The Croats were Catholic the way that the people of South Armagh are Catholic; religion, nation and self merged into an explosive, unstable mixture.

The tragedy of the Serbs raises a variety of difficult and disturbing questions for historians familiar with Nazi crimes. What the Ustasha state did to its Serbs was undoubtedly genocide. Observers as brutal as Mussolini could recognize the reality, even if the word had yet to be invented. But was it a different sort of genocide from the Nazi Final Solution? If not, does the Croatian mass murder campaign make the Nazi extermination of the Jews simply one of many terrible crimes, no longer unique? And what of religion and specifically the role of the Roman Catholic Church? Was Ustasha violence a religious crusade, a Latin jihad? Was it, therefore, less modern, secular, bureaucratic, hence more comprehensible, if not excusable? Are there shades of grey amidst the blackness?

Historians can never answer such questions satisfactorily. They cannot rerun the phenomena with the variables altered. All they can do is look for parallels and make some rough comparisons. Reflecting on the horrors of Pavelić's Croatia may help us to see more sharply the peculiar features of the horrors hidden behind the detached, official language of the Wannsee Protocol.

*

The establishment of a Catholic Croatia and its immediate resort to genocide confronted the Roman Catholic hierarchy in Croatia and the Vatican in Rome with a terrible dilemma. The Nuncio to the Italian government, Monsignor Francesco Borgoncini Duca, a man who made two trips to darkest Calabria to bring the Holy Father's greetings to the Jews interned at Ferramonti Tarsia,[8] rebuked Stiepo Perić, the Croatian minister to the Kingdom of Italy, 'about the well-known atrocities of the Croatians against the Orthodox Serbs and Muslims and the violence perpetrated against them'. As he reported to the cardinal secretary of state, Cardinal Luigi Maglione,

> I added that the Catholic church cannot and will not make propaganda by violence. Jesus said 'go and preach' not 'go and take the people by gun shots'. He replied that 350,000 orthodox had 'converted'. I replied that these conversions did not persuade me very much because for a conversion sentiment was necessary. . . . He said, 'sentiment will come later'.[9]

On the other hand, the Independent State of Croatia, the NDH, enshrined in its constitution and laws the aims that the church had desired for decades and had despaired of achieving: above all, the conversion of the 'schismatics'. As the youthful Archbishop Alojzije Stepinac said to the Regent Prince Paul in 1940,

> The most ideal thing would be for the Serbs to return to the faith of their fathers, that is, to bow the head before Christ's representative, the Holy Father. Then we could at last breathe in this part of Europe, for Byzantinism has played a frightful role in the history of this part of the world.[10]

As for the Jews, the semi-official diocesan weekly *Katolički List* had condemned them frequently during the 1930s as the source of communism, Freemasonry, abortion and irreverence. Jews were aliens and could not be true Croatians.[11] Nor were any tears shed for the destruction of the unitary kingdom of Yugoslavia. The Yugoslav government had, according to Father Ivo Guberina, reader in the University of Zagreb, undermined Catholicism in every way. It built 'splendid Orthodox churches' in towns historically and actually Catholic:

> The government of Belgrade helped both morally and materially the foundation in Croatia of the so-called 'Old Catholics', which was intended as a means to make Catholics go into schism. . . . Going over to Orthodoxy was more or less openly favoured. . . . Mixed marriages at the expense of the Catholic Church were skilfully encouraged. . . . Catholic areas were systematically colonized.[12]

Now at last, as *Katolički List* wrote on 21 April 1941, not quite two weeks after the establishment of the new Ustasha state, the dark days of humiliation were over.

> The NDH is thus a fact established by Almighty Providence on the 1300th anniversary of Croatia's first links with the Holy See. The Catholic Church which has been the spiritual leader of the Croatian people for 1300 years in all its difficult, painful and joyful days now accompanies the Croatian people with joy in these days of the establishment and renewal of its independent state.[13]

The Serbs, observed the new minister of education, Mile Budak,

> are not Serbs but people brought here from the East by the Turks . . . as the plunderers and refuse of the Balkans . . . God is one, and the people that governs is also one: and this is the Croatian people . . . it would be as well for them to know our motto: 'either submit or get out'.[14]

The new state was not, however, the result of a heroic rising by the people of God but of outside intervention. At 5.15 a.m. on 6 April 1941, the *Wehrmacht* crossed the frontiers of Yugoslavia and Greece from the north and the east. Zagreb fell on 10 April, Belgrade on the 12th and six days later Yugoslavia capitulated. On 27 April, German troops after unexpectedly fierce resistance from the Greek and British forces finally entered Athens.

The Germans and their allies redrew the Balkan map. Yugoslavia ceased to exist. On 10 April 1941 the Independent State of Croatia was proclaimed with its capital in Zagreb, its frontiers from the Drau and Danube in the north-east to those parts of the Dalmatian coast left it by the Italians in the south. A line running north-west to south-east divided the new state into German and Italian spheres of influence. Slovenia was split on the same basis with the southern part, including the capital Ljubljana, annexed to Italy, the northern part to Germany. Hungary annexed outright Bačka and Baranja and the region Medjimurje. Bulgaria 'redeemed' what it had always regarded as its ancient provinces of Macedonia and Thrace. Serbia was put under direct German military rule and Serbs and their officers were, according to OKW (High Command of the *Wehrmacht*) instructions, 'to be treated exceptionally badly'.[15] As Mark Wheeler has put it, 'this was no simple military defeat. It was the fracture and destruction of an entire ruling order and of the political and national conception that underlay it.'[16]

The new Croatian state lacked everything. It scarcely had enough cars to drive its cabinet officers about, but it soon developed legislation to please Hitler. Within three weeks of its establishment, it passed legislation defining Jews in racial terms. In the months of May and June 1941, it rapidly passed the laws that the Nazis had taken years to work out:

prohibiting intermarriage and employment of Aryan female servants by Jews, the marking of Jewish stores and persons, compulsory registration of Jewish property, the removal of Jews from the bureaucracy and professions and the 'Aryanization' of Jewish capital. As early as May 1941, some of the Jews of Zagreb were rounded up and sent to the Danica camp and later in the summer to Jasenovac.[17]

The real enemy were the Serbs. As Mark Wheeler writes, the NDH came to power with 'a threefold scheme to rid Croatia of its "oriental minority" – by expelling a third to rump Serbia, forcibly converting a second third to Roman Catholicism and slaughtering the remainder'.[18] The numbers involved were impressive. While the new Croatian state had doubled the territory which the former Yugoslav state had allotted to it as an autonomous region, much of it had inconveniently large settlements of non-Croats. Of the 6,700,000 citizens of the new state, only 3,300,000 were Croats. There were 2,200,000 Serbs, 750,000 Muslims, 35,000 Jews including an estimated 5,000 Jewish refugees, 70,000 Protestants and other minorities.[19]

Hitler left the Independent State of Croatia to the Italians as part of their sphere of influence in the Balkans but negotiations between Italy and the new Croatian state produced no easy agreement. Ante Pavelić, its leader or Poglavnik, modelled himself and his Ustasha movement on Mussolini and fascism. Pavelić owed his and his movement's survival to fascist protection during the 1930s when he and his followers were in exile in Italy. In spite of his debt to Italy and to Mussolini, he was appalled when the Italians annexed historic Croatian lands on the Dalmatian coast. Most of the coast, with its beaches, the Dalmatian islands, the cities of Zara, Dubrovnik, Split and the city and bay of Kotor, either became provinces of metropolitan Italy or were subsequently occupied by the Italian Second Army. Hitler refused to intervene and Pavelić had no choice but to sign a state treaty on 18 May 1941 in Rome.[20]

By the time that Pavelić arrived in Rome, the character of the new regime was clear. Hundreds of Serbs had already been killed within the first three weeks by methods later perfected by the SS *Einsatzgruppen*. Serb men, women and children were forced to dig ditches into which their mutilated bodies were then hurled, often still alive. At Otočac early in May 1941 the usual slaughter was made worse by holding back the Greek Orthodox priest and his son to the end. The boy was cut to pieces under the eyes of his father who was then forced to recite prayers for the dying. At Glina on 14 May, the Serbs were invited to hear a *Te Deum*. Once inside the church, the Ustasha officer asked whether any present had certificates of conversion. Two did. The rest were hacked to death inside the sanctuary.[21]

By early June, the Carabinieri in Split were reporting streams of Serbian and Jewish refugees crossing into Italian territory with tales of atrocities and massacres carried out by the Ustasha.[22] The German general plenipotentiary accredited to the NDH, Edmund Glaise von Horstenau, reported that 'according to reliable reports from countless German military and civil observers during the last few weeks in country and town the Ustasha have gone raging mad'.[23]

He reported that Serbian and Jewish men, women and children were literally hacked to death. Whole villages were razed to the ground and the people driven into barns to which the Ustasha set fire. At one point the Ustasha had thrown so many corpses into the River Neretva near Metkovic that the government began to pay peasants 100 kune for each body hauled out, lest they float downstream into the Italian zone.[24] Neighbours murdered neighbours, as Menachem Shelach points out, people whose families had lived side by side for generations.[25] The Croatian militia were often egged on by local priests. When an Italian junior officer asked a Croatian priest for his authorization, the priest replied, 'I have one authorization and only one: to kill the Serb sons of bitches.'[26] Early the following year Cardinal Tisserant confronted the Croatian emissary to the Vatican, Dr Nikola Rusinović, with the appalling behaviour of Croatian Franciscans.

> I know for a fact that it is the Franciscans themselves, as for example Fr Simić of Knin, who have taken part in attacks against the Orthodox populations so as to destroy the Orthodox Church (in the way you destroyed the Orthodox Church in Banja Luka). I know for sure that the Franciscans in Bosnia and Herzegovina have acted abominably, and this pains me. Such acts cannot be committed by educated, cultivated people, let alone by priests.[27]

Observers within the German Army also disapproved of uncontrolled violence. Early in June 1941 Glaise reported with dismay that the Croatians had expelled all Serbian intellectuals from Zagreb. When he went to see the Poglavnik, Pavelić promised humane treatment for them. The fact that they were only allowed 30 kg of luggage made Glaise suspicious.[28] He had good reason. On 10 July, he reported the 'utterly inhuman treatment of the Serbs living in Croatia', the embarrassment of the Germans who 'with six battalions of foot soldiers' could do nothing and who had to watch the 'blind, bloody fury of the Ustasha'.[29] On 19 July, he wrote:

> Even among the Croatians nobody can feel safe in this land any more. . . . The Croatian revolution is by far the harshest and most brutal of all the different revolutions that I have been through at more or less close hand since 1918.[30]

The Italian representative in Zagreb, Casertano, reported with equal dismay that 'persecutions of Jews are continuing. Foreign influence [i.e. German] is clearly visible in the recent decree prohibiting Jews from circulating in the city before ten in the morning and at any hour in markets or banks.'[31]

Small communities were not spared. The adjutant major of the 32nd Infantry Regiment stationed in Bileca recorded in the unit's war diary on 16 June that 'searches and arrests are continuing day and night. Numerous murders have taken place. Jews and Serbs are being robbed of all their goods by the Ustasha who are profiting from that in their greed for personal enrichment.'[32]

Meanwhile in Zagreb, the NDH had set about reconquering the country for the true faith. In June 1941 all primary and infants' schools belonging to the Serbian church were closed and the 10 per cent tax levied by the state for the Orthodox Church abolished. In July the use of the phrase 'Serbo-Orthodox religion' was forbidden and replaced by the term 'Greco-Oriental'. On 14 July 1941, the Ministry of Justice and Religion issued a decree to the bishops within the territory of the NDH in which it announced that Orthodox converts were forbidden to join the Greco-Catholic Church, that is the Greek-rite churches in communion with Rome, and added

> the Croatian government does not intend to accept within the Catholic church either priests or schoolmasters or, in a word, any of the intelligentsia – including rich Orthodox tradesman and artisans. . . . Reception of the common Orthodox people and the poor is allowed after instruction in the truths of Catholicism.[33]

In a speech to the Sabor (parliament) in February 1942 Pavelić explained that he had nothing against Orthodoxy as such but the Serbian Orthodox Church could not be allowed to exist within the NDH because Orthodox churches were always national. It had been the state religion of the old Yugoslav kingdom, its bishops and priests were all Serbs and hence inadmissible in Croatia.[34]

The Catholic hierarchy within Croatia watched the unfolding events with complicated and conflicting feelings. Archbishop Stepinac, who was a man of deep personal piety and puritan tastes, could not fail to welcome the NDH's new decrees punishing with thirty days in jail those who swore in public, forbidding indecent advertisements and window dislays, and prescribing the death penalty for abortion.[35] The archbishop believed, as he said in a sermon at a penitential rally of 200,000 people at Marija Bistrica in June 1943,

> we are all deeply convinced that this dreadful war with all its evil consequences is a justified punishment of God for so many sins . . . sins of impurity, adultery, disorderly marriages, abortion, contraception, drunkenness, thieving and cheating, lying and swearing, indifference to holy days, to Sunday Mass and the holy sacraments; they all cry to heaven for vengeance.[36]

While the NDH enforced a puritanism which he welcomed, it assumed an authority in matters of faith and doctrine which he could not welcome. The Minister of Justice and Religion bombarded the bishops in the new state with decrees like the one just cited. Wholesale deportations of Jews and Serbs worried him, not least because the NDH apparently made no distinction between those converted to Catholicism and those who were not. The Archbishop began discreetly to protest. On 16 July, he wrote to the Minister of Justice and Religion to complain that: 'it would be against the spirit and duty of the Catholic Church to refuse to receive the whole intelligentsia on principle. Christ came into the world to save all men.'[37]

A week later he wrote directly to the Poglavnik himself:

> I am convinced that these things have been happening without your knowledge and that others may not dare to tell you about them; so I am all the more obliged to do so myself. I hear from many sides that there are instances of inhumane and brutal treatment of non-Aryans during the deportations and at the camps, and even worse that neither children, old people nor the sick are spared. I know that among recent deportees there have been converts to Catholicism, so that it is even more my duty to concern myself with them. Allow me to make a general observation; the measures which have been undertaken would have their full effect if they were carried out in a more humane and considerate way, seeing in human beings the image of God; human and Christian consideration should be shown especially to weak, old people, young and innocent children and the sick.[38]

The archbishop had, in effect, condoned the end but condemned the means. He must surely have known, as General Glaise knew, that the NDH intended to carry out its own Final Solution of the Serb question. An administrative state agency, the Državno Ravnateljstvo za Ponovu (state directorate of renewal) had been charged with the execution of the laws against Serbs, the seizure of their property and resettlement of Croats in vacant Serb villages. A day after the archbishop's letter, the Minister of Education, Mile Budak, speaking in Gospic, made clear that one-third of the two million Serbs would be deported, one-third converted to Catholicism and one-third killed.[39]

While Budak was announcing that genocide was now official in Croatia, the Poglavnik's ally, Adolf Hitler, began his greatest enterprise. At 3.15 on the morning of 22 June 1941, Operation Barbarossa went into effect and German troops crossed the frontiers of the Soviet Union. The communist parties of all the Balkan states now joined the anti-fascist front and in time came to dominate those movements. Yugoslav communists were free to attack the Croatian fascists directly and took to the hills.

Non-communist Serbs had not been sitting idly waiting for extermination. In rump Serbia, bands of irregulars, known as *četniks*, had gathered around the Serb general staff officer Draza Mihailović, who was loyal in his way to the exiled king and the Allies. The Serbs of Montenegro and Croatia, especially those behind the coastal strip in towns such as Knin and Gračac, took up arms. Incidents like the following became common. Two lorries of Italian fascist militiamen, fifty-five blackshirts, two officers and a doctor, set out from Bileca in the hills behind Dubrovnik for Gacko in the mountains of Herzegovina. The transport was caught in a storm of automatic fire and explosions 35 km from Bileca. The militiamen threw themselves to the ground crying, 'Siamo italiani! Siamo italiani!' (we are Italians!) at which point the firing suddenly stopped and a group of sheepish Serbs emerged from the undergrowth to apologize for mistaking the fascists for Ustasha. They also reported that in the next village they had found 200 Serb corpses.[40]

The situation was rapidly becoming intolerable for the Italian occupation forces. As the Serbs took to the hills and fired back, the Italian army got caught in the cross-fire. In the meantime they had to watch as the 'friendly and allied independent state of Croatia' committed atrocities in front of their barracks. On 24 June the governor of Dalmatia, Giuseppe Bastianini, wrote a strong letter to Rome. Italian troops were

> constrained to stand by inactive in the face of such acts carried out under their very eyes . . . I cannot guarantee that in reaction to some act of violence carried out in our presence there will not be an energetic intervention which could collide with the sensibilities and sentiments of the local 'lords and masters'.[41]

The Vatican too had problems with the new state which pressed its claims by every means available. The British minister, for example, demanded that the Holy See condemn 'the brutal and unjustified attack on Yugoslavia' as did the exiled government of the kingdom of Yugoslavia, still accredited to the Holy See.[42] The Croatians pressed hard for full recognition as a Catholic state. When Pavelić came to Rome to sign the state treaty with Italy, the Pope refused to receive him as a head of state but conceded 'an audience without exteriority, as to a private person, as to a simple Catholic'.[43]

In the long run the Vatican could not leave the new state without any direct diplomatic channels, and in late July 1941 Cardinal Maglione informed Archbishop Stepinac that His Holiness intended to send an Apostolic Visitor to the bishops, not a Nuncio to the state. The Pope named a Benedictine father, Monsignor Ramiro Marcone, for this delicate mission.[44] Although Mgr Marcone spoke no Croatian, his secretary, Father Masucci, soon learned it and for the greater part of the war the two Benedictines passed on vital information from and to the Holy See. By August 1941, the Vatican understood only too well what was happening in Croatia. The Roman Catholic archbishop of Belgrade begged the Pope to intervene to prevent 'the violent persecutions being carried out in the kingdom of Croatia against the Orthodox Serbs . . . an outrage to good sense and civil law . . . not to mention Christian charity'.[45]

In November 1941, Bishop Mišić, the Roman Catholic bishop of Mostar, wrote to Archbishop Stepinac:

a reign of terror has come to pass . . . men are captured like animals. They are slaughtered, murdered; living men are thrown off cliffs. The under-prefect of Mostar, Bajić, a Moslem has said – he should keep silent and not utter such things – that at Ljubinje in a single day 700 schismatics were thrown into their graves. From Mostar and Capljina a train took six carloads of mothers, young girls and children ten years old to the station at Surmanci . . . they were led up the mountains and mothers together with their children were thrown alive off the precipices.[46]

The archbishop wrote another letter to the Poglavnik and protested. The episcopal conference met and sent in a protest but at the state opening of parliament in February 1942, the archbishop blessed its proceedings and the Poglavnik.[47] On the first anniversary of the establishment of the NDH, *Katolički List* wrote enthusiastically that

under the former government freemasons, Jews, communists and such people had a big say and abortion was widely practised. . . . One year of freedom and independence and what a rich harvest for the Croatian people. The NDH is a renewal of Zvonimir's Croatia and the Poglavnik follows in his footsteps.

A solemn *Te Deum* was celebrated and the archbishop preached a sermon.[48]

Private protests and interventions continued. The Germans, well informed as always, regarded Stepinac as *judenfreundlich* (friendly towards the Jews)[49] and even the Yugoslav government-in-exile grudgingly admitted in July 1942 that 'according to reports from Serbs in Zagreb Stepinac is behaving well'.[50] Yet he never spoke out or openly criticized Pavelić and his regime. Nor did he imitate his colleague in Slovakia who had a pastoral letter read out, signed by the entire Slovak episcopate, condemning the deportation of the Jews.[51]

The silence of Archbishop Stepinac recalls the greater silence of Pius XII and the Holy See. In October 1942 d'Arcy Godolphin Osborne, British minister to the Holy See, wrote a furious letter to Monsignor Tardini, Vatican under-secretary of state, complaining that if His Holiness granted an audience to Pavelić, it would create a very bad impression in England: 'the Croatian regime over which he presides and his Ustaschi [*sic!*] have been responsible for the murder of some 600,000 Serbs and at the present moment his troops are destroying Serbian villages in Bosnia and exterminating the Serbian population.'

Monsignor Tardini noted that in conversation with the ambassador he had responded that Osborne, who had not been instructed by his government to make such a protest, had exceeded his competence. In the margin he observed 'il Ministro è, da qualche tempo, un po' eccitato' (the Minister is . . . a little excited).[52] Whatever passion or cries of outrage the Vatican archives reveal always come from the outside; for Maglione and his staff the whole world appeared to be 'un po' eccitato'. Harold Macmillan caught the special atmosphere when he had an audience with the Pope in 1944:

> A sense of timelessness – time means nothing here, centuries come and go, but this is like living in a sort of fourth dimension. And at the centre of it all, past the papal guards, and the monsignori, and the bishops, and the cardinals, and all the show of ages – sits the little saintly man, rather worried, obviously quite selfless and holy – at once a pathetic and tremendous figure.[53]

Archbishop Stepinac shared with the Pope the selflessness, the austerity and, from reports of those close to him, the holiness as well. But his world was not timeless. He lived amidst the terrors and dangers of the greatest charnel house in human history. Moreover, as the scanty evidence presented so far makes clear, there can be no question that he did not know what was going on. He was not an old man: he had been consecrated when not yet 40 and was in his mid-forties during the Second World War. He showed great personal courage and dignity both during his trial by the communist regime in 1946 as a war criminal and in the long years of imprisonment which he had to undergo. Some commentators have argued that Pius XII was simply weak. Nobody has ever suggested such a thing about Archbishop Alojzije Stepinac. Why then did he keep silent?

Part of the answer can be read in a circular he published after the bombing of Zagreb on 22 February 1944:

> I raise my voice in bitter protest and justified condemnation against those who do not flinch from any measures . . . and are destroying the living organism of the Croatian people . . . Croats have fought over the centuries to defend the ideals of real human freedom and Christian culture. . . . Because of which the Pope, the greatest defender of real culture and freedom of mankind, gave them the honourable title of 'Antemurale Christianitatis'.

A few days later he declared in a letter to d'Arcy Osborne that 'without exaggeration one can assert that no people during this war has been so cruelly stricken as the unhappy Croatian people':[54] not a view which would have been shared by Jews, Poles, Great Russians, Ukrainians, White Russians, Serbs or Gypsies. Stepinac failed to see that because in the end Croatians were the only people who mattered to him, and with the exception of those Italians he had known as a seminarian, the only people he had ever known. Archbishop Stepinac saw himself as the pastor to his people; he was both archbishop and nationalist. Indeed, as we have seen, nationalism in the Balkans was hardly a secular category; to be Croatian was to be Catholic. In this respect the charges made at his trial in 1946 were correct. He had welcomed the foundation of the NDH; he had repeatedly said prayers and offered thanksgiving for it; he had celebrated with ecclesiatical pomp and splendour its official holidays and its leader's birthday. He had half-condoned atrocities because they were committed by 'our' people and not 'theirs'. The Croatian emissary to the Holy See, Nicola Rusinović, noted with satisfaction during the archbishop's visit to Rome in 1942 that Stepinac was 'really belligerent about the potential enemies of our country. . . . In his attack on the Serbs, the Cetniks and the Communists as the cause of all the evil that has befallen Croatia he produced arguments that not even I knew.'[55]

In a visit to Rome in late May 1943, the archbishop told Prince Lobkow-icz, who had replaced Rusinović as emissary of the Independent State of Croatia to the Holy See, that

> he had kept quiet about some things with which he is not at all in agreement in order to be able to show Croatia in the best possible light. He mentioned our laws on abortion, a point very well received in the Vatican. Basing his arguments on these laws, the Archbishop justified in part the methods used against the Jews, who in our country are the greatest defenders of crimes of this kind and the most frequent perpetrators of them.[56]

Such behaviour may be reprehensible but it is all too common. How many Jews excuse Israeli violations of civil rights, illegal deportations and police brutality 'to be able to show Israel in the best possible light'? After all, if given the chance, 'they' would destroy 'us'. Strong and secure national states can afford tolerance and legality; 'we' have to use every means available. 'We' are threatened with extermination.

It may help to place Archbishop Stepinac's equivocations in more familiar context if I compare him with another prelate, the late Cardinal Tomas O'Fiaich, Archbishop of Armagh and Primate of all Ireland, who died on 8 May 1990. *The Times* in its obituary wrote of him:

> His sense of identity with the Catholic people of South Armagh from whom he sprang and whose spiritual leader he became could be doubted by none who knew him. . . . The very attributes which endeared him to the local people made him appear narrow-minded and one-sided on the broader stage.

What were these attributes? 'Simple habits of speech, behaviour and leisure interests'; for example, he would regularly turn out to support the local Gaelic football team in his hometown of Crossmaglen. He was a passionate

Irish linguistic nationalist and changed his name from Fee to its Gaelic form. He taught Irish medieval history, founded and in due course presided over the association of Irish-speaking priests. He had a brilliant record of firsts and *summa cum laudes* and became lecturer and then professor at Maynooth. In 1974 he became its president. In short, he was for the non-Catholic world the very embodiment of the 'impossible Irishman', loved and revered by his people; as *The Times* put it, 'the right man at the right place at tragically the wrong time'.[57]

In Crossmaglen the time is never right. Since the seventeenth century South Armagh has been a frontier zone, the border between one ethno-religious community and another. Crossmaglen was the site of a famous atrocity in 1791 and of bomb outrages in 1991.[58] Out of Crossmaglen, son of the local primary school teacher, Cardinal Tomas O'Fiaich, a warm, pious and saintly man, rose to be Primate, while remaining not merely the spokesman but the embodiment of Crossmaglen and South Armagh.

The people of Croatia are also a border people. As Archbishop Stepinac reminded his congregation in 1944, the Pope had consecrated them by giving them 'the honourable title of *Antemurale Christianitatis*' or, as Father Ivo Guberina put it 'the bulwark and stronghold of Catholicism and Christianity in its most critical moments'.[59] And the Serbs of the area had been 'planted' by an imperial government in Vienna no less explicitly than London had settled Protestants in Ireland. The Habsburgs had encouraged sturdy Serb peasants fleeing from Turkish rule to settle in the so-called Vojna Krajina, the military districts to the west of Turkish domain. In 1630 the Habsburgs granted these Krajisnici freedom from feudal obligations to the local Croatian feudal lords. The free Serb peasantry became in time like the Jews in eastern Europe, objects of hatred and envy; they were the *Vlasi*, the 'kikes' of Croatia, alien, Orthodox in religion and, above all, under the direct and exclusive administration of the Habsburgs in Vienna. Ethnic tension was not born in 1941. As early as 1869, Ante Starcevic, the 'father of the Croatian nation', described the Serbs in the dehumanizing language which forms the intellectual precondition for genocide:

> They are the race of slaves, beasts worse than any. There are three levels of human perfection: that of the animal, that of comprehension and that of reason. Slavo-Serbs have not quite reached the first level and cannot rise above it.[60]

As Srdjan Trifkovic pointed out in a recent paper, Starcevic merely marked the beginning of a line of thinking which turned Serbs into the 'outgroup' necessary to define an exclusive Croatian identity:

> Whether the scapegoat was the Serb, the Slav, the Jew, the Czech, 'evidence' was collected to dehumanize him and subsequently remove

moral inhibitions in the treatment of him when the time came. However, while to a Nazi 'the Jew' was a necessary social and political concept, to a Frankist or an Ustasa 'the Serb' was more than that: he was an integral part of his Croatness. Without him Croatdom could not be defined, let alone practised.[61]

To be a Serb or a Croat was to be Orthodox or Catholic. As Trifkovic continues,

> In the highlands south of the Sava river, to say that a person was 'Orthodox', 'Catholic' or 'Muslim' conveyed all that one wanted to know about him. His looks, age, social status, temperament, likes and dislikes came a poor second. To the Slovaks and Poles, Catholicism was almost synonymous with national identity; to the Dinaric Croats of the *zadruga* culture, it was more: it *was* their national identity.[62]

Like Archbishop O'Fiaich, Archbishop Stepinac came from the heart of such people, a community defined by religion and by almost nothing else. He was born on 8 July 1898, in Krašić, south-west of Zagreb, into a large, prosperous peasant family. He always saw his pastoral mission in service to those peasant communities from which he, a man of the people, had sprung.

Like the Jews of Israel, the Protestants of Northern Ireland and the Afrikaners in South Africa, the Croatians are surrounded by peoples more numerous than they. They count and recount their numbers. Contraception, known in Croatian Catholic writing as 'the white plague' (*bijela kuga*), offended God's laws and betrayed the Croatian people. Religion and nation demanded the same behaviour. How could a Croatian priest, a man concerned for the future of his people, condemn a state which had not only outlawed abortion but introduced the death penalty for those daring to practise it?

*

The active, powerful presence of Roman Catholicism distinguishes the events in Croatia from those discussed elsewhere in this volume. As a matter of general policy Nazi occupation forces had instructions to avoid or contain contacts with churches and church leaders. In Croatia the Church and its faith provided a part of the ideology in whose name the Ustasha practised genocide. It is tempting, therefore, to draw too dark a line between Nazi modernity and Croatian traditionalism. Much recent research on the pervasiveness of the Nazi racial *Weltanschauung* emphasizes the power of racial dogmas and the almost mystical crusade on which they were set. The cranky theories, superstitions and occult flummery of the SS need to be taken seriously. Membership in the SS involved initiation, symbolic rites and oaths; it celebrated its festivals with mystical ceremonies and solemn formalities. The SS conceived itself as an 'Order'; they were the Jesuits of death.[63] Nor was Hitler immune from such ideas. In a famous outburst, Hitler announced to Hermann Rauschning:

> There cannot be two chosen people. We are the people of God. Does that not explain it all? Two worlds oppose each other! God's man and Satan's man. The Jew is the opposite of man, the anti-human being. The Jew is the creature of another God.[64]

Nor was Croatian genocide all that different from Nazi genocide in its objects. Hitler hated Serbs and placed them among the slave peoples, not worthy of statehood. The Nazi tendency to distinguish among peoples on some scale of biological worthiness encouraged, made possible and ultimately rewarded what Croatians had long wanted to do anyway. There is not much difference between the *Einsatzgruppen* machine-gunning pits full of Jews and the pits and trenches into which the Ustasha piled their victims. Certainly the Germans murdered more people in absolute terms than the Ustasha but those are differences of scale, not kind.

The sole distinction that I can see – and it is crucial – is emotional. Croatians hated Serbs and so they killed them. The majority of Germans – killers, abetters, condoners and uninvolved – cared little one way or the other about the fate of Jews. Hitler's rabid anti-Semitism had almost nothing to do with his successful seizure of power and seemed irrelevant to the *Wehrmacht*, the bureaucracy and the business elites. Even the killers themselves, as Christopher Browning has so chillingly shown in his brilliant new study of a reserve police battalion, had no particular animus against their victims. They even chatted with the occasional German Jew who turned up among the Polish Jews and had to be murdered with them in the pits.[65]

The language and tone of the Wannsee Protocol remind us that the uniqueness of Nazi genocide arises from its coldness, its lack of frenzy, its detached, correct, bureaucratic efficiency, its record-keeping and file references, its memoranda and liaison officers, its timetables and gas canisters, its lists of men, women and children 'deloused', 'resettled', 'specially handled', 'sent east', as problems 'solved', 'settled' and 'clarified', as actions 'to cleanse', 'purify' and 'disinfect'. Nazi genocide speaks the language of accountants, civil servants and public health workers. Occasionally it speaks openly but even then without passion or hate. On 1 August 1941, the HQ of the 2nd SS Cavalry Brigade issued the following order at 10.00 which read in its entirety as follows:

Explicit Order of the Reichsführer SS

All Jews must be shot. Drive Jewish females into the swamps.[66]

By the standards of Wannsee, the SS was overly direct but even in this case where there is no concealment, there is no passion either. The Jews to be shot are units in a murder machine. Disagreeable duty, perhaps, but one which will be carried out with that terrifying German thoroughness and rage for perfection which is the only rage that such killers allow themselves. It is the absence of hatred which makes Nazi genocide stand out in the long annals of human bestiality; it is cold, calculated and efficient murder. The Wannsee Protocol is literally murder's *memorandum*, a thing to be remembered.

NOTES

The primary and secondary sources on which this chapter rests are listed below in the notes. About half the references have been drawn from German and Italian military, political and personal archives. For the student of Croatia during the war, and especially of the relations between the German military and political authorities and the Independent State of Croatia, the personal correspondence of General Edmund Glaise von Horstenau is essential. It can be found in folders 1–13 of the file RH 31 III 'Bevollmächtigter deutscher General in Agram', housed in the West German Federal Military Archive in Freiburg. Glaise von Horstenau had a rank as SS Brigadeführer, equivalent to his *Wehrmacht* rank of Generalleutnant. Hence some of his personal correspondence is housed in the SS files in the Berlin Document Centre. Peter Broucek is the author of a three-volume edition of the papers of Glaise von Horstenau in which much of the material can be found, *Ein General im Zwielicht. Die Lebenserinnerungen Edmund Glaises von Horstenau*, 3 vols (Vienna, 1980, 1983, 1989). The Italian military and diplomatic archives are unusually rich because the Independent State of Croatia was nominally an Italian protectorate. In order to make reference to these primary sources less tedious, I refer to the page and note number in my recent book, *All or Nothing: The Axis and the Holocaust 1941–1943* (London/New York, Routledge, 1990) as follows: 'Steinberg, p. 274, n. 134'. The other primary source used in this paper is the diplomatic documentation published by the Vatican itself in the series *Actes et documents du Saint Siège relatifs à la seconde guerre mondiale*, vols. 4, 5 and 8 (Libreria Vaticana, 1975), which I have abbreviated below as 'StS'. Other references are drawn from secondary sources. I do not, alas, read Croatian.

1 Holm Sundhaussen, 'Jugoslawien', in *Dimension des Völkermords. Die Zahl der jüdischen Opfer des Nationalsozialismus*, herausgegeben von Wolfgang Benz, Quellen und Darstellungen zur Zeitgeschichte, Herausgegeben vom Institut für Zeitgeschichte, Band 33 (Munich, 1991), p. 330.
2 Damir Mirković, 'Victims and perpetrators in the Yugoslav genocide 1941–1945: some preliminary observations', presented at the 22nd Annual Scholars Conference, 'The Holocaust and the German church struggle: religion, power and politics of resistance (1939–1945), 29 February–4 March 1992, University of Washington, Seattle, p. 15.
3 Heydrich to *Einsatzgruppenchefs*, 29 June 1941, Bundesarchiv Koblenz R 70/SU 32.
4 Gedächtnisprotokoll, GO Löhr, 21 November 1942, Bundesarchiv-Militärarchiv, Freiburg im Breisgau, Wehrmachtsbefehlshaber Südost (AOK 12) RH20-12/153.
5 Vladko Maček, *In the Struggle for Freedom* (University Park, Pa, 1957), p. 234.
6 ibid., p. 245.

7 J. S. Conway, 'How shall the nations repent? The Stuttgart Declaration of Guilt, October, 1945', *The Journal of Ecclesiastical History*, vol. 38, no. 4 (1987).

8 Steinberg, pp. 80, 280, n. 117–19.

9 Borgoncini Duca to Cardinal Maglione, 22 September 1941, StS, Vol. 5, No. 95, pp. 244–5.

10 Stella Alexander, *The Triple Myth. A Life of Archbishop Alojzije Stepinac*, East European Monographs Boulder No. CCXXVI (New York, 1987), p. 26.

11 ibid., p. 52.

12 Carlo Falconi, *The Silence of Pius XII*, trans. Bernard Wall (London, 1970), pp. 267–8.

13 Alexander, *The Triple Myth*, p. 90.

14 Falconi, *The Silence of Pius XII*, p. 277.

15 Steinberg, p. 271, n. 43.

16 Mark Wheeler, 'Pariahs to partisans to power: the Communist Party of Yugo-slavia', in Tony Judt (ed.) *Resistance and Revolution in Mediterranean Europe* (London, 1989), p. 124.

17 Raul Hilberg, *The Destruction of European Jews*, revised and definitive edn, 3 vols (New York and London, 1985), vol. 2, pp. 710–11.

18 Wheeler, 'Pariahs', p. 129.

19 Falconi, *The Silence of Pius XII*, p. 274.

20 Steinberg, pp. 24ff for the negotiations that led to the partitioning of the Balkan territories, which all qualified observers considered absurd.

21 Falconi, *The Silence of Pius XII*, p. 271.

22 ibid., n. 56.

23 ibid., n. 57.

24 ibid., p.272, n. 59.

25 Menachem Shelach, *Heshbon Damim. Hatzlat Yehudi Croatiah al yiday ha-italikim 1941–43* (Blood Reckoning. The Rescue of Croatian Jews by the Italians) (Tel Aviv, 1986), p. 30.

26 ibid., p. 31.

27 Falconi, *The Silence of Pius XII*, p. 308.

28 Steinberg, p. 272, n. 63.

29 ibid., n. 64.

30 ibid., n. 65.

31 ibid., n. 66.

32 ibid., n. 67.

33 Falconi, *The Silence of Pius XII*, p. 276.

34 Alexander, *The Triple Myth*, p. 68.

35 ibid., p. 90.

36 ibid., p. 105.

37 Falconi, *The Silence of Pius XII*, p. 281.

38 Alexander, *The Triple Myth*, pp. 71–2.

39 ibid., p. 71.

40 Steinberg, p. 272, n. 68.

41 ibid., n. 69.

42 Osborne to Cardinal Maglione, 7 April 1941, StS, Vol. 4, No. 313, p. 447; Legation of Yugoslavia to Cardinal Maglione, 17 May 1941, ibid., No. 355, p. 498.

43 Note from Mgr Montini, 16 May 1941, ibid., No. 348, pp. 491–2; Note from Mgr Tardini, 17 May 1941, No. 352, p. 495; Note from Mgr Montini, 18 May, No. 358, p. 500.

44 Cardinal Maglione to Archbishop Stepinac, 25 July 1941, ibid., Vol. 5, no. 21, p. 106.
45 Archbishop Joseph Ujcic to Cardinal Maglione, 24 July 1941, ibid., Vol. 5, No. 20, pp. 104–5.
46 Alexander, *The Triple Myth*, p. 80.
47 ibid., pp. 84–5.
48 ibid., p. 90.
49 Steinberg, pp. 80, 280, n. 115.
50 Alexander, *The Triple Myth*, p. 101.
51 Steinberg, pp. 119, 286, n. 132.
52 Osborne to Tardini, 3 October 1942, StS, Vol. 5, No. 498, pp. 736–7.
53 Owen Chadwick, *Britain and the Vatican during the Second World War* (Cambridge, 1986), pp. 302–3.
54 Alexander, *The Triple Myth*, pp. 104–5.
55 Falconi, *The Silence of Pius XII*, p. 314.
56 ibid., pp. 315–16.
57 *The Times*, Obituary, 10 May 1990.
58 J. Smyth, '*The Men of No Property': Irish Radicals and Popular Politics in the Late Eighteenth Century* (London, Macmillan, 1992), p. 49–50. See also pp. 40–1 for South Armagh as a troublespot and 46–7 for the frontier as an ethnic and cultural divide. I am grateful to Dr Jim Smyth, my colleague at Trinity Hall, for helping me to understand the world of nationalism in Ireland. He is, of course, not responsible for the conclusions I draw from his lessons.
59 Falconi, *The Silence of Pius XII*, p. 265.
60 Srdjan Trifkovic, 'The first Yugoslavia and the origins of Croatian separatism', unpublished paper, Hoover Institution, Stanford, Calif., 1991, p. 27.
61 ibid., p. 28.
62 ibid., p. 29.
63 John M. Steiner, 'Über das Glaubensbekenntnis der SS', in Karl-Dietrich Bracher, Manfred Funke and Hans-Adolf Jacobsen (eds) *Nationalsozialistische Diktatur 1933–1945. Eine Bilanz*, Schriftenreihe der Bundeszentrale für politische Bildung, Bonn, vol. 192 (Düsseldorf, 1983), p. 216.
64 ibid., p. 211.
65 Christopher R. Browning, *Ordinary Men. Reserve Police Battalion 101 and the Final Solution in Poland* (New York, 1992), especially, pp. 58ff, 137ff.
66 Reitende Abteilung, SS Kav.-Rgt. 2, 1.8.41, 1000, Bundesarchiv-Militärarchiv, Freiburg im Breisgau, RS 3 – 8/36.

12

HOW FAR DID VICHY FRANCE 'SABOTAGE' THE IMPERATIVES OF WANNSEE?

John P. Fox

When Germany defeated France in 1940, that country contained approximately 300,000 Jews, a significant number of whom were non-French.[1] It is calculated that 76,134 were murdered in the Nazi gas chambers in Auschwitz, Sobibor and Treblinka, or were shot by the Germans in France, or died in French concentration camps established in pursuit of France's own anti-Jewish policies.[2] Approximately 74.6 per cent of Jews in France thus escaped extermination under the Nazi *Endlösung* programme. But in a situation full of paradoxes, which hardly made for good humour in the German camp, the chief paradox is that the majority of the approximately 74,000 Jews deported from France to their deaths in the extermination camps were entrained in 1942. After Germany annexed the unoccupied zone on 11 November 1942, the number of transports and Jews deported dropped significantly.[3]

The 'results' achieved in France for the Wannsee *Endlösung* programme were clearly disappointing for the SS authorities, in themselves and in comparison with elsewhere.[4] They contrasted sharply with the exterminatory imperatives outlined at the Wannsee Conference, albeit expressed in circumlocutory language, which were summed up in Reinhard Heydrich's statement that 'in the course of the practical implementation of the Final Solution, Europe will be combed from west to east'. Apropos the words of Reichsführer-SS Heinrich Himmler at Posnan on 4 October 1943, France was also to be written into his 'page of glory in our history'.[5]

Something obviously went 'wrong' for Germany's Wannsee imperatives in France. Why? Any assessment of that situation requires us to consider two basic issues. First, what features on the German side contributed to their own sense of 'failure'? Second, as with Jacob Gens and other leaders of the eastern *Judenräte*,[6] is it possible or even necessary to 'moderate' the general condemnatory judgements about the leadership of Vichy France, Pierre Laval and Marshal Pétain, concerning their handling of the Jewish question vis-à-vis the German authorities in wartime France?[7] Did those French leaders actually 'sabotage' the French element of Wannsee?

Certainly France became a classic example of the truism that 'what governed the scale of the killings was the degree to which the Germans were able to apply their power'.[8] But because Adolf Hitler 'limited' German power from the outset by permitting Vichy France a privileged place in the Nazi 'European New Order' through the retention of degrees of sovereignty, the Germans had only themselves to blame for anything the Vichy government did to 'sabotage' those imperatives. The situation was such as almost to prompt the question: how was it that the Germans were able to achieve as much as a 25.4 per cent kill rate for Jews there?

The 'special relationship' which came to exist between the Third Reich and Vichy France was to have serious consequences for Germany's anti-Jewish policies in France in two respects. First, retention of sovereignty by the Vichy regime gave it an edge in any negotiations with the Germans. Second, because of Germany's changing fortunes in the war and Vichy's 'positive' attitudes in the Franco-German relationship, it was in Berlin's interest never to risk that regime's overthrow and replacement by a less amenable or even anti-German government. And, since a significant lack of manpower often meant the Germans were dependent upon French assistance, German policy was sometimes hostage to the domestic political fortunes of the Vichy regime.

So ubiquitous was this general aspect that, for example, Himmler was never able to extend the Yellow Star policy, in force in the occupied zone from 7 June 1942, to Vichy territory even after it was taken over by the Third Reich. This was another impediment to the clear identification of Jews, their arrest and deportation. The introduction of the Yellow Star policy in the occupied zone, and the intention to introduce it in the unoccupied zone, were matters of particular concern to the Auswärtiges Amt (German Foreign Office) and the Paris embassy because of the large numbers of non-French Jews likely to be involved, with consequent repercussions on Germany's official relations with states with which it still had diplomatic relations.[9]

Germany's position in France thus epitomized Eichmann's complaints to his Israeli interrogators about how far the extensive state apparatus necessarily involved in Germany's anti-Jewish operations at home and abroad, including that of the Auswärtiges Amt and the German railway system, the *Reichsbahn*,[10] complicated the task of the SS throughout Nazi-occupied Europe:

> it shows that evacuations were not so easy to carry out. No matter how large a German force was present, they couldn't just round up people, put them in freight cars, and ship them out. The whole

evacuation process in the European countries required stubborn, long-drawn-out negotiations.[11]

Beyond the wider political constraints on the Third Reich's position in wartime France, of which the Germans were themselves the authors, Eichmann's reference to 'long-drawn-out negotiations' also pinpoints attention on what, on the German side, was perhaps the most crucial determinant of how far and fast the Wannsee *Endlösung* programme could be pursued in France: the transportation question. The deportation process to the east depended, crucially, upon the 'special' trains, the *Sonderzüge*, which the SS authorities managed to beg and negotiate from the *Reichsbahn* and Ministry of Transport, and which then had to be slotted into complicated pan-European timetables.

But even when the SS authorities obtained their *Sonderzüge*, this was often just the beginning of their troubles. It then became incumbent on the SS to fill them to capacity with Jews and to ensure their prompt departure, otherwise Europe-wide and Auschwitz-Birkenau timetables, once that death factory began its murderous operations in the summer of 1942, could be thrown into disarray. But filling trains in France with the requisite number of Jews was never as easy or straightforward a task as the Germans envisaged, and indeed as the popular perception of Germany's position in France would have it.

It was often the case that the central requirements of the Berlin Wannsee programme, compounded by the necessity of completing tight timetable schedules, resulted in the Germans setting themselves unrealistic quotas of Jews for deportation at the local level in France. Those quotas were often unrealistic because the SS authorities, blind to everything apart from their duty to fulfil the Führer's *Endlösung* imperatives, failed to take sufficient account of important political considerations attaching to Germany's position in France, as well as Germany's remaining international relationships in Europe and the world at large.

Those broad political considerations determined, initially, that stateless and foreign Jews would be the first to be deported from France. But here the SS people were in particular difficulty. They could hardly expect those Jews to volunteer for the deportation process, while those they apprehended often fell short of the totals Himmler and Eichmann wished to remove from France. Moreover, given the diplomatic consequences involved in deporting foreign Jews, the SS was bound to negotiate with the Auswärtiges Amt and the Paris embassy on this question, a key point of bureaucratic procedure for which Martin Luther of that Office had obtained Heydrich's agreement at the Wannsee Conference.[12] But any success the Germans might expect to have in such enterprises required a *modus vivendi* with the Vichy authorities whose police forces would play a crucial role in the process. Finally, as German anti-Jewish actions led to an *anti-German* response from French public opinion, so greater numbers of non-French Jews became 'lost' within the labyrinth of French Gentile society. Trains often left Drancy for Auschwitz-Birkenau below their targeted payload. Indeed, one transport due from Bordeaux on 15 July 1942 was cancelled because only 150 stateless Jews could be found in the city. That caused Eichmann to explode with anger and to wonder aloud if France deserved to be considered as worthy of incorporation into the *Endlösung* programme.[13]

Moreover, the SS authorities faced fierce competition for scarce rolling stock from the *Wehrmacht*, whose struggle on the Eastern Front was unceasing from 1941 to 1945. In September 1942, the *Reichssicherheitshauptamt* (Reich Security Main Office – RSHA) was forced to admit that from 15 November at the latest until spring 1943, no more trains would be made available for deportation purposes.[14]

*

Vichy France has always had a bad press. And, given the severity of its own anti-Jewish policies initiated, without any prompting from the Germans, shortly after Germany's victory in June 1940 and pursued thereafter with a particularly Gallic vengeance, and the indisputable facts of French official and police cooperation in the implementation of German anti-Jewish polices before and after total occupation at the end of 1942, there would appear to be nothing which could possibly redeem the reputation of Vichy France in this respect.

Despite the appalling conditions and loss of life in the French concentration camps for stateless and other foreign Jews, forever a stain upon modern French history,[15] we can be quite certain that Vichy France would never have been associated with any kind of mass extermination programme, had it not been for Adolf Hitler having conceived that notion in the first place, and the Nazi Third Reich implementing it, by combing Europe 'from west to east' after Wannsee.

However, to appreciate the finer aspects of Vichy's alleged role in the Nazi 'Final Solution', it is necessary to bear in mind three points central also to analysis of the east European *Judenräte* under Nazism. First, what 'choice' did Vichy France have when confronted with German demands for specific numbers of Jews for deportation or 'settlement'? Second, what certain 'knowledge' did that regime have of the fate of Jews removed from their control? When 'knowledge' became 'belief' about the extermination policy, how did this affect French policy? And third, was there a 'higher purpose' to any of the strategies employed by Vichy when responding to German demands for Jews? How conscious, for example, were the Vichy authorities that, like the *Judenräte*, they too were being placed in the position of deciding *Mi le-hayim umi le-mavet* ('who shall live and who shall die')? Did Vichy at any time adopt the rationale of the *Judenräte*, summed up in the folk saying, *Chaye shoo is oykh lebn* ('respite of death is also life')?[16]

When the Nazis began to implement the Wannsee programme throughout Europe in 1942, the Vichy authorities certainly volunteered the stateless and foreign Jews for deportation by the Germans from their zone. René Bousquet, General Secretary of the French National Police, began that process on 6 May 1942 when he responded thus to Reinhard Heydrich's statement that the next transports from the occupied zone would consist mainly of stateless Jews, for 'labour purposes' in the east.[17]

The Franco-German negotiations about the deportation of Jews from France over the following months proceeded initially from the Bousquet-Heydrich meeting of 6 May 1942. But it is important to be clear about one thing. There was never any unity of purpose between the two sides because each pursued different objectives. From the outset, the Nazi intention was the extermination of all Jews in France. Himmler made this clear to his subordinates on 23 June 1942, and even the French were eventually told of Germany's intention to deport all Jews from France on 13 August 1942. But what the French were not told on any occasion was the exterminatory purpose of such deportations.[18] The Germans never made that plain to the French, to whom they lied as they did to everyone else, to an extent even to themselves.[19]

What, then, lay behind Vichy France's willingness to allow the Germans to deport non-French Jews from France? The fact is that Heydrich's statement of 6 May 1942 appeared to offer Vichy an *Endlösung* of its own to what had always been regarded as its intractable Jewish problem, the unwelcome presence of tens of thousands of foreigners who were also Jews and who had flooded into the country in the 1930s, and even in 1940.[20] Vichy's admittedly precipitate wish to take advantage of the German 'offer' to remove unwanted elements from France was therefore prompted by two considerations. First, for jingoistic and racialist motives, France could then solve its own 'refugee' problem with German assistance. Second, there was no need for a 'crisis of conscience' since the Germans stated the purpose of such deportations to be 'labour in the east', *Arbeitseinsatz*. It is on this basis alone and no other that Bousquet and other Vichy authorities negotiated with the Germans and instructed French police to round up stateless and foreign Jews for deportation. It is incorrect, therefore, to assume that Vichy France, *consciously* and *deliberately*, pursued its own policy of annihilating Jews through such forms of cooperation with the Nazis. One may certainly accuse the Vichy authorities of callousness and inhumanity in this respect, but not of mass murder.

In dealing with people to whom utter ruthlessness was second nature, the Vichy authorities must, however, also be accused of arrogance and short-sightedness. When Bousquet 'offered' Heydrich the stateless and foreign Jews on 6 May 1942, it was obvious that Vichy officials were confident they could deal successfully with what appeared to be yet another 'negotiating' issue between the Third Reich and a sovereign Vichy France. On 25 June 1942, however, the French were quickly disabused of any such notions when SS-Obersturmführer Theodor Dannecker, Adolf Eichmann's confidant in Paris, told the French that of the Jews to be deported from the occupied zone, the Germans required that a minimum of 40 per cent should possess French nationality. He added that the Germans would accept Jews who had been granted naturalization after the First World War.[21] A fortnight later, on 6 July, Dannecker observed to his RSHA superiors in Berlin that deporting the stateless and foreign Jews was only the first phase of operations in France; the second would comprise Jews naturalized after 1919 and 1927,[22] a notion entirely shared by the German Ambassador, Otto Abetz.[23]

That date, 25 June 1942, probably marks the real nemesis of the Third Reich's Wannsee policy in France, precisely when the SS felt they were about to institute that programme there. While the Third Reich's anti-Jewish policies posed an implicit threat to all Jews in France, until then there had been no blatant threat to *French* Jews, although that would soon have materialized. Dannecker's statement shook the French to the core. But irritation at this obvious threat to one important aspect of French sovereignty, control over its citizens, was probably a more powerful element in the negative response of the French than a sense of altruism for French Jews. For Dannecker's threat raised the horrendous spectre of French police acting against French (Jewish) citizens in the service of the occupying power. If pursued, public order would be at grave risk, as would the political life of the Vichy regime. Neither risk could be taken, and so Dannecker's statement of 25 June 1942 forced the French – in a defensive manner – to formalize a specific policy, as against *ad hoc* soundings of the Germans, on the deportation question. Already on 26 June, the French denied the Germans any promise to hand over Jews from the free zone, while in Cabinet, Laval also denied any such 'agreement'.[24]

When the Franco-German police negotiations resumed on 2 and 4 July 1942, however, it was the Germans who were forced to accept French conditions for the pursuance of only a limited Wannsee programme in France. Desperate to fill the trains Eichmann and others had worked so hard to obtain, and because of general manpower difficulties, the SS negotiators were only able to obtain Bousquet's promise of a joint Franco-German police action against foreign Jews throughout France in return for their acceptance of Pétain's and Laval's condition – approved by the French Cabinet on 3 July – that French Jews were to be left alone. But the manner in which they were told this was, to say the least, ambiguous. The expression used by Bousquet at his meeting with Dannecker on 2 July was that Pétain, together with Pierre Laval, 'agreed to the deportation, *as a first step* (*pour commencer*), of all stateless Jews from the Occupied and Unoccupied zones'.[25]

Did this mean that the Vichy authorities would one day permit *all* Jews resident in France to be deported to the east? Or was it simply a negotiating ploy, designed to give immediate satisfaction to the Germans in the hope that something more advantageous for the French – and French Jews – could be obtained later as part of a wider package of concessions to France granted by Hitler himself? A standard work on the subject, that by Michael Marrus and Robert Paxton, concludes that 'the cardinal point' of Laval's response 'to the final solution' was to try to 'buy off French Jews with stateless and foreign ones'.[26]

Those authors are wrong, however, as is Serge Klarsfeld,[27] to apply any reference to the Final Solution to the Franco-German police negotiations of May to July 1942,[28] the results of which largely set the pattern of Jewish deportations from France for the next two years.[29] When the French agreed, on 2 and 4 July 1942, to the deportation of stateless and foreign Jews, their 'permission', such as it was, was based on what they had been told by the Germans was the purpose of the deportations, 'labour in the east', *Arbeitseinsatz*. Nor was there anything unusual about this since Germany's 'thirst for foreign labour' was one unpalatable and well-known fact of life for occupied Europeans.[30] Such arguments, however, bring us nearer to the heart of the controversy over Vichy France and the Jewish question under Nazism.

To be valid, accusations of *conscious* French complicity in the Nazi programme of mass murder require two conditions to be present. First, that the Vichy authorities, like the Nazis, intended the extermination of the Jews. There is no basis for such an assertion. Second, that the French willingly handed over non-French Jews to the Nazis, *knowing* what their fate would be. Here, a number of difficulties arise, not least of which is when one may, with more than a degree of certainty, establish that point of 'knowledge'. There is also Walter Laqueur's valid point to consider, that 'knowledge' is not always the same as 'belief'.[31]

In this connection, two factors need to be considered. First, Vichy France, like every nation in the world, learned about Nazi atrocities in Poland and Russia after 1939 and 1941. If knowledge of *Einsatzgruppen* operations in Russia was picked up early on by western intelligence[32] and German public opinion,[33] there is no reason to doubt that similar news also reached Vichy. But to attribute to such reports anything other than the exigencies of an especially bitter military conflict would have required flights of imagination possessed by few outside the Third Reich.

Second, even when more definite reports about an extermination policy were directed to France by the BBC from 1 July 1942, fuelled by statements in the underground and communist press about the use of gas on deportees from France, one could hardly expect Vichy officials to be any different from those in London or Washington in disbelieving, in the first instance, that Germany, even the Third Reich of Adolf Hitler, could have embarked on such a path to damnation.[34] During the winter of 1942–3, however, particularly after the Allied Declaration of 17 December 1942 (including the French National Committee) warning the Third Reich of the consequences if it continued with its exterminatory policies,[35] Vichy officials had no choice but to concede the truth of reports of extermination, although for some time afterwards many people, including Jews in France, still could not bring themselves to believe in such horror.[36] But this then raised the vital question: *Quo vadis* Vichy and its involvement in the deportation process?

*

To paraphrase Winston Churchill's aphorism about Soviet Russia, one may only get close to understanding the riddle of Vichy policy in the crucial period 1942–4 if one attempts to unravel the enigma of Pierre Laval, that epitome of political casuistry. Laval, who continually proclaimed that he did not mind soiling his hands in the interests of France,[37] appeared to have outdone his apparent obsequiousness towards the Third Reich in his radio speech on 22 June 1942, when he declared that 'I desire the victory of Germany, for without it, Bolshevism would tomorrow install itself everywhere.'[38]

The public face with which he confronted representations by Quakers, the Vatican and American diplomats about the fate of Jews in France, a matter he regarded as one of domestic concern only, was indeed a callous and cynical one.[39] In August 1942, he told an American Quaker who had come to protest about the deportations that 'these foreign Jews had always been a problem in France and the French government was glad that a change in the German attitude towards them gave France an opportunity to get rid of them'.[40] As to Vatican and American 'interference' in the domestic concerns of France, he rejected their 'moralistic advice' out of hand, not only with degrees of insolence but together with threats to French clergy if they sheltered Jews in church buildings.[41]

Marrus and Paxton are undoubtedly correct to observe that 'some of Laval's attitude' in this respect 'may have been bravado designed to conceal the reality of French subjugation'.[42] This may have been true as regards outsiders, but to other Frenchmen, and to the Germans, he presented another face altogether. On 25 September 1942, for example, he told a private meeting of Prefects that 'every time a foreign Jew leaves our territory, it's one more gained for France'.[43] Laval's best biographer has concluded, therefore, that Laval 'fought very hard for the French Jews'.[44] He did so, but less out of a sense of altruism than as a means of pursuing French political and racial interests.

That altruism was a poor country cousin to political cynicism in Vichy considerations for the French Jews was perfectly illustrated in the wake of the arrests of non-French Jews by the Germans in the occupied zone on 16–17 July, and by the French in the free zone on 26–28 August 1942. The negative feelings these actions produced in the French police forces and public alike, including the Catholic church, and manifested in the widespread 'rescue' of Jews,[45] was also a clear warning to the Vichy regime of what it could expect if, as many people believed, the next victims of deportation were to be the French Jews. In this slightly convoluted manner, the fate of the French Jews moved prominently to centre-stage, at the same time as the Germans began exerting pressure on the French about denaturalization measures in order to spread the net wider for a greater harvest of Jews.[46]

The devious nature of Vichy's response to German demands to denaturalize 'recently' arrived Jews in France – always promising but hardly delivering – can only properly be understood if two considerations are borne in mind. First, that this extension of the deportation process could just about be considered if the Vichy authorities were still able to believe in German statements about *Arbeitseinsatz* in the east. Second, and more crucially, since the French would have to execute such a measure themselves, which would impinge also upon the domestic viability of the Vichy government, this immediately provided them with a supreme negotiating point in their dealings with the Germans.[47] That was seen to be vital from 13 August 1942 when the French were told that German actions against Jews in France had to be considered 'a permanent action which, in their final stages, would also involve Jews of French nationality'.[48] Going far beyond Dannecker's bombshell of 25 June, the potential political dangers of the 13 August declaration for Vichy became especially stark when related to French reactions to the Vichy roundup of 26–28 August.

In response to this complex situation, Laval outdid himself in the oblique manner in which he kept the Germans at bay, and laid the foundations for the 'rescue' of French Jews from the Nazi *Endlösung* programme. Although he professed to dismiss it, it was evident by then that he was also being affected by American and Vatican pressure about the precise fate of Jews deported from France,[49] which itself added to increasing doubts within Vichy circles about how to square the German *Tarnspruch* (camouflage language) of *Arbeitseinsatz* in the east for the Jews with persistent rumours of their extermination.

On 2 September 1942, and ever the disingenuous Machiavellian with more than half an eye on the future stability of Franco-German relations, Laval suggested to SS-General Karl Oberg, the senior SS officer in France, that to avoid discrepancies between French and German statements concerning the fate of deported Jews, he should be given some 'language guidance' on the matter, *Sprachregelung*. Both sides agreed on the statement that the Jews had been sent to Poland for labour purposes.[50] To Oberg, all this seemed perfectly reasonable, while given the paucity of trains likely to be available during the winter, it was not difficult for him to appear 'conciliatory' within the wider framework of Franco-German relations.

But persuading the Germans that he was just as concerned for their public position was only one part of Laval's involved strategy. It was imperative that he, too, obtained something in return. With specific reference to French opposition to the roundup of Jews, Laval successfully urged Oberg not to make further demands for Jews from the free zone, nor to set any more target figures. In return, and well aware of increasing German suspicions about Vichy's delays over the naturalization question,[51] Laval assured the Germans that previous agreements remained valid for the deportation of stateless and foreign Jews, and eventually for those naturalized since 1933.[52]

Laval's achievements on 2 September 1942 could be described as a passive 'holding operation'. Yet immediately, Laval showed that a more positively pro-French strategy lay behind his apparent accommodation with Oberg. Using the moratorium on further German demands for Jews as a starting point, and directly contradicting the assurances he had then given about the post-1933 denaturalization of Jews, Laval began to freeze out the Germans from approaching French Jews by delaying Vichy consideration of such laws.[53] The real significance of Laval's delaying tactics is that at the beginning of September 1942, German plans were still predicated upon a denaturalization law being passed by Vichy.[54]

The positive success Laval gained during the winter of 1942–3 may be gauged by the fact that whereas Himmler made it clear he wished to see German-occupied territory cleared of Jews by mid-1943,[55] by 25 September 1942 even the Reichsführer-SS was forced to accept Oberg's advice that to pursue the matter of French Jews for the *Endlösung* programme would have the 'gravest consequences'. Reluctantly, Himmler agreed that for the immediate future, French Jews were to be left alone,[56] an indication that by the autumn of 1942 Berlin perhaps needed Vichy more than the other way around.[57]

Laval's apparent success, however, was soon threatened by two developments beyond his control which threatened both the French Jews and his overall strategy vis-à-vis the Third Reich. The first was the German annexation of the free zone on 11 November 1942. Although Hitler declared that the armistice was still in effect and the Vichy government still sovereign, the annexation effectively breached that sovereignty, particularly since the SS now extended their powers throughout France.[58] This enabled the Germans, really for the first time, to apply direct pressure on French officials throughout the country to spread the net more widely for Jews intended for deportation to Auschwitz. The second was Hitler's decision, noted by Himmler on 10 December 1942, to order the arrest and deportation of all

Jews and other enemies of Germany in France, although this was only to be done after discussions with Laval.[59]

Despite these radical moves, Germany's success rate for the *Endlösung* programme in France actually worsened after 11 November 1942. The geographical extension of German control in France complicated the manpower aspect of occupation, part of which concerned identifying, arresting and deporting Jews in an increasingly anti-German environment. Previous German doubts about Italy's fidelity to the anti-Jewish cause were exacerbated after November 1942 when the Italians refused point-blank to allow the Germans access to Jews in the French territories they themselves controlled, although that situation changed after Italy's surrender to the Allies at the beginning of September 1943.[60] Finally, Vichy became convinced that the Third Reich had indeed lost the war.[61] The consequences of 11 November 1942, combined with military developments in North Africa and elsewhere in Europe, thus placed the Third Reich and Vichy France on a collision course.

*

While it is entirely valid to reject accusations of a *conscious* complicity in the Nazi policy of extermination by Vichy France during 1942, the picture changes somewhat during and after the winter of 1942–3. When deportations from France resumed in February 1943 because trains once more became available to the SS,[62] no one in the Vichy regime could any longer believe in the German fiction of *Arbeitseinsatz* for Jews deported to the east. Since the French government and police[63] 'cooperated' with the Germans in arresting and concentrating non-French Jews from February 1943 through to 1944, it is justified to accuse Vichy France – in this respect only – of complicity in the Nazi programme of mass murder. In this way, the Vichy authorities could be said to be jointly 'responsible' for the Nazi extermination of some 30,000 or so Jews from France. Nevertheless, that apparently damning picture requires important modification.

The deportation process from 1943, while concentrated on the stateless and foreign Jews, actually intensified Vichy police and government efforts to prevent French Jews from being deported to what was then realized was certain death in the gas chambers in the east. Those efforts took two forms. First, following the resumption of transports on 9 February 1943, the Germans were informed that Bousquet had stated no French police personnel would assist them with any transports that included French Jews arrested because they had infringed anti-Jewish regulations, especially since there was still no official Franco-German agreement on this question. While the Germans were determined that French Jews already caught would be deported alongside stateless and foreign Jews,[64] this indication of French obstructionism served merely to confirm their other doubts about how far they could count on French cooperation.[65] They were fully aware of the effect on Laval of Italy's negative attitude in the Jewish question,[66] of American pressure on Vichy France, and of French calculations that Germany had effectively lost the war. As early as February 1943, they were informed of Pétain's total opposition to the deportation of French Jews.[67]

The second main thrust of Vichy's defence of French Jews was the corollary of what, in March 1943, the Germans envisaged as one way of breaking the deadlock beginning to confront them, and for which they blamed the Italians. This was the denaturalization of tens of thousands of French Jews.[68] But this proved to be the final sticking point for Pétain and Laval who insisted that Vichy reserved to itself any 'solution' to the question of French Jews.[69] In fact, German emphasis on this strategy in March 1943 with regard to naturalizations after 1927 or 1933[70] can be directly attributable to the radio broadcast at the end of February 1943 by Louis Darquier de Pellepoix, French Commissioner-General for Jewish Affairs from 6 May 1942, in which he declared that the government should strip of citizenship all Jews naturalized since 10 August 1927. But none of de Pellepoix's previous proposals to bring about a closer coordination of Vichy anti-Jewish policies with those of the Germans were ever accepted by the Vichy government, while Pétain and Laval treated him with contempt.[71]

There then followed a veritable battle of wills throughout 1943 between the SS authorities and the Vichy government about denaturalization and an effective cut-off date.[72] On 10 June 1943, for example, the Germans were told that Laval and Justice Minister Gabolde had signed a draft denaturalization law, with a cut-off date of 10 August 1927.[73] Although this appeared to give the green light to the SS authorities to organize a massive roundup of Jews to complete the *Endlösung* programme in France,[74] they did not trust Laval because, time and again, he simply avoided committing himself.[75] Nevertheless, the Germans intended to deport those French Jews they had managed to lay their hands on, with or without such a law being ratified by Vichy.[76] Difficulties even with the French police thus appeared to confirm the impression of an underlying French 'sabotage' of Wannsee by 'sympathetic French civilians and officials' whom the Germans accused of spiriting thousands of Jews across the borders into Italian-controlled territories, and of informing Jews of the forthcoming law and massive arrests.[77]

By August 1943, and without any law being signed, the Germans finally realized they had been thoroughly hoodwinked by Laval. Together with Marshal Pétain,[78] Laval withstood intense German pressure to sign what would amount to French 'permission' for the deportation and thus certain death of tens of thousands of French Jews. After meetings with Laval on 7 and 14 August, the SS authorities finally concluded that, with or without a denaturalization law, the French police could no longer be relied upon to participate in a massive arrest programme of French Jews unless Germany's military situation radically improved.[79]

This situation simply caused the Germans to go their own way. Deportations did not cease, albeit with reduced numbers, and Alois Brunner, the 'butcher' of Salonika, was brought in to spread havoc and terror throughout France.[80] By the spring of 1944, on the eve of liberation, the SS was conducting the deportation process practically on its own since all communications between it and Vichy virtually ceased. Yet in the final days of German and Vichy authority, it was, paradoxically, a French force which acted against the Jews with as much vigour as Brunner's 'search and destroy' units. This was the Milice, a paramilitary force created within the veterans' Légion. But even they could hardly hope to succeed where their German paymasters had ultimately failed.[81]

*

Despite the complexities of the French case in the Nazi Wannsee programme, at one level, simple and uncomplicated conclusions may be drawn. The Vichy government cannot be accused, throughout and without qualification, of any *conscious* and *determined* complicity in the Nazi process of extermination. In 1942, the Vichy regime displayed the utmost callousness because it welcomed the deportation of stateless and foreign Jews – for what it thought was 'labour in the east' – for purely French jingoistic and racialist reasons. But it did not then 'collaborate', knowingly and willingly, in the Nazi system of extermination because, for most of that year, it either knew nothing about the extermination programme or, like other observers, found it impossible to believe in such a thing. Its 'protection' of French Jews from German encroachments that year was undertaken more from concern to maintain certain principles of French sovereignty than for altruistic reasons.

From 1943, when it cannot be denied that knowledge of the extermination process was widespread throughout Europe, Vichy France may be accused of *a degree of complicity* in the Nazi extermination process because it did nothing to prevent further German deportation of the non-French Jews. On the other hand, the Vichy authorities and the French people then did a great deal to obstruct German objectives to make the whole of France *judenfrei* by blocking the deportation of the mass of French Jews.[82] Clearly, Vichy actions, compounded by other factors, successfully 'sabotaged' the Wannsee imperatives in France.

Yet there is more to the French case than is immediately apparent from these rather bald observations. Throughout, one is reminded of many of the debating points surrounding the eastern *Judenräte*. But that historical analogy can be taken back even further by asking whether the case of Vichy France and the Nazi Wannsee *Endlösung* programme does not also confront us with the moral issues raised by Mark Antony in his funeral oration for Julius Caesar when he stated, 'the evil that men do lives after them, the good is oft interred with their bones'.

Seen from a Jewish perspective apropos the teachings of Maimonedes concerning the dilemmas involved in the appeasement of an enemy by handing over 'sacrifices' to preserve the rest of the community,[83] the actions of Vichy France indeed paralleled the practical and moral dilemmas of the eastern *Judenräte* when confronted with Nazi demands for Jewish victims for the gas chambers. Does this require us, then, to grant Vichy France a greater degree of 'understanding' because of the human dilemmas involved in its case, especially since, although it 'assisted' in sending over 74,000 Jews from France to their deaths in the Nazi extermination camps, it undoubtedly 'prevented' the extermination of at least over 200,000 others? How laudatory should we be about those deliberate Vichy policies of 'rescue', doubts by Marrus and Paxton about the 'consciousness' of it notwithstanding?[84] That the position would have been far worse had Vichy not acted in the way it did, or had 'allowed' the Germans free rein to pursue whatever policies they wished, there can be no doubt.[85] But who, finally, is to be the *absolute* judge of such matters?

NOTES

1 Cf. Juliane Wetzel, 'Frankreich und Belgien', pp. 105–35, in Wolfgang Benz (ed.) *Dimension des Völkermords. Die Zahl der jüdischen Opfer des National-sozialismus* (Munich, 1991), especially p. 109. Raul Hilberg, *The Destruction of the European Jews* (London, 1961), p. 392, suggests that before May 1940 the Jewish population in France was around 270,000, supplemented afterwards by 40,000 Jewish refugees from Belgium, Holland and Luxemburg who fled from the advancing German *Wehrmacht*. Lucy S. Dawidowicz, *The War Against the Jews* (London, 1975), p. 360, sets the figure in 1940 at around 350,000.

2 Wetzel, 'Frankreich und Belgien', p. 127. For Vichy France and the Jewish question, see Michael R. Marrus and Robert O. Paxton, *Vichy France and the Jews* (New York, 1983).

3 Before 11 November 1942, forty-four transports carrying approximately 41,400 Jews, i.e. 56 per cent of the total to be killed, departed from France with the full cooperation of the Vichy authorities. During 1943 and 1944, however, when the Germans *ostensibly* had total control in France, and when the Wannsee programme was being accelerated in other countries, those figures for France dropped significantly. In 1943, only nineteen transports with 17,800 Jews departed, while in 1944 only fifteen transports carried 14,600 Jews to the east (cf. Wetzel, 'Frankreich und Belgien', pp. 132–3; I have rounded out Serge Klarsfeld's first figures, whose total is lower than the final one arrived at by Wetzel).

4 At the Wannsee Conference of 20 January 1942, France was (inaccurately) listed as having 865,000 Jews in the occupied and unoccupied zones. For two published versions of the protocol of the Wannsee Conference in German and English, see *Akten zur deutschen auswärtigen Politik 1918–1945*, Serie E. Band I. Document 150 (Göttingen, 1969; hereafter ADAP), and Raul Hilberg (ed.),

Documents of Destruction. Germany and Jewry 1933–1945 (London, 1972), pp. 89–99.

5 Gerald Reitlinger, *The Final Solution. The Attempt to Exterminate the Jews of Europe 1939–1945* (London, 1968, second revised and augmented edn), pp. 317–18.

6 The seminal study on the *Judenräte* – Jewish Councils – in Nazi-occupied eastern Europe remains that by Isaiah Trunk, *Judenrat. The Jewish Councils in Eastern Europe Under Nazi Occupation* (New York, 1972).

7 The most valuable biography of Pierre Laval in English remains that by Geoffrey Warner, *Pierre Laval and the Eclipse of France* (London, 1968). See also Hubert Cole, *Laval. A Biography* (London, 1963), p. 122, where it is claimed that Laval was 'violently opposed to racial persecution'.

8 Marrus and Paxton, *Vichy France*, p. 357.

9 Cf. filmed copies of the documents of the German Foreign Office, Library, Foreign and Commonwealth Office, London (hereafter AA): AA 4851/E247657 and E247656, Vermerk Rademacher, Berlin, 18 May 1942 (Inland II geheim: Kennzeichnung der deutschen Juden); idem, E247653–4, Aufzeichnung Woermann, Berlin, 19 May 1942; idem, E247645, Luther/Abetz, Berlin, 21 May 1942; idem, E247635, Abetz/AA, Paris, 21 May 1942; idem, E247644, AA record of Zeitschel communication of Abetz's telegram; ADAP E. II. Document 230, Luther/Paris, Berlin, 21 May 1942; Imperial War Museum, Case XI, FO 646. Document Book 60-B, Document NG-3668, Zeitschel/MBF, Oberg, Paris, 22 May 1942; AA 4851/E247629–30, Abetz/AA, Paris, 5 June 1942. See also Hilberg, *The Destruction*, p. 405; Marrus and Paxton, *Vichy France*, p. 235–40; Robert O. Paxton, *Vichy France, Old Guard and New Order 1940–1944* (London, 1972), p. 184; Reitlinger, *The Final Solution*, pp. 334–5.

10 Cf. the short but informative study by Raul Hilberg, *Sonderzüge nach Auschwitz* (Mainz, 1981), and Heiner Lichtenstein, *Mit der Reichsbahn in den Tod. Massentransporte in den Holocaust 1941 bis 1945* (Cologne, 1985).

11 Jochen von Lang and Claus Sibyll, *Eichmann Interrogated. Transcripts from the Archives of the Israeli Police* (London, 1982), pp. 99, 145–6. See also Dr Rudolf Aschenauer (ed.) *Ich, Adolf Eichmann. Ein historischer Zeugenbericht* (Leoni am Starnberger See, 1980), pp. 309–22; Leni Yahil, ' "Memoirs" of Adolf Eichmann', *Yad Vashem Studies*, XVIII (1987), pp. 133–62.

12 Not surprisingly, the agreement of the Auswärtiges Amt and the Paris embassy was always forthcoming. Yet the manner of Adolf Eichmann's request on 22 June 1942 for formal 'approval' for the transportation of 40,000 Jews from the occupied zone in the period July–August for the purpose of 'labour in the Auschwitz camp' indicated that he felt his actions were not really dependent upon any reply he received: ADAP E. III. Document 26, Eichmann/Rademacher, Berlin, 22 June 1942.

13 Hilberg, *The Destruction*, p. 407; Serge Klarsfeld, *Vichy-Auschwitz. Die Zusammenarbeit der deutschen und französischen Behörden bei der 'Endlösung der Judenfrage' in Frankreich* (Nördlingen, 1989), pp. 406–7, Vermerk Röthke/Dannecker, Paris, 15 July 1942.

14 Klarsfeld, *Vichy-Auschwitz*, p. 464, Aufzeichnung Zeitschel, Paris, 16 September 1942.

15 Marrus and Paxton, *Vichy France*, pp. 165–76.

16 Trunk, *Judenrat*, pp. xxix, xxxi.

17 Klarsfeld, *Vichy-Auschwitz*, p. 57; ADAP E. Band III. Document 283, Bericht 4004, Schleier/Auswärtiges Amt, Paris, 11 September 1942; Marrus and Paxton, *Vichy France*, p. 232.

18 Klarsfeld, *Vichy-Auschwitz*, pp. 390–1, Vermerk Dannecker, Eichmann, Paris, 1 July 1942; ibid., pp. 432–3, Vermerk Röthke/Knochen, Lischka, Hagen, Paris, 13 August 1942.

19 Cf. Marrus and Paxton, *Vichy France*, p. 351:

> the Nazis did their best to hide, from all but a few administrators and security officials, the murder of millions of Jews. . . . In France, the German occupation authorities told their subordinates to use guarded language and to hide the real objectives of the deportations.

Cf. also Hilberg, *The Destruction*, pp. 646–62.

20 Cf. Klarsfeld, *Vichy-Auschwitz*, pp.445–6, Bericht Geissler/Knochen, Vichy, 29 August 1942, for a report on Bousquet's telephone conversation with the Chief of the Swiss Police, during which he exclaimed, 'you know that I am prepared to give Jews to anyone who will take them out of France. If you would like to have them, I'll give you all of them.'

21 Klarsfeld, *Vichy-Auschwitz*, pp. 70 ff.; ibid., pp. 385–6, Vermerk Dannecker/ Knochen, Lischka, Paris, 26 June 1942; ibid., pp. 386–7, Vermerk Röthke, Paris, 26 June 1942.

22 Klarsfeld, *Vichy-Auschwitz*, pp. 399–400, Bericht Dannecker/RSHA, Paris, 6 July 1942. At an RSHA meeting in Berlin on 11 June, it was agreed that an initial figure of 100,000 Jews should be deported from the whole of France. But German uncertainty on how to deal with the French led them to propose a figure of only 10,000 at the meetings of 25 and 26 June. On 27 June, however, Karl-Theodor Zeitschel impressed upon Ambassador Abetz the urgency of pressure upon Pierre Laval to accede to the deportation of 50,000 Jews from the free zone. Cf. Klarsfeld, *Vichy-Auschwitz*, pp. 100–1; ibid., pp. 379–80, Vermerk Dannecker/Knochen, Lischka, Paris, 15 June 1942; ibid., p. 388, Schreiben Zeitschel/Befehlshaber der Sicherheitspolizei und des SD, Frankreich, Paris, 27 June 1942; ibid., p. 389, Aufzeichnung Zeitschel/Abetz, Paris, 27 June 1942; Marrus and Paxton, *Vichy France*, pp. 231, 324.

23 Agreeing on 2 July 1942 to SS requests that 40,000 Jews be transported for 'labour in the Auschwitz camp', Abetz emphasized it had always been the embassy's purpose to exacerbate anti-Semitic sentiment in France. This was especially strong against foreign Jews, just as similar feelings in Germany had been directed against the 'flood' of *Ostjuden*. He felt it would have a positive psychological effect upon most Frenchmen if foreign Jews were deported first, and French Jews drawn into the process only when foreign Jews did not fill the required quotas. This would not mean giving French Jews a privileged position since they would 'likewise vanish in the course of liberating the European countries from Jewry': ADAP E. III. Document 58, tel. nr. 2784, Abetz/ AA, Paris, 2 July 1942. For Abetz's role in wartime France, see my critique of Christopher Browning's conclusions about German 'diplomats' and the Nazi Final Solution entitled 'German bureaucrat or Nazified ideologue? Ambassador Otto Abetz and Hitler's anti-Jewish policies 1940–44', in Michael Graham Fry (ed.), *Power, Personalities and Policies: Essays in Honour of Donald Cameron Watt* (London, 1992), pp. 175–232.

24 Klarsfeld, *Vichy-Auschwitz*, p. 80; Marrus and Paxton, *Vichy France*, p. 233.

25 Klarsfeld, *Vichy-Auschwitz*, pp. 393–7, Aktenvermerk Hagen/Oberg, Paris, 4 July 1942; ibid., pp. 398–9, Vermerk Dannecker/Knochen, Lischka, Paris, 6 July 1942; Marrus and Paxton, *Vichy France*, pp. 233–4. In his post-war defence, Laval wrote of this decision, thus: 'I did all I could, considering the fact that my first duty was to my fellow-countrymen of Jewish extraction whose interests

I could not sacrifice. . . . How could the Jews have been better protected in a country where the Gestapo ran riot?' (Hilberg, *The Destruction*, p. 407).

26 Marrus and Paxton, *Vichy France*, p. 234.

27 Klarsfeld, *Vichy-Auschwitz*, p. 325.

28 Marrus and Paxton, *Vichy France*, compound this error of directly linking Vichy actions and Nazi extermination policy, at least for 1942, in their further discussions on pp. 362–3. Likewise Cole, *Laval*, p. 211–12.

29 Equally misleading are statements in Paul Webster, *Pétain's Crime. The Full Story of French Collaboration in the Holocaust* (London, 1990), pp. 67, 86, 116, 121–2, compounded by faulty translations of key German documents: cf. ibid., p. 109, with Klarsfeld, *Vichy-Auschwitz*, pp. 385–6, Vermerk Dannecker/ Knochen, Lischka, Paris, 26 June 1942, especially the paragraph beginning, 'Auf den Einwand es Leguay'.

30 Marrus and Paxton, *Vichy France*, p. 352. On foreign labour in the Third Reich, cf. Edward L. Homze, *Foreign Labor in Nazi Germany* (Princeton University Press, 1967).

31 Cf. Walter Laqueur, *The Terrible Secret. An Investigation into the Suppression of Information About Hitler's 'Final Solution'* (London, 1980).

32 Cf. F. H. Hinsley, *British Intelligence in the Second World War*. Vol. Two: *Its Influence on Strategy and Operations* (London, Her Majesty's Stationery Office, 1981), Appendix 5, 'The German police cyphers', pp. 669–73. The British 'Postal and telegraph censorship reports on Jewry 1941–42' contains intelligence about the anti-Jewish operations of the *Einsatzgruppen* in Russia obtained by the Allied authorities through radio traffic: Public Record Office, Kew, Home Office Correspondence, HO 213, Vol. 953, GEN. 462/2/6.

33 Cf. David Bankier, 'The Germans and the Holocaust: what did they know?', *Yad Vashem Studies*, XX (Jerusalem, 1990), pp. 69–98; idem, *The Germans and the Final Solution* (Oxford, 1991); Ian Kershaw, 'The persecution of the Jews and German popular opinion in the Third Reich', *Leo Baeck Institute Yearbook* (LBYB), XXVI (1981), pp. 261–89; idem, *Popular Opinion and Political Dissent in the Third Reich: Bavaria 1933–1945* (Oxford, 1983); Hans-Heinrich Wilhelm, 'The Holocaust in National-Socialist rhetoric and writings. Some evidence against the thesis that before 1945 nothing was known about the "Final Solution" ', *Yad Vashem Studies*, XVI (Jerusalem, 1984), pp. 95–127; Jörg Wollenberg (ed.) *'Niemand war dabei und keiner hat's gewußt'. Die deutsche Öffentlichkeit und die Judenverfolgung 1933–45* (Munich, 1989).

34 Marrus and Paxton, *Vichy France*, pp. 347–8.

35 Cf. John P. Fox, 'The Jewish factor in British war crimes policy in 1942', *The English Historical Review*, Vol. XCII, No. 362 (January 1977), pp. 82–106.

36 Marrus and Paxton, *Vichy France*, pp. 348–9.

37 Cole, *Laval*, p. 209.

38 Laval later admitted that he knew his words would be 'like a drop of sulphuric acid . . . on the skin of suffering people', but he maintained that he had included them in order to convince the Germans of his sincerity, so that he could obtain more concessions from them (Warner, *Pierre Laval*, pp. 300–2). In the event, 'a large section of the nation was incensed that a Frenchman should have publicly wished for the triumph of their brutal conquerors' (Cole, *Laval*, p. 208).

39 Cf. Klarsfeld, *Vichy-Auschwitz*, pp. 144–6.

40 Hilberg, *The Destruction*, p. 409; Marrus and Paxton, *Vichy France*, p. 261; Warner, *Pierre Laval*, p. 306.

41 Cf. Klarsfeld, *Vichy-Auschwitz*, p. 436, tel. nr. 212, Bergen/AA, Rome, 18

August 1942; ibid., p. 440, tel. nr. 211, Wöhring/AA, Vichy, 24 August 1942; ADAP E. III, Document 242, Bericht 3732, Abetz/AA, Paris, 28 August 1942; ibid., Document 247, Bericht 3762, Abetz/AA, Paris, 31 August 1942. Laval's threats to the clergy were real: cf. Klarsfeld, *Vichy-Auschwitz*, pp. 450–1, Bericht 3818, Abetz/AA, Paris, 2 September 1942; Hilberg, *The Destruction*, pp. 409–10; Marrus and Paxton, *Vichy France*, p. 272; Webster, *Pétain's Crime*, pp. 125–6.

42 Marrus and Paxton, *Vichy France*, p. 261.

43 Warner, *Pierre Laval*, p. 306.

44 ibid. In his post-war defence, Laval claimed that it was an insult to accuse him of persecuting Jews (Webster, *Pétain's Crime*, p. 50).

45 Hilberg, *Die Vernichtung*, Band 2, pp. 676–7; Klarsfeld, *Vichy-Auschwitz*, pp. 153–7, 162–5; Marrus and Paxton, *Vichy France*, pp. 250–62, 270–9; Webster, *Pétain's Crime*, pp. 120 ff. Cf. Klarsfeld, *Vichy-Auschwitz*, p. 458, for the report of 9 September 1942 by the German Consul in Vichy, Krug von Nidda, about these developments.

46 Klarsfeld, *Vichy-Auschwitz*, pp. 422–4, Vermerk Röthke/Knochen, Lischka, Oberg, Paris 28 July 1942; ibid., pp. 425–6, Bericht SS-Standartenführer/Chef des Generalstabes beim Militärbefehlshaber in Frankreich, Paris, 30 July 1942.

47 Cf. Klarsfeld, *Vichy-Auschwitz*, pp. 426–7, Aktennotiz Hagen, Paris, 1 August 1942, when Bousquet said the French government, including Pétain and Laval, was prepared to consider a denaturalization law. But four days later, Laval already began to drag his feet. He was prepared to agree to such a measure, with a cut-off date of 1933, but emphasized that it had to be dealt with gradually since otherwise the disadvantages would outweigh any advantages (ibid., p. 429, Aktenvermerk Hagen/Heinrichsohn, Röthke, Paris, 4 August 1942).

48 ibid., pp. 432–3, Vermerk Röthke/Knochen, Lischka, Hagen, Paris, 13 August 1942.

49 This point was actually acknowledged by the Germans (ibid., pp. 459–62, Vermerk Röthke/Knochen, Lischka, Hagen, Paris, 12 September 1942).

50 ibid., p. 454, Aktenvermerk Hagen/Oberg, Paris, 4 September 1942. According to Klarsfeld (pp. 101–2), Laval had told his Cabinet colleagues at the decisive meeting on 3 July 1942 that since it was the German intention to create a Jewish state in Europe, there were no problems about sending the stateless Jews to such a place. After the war, he claimed that General Oberg had told him it was the German government's intention 'to set up a Jewish state in Poland'. Laval's private secretary, André Guénier, has written that Laval never suspected what fate awaited the deportees in the east, and that had he known, 'he would have denounced the fact before the civilised world and would have refused any contact with the representatives of a government indulging in such acts of barbarism'. Warner's comment on this erstwhile defence appears to be valid: 'this is hard to credit, but it may just be possible that Laval did succeed in convincing himself that no harm would come to those Jews he handed over to the Germans' (Warner, *Pierre Laval*, p. 306).

51 Klarsfeld, *Vichy-Auschwitz*, pp. 442–3, Vermerk Heinrichsohn/Knochen, Paris, 27 August 1942; ibid., pp. 449–50, Vermerk Röthke, Paris, 1 September 1942.

52 ibid., pp. 451–3, Aktenvermerk Hagen, Paris, 3 September 1942. Cf. ibid., p. 429, Aktenvermerk Hagen/Heinrichsohn, Röthke, Paris, 4 August 1942, for Laval's promise to Knochen on 3 August about the denaturalization of Jews who entered France from 1933. In Laval's view, and probably not his alone, such Jews – inevitably refugees from Nazism – were undoubtedly still 'foreign' and had no valid claim to that jealously guarded Holy Grail, French citizenship.

53 ibid., pp. 456–8, Vermerk Röthke/Knochen, Lischka, Hagen, Paris, 9 September 1942; ibid., pp. 459–62, Vermerk Röthke/Knochen, Lischka, Hagen, Paris, 12 September 1942.

54 ibid., p. 453, Vermerk Ahnert, Paris, 3 September 1942.

55 ibid., pp. 456–8, Vermerk Röthke/Knochen, Lischka, Hagen, Paris, 9 September 1942, the record of Röthke's conversation with Leguay on 8 September from which the Germans first realized that Laval's assurances to Oberg on 2 September could not be relied upon. This was further acknowledged in an assessment by Röthke (ibid., pp. 459–62, Vermerk Röthke/Knochen, Lischka, Hagen, Paris, 12 September 1942).

56 ibid., p. 469, Fernschreiben Knochen/RSHA Berlin, Paris, 25 September 1942.

57 Abetz's own frustration about the difficulties confronting Germany's efforts to extend the Yellow Star policy to Jews of many more nationalities in France, led him to exclaim that 'enemy propaganda' was thereby enabled to categorize the Third Reich's anti-Jewish actions simply as questions of 'nationality'. He was deeply offended that these policies were not seen in their true light, as a 'racial question': AA 2257/478665–6, Bericht 1738, Abetz/AA, Paris, 7 September 1942 (Inland II geheim. 55: Juden in Frankreich).

58 Marrus and Paxton, Vichy France, pp, 302ff.

59 ibid., pp. 304–5; Norman Rich, Hitler's War Aims. Volume II: The Establishment of the New Order (London, 1974), p. 230.

60 Cf. Hilberg, The Destruction, pp. 413–18; Klarsfeld, Vichy-Auschwitz, pp. 194–9, 206, 213–15, 218–28, 233–5.

61 Cf. Hilberg, The Destruction, p. 411.

62 Cf. Eichmann's letter of 19 December 1942 to Knochen about such arrangements: Klarsfeld, Vichy-Auschwitz, p. 476, Schreiben Eichmann/Knochen, Berlin, 19 December 1942; ibid., p. 476, Schreiben Knochen/RSHA Berlin, Paris, 31 December 1942; ibid., p. 479, Erlaß Knochen/Sipo Kommandos, Paris, 26 January 1943.

63 Klarsfeld, Vichy-Auschwitz, p. 495, Bericht Lischka/Müller, Paris, 24 February 1943, on the participation of French police in arresting 2,000 Jews in 'the old and newly-occupied territories'. Cf. Marrus and Paxton, Vichy France, pp. 306–10.

64 Klarsfeld, Vichy-Auschwitz, pp. 486–7, Vermerk Röthke/Knochen, Paris, 10 February 1943; ibid., p. 513–15, Vermerk Röthke/Lischka, Hagen, Paris, 23 March 1943.

65 Continued French opposition to the Yellow Star forced Helmut Knochen to admit to Gestapo chief Heinrich Müller in February 1943, that 'in the newly-occupied zone, the French Government remains sovereign' (ibid., pp. 489–91, Knochen/Müller, Paris, 12 February 1943).

66 The Auswärtiges Amt, the Paris embassy, and the Sicherheitsdienst forces acknowledged that immediate and full implementation of German anti-Jewish measures in the recently occupied 'free' zone was unlikely, given the obstructionist attitude of the Italians in their zones of France (Klarsfeld, Vichy-Auschwitz, p. 475, Erlaß 5884, Luther/Paris, Berlin, 14 December 1942; ADAP E. V. Document 69, Bericht 508, Schleier/AA, Paris, 23 January 1943; Klarsfeld, Vichy-Auschwitz, p. 488, Schreiben Achenbach/Röthke, Paris, 11 February 1943).

67 Marrus and Paxton, Vichy France, p. 305. That Germany's total occupation of France did not presage a total implementation of the Wannsee imperatives in France (or any other German anti-Jewish measures) was perforce admitted in two communications from Helmut Knochen, Befehlshaber der Sipo-SD (Com-

mander of the Security Police – Security Service) in Paris to Gestapo chief, Heinrich Müller, in February 1943 following his discussions with representatives of Bousquet: Klarsfeld, *Vichy-Auschwitz*, pp. 489–91, Schreiben Knochen/ Müller, Paris, 12 February 1943 and pp. 493–4, Schreiben Knochen/Müller, Paris, 22 February 1943; Marrus and Paxton, *Vichy France*, pp. 315–21. Knochen's reference to Pétain's attitude having a negative effect upon the French police appeared to be confirmed during March 1943 when the latter refused to be involved in transports from Drancy containing French Jews. German complaints on this score were compounded by those concerning Vichy's continuing obduracy on the denaturalization question (Klarsfeld, *Vichy-Auschwitz*, pp. 515–16, Aktenvermerk Hagen/Oberg, Paris, 25 March 1943).

68 Cf. Klarsfeld, *Vichy-Auschwitz*, pp. 230–3, 238 ff.

69 ibid., pp. 513–15, Vermerk Röthke/Lischka, Hagen, Paris, 23 March 1943; ibid., p. 519, Bericht Knochen/Eichmann, Paris, 29 March 1943.

70 ibid., *Vichy-Auschwitz*, pp. 501–2, Vermerk Röthke, Paris, 6 March 1943; ibid., pp. 516–18, Vermerk Röthke/Knochen, Paris, 27 March 1943.

71 Marrus and Paxton, *Vichy France*, pp. 286–301, 324.

72 The Germans constantly pressed for an early cut-off date of 1927, while the Vichy governemnt at first attempted to stand fast on the date of 1 January 1932: Klarsfeld, *Vichy-Auschwitz*, p. 521, Aktenvermerk Hagen, Paris, 12 April 1943; ibid., p. 522, Vermerk Röthke/Knochen, Paris, 12 April 1943; ibid., pp. 526–7, Bericht Knochen/Oberg, Paris, 21 May 1943. The Vichy government, however, was particularly ill-served by Darquier de Pellepoix who entirely supported the German objective of the 1927 date (ibid., pp. 529–30, Vermerk Röthke/Knochen, Paris, 25 May 1943).

73 ibid., p. 530, Vermerk Röthke/Knochen, Paris, 11 June 1943.

74 ibid., pp. 530–5, Vermerk Röthke, Paris, 14 June 1943; ibid., p. 535, Auszug aus Besprechungsniederschrift zwischen RFSS und SS-Gruf. Oberg am 8.6.43., Hagen, Paris, 16 June 1943; ibid., p. 538, Bericht Knochen/Müller, Paris, 28 June 1943.

75 ibid., pp. 537–8, Auszug aus Besprechungsniederschrift mit Secrétaire Général à la Police Bousquet am 23.6.43., Hagen, Paris, 29 June 1943; ibid., pp. 543–4, Vermerk, Röthke, Paris, 16 July 1943.

76 ibid., pp. 542–3, Bericht Röthke/SS-Obersturmbannführer Ehlers (Brüssel), Paris, 15 July 1943; ibid., pp. 545–7, Vermerk Röthke/Schmidt, Paris, 21 July 1943.

77 ibid., p. 282; ibid., pp. 545–7, Vermerk Röthke/Schmidt, Paris, 21 July 1943; ibid., pp. 547–8, Vermerk Röthke/Lischka, Paris, 31 July 1943.

78 ibid., pp. 554–5, Aufzeichnung Schmidt, Paris, 24 August 1943; ibid., p. 555, Aufzeichnung Schmidt, Paris, 24 August 1943; ibid., pp. 555–6, Aufzeichnung Schmidt, Paris, 24 August 1943; ibid., p. 556, Aktenvermerk Hagen, Paris, 25 August 1943; ibid., p. 557, Schreiben Pétain/de Brinon, Vichy, 24 August 1943; ibid., pp. 557–8, Fernschreiben Knochen/Kaltenbrunner, Paris, 25 August 1943; Warner, *Pierre Laval*, p. 376.

79 Klarsfeld, *Vichy-Auschwitz*, pp. 550–1, Aktenvermerk Hagen/Oberg, Paris, 11 August 1943; ibid., pp. 551–3, Vermerk Röthke/Knochen, Paris, 15 August 1943; ibid., pp. 559–60, Aktenvermerk Hagen, Paris, 26 August 1943; Cole, *Laval*, pp. 232–3; Hilberg, *The Destruction*, p. 417; Marrus and Paxton, *Vichy France*, pp. 325–6; Warner, *Pierre Laval*, pp. 374–6.

80 Cf. Klarsfeld, *Vichy-Auschwitz*, pp. 241–2, 252–3, 279–80, 284–5, 311, 315–16.

81 Hilberg, *The Destruction*, pp. 418–19; Marrus and Paxton, *Vichy France*, pp. 329–39; Warner, *Pierre Laval*, p. 377.

82 Marrus and Paxton, *Vichy France*, p. 343, suggest that 'close to one third of the total' exterminated were French citizens. Paxton, *Vichy France. Old Guard and New Order*, p. 183, on the other hand, suggests that only about 6,000 French Jews were deported. Klarsfeld, *Vichy-Auschwitz*, p. 320, concludes that approximately 24,500 French Jews died.

83 Cf. Trunk, *Judenrat*, pp. xxix, xxx, 422, 426, 428.

84 Marrus and Paxton, *Vichy France*, pp. 345–6.

85 This was the main argument put forward by Xavier Vallat, former French Commissioner-General for Jewish Affairs, at his post-war trial: 'so, the basic question is this: was it better that the French government concern itself with the Jewish problem or leave the entire material and moral responsibility for it to the occupation authorities? As for me, I think it was better that the French Government got into it' (Paxton, *Vichy France. Old Guard and New Order*, p. 365). Paxton, wrongly in my view, concludes (p. 372), that 'the shield theory [of Vichy] hardly bears close examination'. There was a 'shield', and it worked.

13

GERMAN PUBLIC AWARENESS OF THE FINAL SOLUTION

David Bankier

The widely discussed issue of what the German public knew of the Holocaust has been dealt with by recent historical literature.[1] Scholars who examined this topic have shown that the main source of information on the mass shootings were soldiers serving on the Eastern Front who witnessed or participated in them. For example, in a letter that reached the Security Service after it was sent to Ribbentrop's wife in November 1944, a private from Saxony asked, *inter alia*:

> do you really think we soldiers don't know what bestial murders have been perpetrated by our SS in Russia? Where for example are the 145,000 Jews of Lemberg who were there when they were transported little by little on trucks and shot not far from Lemberg?[2]

For some, the killings left indelible scars in their memories and the burden of guilt made it difficult to live in peace with their conscience. For others, these were just 'wonderful times'.[3]

As to the gassing, it is clear that by 1943, the use of gas as a killing method had become fairly widely known.[4] Even soldiers who served on the Western Front knew what their comrades were doing to the Jews in the east. An informer planted in a German POW camp in Italy referred to the soldiers' conversations on how the Jews were exterminated in Poland: trucks, railway cars and barracks were filled with Jews and gas was pumped in. The gas, it was said, destroyed the skin and the bodies melted together forming a pyramid in the gas chamber.[5] This, as well as other examples,[6] suggests that different pieces of information on how the gassing was done became associated together and were worked up in the mind till they became organized images. Thus, many who heard the incredible stories supplied the details of how this was done from their imaginations, as this was the only way they could envisage something so incredible. To be sure, much of the knowledge that people had was uncritical and unsifted but it was there; it was just that the more it had been filtered, passing from person to person, the less precise the information.

This explains the stories of gassing tunnels, mass electrocution plants or, as in the above example, of gas that melted the skin.[7]

It is also clear that knowledge of the mass murders was not confined to soldiers. Many ordinary civilians possessed enough information to make them realize, if not the extent, at least the direction of Nazi policy. For example, an American intelligence report written in the last month of the war stated that nearly every German living in the area occupied by the American Army had some knowledge of the atrocities which had been committed. A surprisingly large number admitted to knowledge of the gas vans and how they were used.[8] Having established that there was widespread knowledge of the killings, we may go a step further and ask: what feelings did this information generate?

In November and December 1944, a team of American intelligence officers of the 12th Army Group interviewed German civilians in evacuation centres and small towns around Aachen. The team submitted students, teachers, workers, policemen, civil servants, engineers, shopkeepers and housewives to intensive and prolonged interrogations, probing their attitudes and opinions. Although this was not a scientific cross-section of the population, it reflected the views of a typical mixed population encountered by the Allied troops. The American officers tried to discover where and how the interviewees formed their opinions and to what extent these mirrored the views of those with whom they were associated. Many were eager to speak openly for the first time in years, others said what they thought would please the conqueror. The officers reported the prevalence of a strange sense of guilt about the Jews, an uneasy feeling and, frequently, an open admission that a great wrong had been committed. This was coupled with a fear of revenge and a dread of hearing the worst. So many Germans had heard rumours about the horrors that had been inflicted on the Jews in Poland that they simply dared not face the whole truth. Almost everybody said that attacking the Jews was Hitler's greatest error and all the blame was on the Führer.[9]

A few months earlier a psychological warfare unit of the US Army also detected: 'a latent and possibly deep-rooted sense of guilt, owing to the brutalities committed by the German armies in Europe, particularly in the east and against the Jews'. It stated that: 'Germans have resigned themselves to the idea of retribution and only hope that the Americans would moderate the rage of those who will punish them. But the idea of punishment they do accept.'[10]

It could be argued, however, that to have information is one thing and to understand its meaning and internalize it, quite another. Furthermore, since the annihilation of the Jews was perceived as a collective crime, it may have been natural for the people to try to maintain a 'normal life' by avoiding the topic so as to dissociate themselves from it. An interesting example of this tendency is furnished by the diary of a Berlin woman. She recounts an experience of soldiers travelling on the train who commented on the discovery of the mass graves of Polish officers in Katyn: 'a war is a war, they said, you just have to dig one hundred kilometres further and you'll find the corpses of 10,000 Jews.'[11] She added that this comment was heard by all the travellers and nobody said anything. The silence of the train passengers is meaningful because it suggests that people might have sensed that if they were to block off this information, the consequences would not have to be acknowledged. Yet, as in this incident, when it was forced on to their attention, the listeners distanced themselves from it and erected a collective taboo.[12] If this was the case, how was the awareness of genocide maintained? How was it that it continued generating the afore-mentioned anxieties detected by American intelligence? In this chapter I will point out the factors that made it possible for the information on the extermination of the Jews to be acknowledged, internalized and integrated into people's perception and interpretation of wartime reality.

*

In discussing the question of awareness of the extermination we must bear in mind that the idea of mass murder – not only of Jews – was in the air and that a good many Germans were psychologically prepared to accept the reality of genocide. As early as December 1939, officials planning Poland's future were advising the destruction of the Jewish 'subhumanity' living in the ghettos;[13] in April 1940, the Nazi magazine NS Volksdienst suggested that it would be desirable to exterminate through euthanasia *one million people*.[14] We can, therefore, postulate that many Germans were mentally conditioned to receive the news of the extermination of Jews and that the Final Solution was not internalized in a mental vacuum. When the invasion of the Soviet Union began, particularly, the German public was fully aware that the atrocities taking place there were unusual for an ordinary war. It is true that the magnitude of the atrocities against Russian civilians also created the psychological framework in which the public could submerge the specific annihilation of the Jews. Nevertheless, the killings perpetrated by the *Einsatzgruppen* were not always fitted into this mental matrix; many Germans perceived them in their own right and realized the gravity of the crime committed by the Nazi state.

For the churchgoing population, ministers were an important factor in heightening awareness of the extermination. When people tried to relegate the horrible truth to the back of their minds, certain clergymen prevented this by integrating it into their services. For example, in sermons delivered in December 1943 and March 1944, Catholic Archbishop Frings unre-servedly condemned the killing of innocent people just because they belonged to another race.[15] Perhaps some decent priests dared to break the taboo because, when their congregations sought to eliminate, or at least reduce, the inconsistencies between their Christian values and the rumours they heard about genocide, a self-imposed wilful ignorance set in. This forced the priests to confront a fundamental matter of Christian moral theology: the question of 'vincible ignorance'. Clergymen such as Frings realized that people made no effort to acquire information so as to avoid the transgression of moral boundaries. He therefore purposely raised awareness of the crime, hoping to remove the believers' voluntary ignorance by means of a moral effort.

The letter of Archbishop Theophile Wurm of Württemberg to the Ministry for Ecclesiastical Affairs and to Hitler deserves to be mentioned in this context. Speaking in the name of 'countless Germans', his letter was unambiguously worded:

> The steps taken in the occupied territories have become known in our homeland. [They] are widely discussed and burden most heavily the conscience and strength of countless men and women among the German people who suffer from it more than from their daily sacrifices.[16]

This document is highly informative because it shows that for many of the churchgoing public there was severe inner conflict when information on mass murder could no longer be ignored. At the beginning, people tried to disregard the thorny issue which challenged deep-rooted religious values such as the sanctity of human life or Luther's concept of individual responsibility. This evasion worked because the retreat behind abstract images of 'the Jew' devalued the victim and helped the individual to avoid coming to grips with the moral significance of endorsing Nazi policy. This was so even when it was realized that an 'understanding' of the need for a solution to the Jewish problem paved the way to mass murder. Yet, by 1943, when the fear of defeat counterbalanced loyalty to Hitler, believers were forced to think about the consequences of years of accommodation and acquiescence to the Nazi system.

However, the fact that by 1943 the delusion began to break down does not necessarily mean that widespread self-reproach set in and that people renounced their anti-Semitic beliefs. It is against a background of entrenched anti-Semitic conformity, which had only just begun to be challenged by critical protests, that the statement of a foreigner who left Berlin in 1943 is best viewed. He asserted that: 'feelings were certainly strong against Jews in general, but what the regime had done to them was considered by nearly everyone to be excessive'.[17] This assessment of public attitudes is particularly noteworthy not only because it captures the extent to which vicious anti-Semitism was woven into German society, but also because it indicates that even when objecting to genocidal policy, basic anti-Semitic dispositions remained unchanged. The reason why the desire to remain consistent prevented people from divesting themselves of their anti-Semitic beliefs can be explained. Quitting at this stage would have meant not only abandoning their past support of the Nazis, but a complete revision of their political and cultural identity. Moreover, anti-Semitic feelings remained and perhaps increased not despite but because of the awareness of the extermination. Just as, for centuries, the living Jews served as testimony of the truth of Christianity, so the murder of the Jews made them a symbolic representation and testimony to the most shameful chapter of German history.

Another factor that carried the mass murder of the Jews to the threshold of people's consciousness was the fear of Jewish revenge in case of Germany's defeat. Anti-Semitism had always featured prominently in Nazi propaganda, but steering the Jewish issue to the centre of public interest in wartime was crucial: the British, the Americans and the Russians were concrete enemies; they were there, they were fighting and could be seen. But the main enemy, the mythical Jew, was an invisible one and therefore had to be brought permanently to public attention.

By 1943 it was clear to Goebbels how far Nazism had gone: 'On the Jewish question, especially, we have taken a position from which there is no escape,'[18] he wrote. Particularly after the catastrophic defeat on the Russian front, everyone in Germany was to be made aware that there was no turning back. This is why the themes of 'total war' and 'all are in danger' dominated the slogans of the time and why Nazi propaganda concentrated its efforts on convincing the public that, should Germany lose the war, the Jews would destroy the whole German people; therefore, there were only two alternatives left for the Germans: either perish or win the war at all cost. Goebbels made this point plain in his diary: 'in the first half of the war propaganda was made with optimism, now it would be made with pessimism'.[19] Indeed, already in his broadcast comments on the battle of Stalingrad in January 1943, the High Command spokesman, General Dittmar, spoke of a battle in which everyone knew what fate would await him in the event of defeat.

As the fortunes of war turned against Germany, and the loyalty of the population was considered in doubt, the anti-Semitic agitation was stepped up on Hitler's direct orders. Goebbels wrote in his diary on 8 and 10 May 1943, 'The Führer argued that anti-Semitism must again become the focal point. . . . The Führer attaches great importance to a powerful anti-Semitic propaganda. . . . He is immensely pleased with our sharpening up the anti-Semitic propaganda in the press and radio.'[20] So as to implement the Führer's will, secret circulars were passed among party officials instructing them to increase anti-Semitic indoctrination. The orders were unambiguous:

The German press should not be satisfied with writing an anti-Semitic article every third day but has to become an anti-Semitic press. . . . The Jewish question must remain at the core of our political attitude . . . [and] it should become impossible to speak of the war without at the same time raising the Jewish question.[21]

Indeed, in the spring of 1943, 70–80 per cent of radio broadcasts were devoted to the Jewish question, with the propaganda apparatus highlighting the fate awaiting Germany should the Jews take revenge.[22] It is clear that hammering on the theme of national solidarity in the crusade against the Jews, and on their revenge should Germany be defeated, made it harder for people not to reflect on their share in the Final Solution. For the fanatics, the frenzied anti-Semitic drive reinforced stereotypical prejudices against the Jews, reassured them and helped them to justify the crimes. In contrast, for those Germans who had doubts or had begun to lose their faith in Hitler, keeping the Jewish issue permanently on the agenda inevitably offset the instinctive need to repress the awareness of genocide.

A remarkable example of how the incessant anti-Semitic propaganda triggered awareness of the Nazi extermination policy is provided by the public reactions to the finding of the mass graves of Polish officers at Katyn and Winnitza. The media's campaign on the Katyn revelations, launched in the spring and summer of 1943, sparked a variety of responses. A Bavarian SD reporter alluded to public concern that the Russians might find the graves of Jews killed systematically by German troops. Others commented: 'Neither did we treat the Jews differently but eliminated the enemy ruthlessly.' Some church circles were openly hostile and vented their suspicions that the mass graves were of Poles and Jews killed by Germans. An Austrian priest, for example, sharply criticized the hypocrisy of the Germans who themselves had violated fundamental human rights: 'People who have on their conscience the murder of hundreds of thousands of Jews, Poles, Serbs and Russians should not be shocked by acts of this kind.'[23] We encounter the same reactions in July of that year. When Goebbels engineered a similar campaign seeking to capitalize on the discovery of the mass graves in Winnitza, some people affirmed that the Nazis, who had thrown overboard all human behaviour, could have no moral claims:

> The repugnant and inhuman behaviour of the SS towards the Jews calls for God's punishment of our people. If there is no revenge there is no divine justice. The German people took upon itself a crime for which it cannot expect mercy or forgiveness.[24]

Why were the Katyn graves linked to the annihilation of the Jews?

To be sure, Nazi propaganda generated an association of two instances of mass murder, but there was more to it than that. It has to be borne in mind that the Katyn campaign was heavily blended with anti-Semitic clichés and was propagated as part of the gigantic anti-Semitic drive launched at the time. On 5 February 1943, Goebbels had instructed the press that:

There is for every chief editor in the months to come but one watchword: give battle to Bolshevism and Jewry . . . [they] must place coldly and clearly before our readers the question and answer as to what awaits Europe if it falls victim to Bolshevism, the henchman of Jewry.[25]

Goebbels gave a personal example of how this was to be done. His rhetorical question 'Wollt Ihr den totalen Krieg?' (Do you want Total War?) posed to the crowd assembled on 18 February 1943 at the Berlin Sportpalast was a calculated blend of idealism and terror. Portraying international Jewry as the incarnation of evil, the demon of decay and a world plague, he over and over again threatened what would happen if the total mobilization should fail: Jewish leaders of western plutocracies and their Jewish liquidation squads would enforce the Bolshevization of the Reich and of the whole of Europe.

In April 1943, at the height of the campaign on Katyn, Goebbels also distributed a 'Jewish School Calendar' which quoted statements allegedly made by Jews on their intention to take revenge on the Gentiles for their anti-Semitism. Hence, when the German News Agency reported that the Jewish-Bolsheviks perpetrated the mass murder of Katyn; that the Jews ruled the Soviet secret police and that its chief, the Jew Lazar Kaganowich, pulled the strings for Stalin and that they were using pan-Slavism for their purposes, it is scarcely surprising that people linked the Bolsheviks' atrocities to the Jews: the Bolsheviks killed the Polish officers, but the Jews masterminded the executions. Thus, when the Nazis brought up the theme of Jewish revenge, it was but natural to reflect on the implications of the Katyn affair: if this is what the Jews did to the Poles, there was good reason to fear Jewish retaliation for what the Germans did to the Jews.

The reactions to the Allied bombings also indicate that fears over Jewish revenge heightened the awareness of genocide. Letters written by German citizens mirror the shattering effect of the aerial raids on people's morale. A Hamburg civilian recorded:

We often think our last hour has come. Such nights are frightful. We were again in the cellar. . . . If the pipes burst we should be burned to death, it is better to be killed at once. . . . And there is no end in sight. Oh for peace.[26]

A woman from Hovestadt wrote:

Walter is in Bremen . . . and the air raids get on his nerves, which not being strong make him unable to stand the many disturbed nights and broken sleep . . . Gisela remarked the other day that what she would like was a good-sized bomb to send us all to heaven.[27]

It is no coincidence that people invested the bombings with a meaning which stretched far beyond their own, visualizing them in terms of Jewish revenge. The Nazis had made it a commonplace to state that the Jewish war aim was Germany's annihilation and the air raids seemed to be only the first stage of this.

At an early stage of the war the bombings were attributed to Jewish treachery: Goebbels spread the rumour that Jews had informed the British about the anti-aircraft guns deployed in the areas which were attacked.[28] But from 1943 on, as it was impossible to claim that Jews were active in Germany, Goebbels focused instead on the alleged culpability of world Jewry. Emphasizing that the Jews were behind the air raids, however, had perverse consequences: it prompted people to link the bombings to the Final Solution and to envisage 'Jewish revenge' as a retribution for what Germany had done. Munich Catholics, for example, observed in the bombing and the certain loss of the war, God's punishment for the persecution of the Jews. Similarly, the raids on Kiel, Essen and Hamburg led people to argue that the Nazis were to be blamed because the Allied bombings were a quid pro quo for the extermination policy.[29]

The closer defeat came, the more anxiety over Jewish revenge made inroads into the population, particularly when Germany's positions began deteriorating considerably on all fronts. By mid-1943 the Russians staged a summer counterattack, recapturing Kharkov, Orel and Stalino and forcing the Germans to yield ground. In the west, the Allied bombing was intensified and extended: American bombers penetrated in day raids as far as Stuttgart, Regensburg and Schweinfurt. In the south Mussolini's regime collapsed and Italy surrendered unconditionally. In the following months, the hopes of a new Dunkirk after the Salerno landing proved false, and the retreat expected to stop at the Dnieper continued. In the diplomatic arena the Moscow conference extinguished wishful thinking of disunity among the Allies as well as hopes of a separate peace. Needless to say, in the face of this reality the Nazis feared that defeatist attitudes would gain ground. This certainly underlay the initiatives taken at the time. In the autumn of 1943, again under direct instructions from Hitler, Goebbels renewed his attempts to bolster the nation's will-power and faith in Nazism. The propaganda, naturally, blamed the Jews for the military setbacks but it seems that the argument that Jews were pulling the strings behind the Allies backfired. It prompted criticisms including the one that Germany's predicament was to be laid at the Nazis' door for their horrible way of carrying out the Final Solution.

This public mood can be discerned by carefully reading between the lines of newspapers. It is noteworthy that notwithstanding the fact that the media were subservient to the totalitarian regime, much can be inferred from the arguments put forward by the press. Thus, for example, to meet questions posed by the public, a Nazi paper listed fourteen arguments of 'what might be said' and tried to rebut them one by one. It is reasonable to assume that the Nazi press would not invent such questions but would rather address itself to what was heard and that these questions were being expressed in a much sharper form than it was thought advisable to reproduce in the papers. The fact that a newspaper editor sought to contradict the argument that 'world Jewry would not have fought Germany had it not so radically solved the Jewish question', shows that he was reacting to a prevailing view that the Germans were suffering the adverse consequences of the Nazis' extermination of the Jews.[30]

This tension between the regime's projection of anti-Semitic propaganda and the withdrawal of the public from it, because it made people aware of what the Nazis had done, lasted till the end of the war. Thus, when the press highlighted in a sensationalist manner the behaviour of Russian soldiers to civilians in east Prussia, this line again rebounded when it made people aware of their own crimes. The criticism voiced in early November 1944, when the press reported on atrocities perpetrated by Soviet troops in east Prussia, illustrates this point. An informer monitoring the reactions of the public noticed that:

> On reading these articles people immediately think . . . did we not slaughter the Jews by the thousands? Don't soldiers repeatedly tell of Jews who had to dig their own graves in Poland? . . . We have only shown the enemy what they can do with us should they win.[31]

Finally, the third and perhaps the major factor that made the people aware of what was happening to the Jews was the public statements of the Nazi leadership itself. Since the extermination of the Jews was a secret state matter, this contention might, at first, seem paradoxical. However, in considering the many references made by the leadership to the extermination one must conclude that these were not slips, but rather that the secrecy was purposely broken. On certain issues Hitler spoke cryptically, in order to get his message across without actually revealing his plans; but whenever he referred to the Jewish question, he made no secret of his intentions. For example, in his 1942 New Year message he stated: 'The Jew will not exterminate the peoples of Europe; he will be the victim of his own machinations instead.' In other statements he reassured the Germans in no uncertain terms that the final result of the war would be the extermination of the Jews.[32]

Goebbels was no less explicit in the signals he sent to the public. In his editorials he made it plain that those who aimed at the complete annihilation of their enemy must reckon with similar consequences in the event of defeat. To put it in his words: 'When the Jews planned the total destruction of the German people, they signed their own death warrant.'[33] For those who dismissed this as just rhetoric, a figure of speech or an empty metaphor, Robert Ley, Head of the German Labour Front, 1933–45, formulated Germany's war aims in the clearest terms: 'We swear we are not going to abandon the struggle until the last Jew in Europe has been exterminated and is actually dead.'[34]

It is small wonder, therefore, that in the face of these statements from the highest political level, people drew only one logical conclusion: the Jews will be literally annihilated. For example, when the notorious article 'The Jews are guilty' was published in Das Reich on 16 November 1941 it was met with the comment: 'Having read Goebbels's article in which old people, women and children are made responsible for the death of German soldiers, you can only expect the extermination of the Jews.'[35] Furthermore, evidence that people understood exactly what Hitler meant emerges forcibly from some of the reactions to Hitler's speeches. Surveying the comments on one of Hitler's addresses, the SD noted that a few people whose sense of human dignity was outraged were unambiguously critical: 'Nobody has the right to exterminate another people,' they said. Others, however, even some who held anti-Jewish prejudices and endorsed Hitler's total war against the Jews, coupled their enthusiasm with caution and objected:

'Germany could have solved the Jewish question differently, more humanely.' 'Obviously, the Jews were malignant but we could have let them leave after 1933.' 'Germans in America will suffer because of it.'[36]

Why did the Nazi leaders themselves break the terrible secret? I would argue that calling public attention to what was happening to the Jews fulfilled three important functions.

First, it aimed at liberating people from moral responsibility. In order to free the public from residual scruples and moral inhibitions, the Nazis emphasized that the extermination policy was unavoidable because it was dictated by the crimes committed by the Jews. The alleged lack of alternatives and the emergency excused everything since the Jews were the aggressive persecutors and the Germans their innocent victims.

Second, for those who wished to believe that the Führerprinzip (principle of absolute leadership) created a system of non-responsibility, a sense of shared liability was imposed. The Nazis thus sought to bind the nation more firmly together and prevent responsibility for the Final Solution being laid exclusively on Nazi shoulders. Particularly from 1943 on, in order to rebut the view that in the event of defeat the Bolsheviks would only hang Nazis, Hitler sought to implicate the Germans collectively and make everyone accountable for the Final Solution. By diffusing what Karl Jaspers called 'political guilt', the Nazi leaders sought to make every German share the crimes committed by the regime in the name of the nation and so become liable for the consequences of deeds done by the Nazi state.[37]

Third, imposing political co-responsibility, the Nazi leaders assumed, would make people realize that there was no way back. As Hitler told Heydrich and Himmler: 'it is not a bad idea that public rumour attributes to us a plan to exterminate the Jews. Terror is a salutary thing.'[38] Hence, in referring to the Final Solution the Nazi leaders were warning the German people that all bridges had been burned. They reminded them of what Dr Faust told someone who wanted to rescue him: 'I have gone further than you think and have pledged myself to the devil with my own blood to be his in eternity, body and soul.'[39] The Nazis believed, correctly it seems, that this would make everybody fight to the bitter end.

Summing up, we can draw the following conclusions: First, the view found among the general public, and also in some scholarly works, that very little was known about the extermination at the time, or that only unsubstantiated rumours about the Jews' fate circulated in Germany, is untenable. Second, on the basis of the available evidence it is equally untenable that the German people failed to comprehend the significance of the Nazis' genocidal policy. The evidence presented in this paper helps us to assess not only what the German population actually knew, but also how the awareness of the extermination shaped the public's reactions to the regime's political stimuli and how it affected its intepretations of war-time reality.

NOTES

The research for this paper was carried out with the support of the Wingate Foundation.

1 Marlis Steinert, *Hitler's War and the Germans* (Ohio University Press, Athens, Ohio, 1977), pp. 132–47; Lawrence D. Stokes, 'The German people and the destruction of the European Jews', *Central European History*, 6 (1973), pp. 167–91; Walter Laqueur, *The Terrible Secret* (Weidenfeld & Nicolson, London, 1980), pp. 17–32; Otto D. Kulka, ' "Public opinion" in National Socialist Germany and the "Jewish Question" ', *Zion*, 40 (1975), pp. 186–290 (in Hebrew); Sarah Gordon, *Hitler, Germans and the Jewish Question* (Princeton University Press, Princeton, NJ, 1984); Ian Kershaw, *Popular Opinion and Political Dissent in the Third Reich* (Clarendon Press, Oxford, 1984); David Bankier, *The Germans and the Final Solution* (Basil Blackwell, Oxford, 1992), pp. 101–15.
2 Steinert, *Hitler's War*, p. 285.
3 See Ernst Klee, Willi Dressen and Volker Riess (eds) *'Schöne Zeiten'. Judenmord aus der Sicht der Täter und Gaffer* (Fischer, Frankfurt a.M., 1988).
4 Bankier, *The Germans*, pp. 110–12.
5 OSS report, 21 June 1944, National Archives, Washington (hereafter NAW), RG 226/80227 box 910.
6 Lili Hahn, ... *bis alles in Scherben fällt. Tagebuchblätter 1933–1945* (Braun, Cologne, 1979); Ludwig Haydn, *Meter immer nur Meter. Das Tagebuch eines Daheimgebliebenen* (Scholle, Vienna, 1946).
7 British Legation, Bern to Foreign Office, 17 September 1941, Public Record Office, London (hereafter PRO), FO 371/26513; British Embassy, Madrid to

Foreign Office, 12 April 1943, PRO, FO 371/34429; Lisbon Legation to Political Intelligence Department, London, 1 April 1943, PRO, FO 371/34429; Bankier, *The Germans*, pp. 109–14.

8 Notes on a trip through occupied Germany, 18 April 1945, NAW, RG 226, Entry 16, File 125864.

9 NAW, USA Army report of 19 December 1944, NAW, RG 226/129320 box 1446.

10 US Army, Psychological warfare estimate, 13 October 1944, NAW, RG 226, Entry 16, File 118485.

11 Steinert, *Hitler's War*, p. 143.

12 Frank Stern, *The Whitewashing of the Yellow Badge. Antisemitism and Philosemitism in Postwar Germany*, (Pergamon, Oxford, 1992). See also: Michael Müller-Claudius, *Der Antisemitismus und das deutsche Verhängnis*, (Josef Knecht, Frankfurt a.M., 1948), pp. 166–76; Alexander and Margarete Mitscherlich, *Die Unfähigkeit zu Trauern. Grundlagen kollektiven Verhaltens* (Piper, Munich, 1977).

13 Götz Aly and Susanne Heim, 'The economics of the Final Solution: a case study from the General Government', *Simon Wiesenthal Center Annual*, 5 (1988), pp. 6–7.

14 Robert J. Lifton, *The Nazi Doctors* (Basic Books, New York, 1986), p. 65.

15 Donald J. Dietrich, *Catholic Citizens in the Third Reich*, (Transactions Press, New Brunswick, 1988), p. 238.

16 Wolfgang Scheffler, *Judenverfolgung im Dritten Reich* (Colloquium, Berlin, 1964), doc. 31. Cf. Frank M. Buscher and Michael Phayer, 'German Catholic bishops and the Holocaust, 1940–1952', *German Studies Review*, 11 (1988), p. 465; Guenter Lewy, *The Catholic Church and Nazi Germany* (Weidenfeld & Nicolson, London, 1964), pp. 284–95.

17 British Embassy in Lisbon to Foreign Office, 12 March 1943, PRO, FO 371/34428. See also the results of a survey conducted among German POWs captured between November 1943 and January 1944, NAW, RG 226, 619336 box 719.

18 Louis Lochner, *The Goebbels Diaries* (Award, New York, 1971), p. 299.

19 Günter Moltmann, 'Goebbels' speech on total war, February 18, 1943', in Hajo Holborn (ed.) *Republic to Reich* (Vintage, New York, 1973), p. 326. Cf. the OSS reports of October 1942, NAW, RG 226, Entry 16, File 25583 and of 17 August 1944, NAW, RG 226 x1 1377 box 19.

20 Lochner, *The Goebbels Diaries*, pp. 375, 400.

21 Raul Hilberg, *The Destruction of the European Jews* (Quadrangle, Chicago, 1961), p. 656. See also Goebbels's instructions of 10 May 1943, NAW, RG 226 OSS, 190, box 32, Bern-51-OP-22.

22 Lochner, *The Goebbels Diaries*, p. 411.

23 Heinz Boberach (ed.) *Meldungen aus dem Reich* (Pawlak, Herrsching, 1984), 19 April 1943, 26 July 1943; SD Würzburg, Außenstelle Bad Brückenau, 16 April 1943, Staatsarchiv Würzburg (hereafter StA W), SD 12; SD Hauptaußenstelle Würzburg, 7 April 1943, StA W, SD 37; Stokes, 'The German people', pp. 186–7; Steinert, *Hitler's War*, p. 143; Kulka, 'Public opinion', p. 251–3; Kershaw, *Popular Opinion*, p. 365. On the Katyn affair in Nazi propaganda, John P. Fox, 'Der Fall Katyn und die Propaganda des NS-Regimes', *Vierteljahrshefte für Zeitgeschichte*, 30 (1982), pp. 462–99; excerpts of the party chancellery reports for the period 6–12 June 1943, Bundesarchiv Koblenz (hereafter BA), NS 6/415; SD Abschnitt Linz, report on the impact of press and radio in the period 5–8 May 1943, BA, NS 6/415.

24 On the reactions to the Winnitza discoveries: Boberach, *Meldungen*, 26 July 1943; Kulka, 'Public opinion', p. 251.
25 G. Bording Mathieu, 'The secret anti Juden Sondernummer of 21st May 1943', *Yearbook of the Leo Baeck Institute* (1981), p. 293.
26 Postal and Telegraph Censorship Report on Germany, 4 November 1941, PRO, FO 371/26512.
27 ibid., 14 November 1942.
28 Steinert, *Hitler's War*, pp. 136–7; see also the report of a neutral observer on Hamburg, NAW, RG 226/48742, box 412.
29 USA Consulate general, Geneva, 29 October 1943, NAW, RG 226/56939, box 656; SD Hauptaußenstelle Würzburg, 27 July 1943; RP Augsburg, 10 May 1943, Bayerisches Hauptstaatsarchiv, MA 106703; SD Würzburg, Außenstelle Bad Brückenau 22 April 1943, StA W, SD 12; SD Abschnitt Halle, 22 May 1943, BA, NS 7/406; Steinert, *Hitler's War*, pp. 143–4, 288, 305; Kershaw, *Popular Opinion*, p. 369, Kulka, 'Public opinion', p. 250.
30 See the article of Hermann Hirsch in *Stuttgarter NS-Kurier*, 2 September 1943. Cf. Klaus Schickert, 'Kriegsschauplatz Israel', in the Hitler Youth journal *Wille und Macht*, of September/October 1943. See also Frank Trommler, ' "Deutschlands Sieg oder Untergang". Perspektiven aus dem Dritten Reich auf die Nachkriegsentwicklung', in Thomas Koebner, Gert Sautermeister and Sigrid Schneider (eds) *Deutschland nach Hitler* (Westdeutscher Verlag, Opladen, 1987), pp. 214–28.
31 Steinert, *Hitler's War*, p. 288.
32 Hitler referred to his Jewish policy in his public speeches on 30 January 1941, 30 January 1942, 24 February 1942, 30 September 1942, 8 November 1942, 24 February 1943 and 21 March 1943. See Max Domarus, *Hitler, Reden und Proklamationen 1932–1945* (Loewit, Wiesbaden, 1963).
33 *Das Reich*, 9 May 1943.
34 Cesar C. Aronsfeld, ' "Perish Judah". Nazi extermination propaganda 1920–1945', *Patterns of Prejudice*, 12 (1978), p. 24. By mid-1942 the press led by the *Schwarze Korps*, revived Hitler's 'prophecy' of 30 January 1939 and asserted that economic elimination would not suffice. Robert Ley in his article 'Die Judenwiege der Neuzeit' in *Angriff* of 12 June 1942 also made it clear that the occupation of the Soviet Union would lead to the extermination of the Jews.
35 Jochen Klepper, *Unter dem Schatten deiner Flügel. Aus den Tagebüchern 1932–1942* (DTV, Munich, 1976), entry for 20 November 1941.
36 SD Leipzig, Außenstelle Leipzig, 26 August 1942, BA, NS 29/52.
37 Karl Jaspers, *Die Schuldfrage. Ein Beitrag zur deutschen Frage* (Artemis, Zurich, 1947). On Hitler's threats of what would happen should the Jews win, see also his speech on 30 January 1944, *Domarus*, vol. III, pp. 2084–5. See also the report of an Italian officer formerly attached to the embassy in Berlin that people feared the consequences of what they did and Hitler exploited these feelings in his propaganda, December 1943, NAW, RG 226/54577, box 623. Cf. the intelligence report of 3 February 1945, on the Nazi Party attempts in the press, in the speeches of Gau and Kreisleiter and at party evening courses, to bolster up German morale by stressing the responsibility of the entire German people for the war and its consequences, NAW, RG 226 OSS 190 E Bern 86; Bern OSS OP 31.
38 Hugh R. Trevor-Roper, *Hitler's Table Talk 1941–44* (Weidenfeld & Nicolson, London, 1973), p. 87.
39 Lifton, *The Nazi Doctors*, p. 428.

14

RESCUE THROUGH STATEHOOD

The American Zionist response to the Holocaust

Aaron Berman

During the refugee crisis of the 1930s the Roosevelt administration displayed its inability and apparent unwillingness to come to the support of endangered European Jews. As American Jews desperately searched for an answer to their European kin's plight, they discovered that the small American Zionist movement seemed to have a practical answer to the need of European Jewry for a haven. The result was a steady growth in the membership rolls and treasuries of the Zionist Organization of America (ZOA) and Hadassah, the two largest Jewish nationalist organizations in the United States, and their smaller cousins, the socialist Poalei Zion and Orthodox religious Mizrachi.

When news of the Holocaust reached the United States, the Zionist movement was clearly the most dynamic force in Jewish North America. One would have expected that American Zionists, blessed with charismatic leaders like Rabbis Stephen S. Wise and Abba Hillel Silver, would have responded to the genocide of European Jewry by unleashing an aggressive and audacious lobbying campaign to force the Allies to come to their rescue. Historians tell us, however, that the American Zionists failed to mount such an effort. This chapter contends that the American Zionists' response to the Holocaust did not reflect a callousness on their part to Jewish suffering or their inability to believe the terrible news reaching them from Europe. Rather, critical events that occurred *before* American Jews learned of the Nazi genocide fundamentally shaped the way they received and responded to the news, leading them to conclude that the only real answer to the Holocaust was the establishment of a Jewish state in Palestine.[1]

*

Shortly after their seizure of power, Nazi anti-Semitic restrictions forced many German Jews to consider flight. Unfortunately, they faced a situation unlike that encountered by the millions of Jews who had fled Europe in the nineteenth and early twentieth centuries. The open doors of an expanding United States were now closed, shut by the passage of the 1924 National Origins Act. The Depression strengthened the nativism of the American public, and economically ravaged European nations were also generally unwilling to open their doors to needy Jews. There seemed to be only one society in all the world willing to accept large numbers of Jews: the *Yishuv*, the Jewish community of Palestine.[2]

American Zionists, whose costly efforts had helped prepare Palestine to serve as one of the few available refugee havens, enthusiastically accepted the challenge of providing German Jews with a much needed home. They quickly learned that a mutually beneficial relationship existed between their efforts to rescue German Jewry and the advancement of the Zionist movement in America. As early as April 1933, Stephen Wise had written to Louis Brandeis: 'We feel that time has come which almost parallels the 1914 situation, and that we may now be able to reawaken the interest of American Jews in Palestine and Zionism.' Many American Jews were realizing that Zionism seemed to offer a simple and practical solution to the refugees' plight. While other Jewish organizations futilely attempted to convince Adolf Hitler to alter his anti-Semitic policies, Zionist settlements in Palestine offered German Jews security and a future.[3]

While American Zionists prospered in the years following Hitler's rise to power, their use of the refugee crisis was not callous or Machiavellian. Jewish nationalists understood that both Palestine and Zionism would benefit as a result of the refugees' plight, but they knew that their primary mission was to aid their less fortunate brethren. From 1933 to 1936, no contradiction existed between working to rebuild Palestine and aiding Jewish refugees. Hitler's treatment of the Jews under his control was clearly not improving in these years, and emigration to Palestine was the sole solution available to many of his victims. The first priority of American Zionists was clearly to rescue as much of German Jewry as they could. American Zionists were proving in these years that you could 'have your cake and eat it too'. They were in the rare and enviable position of being able to help themselves and save others. Unfortunately, events soon began to unfold that seriously altered their priorities and undermined their optimistic perception of the future.

The exodus of Jews from Europe that began in 1933 led to the dramatic growth of Palestine's Jewish community. An official British census in 1931 had found that 175,000 Jews comprised 17 per cent of Palestine's total population. By mid-1936, Zionist leaders could proudly claim the loyalty of 28 per cent of Palestine's population. While many Zionists in the United States and Palestine believed that their dream was well on the way to fruition, they had, in fact, seriously underestimated Arab opposition. In April 1936, latent Arab resentment turned into a full-scale revolt against

Zionist settlers and British colonial officials. The intensity and longevity of the revolt physically challenged Zionists in Palestine, but ideologically and intellectually challenged supporters of Jewish nationalism in the United States. Suddenly, American Zionists, who had been concentrating their efforts on proudly portraying Palestine as the most effective solution to the refugee crisis, found themselves having to defend the very right of Jews to build a national home in the Holy Land.[4]

Less than a week after the outbreak of the Arab revolt, the *New York Times* called the conflict between Jews and Arabs 'irreconcilable' and concluded that neither Jews nor Arabs 'no matter what the pretensions of extremist leaders, can reasonably look forward to sole control over Palestine'.[5] In December 1936, Albert Viton in a two-article series for the *Nation*, attacked the Zionists for claiming to be a 'movement of liberation' for the native Arab population, when they were increasingly playing a 'reactionary role'. He concluded that there could be no peace in Palestine as long as Zionists clung to their dream of a Jewish state. Millions of Jews might have to escape European persecution, he added, but Palestine would not be able to offer them security.[6]

Rabbi Philip Bernstein, a rising young leader of the ZOA, responded to Viton's attack. Before the Arab revolt, Zionists had conceived of Palestine as the means through which the Jewish refugee problem could be solved. Now, Bernstein altered the equation and used the refugee crisis as a weapon to defend the Jewish position in Palestine. He pointed to the horrible condition of Jews living in Germany, and forecast that heightened anti-Semitism would ensure that their problems would continue even if Hitler's regime was to be overthrown. Emigration offered the only immediate salvation for European Jewry, but where, he poignantly asked, would Jewish refugees go if denied access to Palestine?[7]

Even as Bernstein and other Zionists struggled to respond to the Arab revolt, a Royal Commission of Inquiry arrived in Palestine to determine for itself why Arab Palestinians so violently resisted Jewish settlement. In April 1937, Zionists learned that the Peel Commission was considering the division of Palestine into separate Jewish and Arab states. Palestine's partition intrigued Chaim Weizmann, who reasoned that statehood would free both the Zionists and the refugees from the burden of endless negotiations with British officials who controlled all their futures. The surrender of territory would be a high but not disastrous price to pay for autonomy.[8]

By contrast, among American Zionists, the rumoured British division of Palestine met with almost universal derision. The ZOA and Hadassah vowed to fight any partition plan. Hayim Greenberg of the socialist *Jewish Frontier* condemned any 'Balkanization' of the Holy Land, while the orthodox Mizrachi Zionist organization announced that the British division of Palestine would be a crime as heinous as the 'Italian rape of Ethiopia'. When the Peel Commission, on 7 July 1937, formally recommended the partition of Palestine into Jewish and Arab states, outraged American Zionists focused their attention on Zurich, Switzerland, where the Twentieth Zionist Congress would consider the British proposal.[9]

The delegates meeting in Zurich in August 1937 reflected the factionalized world of Jewish nationalism. Chaim Weizmann presented the case for partition, warning that if the Jews rejected the Peel scheme, the British would permanently restrict Jewish immigration to Palestine. Jews would be doomed to remain a minority in the Holy Land and the Zionist dream of a national home would die. A Jewish state in a divided Palestine was not an ideal situation, but it would guarantee Jewish autonomy and control of immigration into at least part of the land of Zion.[10]

ZOA leaders Robert Szold and Stephen Wise were among those who challenged Weizmann's pro-partition position. They argued that the Palestine Mandate was workable and that difficulties could be overcome. Szold predicted that a Jewish state would be unable to absorb the large number of Jews seeking to escape from Poland and Germany, and he warned that this would break the morale of the Jewish pioneers in Palestine whose strength and courage were 'based on their hope that they are assisting in the solution of the Jewish problem'.[11]

The struggle at Zurich was long and bitter. Weizmann's argument won some support among American Zionists, resulting in a serious split in the ZOA and Hadassah delegations. Silver, Wise, Szold and their supporters (including Louis Brandeis back in the United States) opposed Weizmann and the division of the Holy Land, while those delegates, including Louis Lipsky, who had supported Weizmann in the past continued to do so. Finally, the Zionist Congress passed a resolution authorizing the Zionist Executive to negotiate with the British in the hope of winning better boundaries for the proposed Jewish state. The resolution, however, prohibited the Executive from agreeing to any particular proposal without first getting the approval of another World Zionist Congress.[12]

The Zurich resolution did not prevent the outbreak of an intense conflict over partition which threatened to divide American Zionists. The bitter battle reflected the belief of both factions that they were fighting to protect the future of the Zionist experiment in Palestine, upon which the very existence of the Jewish people depended. Opponents of partition, including Robert Szold, Louis Brandeis and Abba Hillel Silver, were struggling to preserve the birthright of the Jewish people. They were convinced that partition would not solve the Jewish problem because a divided Palestine would not be able to support a viable Jewish state. Pro-partition advocate Louis Lipsky also claimed to be fighting for the survival of the Jewish people. On the night of 30 December 1937, at a meeting of ZOA leaders, Lipsky warned that Great Britain would respond to a Zionist rejection of partition by repealing the Balfour Declaration and by completely abandoning the Jewish national project.[13]

Zip Szold of Hadassah strongly disagreed with Lipsky, but also perceived herself to be defending the Jewish future. Presenting her own variation of an argument often used by anti-Zionists, she claimed that a partitioned Palestine would not have the absorptive capacity to satisfy the demand of European refugees for a new home. According to Szold, the pro-partitionists' 'complete disregard for future generations of Jews is entirely out of harmony with Jewish tradition and with the realistic emergencies which face Jewish survival at the present moment.'[14]

Finally, after months of tension, the British themselves put an end to the partition controversy when London announced that it was no longer pursuing the Peel Commission's plan. The defeat of partition seemed to return Zionists to the situation that had existed before Lord Peel set foot in the land of Palestine. However, while the partition controversy might not have radically altered the external political realities of the Middle East, it did profoundly affect the mind-set of American Zionists.

Before the Arab revolt of 1936 and the Peel Commission that followed, American Zionists had focused their attention on the plight of European Jewry. Wise, Silver, Szold, Brandeis and Lipsky all expected Palestine to be the destination of most Jewish refugees, and they understood that the Zionist movement in America would win new respect and support with every refugee that the *Yishuv* successfully absorbed into Palestine. Satisfied that events had proved Theodor Herzl correct, American Zionists set out to transform Palestine into a haven for refugees. However, the Arab riots of 1936 and the British reaction to them subtly changed the priorities of American Jewish nationalists.

Arab violence and the fear that it would seriously undermine British support for the Zionist programme led Jewish nationalists in the United States to turn their main attention away from the European refugees to the survival of Jewish Palestine. Upset over the British failure to crush the Arab revolt and suspecting that partition would be recommended by the Peel Commission, Brandeis and other American Zionists concluded that London was determined 'to prevent Jewish development from becoming too powerful in the Near East'. Accordingly, discussions among Zionist leaders and between them and American officials began to focus more on the Palestine situation than the plight of German Jewry. In fact, as the struggle over Palestine's future continued, Zionists began to use the refugee crisis as a *means* to defend their stake in the Holy Land, just as both sides of the partition debate argued that the well-being of the refugees depended on their victory.[15]

Zionist organizations did not ignore the worsening plight of European Jewry in this period. They collected money for relief work, and protested against the persecution of European Jewry. Nonetheless, American Zionists increasingly concentrated on what the Diaspora could do for Paletine, rather than what the Jewish homeland could do for the world's Jews.

Palestine, in the opinion of American Zionists, offered needy Jews 'permanent reconstruction' while other resettlement efforts promised only 'temporary relief'. If American Jewry was to save its European co-religionists, it would first have to defend Palestine. In the words of one ZOA leader:

> Would it not be morally indefensible for the American Jewish community, living in security and comfort in the great and free land, to keep silent as they see their brothers in their tragic plight . . . being threatened with the deprivation of their last cherished hope for a better future for themselves and their children?[16]

Unhappily for Zionists, the British in 1939 responded to the failure of the Peel mission with a new White Paper that severely limited Jewish immigration to Palestine, ensuring that when that land became independent it would be an Arab, not a Jewish nation. When the Second World War broke out in September 1939, Zionists hoped that the British would disavow the 1939 White Paper and renew their alliance with them. London, however, continued to enforce the White Paper, even refusing haven to boatloads of Jews desperately fleeing Nazi armies.

Angered and disillusioned by Britain's rejection of the Zionist cause, *Yishuv* leaders by late 1940 began to reconsider their tactics and goals. Armed struggle against the British was, at least for the moment, completely out of the question. The *Yishuv* simply was materially unprepared for revolution, nor could Jews, in good conscience, do anything that might contribute to Hitler's triumph. Instead, David Ben-Gurion, in consultation with several of his closest advisers, decided that the Zionist movement must alter its timetable. Sovereignty could no longer remain the distant long-term goal of the movement. Recent experience with the British proved that large numbers of Jews would enter Palestine only when the Zionists themselves were free to establish and administer the territory's immigration policies. Therefore, it was imperative for Zionists to mount, as quickly as possible, a powerful pro-statehood political campaign. Ben-Gurion understood that the success of this venture would depend, in no small measure, on the ability of American Zionists to become a potent political force. As Ben-Gurion said in November 1941: 'There was no doubt that England will be influenced by what America says, and it was most important to develop political Zionism in America.'[17]

During two long stays in the United States, Ben-Gurion explained his views to American Zionist leaders. At a meeting on 5 December 1940, Ben-Gurion predicted that the European war would destitute four to five million Jews. Palestine could easily absorb these victims of anti-Semitism, he claimed, but the British White Paper threatened to prevent Zionism from accomplishing its mission of mercy. Statehood, Ben-Gurion argued, was the only 'means' through which future Jewish emigration to Palestine could be ensured.[18]

Nahum Goldmann, a German-born Zionist who attended the meeting as a representative of the Jewish Agency in Washington, immediately recognized that using a post-war refugee problem to justify the establishment of a Jewish state could be a very effective tactic. American Jews were extremely concerned about the fate of European Jewry and feared that powerful nativist sentiment would prevent the refugees from finding a home in the United States after the war. Therefore, if Zionists could respond to American Jews' dismay about the callousness of their Christian neighbours by proposing a dramatic solution to the predicted post-war refugee problem, wide public support would follow.[19]

Ben-Gurion's persistent arguing of his case and Britain's uncompromising enforcement of the White Paper steadily convinced most American Zionist leaders to accept the goal of statehood. In late 1941, they began preparations for a major conference, where the entire Zionist movement in the United States could formally unite around the goal of immediate statehood.

Finally, on 6 May 1942, 586 American Zionists and 67 foreign guests met at New York's Biltmore Hotel for the Extraordinary Zionist Conference, which would plan the redemption of the Jewish people. The gathering delegates knew that they were meeting at a time of grave danger, but did not know that Adolf Hitler had already begun his Final Solution to the refugee problem. However, Chaim Weizmann and his compatriots were aware that Nazi rule subjected European Jewry to starvation, persecution and murder.[20]

At the Biltmore Conference, Weizmann eloquently explained why the suffering of European Jewry would not end with the defeat of the Nazis. He predicted that 25 per cent of east European Jewry would perish as a result of Nazi brutality and atrocities. The four million homeless Jews who survived the war would 'float' between heaven and hell. The United States and its Allies would not absorb many of these survivors. Palestine was the only practical solution to this dilemma and Weizmann argued that 'the very weight of the tragedy and the lack of a rational solution except through Palestine, will . . . focus and force the attention of the world to this solution.' The Biltmore audience enthusiastically responded to Weizmann's declaration: 'I would like to relieve the non-Jewish world of the trouble of settling our problems. We can do it ourselves. We can do it ourselves, and with God's help, we shall do it ourselves.'[21]

Palestine's importance to the solution of a post-war refugee problem, as outlined by Weizmann and other speakers at Biltmore, became the primary basis for pro-Zionist agitation and diplomacy among the Christian public and leaders during the years following the Biltmore Conference. After Biltmore it would be refined and polished. Zionists would not only argue that a large body of Jewish refugees would require a home, but that the security of the Christian world depended upon their settlement in Palestine.

German armies had spread anti-Semitism throughout Europe. A large number of destitute and stateless Jews in Europe after the Second World War would allow a new demagogue like Hitler to use anti-Semitism and Jewish scapegoats to seize power. A Third World War would thus surely emerge out of the ruins of the Second World War.[22]

The delegates at Biltmore realized that this type of argument played to what they believed was the selfish self-interest of Christian leaders who would never be moved by humanitarian appeals to aid the Jews. However, they also knew that their own support of Jewish statehood rested on other rationales. Most of them had been Zionists long before Hitler came to power in Germany, and their commitment to Jewish nationalism went beyond any need to solve an immediate Jewish refugee crisis. They were fully convinced that Zionism would solve, once and for all times, the 2,000-year-old problem of anti-Semitism.

Of all the Zionists at Biltmore, Abba Hillel Silver most clearly articulated the belief that Jewish statehood was not merely a practical solution to Nazi persecution. For Silver, like many Jews, Jewish history for 2,000 years seemed to be one long chain of persecution and tragedy. He could see nothing unique about the experience of Jews in Nazi-occupied territories. Their plight was no different from that of their ancestors who had endured forced conversions, expulsions, inquisitions and pogroms. Anti-Semitism predated Hitler and the defeat of the Nazis, he predicted, would not be the final cure to this affliction. As a Zionist, Silver believed that the entire course of Jewish history could be changed by the bold act of re-establishing the Jewish state destroyed two millennia before by the Roman Empire. The American people, he said, had to understand that 'the ultimate solution of the Jewish problem must finally be sounded, and the ultimate solution is the establishment of a Jewish Nation in Palestine.'[23]

Following Silver's address, the conference overwhelmingly ratified a declaration making the creation of a Jewish commonwealth the immediate and major goal of the American Zionist movement. In the propaganda they prepared for Christian consumption after Biltmore, Zionists argued that only a Palestinian Jewish nation could solve the post-war refugee problem. However, the radical promise to solve the 'Jewish problem' and to end Jewish persecution was especially effective in winning the support of the American Jewish masses who were grieving for their suffering European brethren. As American Jews became more aware of the magnitude of Nazi murder and destruction, the Zionist plan to revolutionize Jewish existence became almost irresistibly attractive.

The triumph of Jewish statehood at Biltmore cheered American Zionists, but in August, three months after the conference, Stephen Wise received a distressing message from Dr Gerhart Riegner, informing him that the Germans were systematically murdering the Jews of Europe. Riegner, representing the World Jewish Congress in Geneva, had asked American diplomats to inform Wise of the terrible news, but State Department officials, characteristically insensitive and possibly influenced by anti-Semitism, decided not to inform the rabbi. Wise nevertheless learned of Riegner's message from Jewish leaders in Britain, and approached Under-Secretary of State Sumner Welles, who asked him to keep the information confidential until it could be verified. When Welles finally authorized Wise to release the news, the rabbi immediately held a press conference on 24 November 1942.[24]

Wise's announcement was electrifying. Jewish leaders quickly declared a day of fast and mourning, and at Wise's initiative, a delegation of American Jewish leaders met with President Roosevelt. The President offered his condolences and sympathy, but suggested no plan for the immediate salvation of European Jewry.[25]

By this time it was apparent to American Jewish leaders that the immediate fate of European Jews could be determined only by the Germans who sought to destroy them or the Allies who might be able to rescue them. Only Roosevelt and Churchill had the means necessary to threaten Germany and its satellite states with retribution, to launch rescue operations and to pressure neutral states that bordered the Reich to offer haven to escaping Jews. Accordingly, representatives of major Jewish organizations formed the Joint Emergency Committee on European Affairs which existed for only a few months, but did lobby the American government to rescue European Jewry. American Zionists were in the forefront of these efforts, which included sponsoring mass rallies throughout the nation calling for government action on rescue.[26]

The most important of the American Jewish mass meetings was the 'Stop Hitler Now' rally organized by the American Jewish Congress with the cooperation of the American Federation of Labor and the Congress of Industrial Organizations. On 1 March 1943, over 21,000 people jammed into New York's Madison Square Garden as an expression of support for the millions of European Jews threatened with extinction. Jewish leaders presented an eleven-point rescue programme to the rally which included a call for the creation of an intergovernmental rescue agency.[27]

American Zionists, particularly Stephen Wise, played important roles in the organization of the 'Stop Hitler Now' rally. The left-wing Zionist journal of Hashomer Hatza'ir, *Youth and Nation* hoped that American Jewish pressure would force the Roosevelt administration to lead the rescue of European Jewry.[28]

American and British Jewish pressure did, in fact, force a response from the Allied governments. In early March 1943, Washington and London announced that they would hold a conference to develop plans to aid European Jewry. British and American officials originally intended to have the rescue conference in Ottawa, Canada, but they later decided to switch the location to Bermuda where reporters and the representatives of Jewish

organizations would be less likely to intrude on the privacy of the conferees.[29]

When the Bermuda Conference opened on 19 April 1943, American
Zionists hoped that the Allies would develop a plan for the salvation of
European Jewry. Tragically, however, the Bermuda Conference failed to
change the fate of the millions of Jews destined for the gas chambers. The
American representatives to the conference announced that the most
efficient way to rescue European Jewry was to ensure a speedy Allied
victory and implied that the Jewish rescue proposals would hinder the war
effort. America's refusal to consider any plan involving a breaching of the
nation's immigration quota handicapped the Bermuda Conference from
the day of its opening, as did the British refusal to deviate from the White
Paper restrictions. Despite optimistic statements following the conference
by the participants, the Bermuda Conference rescued no one.[30]

The obvious decision of the Allies to abandon European Jewry to its
fate reconfirmed for American Zionists all the lessons they had learned
during the previous decade. Over and over again, Christian governments
had demonstrated their callousness to Jewish suffering, and their unwillingness to be moved by humanitarian pleas for Jewish survival. It was clear
that if Jews were to be saved, Jews themselves, and particularly American
Jews, would have to shoulder the burden. In a 2 May address to the
National Conference for Palestine, Abba Hillel Silver condemned the
Bermuda Conference. Silver angrily proclaimed that, 'the enemies of Israel
seek us out and single us out, but our friends would like to forget our
existence as a people.' He concluded that this latest tragedy of persecution
must be the last ever suffered by Jewry. He declared, 'we now wish to be
noble and free and as a free people in its own land.'[31]

The day after Silver's angry speech, leading American Zionists met to
discuss the Allies' failure at Bermuda. Moshe Furmansky, a left-wing
socialist Zionist, suggested that American Zionists immediately organize a
mass protest campaign against the White Paper's restriction on Jewish
immigration to Palestine. Nahum Goldmann seconded Furmansky's proposal, but added that if Zionists wanted to conduct a massive attack on
the White Paper, they would have to cease demonstrating against the
massacre of European Jewry. Goldmann explained that the Zionists' limited
resources made it impossible to engage in two major campaigns at the
same time. Rabbi Wolf Gold, a leader of Mizrachi, the Orthodox Jewish
Zionist organization, disagreed with Goldmann. He believed that action
against the White Paper was 'long overdue', but he did not understand
why it would preclude mass action against the Nazi extermination programme. Gold maintained that the two issues could be linked together,
since the only answer to the problem of rescue was to open the gates of
Palestine.[32]

While Gold and Goldmann disagreed about the relationship of a drive to press the government to attempt rescue and an anti-White Paper campaign, no one at the meeting questioned whether Nazi extermination policies threatened to undermine the Zionist argument for Jewish statehood. Long after Stephen Wise's terrifying November 1942 announcement, Zionists continued to insist that a large number of homeless Jews would survive the war and that the only practical solution to their plight would be resettlement in a Jewish state. The Zionists, after all, believing that Christians would never be motivated by charity, had constructed a complex argument for Jewish statehood that required the existence of a substantial number of Jewish refugees at the end of the war. If these Jewish refugees were not present, Zionists must have feared, they would be left with no effective argument with which to approach the Western governments. Understandably, then, few American Zionists were able to comprehend that Nazi gas chambers threatened to solve the 'Jewish problem' in a most gruesome manner.

In mid-1943, one lone voice within the councils of American Zionism questioned the logic of remaining loyal to the Biltmore resolution's demand for a Jewish commonwealth while the Holocaust continued. On 1 June 1943, Chaim Weizmann, then in the United States for an extended visit, attended a meeting of American Zionist leaders. Zionists, he said, had to consider seriously the implications of the Nazi extermination of European Jewry. Where, he asked, would the millions of Jews who were supposed to go to Palestine (and were necessary to create a Jewish majority there) come from? Weizmann urged Jewish nationalists to abandon 'old methods' and 'slogans' and to seek out new strategies and positions. These, however, he did not specify.[33]

Weizmann's stark and depressing analysis of the problems confronting the Zionist movement sparked a lively discussion among the American Zionist leaders. Rabbi Meyer Berlin, a Palestinian leader of Mizrachi who was also on a visit to the United States, argued that such a bleak portrayal of the Zionist future would be strongly opposed in Palestine where the *Yishuv* generally believed that peace would bring the implementation of the Biltmore programme. He insisted that no one could accurately forecast how many Jews would survive the 'massacres' in Europe; millions of Jews might well endure.[34]

The *furor* caused by Weizmann's comments continued after the meeting. On 25 June Weizmann wrote to Stephen Wise that his remarks at the meeting 'have been construed as a deviation from the Biltmore program and that as a result a cable has been sent to Palestine in protest against this "heresy" '. Subjected to censure and criticism, Weizmann retreated from his position. Publicly, he followed the orthodox Zionist line, while he privately worried about the consequences of European Jewry's demise on the Zionist programme.[35]

As Chaim Weizmann despaired about the effects of mass extermination on Jewish nationalism, and while Allied planning for the Bermuda Conference continued, Zionists prepared to continue the work they had begun at the Biltmore Hotel in May 1942. Now that American Zionists were united around the statehood goal, they began to organize a national conference representing all American Jews, which would endorse the Zionist programme.

On 29 August 1943, 500 delegates elected by their communities or selected to represent major Jewish organizations gathered at the Waldorf Astoria for the opening of the American Jewish Conference. A majority of the delegates were Zionists, reflecting the organizational successes of the Zionist movement. However, to ensure the participation of the prestigious American Jewish Committee which remained hostile to Jewish statehood, Zionist leaders agreed to a compromise under which the conference would endorse a call for ending White Paper immigration restrictions, but would not specifically mention statehood.[36]

Although the issue of Zionism promised to be the dominant issue at the conference, the plight of European Jewry was an ever-present concern. To symbolize the seriousness of the occasion, delegates gathered in a room decorated only with the flags of the United States and the Zionist movement. Following a memorial service, B'nai B'rith president Henry Monsky welcomed the delegates and chastised the Allies for failing to undertake 'practical measures for the relief of the millions who have been persecuted, pillaged, pilloried and devastated'. He then demanded that the British White Paper of 1939 be withdrawn, but avoided calling for the immediate creation of a Jewish state in Palestine.[37]

Other speakers at the American Jewish Conference followed the trend set by Monsky and avoided asking the conference to endorse the Biltmore resolution's demand for the immediate creation of a Jewish state. However, not all American Zionists were pleased with the abandonment of the Biltmore programme. One of the disgruntled delegates, Emanuel Neumann, approached Abba Hillel Silver and asked him to speak in favour of Jewish statehood. Silver was not scheduled to appear before the conference, but Neumann hurriedly arranged for him to address the delegates on Monday night, 30 August 1943.[38]

Silver, then 50 years old and at the peak of his capabilities, proved more than able to meet the task that Neumann set for him. In a masterful speech, he championed the ideal of Jewish statehood and defeated all those who had sought compromise. The powerful response to his speech came not from the uniqueness of what he said, but rather because he eloquently summarized all that American Jewry had learned and experienced in their previous encounters with anti-Semitism and with 'friendly' Christian governments. He brilliantly reflected the concerns and hopes of American Jews who were living through the hell of a war in which millions of their brethren were being butchered while their own government did nothing to stop the slaughter.[39]

Calling on his audience to look beyond the war years, Silver warned that many Jews were falsely hoping that the Second World War would achieve 'what an Allied victory failed to give them after the last war'. International treaties and guarantees of minority rights were useless because they ignored the principal cause of Jewish suffering, 'the immemorial problem of our national homelessness'. All Jewish history since the exile from Palestine consisted of one long line of tragedies. He explained that, 'There is a stout black cord which connects the era of Fichte in Germany with its feral cry of "hep, hep", and the era of Hitler with its cry of "Jude verrecke".' There was only one solution for the 'persistent emergency', the 'millennial tragedy' of Jewish life. 'There is but one solution for national homelessness. That is a national home!'

Silver asserted that there could be no compromise on the commonwealth demand, because Jewish statehood was the 'cry of despair' of a people who had suffered yesterday, were suffering today, and would probably suffer tomorrow if their prayer was not answered. Great Britain's betrayal of its Balfour Declaration pledge clearly proved that Zionists could not rely on the goodwill of Christian governments which would only protect the Jews if it served their own national interests. Silver proclaimed that the 'crucifixion' of the Jewish people must end, saying:

> From the infested, typhus-ridden ghetto of Warsaw, from the death-block of Nazi occupied lands, where myriads of our people are awaiting execution by the slow or the quick method, from a hundred concentration camps which befoul the map of Europe, from the pitiful ranks of our wandering hosts over the entire face of the earth, comes the cry: 'Enough; there must be a final end to all of this, a sure and certain end.'[40]

As Silver finished speaking, the conference audience spontaneously arose and sang 'Hatikvah', the Zionist anthem. The highly emotional ovation that followed seemed to seal Silver's victory over those who had attempted to avoid the statehood issue.[41]

The conference's Palestine Committee, charged with the wording of a Palestine resolution to be presented to all the delegates, discussed Silver's call for the historical rescue of the Jewish people. Robert Goldman, a Zionist representing the Union of American Hebrew Congregations, directly confronted Silver's thesis that the best response to Hitler's extermination policies was immediately to create a Jewish state so that future persecution would be impossible. Goldman told the Palestine Committee that American Jewry faced two problems. The long-range problem was the need to create a Jewish state. The 'immediate problem', he continued, 'is rescue; and I don't care what else you say or how you characterize it, or what you say about me for saying it, that is the immediate problem and that is the problem that we should be concerned with.' Goldman insisted that the first task of American Jewry was to save their European kin and he warned that

> if the long-run problem which we want to project is going to interfere with the solution of the immediate problem ... you have no right to insist on that problem that may result in the loss of thousands and hundreds of thousands more Jews that could otherwise be saved in the next few years.

Some British and American officials, he explained, were totally opposed to increased Jewish immigration to Palestine, while others supported opening Palestine's doors as a humanitarian response to Hitler's extermination policies. If Zionists insisted on demanding statehood, Arab opposition in the entire Middle East would intensify, making it impossible for proponents of increased immigration to win their case. If this happened, hundreds of thousands of Jews would be left 'in places where they cannot be rescued'.[42]

Proponents of Jewish statehood on the Palestine committee wasted little time before challenging Robert Goldman's position. Emanuel Neumann delivered the most articulate and vigorous condemnation of a 'rescue-first' strategy. The 'immediate problem' facing the conference, he said, was not peculiar to the Jews of their day. For centuries, Jews had been in a 'permanent state of emergency'. He charged that Jewish leaders always concerned themselves with the 'immediate problems', thereby ignoring the underlying cause of their suffering and persecution. Had Jews dealt with the problem of 'homelessness' earlier, he speculated, 'either a Hitler would not have arisen in our time, or, if one had, we might have had a country under Jewish control in which Jews of Germany and other lands could have been received – and received in large numbers.' Neumann complained: 'It has been our misfortune throughout our history that we have not been able to look ahead, to plan ahead, and to provide this radical solution.' If American Jewry in 1943 failed to put an end to the long history of Jewish suffering by supporting the creation of a commonwealth in Palestine, Neumann concluded, 'we shall be contemptible in our own eyes'.[43]

Neumann's and Silver's argument won many more supporters than did Goldman's. With the exception of four delegates, including the representatives of the American Jewish Committee, the entire American Jewish Conference voted for a resolution demanding the establishment of a Jewish commonwealth in Palestine.[44]

After the American Jewish Conference, American Jewry joined the Zionist crusade. Under Silver's leadership they organized congressional and popular support for the creation of a Jewish commonwealth in Palestine. Sadly, concentration on the statehood issue left few resources for an

241

immediate rescue campaign. As Nahum Goldmann correctly sensed in May 1943, Zionists simply were not powerful enough to carry out two aggressive political campaigns. As a result, the extremely efficient lobby and propaganda machine fashioned by the American Zionists championed Jewish statehood, not the rescue of European Jewry.

Zionists at the time, however, could not actually recognize that there were two campaigns. The Arab revolt, the partition controversy and Britain's inhumane White Paper policy had convinced them that the Zionist presence in Palestine, the key to Jewish survival, was threatened with destruction. Accordingly, they launched *their* rescue campaign well before they learned of the Holocaust. The news of the extermination and the Allies' disgraceful failure to respond to the mass murder reconfirmed the American Zionists' belief that Christian governments would not be moved by humanitarian pleas and that Jews must take their destiny into their own hands. They left the American Jewish Conference religiously believing that the creation of a Jewish state would save future generations of Jews from other Auschwitzes and Treblinkas. Morever, they firmly held that their experiences with Christian governments proved that any rescue campaign, which would have had to be based on humanitarian appeals, would be doomed to failure.

American Zionists were ideologically and politically unable to give the rescue of European Jewry priority over the creation of a Jewish state. They could not distinguish between the rescue issue and the statehood issue which seemed to be inextricably linked by the Zionist view of Jewish history and by their own experiences since Hitler's rise to power in 1933. They resolved to put an end, once and for all, to Jewish suffering. The Second World War, which Zionists expected would end with the redrawing of the world's boundaries, seemed to offer them one last chance to achieve their goal. For American Zionists, failure to seize the time would be criminal.

NOTES

1 There is a rich literature on the American response to the Holocaust. Among the best works are: David S. Wyman, *The Abandonment of the Jews: America and the Holocaust* (New York: Pantheon, 1984); Henry L. Feingold, *The Politics of Rescue: The Roosevelt Administration and the Holocaust 1938–1945* (New Brunswick, NJ: Rutgers University Press, 1970); Arthur Morse, *While Six Million Died* (New York: Random House, 1968); Saul S. Friedman, *No Haven for the Oppressed* (Detroit: Wayne State University Press, 1973); Yehuda Bauer, *American Jewry and the Holocaust: The American Jewish Joint Distribution Committee, 1939–1945* (Detroit: Wayne State University Press, 1981); Richard Breitman and Alam M. Kraut, *American Refugee Policy and European Jewry, 1933–1945* (Bloomington: Indiana University Press, 1987). Also see Dina Porat, *The Blue and the Yellow Stars of David: The Zionist Leadership in*

Palestine and the Holocaust, 1939–1945 (Cambridge, Mass.: Harvard University Press, 1990).

2 On US refugee policy in the 1930s, see David S. Wyman, *Paper Walls: America and the Refuge Crisis, 1938–1941* (Amherst: University of Massachusetts Press, 1968).

3 Wise to Brandeis, 5 April 1933, Brandeis Records, Microfilm Roll No. 22, Zionist Archives and Library (hereafter ZAL). For a full discussion of the Zionist response to the refugee crisis, see Aaron Berman, *Nazism, the Jews, and American Zionism 1933–1948* (Detroit: Wayne State University Press, 1990), Chapter I.

4 *Palestine Department of Migration Annual Report, 1934* (Jerusalem: 1935), p. 13; *1935* (Jerusalem: 1936), p. 10; *1936* (Jerusalem: 1937), p. 9. For a detailed dicussion of the American Zionist response to the Arab revolt and the partition controversy which followed, see Berman, *Nazism, the Jews and American Zionism*, Chapter II.

5 *New York Times*, 21 April 1936, p. 22.

6 Albert Viton, 'The fate of Zionism,' *Nation*, 19 December 1936, pp. 725–8; Albert Viton, 'A solution for Palestine', *Nation*, 26 December 1936, pp. 756–8.

7 Philip Bernstein, 'Promise of Zionism', *Nation*, 2 January 1937, pp. 12–15.

8 Arthur Lourie to Stephen Wise and Louis Lipsky, 4 April 1937, Brandeis Records, Microfilm Roll No. 26, ZAL; Chaim Weizmann, *Trial and Error: The Autobiography of Chaim Weizmann* (New York: Schocken Books, 1949, reprint 1966), pp. 319–20.

9 'Hadassah petition to the U.S. Secretary of State and the British Ambassador in the U.S. – May 1937 – passed at the Hadassah Spring Conference', attached to minutes of Hadassah National Board Meeting, 11 May 1937, Hadassah Papers, ZAL; Minutes of Hadassah National Board Meeting, 2 June 1937, Hadassah Papers, ZAL; 'Rejected', *New Palestine*, 30 April 1937, p. 4; Greenberg, 'Balkanization of Palestine', *Jewish Frontier*, May 1937, pp. 12–14; 'Cantonization – an experiment in geographic surgery', *Jewish Outlook*, May 1937, p. 4.

10 Weizmann, *Trial and Error*, p. 386; Walter Laqueur, *A History of Zionism* (New York: Holt, Rinehart & Winston, 1972), p. 518; Jacob C. Hurewitz, *The Struggle for Palestine* (New York: Schocken Books, 1950, reprint 1976), p. 77; Norman Rose, *Chaim Weizmann: A Biography* (New York: Viking, 1986), pp. 325–7. See reprints of Weizmann's address in 'The Zionist Congress debates', *Jewish Frontier*, September 1937, pp.22–5; 'A basis for the growth of Jewish life', *New Palestine*, 3 September 1937, pp. 4–5.

11 Szold to Mack, 16 August 1937, Brandeis Records, Microfilm Roll No. 26, ZAL. Also see: Melvin Urofsky, *A Voice that Spoke for Justice: The Life and Times of Stephen S. Wise* (Albany: State University of New York Press, 1982), pp. 286–7; *New York Times*, 9 August 1937, p. 5; 'Answer to Britain is "Non Possumus"', *The New Palestine*, 3 September 1937, pp. 5–6.

12 *New York Times*, 12 August 1937, p. 1; Weizmann, *Trial and Error* p. 387; Laqueur, *History of Zionism*, p. 520; 'Congress and Agency Act', *Jewish Frontier*, September 1937, p. 27.

13 Szold to Brandeis, 31 December 1937, Brandeis Records, Microfilm Roll No. 26, ZAL. Also see Louis Lipsky, 'Toward a Jewish state', *New Palestine*, 3 September 1937, p. 3.

14 'Mrs Szold's presentation of the anti-partition position', attached to minutes of Hadassah National Board Meeting, 2 March 1938, Hadassah Papers, ZAL.

15 Report on meeting of Louis Brandeis, Eliezer Kaplan and Stephen Wise, 7

February 1937, Brandeis Records, Microfilm Roll No. 26, ZAL; Report on visit of Stephen Wise to Franklin Roosevelt, 5 October 1936, Brandeis Records, Microfilm Roll No. 25, ZAL.

16 Transcript of 1937 ZOA Convention, p. 418.

17 Monty Noam Penkower, *The Jews Were Expendable: Free World Diplomacy and the Holocaust* (Urbana: University of Illinois Press, 1983), pp. 50–3; Monty Noam Penkower, 'Ben Gurion, Silver and the 1941 UPA National Conference on Palestine: a turning point in American Zionist history', *American Jewish History* LXIX (September 1979), pp. 66–91; Yehuda Bauer, *From Diplomacy to Resistance* (Philadelphia: Jewish Publication Society of America, 1970), Chapter 6; Michael Bar-Zohar, *Ben-Gurion: A Biography*, trans. Peretz Kidron (New York: Delacorte Press, 1978), pp. 101–5. For a discussion of the American Zionists' adoption of Jewish statehood as their immediate goal, see Berman, *Nazism, the Jews and American Zionism*, Chapter III.

18 'Report of a meeting with Mr Ben-Gurion held at the Winthrop Hotel', 5 December 1940, Emanuel Neumann Papers, Ben-Gurion file, ZAL.

19 'Report of a meeting with Mr Ben-Gurion held at the Winthrop Hotel', 5 December 1940, Neumann Papers, Ben-Gurion file, ZAL.

20 'Extraordinary Zionist Conference, New York 1942, Stenographic Protocol', pp. 13–14, 278, ZAL. Also see American Emergency Committee for Zionist Affairs Minutes, 5 May 1942, Emanuel Neumann Papers, American Zionist Emergency Committee file, ZAL.

21 Weizmann, 'Extraordinary Zionist Conference, New York 1942, Stenographic Protocol', pp. 20–40, ZAL.

22 See, for example, Leon Feuer, *Why a Jewish State* (New York: R. R. Smith, 1942).

23 Silver, 'Extraordinary Zionist Conference, New York 1942, Stenographic Protocol', pp. 456–78, ZAL.

24 For a discussion of the American Zionist response to the Holocaust, see Berman, *Nazism, the Jews and American Zionism*, Chapter IV.

25 *New York Times*, 26 November 1942, p. 16; Eliyho Matzozky, 'The response of American Jewry and its representative organizations between November 24, 1942, and April 19, 1943, to mass killings of Jews in Europe' (Master's thesis, Yeshiva University, 1979), pp. 13–14, Chapter 3; Wyman, *Abandonment of the Jews*, pp. 71–3.

26 Wyman, *Abandonment of the Jews*, pp. 93–8, 102–3, 109–11, 120–1, 168–9; Edward Pinsky, 'American Jewish unity during the Holocaust – the Joint Emergency Committee, 1943', *American Jewish History*, LXII (June 1983), p. 477–94.

27 *New York Times*, 2 March 1943, p. 2; Feingold, *Politics of Recue*, pp. 176–7; Wyman, *Abandonment of the Jews*, pp. 88–9; 'Program action on the rescue of Jews in Nazi occupied territories adopted by the Joint Committee on the European Emergency Jewish Situation', n.d., Abba Hillel Silver Papers, Manson File I–81, Abba Hillel Silver Memorial Archives, The Temple, Cleveland, Ohio (hereafter AHSMA).

28 'End the conspiracy of inaction', *Youth and Nation*, March 1943, pp. 3–4.

29 Wyman, *Abandonment of the Jews*, p. 108.

30 For background on the Bermuda Conference, see Wyman, *Abandonment of the Jews*, Chapter 6; Feingold, *Politics of Rescue*, Chapter 7; Morse, *While Six Million Died*, Chapter III; Friedman, *No Haven for the Oppressed*, Chapter 7.

31 Silver's 2 May 1943 address can be found in Abba Hillel Silver, *Vision and*

Victory: A Collection of Addresses, 1942–1948 (New York: Zionist Organization of America, 1949), pp. 1–12.

32 American Emergency Committee for Zionist Affairs (AECZA) Minutes, 3 May 1943, No. 59, ZAL.

33 Minutes of AECZA Office Committee meeting, 1 June 1943, Silver Papers, AHSMA.

34 ibid.

35 Weizmann to Wise, 25 June 1943, letter No. 42 in *The Letters and Papers of Chaim Weizmann*, Series A. vol. XXI, ed. Barnet Litvinoff (New Brunswick, NJ: Transaction Books, Rutgers University, 1979). Also see Weizmann to Weisgal, 23 August 1943, letter No. 58 in ibid.; and Weizmann to Weisgal, 13 April 1944, letter No. 151 in ibid.

36 On the American Jewish Conference, see Berman, *Nazism, the Jews and American Zionism*, pp. 108–12.

37 Alexander S. Kohanski (ed.) *The American Jewish Conference: Its Organization and Proceedings of the First Session* (New York: American Jewish Conference, 1944), pp. 56–7, 67–70.

38 Emanuel Neumann, *In the Arena* (New York: Herzl Press, 1977), p. 191; Samuel Halperin, *The Political World of American Zionism* (Detroit: Wayne State University Press, 1961), p. 234; Melvin Urofsky, *We Are One!: American Jewry and Israel* (Garden City, NY: Anchor Press, 1978), p. 27.

39 For a biography of Silver, see Marc Lee Raphael, *Abba Hillel Silver: A Profile in American Judaism* (New York: Holmes & Meier, 1989).

40 Silver's address can be found in Silver, *Vision and Victory*, pp. 13–21; and Arthur Hertzberg (ed.) *The Zionist Idea: A Historical Analysis and Reader* (New York: Atheneum, 1959, reprint 1973), pp. 592–600.

41 Rose Halprin noted that 'Dr Silver's magnificent address won over to the cause of Palestine many unaffiliated and previously unenthusiastic persons.' Minutes of Hadassah National Board Meeting, 8 September 1943, Hadassah Papers, ZAL.

42 'Minutes of the Palestine Committee, American Jewish Conference Sessions held Aug. 31 through Sept. 1, 1943', pp. 73–7, ZAL.

43 ibid., pp. 218–36.

44 ibid., pp. 266–70; Kohanski, *American Jewish Conference*, pp. 178–81.

15

DIFFERENT WORLDS
British perceptions of the Final Solution during the Second World War

Tony Kushner

The British novelist, Martin Amis, has written that at the railway station in Treblinka, 'the four dimensions were intriguingly disposed. A place without depth. And a place without time.' If there is a need, as Michael Marrus suggests, 'to integrate the history of the Holocaust into the general stream of historical consciousness', it does not imply that the Holocaust can be made explicable by 'normal' methods of historical enquiry.[1] The Holocaust does not exist outside history, yet its very study challenges many of the basic assumptions of the historical profession; hence the importance of the remarks of Claude Lanzmann that 'any Work that would do justice to the Holocaust must take as its first principle the shattering of chronology.'[2] In terms of the perpetrators, even the most extreme intentionalist interpretation of Nazi policy towards the Jews acknowledges a degree of confusion, opportunism and contradiction in the various stages of persecution and destruction (and especially the significance of local variation in all the bureaucratic processes). The study of the Holocaust (or at least modern perceptions of it) has become too Auschwitz-centred, lending it a deceptively simple chronological framework. For the survivors, it has been suggested that 'the Holocaust has a different beginning for each victim'. With the massive growth of Holocaust testimony in recent years – whether on film, paper or tape – it is no longer justifiable to write Holocaust history without reference to the victims and survivors. Yet the inclusion of their voices poses immense problems for historians faced with the task of providing a 'logical' framework from which to make sense of these many individual chronologies. To quote Lanzmann again: 'The chronological account that begins with the boycott in April 1933 and leads us *naturally* into the gas chambers at Auschwitz or Treblinka is . . . rather dismally flat and one-dimensional.'[3]

Holocaust history can no longer be written in its initial form (that is with only passing reference to the Jews themselves). Nor can it be studied as a purely Nazi or Nazi-influenced phenomenon: the role of the outside world must also be considered if a truly comprehensive and synthetic approach is to be achieved. Yet the inclusion of the reactions and responses of the free world creates even greater problems in terms of providing a straightforward Holocaust chronology. The Allied countries and those under Nazi control inhabited different moral universes during the war. Information about the crimes committed against the Jews in the latter was received with varying time-lags in the former. The assimilation of that information, however, occurred at even more differing rates. Indeed, this chapter will argue that in the British case, understanding that there was a Nazi plan to exterminate all the Jews, and that in many parts of Europe it was largely carried out, did not occur until well after the liberation of the camps in 1944 and 1945. It will explore the impact of the news concerning the destruction of European Jewry, looking at the British state, public and Jewish minority but eschewing a top–down approach where popular opinion is merely assumed to have been conditioned from above by both government and press. Instead, this chapter will attempt a social history of Allied knowledge of the final solution providing a history from below which is neither patronizing or apologetic about British popular mentalities. Mary Nolan has suggested with regard to the German *Historikerstreit* (the historians' debate which developed in the 1980s on the nature of Nazism) that the right there 'has challenged social historians to connect everyday life and high politics, and to rethink each in the light of the other'. She suggests that the *Historikerstreit* 'serves as a deserved reprimand to Left historians who have ignored anti-Semitism, racism, and the Final Solution'.[4] Here the emphasis will be on the *ideological* underpinnings of British responses, whether from the state, public, media or Jewish minority. It will argue that ideological factors, which have been marginalized in favour of explanations concentrating on either the quality of information received in the west or psychological avoidance of 'atrocity stories', are crucial in determining the unique chronology (or, more accurately, chronologies) connecting the United Kingdom to the Holocaust in the war.

I

In the early 1960s Andrew Sharf, sponsored by the Institute of Race Relations, carried out the first major research into Allied knowledge of the Holocaust in a study published as *The British Press and Jews under Nazi Rule* (1964). Sharf stressed that any British incomprehension of the enormity of Nazi crimes was due to 'the psychological commonplace that, with the best will in the world, it is hard to grasp the meaning of suffering wholly outside one's immediate experience and for which, moreover, there is very little historical precedent'. He did consider, however, whether 'the inadequate response to Jewish suffering in Europe [was] also the result of widespread dislike of Jews in England'. Sharf concluded that the latter factor only operated in the case of a small minority and more important was 'an inveterate British inability to grasp imaginatively what could happen on the continent of Europe'.[5] The lack of comprehension was not, in Sharf's view, due to a shortage of information because for all stages of Nazi anti-Semitism, including the extermination process, the British 'Press knew well and printed accurately exactly what was happening'. Writing four years later, Arthur Morse in a study of American and British 'indifference' to the Jewish plight in the war also assumed full knowledge on behalf of the leading Allied nations.[6] It was not until Walter Laqueur's *The Terrible Secret* (1980) that a more sophisticated analysis emerged. In particular, Laqueur asked with regard to the Allies and the news of the Holocaust 'what is the meaning of "to know" and "to believe"?' Laqueur analysed both the quality and quantity of information available and concluded that 'all the evidence shows that news of the "Final Solution" had been received in 1942 all over Europe, even though many of the details were not yet known.'[7]

Laqueur partly followed Sharf in his explanation of why this information was not believed – a psychological mechanism to reject that which is unacceptable. Similarly Laqueur rejected the explanation of anti-Semitism (although he did not deny its existence in the case of several British Foreign Office officials who came into direct contact with the information received). Ultimately, however, he concluded that 'when the veracity of the information becomes incontrovertible, continued resistance to it becomes almost inexplicable'.[8]

All these authors dealing with the question of Allied knowledge of the Holocaust, as well as Martin Gilbert who followed with his *Auschwitz and the Allies* (1981), were concerned with the various Allied governments (or governments-in-exile), press or Jewish leadership.[9] Laqueur did acknowledge that: 'It is important to know how widely the information was distributed and whether it was read and accepted.' Nevertheless, Laqueur acknowledged that this was 'usually more difficult to document' although he posited from the partial evidence, mainly relating to state officials, that:

> the fact that some information has been mentioned once or even a hundred times in secret reports or in mass circulation newspapers does not necessarily mean that it has been accepted and understood. Big figures become statistics, and statistics have no psychological impact. Some thought that the news about the Jewish tragedy was exaggerated, others did not doubt the information but had different priorities and preoccupations.[10]

In the United Kingdom a unique archive exists which includes the diaries of roughly 500 men and women who wrote for at least some of the period of the Second World War and beyond. These people were writing for the organization Mass-Observation which was set up in 1937 to investigate everyday British social life. Through their eyes, in conjunction with other similar materials as well as the press and government records, a new perspective can be found on British perceptions of the Holocaust. Moreover, some of the mysteries of incomprehension that have been referred to can be, if not totally solved, then at least teased out to reveal all their complexities and contradictions.[11]

II

In late October 1939 the British government published a White Paper on German Atrocities. All the details of the White Paper referred to the pre-war period yet, in terms of material on the Jews and the reaction to it, a pattern was set which (with one major exception) would be in operation for the rest of the war. First of all, the British government had wanted to avoid 'atrocity' propaganda but had been goaded into the White Paper by Nazi accusations about British concentration camps in South Africa before 1914. Second, it was unhappy about using stories about Jews, partly because officials distrusted Jewish sources but mainly due to a reluctance to identify in any way with the Jewish plight or somehow connect the British war effort with the protection of the Jews.[12] Public reactions to the White Paper indicate how important it is to take seriously the interrelationship between state and popular opinion in this area.

The queues and orders for copies of the White Paper might suggest it had a degree of success, but, sales apart, the document was another failed venture in terms of the British government's official information and propaganda at the start of the war.[13] A month earlier, the disastrous Ministry of Information poster campaign, '*Your* Courage, *Your* Cheerfulness, *Your* Resolution, Will Bring Us Victory', had actually emphasized the distance between state and public at the beginning of the conflict.[14] Responses to the White Paper reveal that again the British public believed they were being manipulated by the government. Official statements that the material had hitherto been suppressed so as not to risk the chances of peace with Germany were regarded as

Absolute . . . and perfect rot.

I now feel that a stronger and less grandmotherly government would have had the honesty to publish the account in peace-time, while a more honourable government would have refrained from doing so in war.

All these details [concerning the horrors of the German concentration camps] were known last September and yet we signed at Munich.

249

This is the limit of hypocrisy unless it is more sinister and is the beginning of a hate campaign.

I hate the inconsistency of policy, that kept it all quiet while we were busy buying off the Nazis' Western threats at the expense of Austria, Czechoslovakia, the Ukraine, etc., and now brings out the story full-blast with exclamations of righteous horror.

With regard to the [White Paper] on seeing this I thought [to] myself 'How come the atrocity stories'. This opinion was shared by my sister who said she supposed people were not being sufficiently enthusiastic about the war, so the Government had to whip up some hate.[15]

Few actually doubted the information contained in the White Paper and those who did were often sympathetic to the Nazi regime. Others were aware of the false atrocity stories of the First World War which along with scepticism about the press after 1918 heightened public cynicism about any 'official' news. Yet it was on such grounds that a university librarian from Leeds who, while accepting the validity of the reports, still 'thought it was a thoroughly bad thing to publish it *as propaganda – as atrocity-stories*'.[16] The government's later claims that its first attempt at 'atrocity' propaganda had been counterproductive were only partially justified – the White Paper did not lead to any sympathy towards Nazi Germany, indeed the reverse was true, but it did heighten public concern that they were being treated like children by the state. Also of great significance was the absence of any public debate of the fact that atrocities in the German concentration camps had been particularly committed against Jews. The state itself was partly responsible for this absence: it was decided to emphasize in 'the first few documents [ones] which are not so sensational as the Jewish ones but which show that perfectly good Aryans such as Niemoller and the German Catholics have also had to suffer'. There was material on Jews in camps such as Buchenwald and also on the events of Kristallnacht in Germany and Austria but these elicited no specific comment from the public.[17]

Several clear tendencies emerged from the White Paper. First, all future Nazi crimes would be viewed through the prism of 'atrocities' and thus run the risk of being dismissed as manipulative propaganda. Second, 'atrocities' would be connected to the German concentration camps of the late 1930s. The White Paper helped to break down the reluctance in Britain before the war to accept the brutality of these camps. Nevertheless, it was assumed that such camps were the limit of Nazi inhumanity and there was no idea in 1939 that the war could mean, as Hitler had expressed in January 1939, one of extermination against the Jews.[18] In spring 1945 camps such as Buchenwald and Belsen were liberated. The disclosures from the camps were generally linked by the British public to what they believed in 1939. The possibility of *death* camps such as Treblinka thus bypassed most people in Britain until well after the end of the war.[19] Third, the British state refused to emphasize any Jewish themes in its atrocity propaganda. Comments about the use of 'perfectly good Aryans such as Niemoller' by officials in the White Paper indicated a wider tendency to see the Jews as undeserving of sympathy (or at least a fear that this was how the British public felt about this aspect of Nazism). In the summer of 1940 George Bernard Shaw was stopped by the British government from making a broadcast about the persecution of the Jews for fear of upsetting public opinion, particularly in the United States. In 1941 the refusal to identify with the Jews as specific victims of the Nazis was made explicit by the Ministry of Information where 'horror stuff . . . must be used very sparingly and must deal always with treatment of indisputably innocent people. Not with violent political opponents. And not with Jews.'[20]

The avoidance of the Jewish issue requires some explanation: the British government consciously turned down in the first part of the war a chance to expose the most brutal aspect of its enemy's policies. At the heart of the state's reluctance to stress Nazi anti-Semitism was the existence of a powerful liberal discourse concerning the Jews. It on the one hand abhorred violence against the Jews as a minority group but, on the other, made it very difficult to accept the reality and scope of Nazi cruelty. Rather than seeking explanations at the level of plain hatred, many in Britain looked for a rational explanation for Nazi anti-Semitism.[21] Anti-Semitism was assumed to be the result of Jewish difference; antagonism was seen to be a natural reaction to the irritant of Jewish particularity. The *level* of Nazi anti-Semitism could not, however, be explained by this classic liberal assimilationalist theory. The response was thus to ignore evidence to the contrary, or, less frequently, to suggest that stories of persecution were subject to Jewish exaggeration.[22] The popular British image of 'the Jew' during the war was still one of a powerful, international figure which again did not match the reality of Jewish powerlessness exposed in the Holocaust.[23] Moreover, many government officials believed that to stress *Jewish* sufferings was also against liberal, universalist principles and their liberal perspective did not allow them to see that the Jewish case might be unique. As Frank Roberts, a senior official in the Foreign Office, put it as late as May 1944: 'The Allies rather resent the suggestion that Jews in particular have been more heroic or long-suffering than other nationals of occupied countries.'[24]

III

The net result at the start of the war was an unawareness on a popular level that the war had already brought disaster to the Jews of Europe. Just a couple of Mass-Observers in the first three months of the conflict referred to the fate of Jews in Poland. It is significant that when one of these received information on the BBC news that the Polish Jews were being treated even worse than the Poles by the Germans, she still considered it to be '80% . . . propaganda and exaggeration'. She was not convinced until she saw photographic evidence from the American *Time* magazine. Otherwise the British perception of German atrocities was still confined to the image of the concentration camp.[25] In terms of the Jewish minority in Britain, the start of the war was a bleak period for the refugees from Nazism, especially the child refugees who had left parents behind and now feared that they would never see them again. Yet for Anglo-Jewry as a whole the significance of the start of the war for their co-religionists on the continent had not sunk in. A columnist in the *Zionist Review* commented at the start of 1940: 'Speak to the average English Jew and he will agree that the Jews in what was once Poland are having an appalling time. It is questionable, however, whether one in a hundred here realises the full nature of the tragedy.' As the war progressed and the position of the Jews deteriorated, Anglo-Jewry's perception of the plight of European Jewry slipped ever further away from the grim reality. Why was this the case?[26]

In terms of evidence, Anglo-Jewry was in a privileged position: weekly journals such as the *Jewish Chronicle* and the *Zionist Review* provided constant news about developments in Europe (although it was not always prominently displayed or emphasized editorially).[27] Family correspondence provided another source of information although it inevitably declined as the war progressed. Yet Anglo-Jewry, as a whole, shied away from such evidence. On one level the news was too hard to take and if it was true it could only cause frustration to those unable to influence events. A degree of psychological avoidance on behalf of Anglo-Jewry undoubtedly did take place.

Samuel Rich, a minor Anglo-Jewish religious and communal figure, provides a classic example of these tendencies. In the 1930s he had been very active in the refugee movement and was appalled by Nazi brutality. After less than a year of the war, however, he was resigned to the fate of the Jews in Europe and became increasingly concerned just with the survival of his own family and Anglo-Jewry. In July 1940 Rich wrote in his diary that 'S[tephan] Wise called, he's to go to Lisbon as European "boss" of the Jewish World Congress.' Rich added: 'They've no idea of the impossibility of European work *now*.' Thereafter, the Jews of Europe rarely featured in Rich's prolific diary writing.[28]

Yet to understand this avoidance properly, it is important to take into account the pressures operating on Anglo-Jewry in the war. They were not only suffering all the hardships associated with life on the Home Front but were also afraid of the possibility of domestic anti-Semitism developing. Indeed its major papers and communal organizations (including alternative groups on the Left) devoted enormous resources and time to combating anti-Semitism in Britain during the war.[29] Anglo-Jewry during the conflict was a frightened community tied up with its own defence and the pressures operating on it to keep Jewish traditions alive in unfavourable circumstances. The distance from the events in Europe but also the domination of a domestic agenda was illustrated by a remarkable letter from the Chief Rabbi, Joseph Hertz, to the Archbishop of Canterbury in June 1942, exactly at the point when the first news of the Final Solution reached Britain. Hertz wrote with regard to religious dialogue, and the possibility of it leading to Jewish apostasy, that 'There are things that I fear more than pogroms.' Anglo-Jewry had neither the moral energy, vision or self-confidence, nor the financial resources to confront the horrors facing the Jews of Europe. Moreover, it was also imbued with liberal values and did not want to emphasize the specific Jewish plight for fear of alienating itself from state and public. Highly visible protests on behalf of persecuted Jewry were rejected as these themselves might create anti-Semitism in Britain.[30] The net result was that for all but an exceptional minority, Anglo-Jewry was left deeply shocked and with a lasting sense of guilt by the disclosures in 1945 relating to the Final Solution. Slowly after the war Anglo-Jewry started to grasp the full implications of what had happened to the Jewish communities of Europe. Nevertheless its sense of shame led to a silence that was not overcome until recent years.[31]

IV

It is thus important to understand that when the first news of the Final Solution reached Britain in the summer of 1942 it would be received by the state, public and Jewish community in a specific light. Past considerations of atrocities, attitudes towards Jews and the general state of the war would be as important as the news itself. The frustrations of those attempting to communicate the knowledge to those who seemed reluctant to 'use [their] imagination' in the period up to the end of 1942 were immense. Individuals such as Richard Lichtheim, Gerhard Riegner and Jan Karski who passed on the first reports faced disseminating information that was simply unacceptable: the mass-scale persecution of the Jews was extraordinarily difficult for a liberal-dominated society to accept.[32] A plan to exterminate totally the Jews proved to be a concept that was impossible for all but a tiny minority of both the British state and public to assimilate.

By the summer of 1942 the British public, at least, was out of touch with the position of European Jewry. In January 1942, ironically at the same time as the Wannsee Conference, the British press gave some publicity to a Soviet Union note on German atrocities. The Soviet account paid little attention to the Jews and these limited references made little impact in Britain.[33] Throughout 1942 more information became available about the mass killings perpetrated by the *Einsatzgruppen* in eastern Europe and in June 1942 the *Daily Telegraph* published a report of the Jewish labour *Bund* in Warsaw. The report referred to the mass shootings and liquidation of the ghettos but also to the use of gassing at Chelmno. It reported that already 700,000 Polish Jews had been killed and that the Nazis were intent on killing all the Jews in Europe. This information, along with other Polish details, received widespread coverage in the British press in late June/early July 1942.[34] It is significant, however, that Mass-Observation diaries would suggest that the impact of this news on the British public was minimal and some of the press reported it in terms of a pogrom rather than a systematic programme of mass killing.[35] Indeed, the news of an actual extermination programme in the second half of 1942 actually confirmed the view that atrocities in the form of massacres were taking place rather than a deliberate plan of extermination. Both the British state and the public remained one crucial step behind in their understanding of Nazi anti-Semitic policy in 1942. Thereafter, only a few in Britain before 1945 were able to grasp that something remarkably different to previous massacres in war or on a different plane to the pre-war camps was occurring in Nazi Europe.

In August 1942 Gerhard Riegner, representative of the World Jewish Congress in Geneva, sent a telegram to Washington and London that he had received an 'alarming report' about a plan in which all the Jews in countries occupied or controlled by the Nazis would 'be exterminated at one blow to resolve once and for all the Jewish Question in Europe'. David Allen in the Foreign Office was aware of all the deportations and the destruction in the Warsaw Ghetto yet he could not see that 'this rather wild story' confirmed that there was a policy to ' "exterminate at one blow". The German policy seems to be rather to eliminate "useless mouths" but to use able bodied Jews as slave labour'.[36] More and more evidence came to the west in 1942, yet officials such as Allen were reluctant to accept that the anti-Jewish massacres were 'the result of a plan drawn up on a given date at Hitler's headquarters'.[37] In December 1942 pressure grew from the Polish government in exile and Jewish and pro-Jewish lobbyists for an Allied declaration. The Foreign Office was opposed to such a move, not wishing to emphasize the particularity of the Jewish fate. If there was to be a declaration, Allen believed it should 'avoid specific reference to the *plan* of extermination'. Similarly Eleanor Rathbone, a great campaigner on behalf of the persecuted Jews, found that in early December 1942 the Political Warfare Executive, responsible for British propaganda abroad, 'don't feel sufficiently satisfied that Hitler actually signed a decree for mass extermination'.[38]

On a popular level, similar sentiments were expressed. The widespread reports in the press on the atrocities committed in Poland, followed by the Allied declaration in the middle of the month, created much anguish but there was disbelief that there could actually be a plan of extermination.

As a Mass-Observer from Bury St Edmunds wrote: 'I quite believe many are getting massacred, but I can't understand *any* Government deliberately ordering it.'[39] A minority thought they were part of a deliberate hate campaign or were the result of Jewish or Soviet invention, a theme with some resonance in pacifist and right-wing Catholic circles.[40] The popular writer Douglas Reed (who was one of the first to present a theory of Holocaust denial) also provided some support for those who were convinced that the Jews were a powerful world menace rather than a desperately persecuted and disappearing minority.[41] Yet even if few realized the full horror of what was happening in Europe, there was still a great awareness that the Jewish plight was dire.

The government's Home Intelligence report at the end of December 1942, summarizing the public's response to German atrocities observed that the Jews had: 'Abroad – greatest sympathy; in England – general feeling that they badly want controlling'.[42] There is indeed much evidence from the Mass-Observation diaries, Home Intelligence reports and many other sources that the news from Europe caused people to be 'more conscious of the Jews they do not like here'.[43] Such tendencies actually revealed the tenacity of liberal beliefs in Britain concerning the Jews: Jews in Britain were blamed for the existence of anti-Semitism. Nevertheless, it was assumed that no Jewish activities in Europe could possibly have deserved the treatment received and thus actual support for Nazi techniques was relatively rare.[44] The liberal imagination may have made it hard to accept the reality of such irrational facts as the planned extermination of the Jews, yet there was still widespread sympathy for the Jews and a desire that the government increase its efforts to help them (a detail that escaped the attention of those who drew up the Home Intelligence reports). The Allied declaration thus had the effect feared by the British government – leading to public demands for the specific *rescue* and *saving* of Jews rather than a pious announcement that those responsible would be punished after the war.[45] News of the Holocaust peaked in Britain during December 1942 and January 1943. Thereafter, although there was much more detail available, particularly about the death camps, neither the government nor the press was anxious to give it much attention. What then was the impact of this sudden rush of information at the end of 1942?

Aside from the significant but numerically small number who for ideological reasons denied the reality of the persecutions, others could be found who avoided 'the word "Jew" in the paper[s]' because 'the news about [them] is so dreadful that it is almost pas[t] bearing'.[46] Another Mass-Observer, a left-wing electrician from Blackburn, provided a revealing account of the process of 'knowing and believing'. His diary included the use of newspaper stories which he had noted. Throughout early December 1942 he recorded headline after headline, mainly from the *Manchester Guardian* (a newspaper which Eleanor Rathbone told its editor had 'done more than all the rest of the British press put together' to outline the persecution of the Jews), relating to the 'Plight of the Jews, mass annihilation'. Yet it was not until 10 December that he reported any personal reaction: 'It wasn't until I read in such details in the *Guardian* today that I realised the enormity of the crime against the Jews. It seems that the evidence is irrefutable.'[47] It took constant repetition of the Jewish plight and the reinforcement of an official announcement to make any lasting impression. This only occurred once in the war and even then there was great reluctance to accept that the news amounted to a plan to exterminate the Jews. A handful of individuals, including Victor Gollancz and Eleanor Rathbone, realized that what was happening to the Jews 'is part, not of war, but of a quite deliberate policy, openly proclaimed, of exterminating the Jewish population of Europe'.[48] Few in Britain, it must be suggested, accepted the Gollancz–Rathbone position that the Jews were systematically being exterminated. Nevertheless, many hundreds of thousands not only acknowledged that the Jews were undergoing terrible hardships in the war but also followed these campaigners in the first few months of 1943 in demanding that the government provide help to 'rescue the perishing'.[49]

In the first six months of 1943, Gollancz, Rathbone and others, organizing through the National Committee for Rescue from Nazi Terror (hereafter the National Committee), desperately tried to keep the issue of the Jews alive in Britain. They did so without the support of the government who were thoroughly embarrassed about the topic and actually wanted it to fade away in terms of public concern. Officials believed that nothing could be done and that it was senseless to provoke an emotional response by pretending otherwise.[50] By the summer of 1943 the National Committee was struggling to keep the issue alive: the public, they believed, had become 'hardened to atrocities' and the press, following the government, devoted less and less time to the persecution of the Jews. By late 1943, when graphic details of the death camps were known, disbelief in both government and public was increasing again. From being on the verge of accepting that something unique was happening to the Jews by the end of 1942, just a year later accounts of destruction were being rejected as 'atrocity propaganda'.[51] In the spring and summer of 1944 the quite blatant, open deportation and subsequent extermination of Hungarian Jewry in the death camps of Poland elicited next to no public response or press interest. The liberation of the Maidanek and Auschwitz camps in August 1944 and January 1945 respectively were also minor stories as far as the British press was concerned – doubted as Soviet atrocity-mongering and rarely connected to the Jewish disaster.[52] By the end of the war in Europe the British population had little or no idea of the nature or scale of the Final Solution. Even senior Foreign Office officials who had received detailed accounts of the death camps had failed to assimilate the significance of the information.[53] From the summer of 1943 until the spring of 1945 quite remarkably, British understanding of the Holocaust declined (even though the detailed evidence available in the west actually increased). How did this paradoxical situation come about?

V

In December 1943 the question of a new United Nations declaration on behalf of the Jews was raised in the British Foreign Office. It was requested by A. L. Easterman of the British section of the World Jewish Congress but rejected on the grounds that the last declaration had not lessened persecution and had provided ammunition for the Germans to embarrass the Allies. Moreover, 'among Jews it raised hopes and expectations of action to rescue Jews – expectations which have worried [the] Refugees Department ever since, particularly since the war situation has very largely prevented their fulfilment.'[54] Throughout 1943, the Foreign Office had convinced itself that there was nothing that could be done to help the Jews and 'that vociferous public pressure about [Jewish] refugees [in Europe] is decidedly against the interest of the refugees themselves'.[55] It continued its reluctance to regard the Jews as a special case, as we have seen with the comments of Frank Roberts in spring 1944 concerning resentment of the suggestion that Jews had been 'more heroic or long-suffering than other nationals of occupied countries'. Thus the British state gave little lead in terms of publicity on behalf of the Jews from 1943 until the end of the war.

As 1944 progressed, accounts from Auschwitz-Birkenau and other camps were given greater credence by British officials, although continuing doubts that they might be subject to 'Jewish' exaggeration lingered even in 1945.[56] Nevertheless, the British state grimly held on to its liberal-inspired views and refused to regard the Jews or the persecution of the Jews as a separate issue deserving special attention. The Foreign Office especially resented the activities of the War Refugee Board in the United States which it saw as a Jewish publicity stunt with no real chance of success. Ultimately the Foreign Office believed it was designed as a particularistic sop to the Jewish voters of New York.[57] The British state thus kept its distance from the Jewish tragedy in the last half of the war. It was a side issue in the conflict that did not fit British war strategies (hence the decision not even to take the minor risk of bombing Auschwitz in the summer of 1944).[58] Moreover, the destruction of European Jewry should not, according to liberal principles, have been happening in the first place. Jews were, at worst, in the view of British state officials, an irritant in Europe but the solution was for them to be treated as nationals of existing states which would help integration; mass extermination was not the answer and there was thus incredulity about the scope of the disaster.

The British public shared many of the same assumptions and it was only

257

with the momentum built up at the time of the December 1942 declaration that the fate of the Jews made much of an impact. Without the reinforcement of state interest, the issue slipped further from popular consciousness and was relegated to the dubious category of 'atrocity stories'. The British press, which had been energetic in its coverage of the Jewish plight in the last few months of 1942, followed the state in giving less coverage to the subject after the declaration of 1942. Harold Nicolson, MP, of the National Committee, wrote in November 1943 that 'the Press was bored with atrocity stories'.[59] Limited coverage was given to the Hungarian Jews in 1944 and there were a few articles on the liberation of Maidanek in August of that year although not all of these mentioned that Jews had been the major victims of the camp.[60] The evidence of the Holocaust in its final stages was available: a reading of the weekly journal of the National Committee, News from Hitler's Europe, gives a comprehensive and quite accurate account of the Jewish fate from its first issue in October 1943. The evidence was also present in the mainstream national press but only in piecemeal and unprominent form.[61] Again, with a few notable exceptions, there was a reluctance to connect the plight of the Jews with the British war effort. Without that bond, it is not surprising that a boredom threshold was soon reached: the stories concerning the Jews only had appeal as 'atrocities'; there was no attempt to identify with the victims on a human level. There is thus an irony in that the British inability to *understand* Nazi anti-Semitism, due to the prevalence of liberal ideology, was also matched by a refusal to connect to the specifically Jewish tragedy because of an exclusive British (or more frequently English) nationalism.[62]

By late 1943 the British public again placed the Jewish tragedy in Europe in the category of 'atrocities' – that is, stories which may or may not have been true. As the news of the methods employed in the Final Solution percolated through in 1943 and 1944, it tended to be rejected as too fantastic. Arthur Koestler produced a short account of a journey of a cattle wagon taking Jews to their death, 'The Mixed Transport', in a progressive literary magazine in October 1943. He pointed out how three million Jews had died, by the use of gas among other ways. Readers expressed doubts about the authenticity of his piece. Koestler was furious that it was rejected as 'atrocity propaganda', replying publicly that 'There is no excuse for you – for it is your duty to know and to be daunted by your knowledge.'[63]

Koestler was perhaps asking a lot of the public, yet there were some in Britain who were prepared to acknowledge the appalling reality of the Jewish plight and to campaign on behalf of the Jews. Marginalized by the British state and with limited support more generally, their task was a lonely one, often offering the prospect of moral and physical exhaustion. The toll was indeed immense: few of the original executive of the National Committee survived the war. Eleanor Rathbone, the leading force, was exhausted by her campaigning and died early in 1946; Victor Gollancz

suffered a nervous breakdown in 1943 partly due to his constant campaigning on this tragic subject.[64] These were exceptional people – outsiders in
society such as Gollancz and Harold Laski in the world of Anglo-Jewry
or James Parkes in the Church of England.[65] Rathbone, perhaps the most
determined campaigner, was motivated by a lifelong role of carrying out
what she saw as her duty as one from the privileged classes – that of an
international servant alleviating human misery across the world.[66] All these
individuals operated within a progressive liberal framework, yet it was one
that was ahead of its time in accepting plurality and also the possibility of
mass evil in the world which had to be confronted. A married couple, the
Ws, both Mass-Observers, provide us with rare insights into the minds of
those exceptional individuals who were at least prepared to confront the
reality of events in Europe. Their moving testimony indicates the difficulty
of acknowledging the horror and ultimately the powerlessness in doing so
given the stance taken by the British government. They were prepared for
an identification and soul-searching that the British state, with its crude
mixture of exclusive nationalism and redundant liberalism, could not tolerate. As Mrs W, a railway clerk, wrote in October 1944: 'I cannot write
what I feel about all this evil. My soul cries out in distress. I am a Jew, a
Pole, a Greek, I am all women who are tortured, all children who are
hurt, all men who die in agony'.[67]

A month earlier Mr W, then a radio operator, had given his reaction to
the news concerning the Nazi death camps:

> we hear that they are going to slaughter all the Poles in the concen-
> tration camps of Oswiecim & Warsaw. . . . When I first heard about
> such things, many years before the war, they threw me into a state
> of sick horror from which it took me as much as a day to recover. . . .
> Part of my intellect, which regards human life as supremely valuable
> & the only ultimate good, continually argues with me that I ought
> now to live perpetually in such a state. . . . But of course it is imposs-
> ible to live perpetually in contemplation of such things & remain
> sane. In practice I find I think of them comparatively little. For five
> minutes or so when I read an account in the newspapers, or my
> thoughts drift off to something else. Very occasionally, when I laugh,
> something inside me asks what right have you to laugh in a world
> where such things are? But it is only for a moment. No doubt it is
> inevitable & necessary. I tell myself however little I think of these
> things they have entered too deeply in my heart's core for me to be
> in any danger of really forgetting them. I hope I am not mistaken.
> For they appear to make very little impression on most people. One
> still meets some who try to make out that these stories are not true,
> that they are lies, or propaganda, or rumours, or what not. Perhaps
> this is one of the greatest of problems for civilised life; how is one

to combine a sense of universal responsibility with ordinary day-to-day sanity.[68]

Mr W was exceptional in his willingness, as at the time of the Warsaw Ghetto rising, 'to produce a concrete picture' of what was implied by the death of 'umpteen million Jews . . . in Poland since 1939'.[69] Few others recognized the scale and nature of the Jewish tragedy in the latter stages of the war, although it would be wrong from this to deduce that it was due to a widespread antipathy towards the Jews and therefore an indifference to their fate. After the declaration of December 1942 rumours abounded that the government had refused to allow Jewish refugee children from Europe into the British Empire because it feared it would lead to domestic hostility. Mr W commented 'Can it really be true that anti-Semitism in this country is too strong to allow of it?' His incredulity was not misplaced, but he, like others working on behalf of persecuted Jewry, spent much time and energy in combating the racialism which their government claimed was a reason for inaction.[70] Government passivity due to its lack of faith in the British public, but also the dominance of a monocultural liberal ideology across state and society, ensured that there was little conception of the reality of the Final Solution, let alone an understanding of the impact of the Holocaust on European Jewry as the war came to an end. For a few Jews (and particularly the refugees) and a limited number of Christians, 'Victory in Europe' day could not be celebrated with any joy; but for the vast majority of the British population at this time, Auschwitz remained a million miles away.[71]

VI

In his autobiography, James Parkes related his experiences with Foreign Office censorship in the war in relation to a work on anti-Semitism in Europe. In the first draft Parkes gave a figure of 50,000 Jews murdered, yet the Foreign Office crossed off a nought. With more news of destruction, in the second draft Parkes revised his figure up to half a million, yet the Foreign Office reverted to his original total. 'When they did the same to five million, I gave up, and no figure is mentioned in the book.'[72] Even allowing Parkes some literary licence, his account summarizes the problem of comprehension in Britain concerning the scale of the Jewish disaster. In terms of chronology, both state and public were always at least one stage behind the events in Europe. Ironically in this they were mirrored by the Nazis at the Wannsee Conference itself – the total of Jews in Britain given there who were to be killed actually corresponds to the statistics from 1933 (that is before the new influx of refugees swelled the population of British Jewry by nearly one-quarter). The initial disclosures from the camps in spring 1945 did little to improve matters in Britain: they did not relate to death camps as such and were connected to pre-war atrocities in the public mind rather than the destruction of European Jewry. The state, in terms of official films, and the media in general continued its adherence to liberal values and referred to victims by nationality and not by race. The Nuremberg trials provided a little more knowledge of the destruction of six million Jews as did publications such as *The Diary of Anne Frank* and *Scourge of the Swastika* in the 1950s and the Eichmann trial in the 1960s. Yet even as late as 1975 the showing in Britain of a documentary on the Holocaust brought this comment from a prominent press figure: '[in my office the] next day, among colleagues and friends, the sense of shock was palpable. . . . Why had we never been told before?' A recent poll suggests that now over three-quarters of the British population are aware of the significance of Auschwitz although the figure drops remarkably for the younger generation. It has thus taken a long time for Britain to face up to the reality of the Holocaust and the process is still far from complete.[73]

The diary of the Ws and of other Mass-Observers from the war indicates that the contemporaries Blanche Dugdale and Arthur Koestler as well as subsequent historians such as Andrew Sharf and Walter Laqueur were right to suggest the importance of psychological barriers in the process of 'believing'.[74] Yet psychological factors did not work in isolation; they operated in an ideological and cultural framework and context. In Britain the centrality of both liberalism and 'Englishness' to national identity made it hard for the public to identify with the Jews, especially given the lack of lead by the state. In Britain on a governmental and popular level Jews were blamed for the existence of anti-Semitism, a philosophy internalized to a large extent by Anglo-Jewry itself. The existence of genocidal anti-Semitism on the scale operated by the Nazis was thus hard, if not impossible, to explain and therefore much available evidence remained unassimilated. A small but important minority were able to move beyond such an ideological straitjacket and identify with and fight on behalf of the Jews. It is thus significant, returning to the Ws, that to them their 'Welshness' made it easier for them to reject a more exclusive approach to the world and to allow them to include the fate of the Jews in their moral universe.[75] Another small group in Britain developed the alternative strategy of strident dismissal of stories concerning the persecution of the Jews. The British roots of what has become known as 'Holocaust denial' are disturbingly deep. Yet the major tendency in Britain during the war was neither denial nor identification, but silence. The impact of the Final Solution and the Holocaust in general was, ultimately, negligible.

In conclusion, this chapter reveals the importance of social history to the study of the Holocaust. It shows that if the policies of the state are analysed in isolation from popular responses, then a warped and narrow interpretation will follow (ironically mirroring the elitist and essentially patronizing philosophy of the British government itself over this issue in the war). Finally, while rejecting the idea that the British public were too anti-Semitic to consider helping the Jews, it must be suggested that adherence to a monocultural liberal ideology by state and public led to a total failure of imagination in Britain with regard to the Final Solution. It thus may be appropriate to close with a Mass-Observer confronting a crossword puzzle in the war. It reveals the tragicomedy when British liberal understatement was combined with the horror of Nazi crimes against humanity: 'Do a crossword. One clue says: "Hitler doesn't like them." Four letters, the second letter E. I fill in "Reds", but of course it's wrong, it should be "Jews".'

Only in Britain could Hitler be transformed into a golf-club anti-Semite.[76]

NOTES

I should like to thank the Trustees of the Mass-Observation Archive for permission to make use of their material. I am particularly gratful to Joy Eldridge and Dorothy Sheridan at the archive and Mag Kushner for her help with some of the diary material.

1 Martin Amis, *Time's Arrow* (London, 1991), p. 151; Michael Marrus, *The Holocaust in History* (London, 1988), p. xi.

2 Claude Lanzmann, 'Shoah as counter-myth', *The Jewish Quarterly*, vol. 33 (Spring 1986), p. 11. See Yehuda Bauer, 'Against mystification', in his own *The Holocaust in Historical Perspective* (London, 1978), pp. 30–49 for a sensible analysis of the strengths and limitations of the historical approach.

3 Ian Kershaw, 'Hitler and the Holocaust', in his own *The Nazi Dictatorship* (London, 1989), pp. 82–106, on the functionalist/intentionalist debate. Christopher Browning, *Fateful Months: Essays on the Emergence of the Final Solution* (2nd edn, New York, 1991), pp. 3–38, provides a brilliant, balanced account of the importance of central Nazi as against local initiatives in 1941 with regard to the murder of the Jews. Arno Mayer, *Why Did the Heavens Not Darken? The 'Final Solution' in History* (London, 1990), is particularly unhelpful in minimizing the genocidal aspects of ghettoization policy and the activities of the *Einsatzgruppen*; Lawrence Langer, *Holocaust Testimonies: the Ruins of Memory* (New Haven, 1991), p. 66; Lanzmann, 'Shoah as counter-myth', p. 12.

4 Mary Nolan, 'The *Historikerstreit* and social history', in Peter Baldwin (ed.) *Reworking the Past: Hitler, The Holocaust and the Historian's Debate* (Boston, 1990), pp. 225, 242–4.

5 Andrew Sharf, *The British Press and Jews Under Nazi Rule* (London, 1964), pp. 194, 209.

6 ibid., p. 113; Arthur Morse, *While Six Million Died* (London, 1968), p. 199.

7 Walter Laqueur, *The Terrible Secret* (London, 1980), pp. 3, 197; idem, 'Hitler's Holocaust: who knew what, when and how?', *Encounter*, vol. LV (July 1980), p. 24.

8 Laqueur, *The Terrible Secret*, Chapter 3 and p. 208, and 'Hitler's Holocaust', p. 24.

9 Martin Gilbert, *Auschwitz and the Allies* (London, 1991, 1st edn 1981); Deborah Lipstadt, *Beyond Belief: The American Press and the Coming of the Holocaust 1933–1945* (New York, 1986), makes limited use of opinion poll material on

popular attitudes in the United States but her study is essentially concerned with the press, using White House press cutting material in an impressive account.

10 Laqueur, *The Terrible Secret*, pp. 66, 99.

11 See N. Stanley, 'The extra dimension: a study and assessment of the methods employed by Mass-Observation in its first period' (unpublished PhD thesis, Birmingham Polytechnic, 1981), and Dorothy Sheridan, *The Mass-Observation Archive; Guide for Researchers* (University of Sussex, 1991), for this organization and its surviving material. While the Observers did not provide a perfect match of the British population at this time, their diaries are of sufficient quantity and quality to provide a deep insight into British popular thinking in the war. See Angus Calder, 'Mass-Observation 1937–1949', in Martin Bulmer (ed.) *Essays on the History of British Sociological Research* (Cambridge, 1985), pp. 133–5, for a defence of Mass-Observation in terms of its correspondents' backgrounds.

12 *Papers Concerning the Treatment of German Nationals in Germany 1938–9* Cmd 6120 (London, 1939); see Public Record Office (PRO) FO 371/23105 C16788 for the emergence of this issue in September/October 1939.

13 For its sales success, see Robert Kee, *The World We Left Behind: A Chronicle of the Year 1939* (London, 1984), p. 329, and Mass-Observation Archive (M-O A): D5039.9, 1 November 1939, who was told by a newsagent friend that he 'had more orders for the Concentration Camp White Paper than . . . for any other'; Sharf, *The British Press*, pp. 85–7, for the generally positive response on behalf of the national and local British press.

14 Ian McLaine, *Ministry of Morale: Home Front Morale and the Ministry of Information in World War II* (London, 1979), p. 31; Angus Calder, *The People's War: Britain 1939–45* (London, 1969), pp. 61–2.

15 M-O A: D5291, 31 October 1939; D5145, 31 October 1939; D5173, 31 October 1939; D5276, 3 November 1939; D5295, 1 November 1939.

16 The only national paper to cast doubt on the White Paper was *Truth*, 3 November 1939. For popular disbelief as a form of pro-Nazism, see M-O A: D5416, 31 October 1939 and D5145, 31 October 1939 for criticism of the government's use of the material as atrocity stories.

17 For later belief that the campaign had backfired, see Sargent minute, 5 February 1940, in PRO FO 371/24422 C2026 and Fraser minute, 10 February 1942, in PRO INF 1/251 Pt 4; Roberts to Stevens, 16 October 1939, on Niemoller etc. in PRO FO 371/23105 C16788.

18 For the relevant section of Hitler's speech, 30 January 1939, see Lucy Dawidowicz (ed.) *A Holocaust Reader* (New York, 1976), pp. 32–3. Sharf, *The British Press*, pp. 97–8, produces British examples of press headlines from before the war about the Nazis' threats to 'annihilate' or 'exterminate' the Jews. Bauer, 'The Holocaust and American Jewry', in his *The Holocaust in Historical Perspective*, p. 7, makes the important point that such terminology before 1945 had a different meaning and should 'not indicate a knowledge or a serious prediction of the mass murder of millions of human beings'.

19 See the Mass-Observation diaries in April–May 1945 particularly, and T. Kushner, 'The impact of the Holocaust on British society and culture', *Contemporary Record*, vol. 5, no. 2 (1991), pp. 357–9; Laqueur, *The Terrible Secret*, pp. 1–2; Jon Bridgman, *The End of the Holocaust: The Liberation of the Camps* (London, 1990), p. 34.

20 Michael Holroyd, *Bernard Shaw*, vol. III *The Lure of Fantasy* (London, 1991),

p. 433; memorandum: 'Plan to combat the apathetic outlook of "What have *I* got to lose even if Germany wins" ', 25 July 1941, in PRO INF/251 Pt 4.

21 For a fuller development of this argument, see Tony Kushner, 'Beyond the pale? British reactions to Nazi anti-Semitism, 1933–39', in Tony Kushner and Kenneth Lunn (eds) *The Politics of Marginality: Race, the Radical Right and Minorities in Twentieth Century Britain* (London, 1990), pp. 143–60.

22 See the directives on Jews in M-O A: October 1940 and March 1943.

23 M-O A: FR 523B summarizes the information obtained in the October 1940 survey. Jews scored heavily in categories such as 'predatory' or 'a problem' but less so in the section on 'deserv[ing] sympathy'.

24 Frank Roberts, 11 May 1944, in PRO FO 371/42790 W7937.

25 M-O A: D5182, 30 October 1939. See also D5291, 3 November 1939.

26 For a moving account of the impact of war on the child refugees, see the collective diary from a hostel in Southport, 12 February 1939 to 12 February 1940: 'Our first year in "Harris House" ', Manchester Jewish Museum; 'Do we realise?', *Zionist Review*, 4 January 1940.

27 Richard Bolchover's *British Jewry and the Holocaust* (Cambridge, 1993) provides the fullest account of this subject and there will also be a valuable chapter in David Cesarani's forthcoming history of the *Jewish Chronicle* – the most influential Jewish paper in Britain. Previous work such as Meir Sompolinsky, 'The Anglo-Jewish leadership, the British government and the Holocaust' (unpublished PhD, Bar Ilan University, 1977), and Bernard Wasserstein, 'Patterns of Jewish leadership in Great Britain during the Nazi era', in Randolph Braham (ed.) *Jewish Leadership During the Nazi Era* (New York, 1985), pp. 29–43, concentrate on the Jewish elite and its relationship with the British state.

28 For Rich see his diary entry of 2 July 1940 in University of Southampton archives, AJB 217.

29 See Tony Kushner, *The Persistence of Prejudice: Antisemitism in Britain During the Second World War* (Manchester, 1989), particularly Chapters 1, 2 and 6, for the pressures operating on Anglo-Jewry in the war and its responses to domestic anti-Semitism.

30 Hertz to Temple, 23 June 1942, in Chief Rabbi's papers, 2805/124, Greater London Record Office. The Board of Deputies of British Jews had only minimal resources to fight on behalf of the Jews – see memorandum, November 1943 in its own archive E3/536 F1. Anglo-Jewry as a whole was attacked for its financial contribution to rescue work in the war by the *Yishuv* as Dina Porat has shown in her *The Blue and the Yellow Stars of David: The Zionist Leadership in Palestine and the Holocaust, 1939–1945* (London, 1990), pp. 105–6. Undoubtedly some wealth within the community was not utilized, yet it must not be forgotten that support of the refugees throughout the 1930s and into the Second World War had drained Anglo-Jewry to the extent that the British government was forced to intervene in 1940 by providing assistance and loans. Opposition to public protests on behalf of the Jews is referred to in PRO INF 1/292 22–29 December 1942 and by A. Gordon in *Zionist Review*, 18 December 1942.

31 See 'Gag is put on Holocaust', *Jewish Chronicle*, 17 May 1985, and letter of Bernard Slater to *Jewish Chronicle*, 20 June 1986. For the silence after the war, see Howard Cooper and Paul Morrison, *A Sense of Belonging: Dilemmas of British Jewish Identity* (London, 1991), pp. 88–94 particularly.

32 Lichtheim, 18 September 1942, quoted by Gilbert, *Auschwitz and the Allies*, p. 70. For Riegner, see Laqueur, *The Terrible Secret*, appendix 3, and his own 'A warning to the world' (Stephen Wise Lecture, Hebrew Union College-Jewish

Institute of Religion, Cincinnati, 17 November 1983); Jan Karski, *Story of a Secret State* (London, 1945), and David Engel, 'Jan Karski's mission to the west, 1942–1944', *Holocaust and Genocide Studies*, vol. 5, no. 4 (1990), pp. 363–80.

33 See Laqueur, *The Terrible Secret*, pp. 69–70, and M-O A: D5423, 12 January 1942; D5004, 17 January 1942; D5098, 7 January 1942, for their limited impact.

34 *Daily Telegraph*, 25 June 1942; Yehuda Bauer, 'When did they know?', *Midstream*, vol. 14 (April 1968), pp. 51–8, reproduces the Bund report; see Sharf, *The British Press*, pp. 92–3, and 'The greatest pogrom', *Zionist Review*, 3 July 1942, for general press reactions.

35 Only one Mass-Observer commented on the 'spate of German "atrocity" stories' and he 'wonder[ed] how many [were] true' in M-O A: D5230, 20 June 1942; 'Greatest pogrom', *Daily Mail*, 30 June 1942. See also the comments of the Chief Rabbi referred to earlier in Note 30.

36 See Allen minute, 10 September 1942, in PRO FO 371/30917 C7853.

37 Allen, 27 November 1942, and Roberts, 1 December 1942, in PRO FO 371/30923 C11923.

38 David Engel, *In the Shadow of Auschwitz: The Polish Government-in-Exile and the Jews, 1939–1942* (Chapel Hill and London, 1987), pp. 191–202; Allen, 27 November 1942, in PRO FO 371/30923 C11923; Rathbone to Crozier, 4 December 1942, in *Manchester Guardian* archive, 223/5/47.

39 M-O A: D5271, 10 December 1942.

40 M-O A: DR 2925, 1393, 2804 March 1943; *Catholic Herald*, 24 December 1942; *Catholic Times*, 24 December 1942; *Peace News*, 14 August 1942; *New Leader*, 19 December 1942; *Socialist Appeal*, January 1943.

41 For Reed, see Kushner, *The Persistence of Prejudice*, pp. 99–101, 198, and M-O A: DR March 1943 for his influence.

42 PRO INF 1/292, 22–29 December 1942.

43 PRO INF 1/292, 29 December 1942–5 January 1943 and their reports from December 1942 to March 1943.

44 Mass-Observation diaries for December 1942 and January 1943 and its survey on the Jews in March 1943 indicated that although some wanted no more Jews to come to Britain, most were ashamed of the government's inaction – although they harboured dislike of the Jews themselves.

45 See *Hansard* HC vol. 385, cols 2082–9, 17 December 1942, and PRO FO 371/32681 W14673 for the declaration.

46 M-O A: D5460, November/December 1942.

47 M-O A: D5173, November/December 1942 and 10 December 1942 especially.

48 Victor Gollancz, *Let My People Go* (London, 1943), p. 1.

49 Eleanor Rathbone, *Rescue the Perishing* (London, 1943). Evidence of public concern is produced in later editions of Gollancz's and Rathbone's pamphlets. See also PRO FO 371/36651.

50 This campaign and the government's response to it is dealt with in Tony Kushner, 'Rules of the game: Britain, America and the Holocaust in 1944', *Holocaust and Genocide Studies*, vol. 5, no. 4 (1990), pp. 385–7.

51 Gollancz, 13 April 1943, in National Committee Executive meeting in Parkes papers, University of Southampton archive 15/057 file 1; Harold Nicolson to the Executive, 24 November 1943 15/057 file 2. For official disbelief, see the minutes of Roger Allen and William Cavendish-Bentinck, 27 August 1943, concerning the use of gas chambers in PRO FO 371/34551 C9705.

52 The Mass-Observation diarists made no mention of the Hungarian Jews in the spring and summer of 1944. Home Intelligence did report some concern – see PRO INF 1/292, 18–25 July 1944, but it was less vocal and intense than eighteen

months earlier. See *Jewish Chronicle*, 30 June 1944, for a confirmation of this analysis; for Maidanek, see *The Times*, 12 August 1944, and *The Illustrated London News*, 14 October 1944, for a major feature which failed to mention the Jews once. The BBC refused to use the story believing it to be Soviet propaganda – see Alexander Werth, *Russia at War 1941–1945* (London, 1964), pp. 890–4. For Auschwitz, see *The Times*, 8 May 1945.

53 See file PRO FO 371/51185 for official reactions to the liberation of Auschwitz and, more generally, John Conway, 'The first report about Auschwitz', *Simon Wiesenthal Centre Annual*, vol. 1 (1984), pp. 133–51.

54 Randall minute, 14 January 1944, in PRO FO 371/36673 W17929.

55 Henderson minute, 28 September 1943, in PRO FO 371/36666.

56 See Henderson minute, 11 January 1945, on Jewish 'exaggeration' in PRO FO 371/51134 WR89 but dissension from H. Beeley, minute 16 January 1945.

57 Kushner, 'Rules of the game', pp. 389–94.

58 See Gilbert, *Auschwitz and the Allies*, Chapter 31.

59 Nicolson, 24 November 1943, Parkes Papers 15/057 file 2, University of Southampton archive. See also Sharf, *The British Press*, p. 89.

60 See Note 52 for details of the press and public in 1944.

61 *News from Hitler's Europe* gathered material from sources such as the Jewish Telegraphic Agency. It was then circulated to all the national press. See Sharf, *The British Press*, p. 115, for reporting of the Hungarian Jewish crisis.

62 See Mclaren to Calder, 3 January 1945, in PRO FO 898/422 and George Orwell in *Tribune*, 11 February 1944, for a belief that the public was growing sceptical about 'atrocity stories' towards the end of the war; Sharf, *The British Press*, pp. 71–2, on the loaded nature of the word 'atrocity' in Britain by the time of the Nazi era. See Patrick Wright, *On Living in an Old Country* (London, 1985), *passim*, on British exclusivity and the Second World War.

63 In *Horizon*, vol. 8 (October 1943), pp. 244–51, and correspondence (November 1943), p. 362 and (December 1943), p. 433. This prompted his article 'On disbelieving atrocities', *New York Times*, 9 January 1944.

64 For an appreciation of her work for persecuted Jews by a fellow campaigner, Victor Gollancz, see *AJR Information*, no. 2 (February 1946); Ruth Edwards, *Victor Gollancz* (London, 1987), pp. 376–7; *News from Hitler's Europe*, 3 July 1945.

65 Kingsley Martin, *Harold Laski* (London, 1953). For Laski's concern, see letter to Churchill, 1 July 1943, in PRO PREM 4/51/6 and to Eden, 5 August 1943, in PRO FO 371/36664; James Parkes, *Voyages of Discovery* (London, 1969).

66 Mary Stocks, *Eleanor Rathbone* (London, 1949).

67 M-O A: D5460, 24 October 1944.

68 M-O A: D5233, September 1944.

69 M-O A: D5233, May 1943. He was prompted to write after the death of Leslie Howard, commenting how much more impact was made with an individual tragedy rather than huge statistics which were hard to comprehend in their scope.

70 M-O A: D5233, January 1943. See also M-O A: D5402, 8 January 1943; D5065, 26 December 1942; D5215, 30 January 1943; D5271, 24 December 1942; Dd5375, 17 December 1942 for criticism of the British government; Kushner, 'Rules of the game', pp. 388–9, for the energy spent in combating anti-Semitism among campaigners.

71 Isaiah Berlin, interviewed by Ramin Jahanbegloo in *The Jewish Quarterly*, vol. 38 (Autumn 1991), pp. 18–19, indicates some of the problems of comprehension which confronted Anglo-Jewry with regard to the Holocaust during the war.

See also Cooper and Morrison, *A Sense of Belonging*, p. 87. See J. Lieberman, *He Came to Cambridge: Rabbi David Samuel Marguiles* (Royston, Herts., 1982), p. 19, for an alternative perspective on VE Day.

72 Parkes, *Voyages of Discovery*, p. 180.

73 The minutes of the Wannsee Conference are reproduced in Dawidowicz, *A Holocaust Reader*, pp. 73–82. See p. 76 for England, and Hannah Neustatter, 'Demographic and other statistical aspects of Anglo-Jewry', in Maurice Freedman (ed.) *A Minority in Britain* (London, 1955), pp. 55–133, for more accurate figures. See Kushner, 'The impact of the Holocaust', p. 357–69, for post-war developments; Philip Norman in *The Independent on Sunday*, 25 August 1991, for the impact of the documentary 'Genocide' in 1975 and *The Daily Mail*, 26 August 1989, for contemporary belief about the Holocaust. There are no comparative statistics for the war – unlike the United States.

74 Blanche Dugdale, 'To bear witness', *Zionist Review*, 4 December 1942, and also in *The Spectator*, 11 December 1942. For Koestler, see Note 63.

75 Internalization of anti-Semitism within Anglo-Jewry is dealt with in Kushner, *The Persistence of Prejudice*, pp. 127–9; Mrs W thus wrote in 1946 that 'I remember all the dreadful things that have happened to them, just because they were Jews and might just as well happen to me because I am Welsh' in M-O A: DR5460, July 1946.

76 M-O A: D5228, 4 October 1939.

16

ENMITY, INDIFFERENCE OR COOPERATION

The Allies and Yishuv's rescue activists

Dalia Ofer

THE BACKGROUND

Until December 1941, when the USA was attacked and became a belligerent, American diplomats had been an important source of information concerning the fate of European Jewry under Nazi occupation. After the United States entered the war, Europe became more isolated and information less accessible. However, the Soviet press, a variety of informers, representatives of the underground movements and Germans passed information to the west via neutral countries. The fate of the Jews was included in many reports, while some were entirely dedicated to the situation of the Jews.

In the summer of 1941, the Jewish Telegraphic Agency informed the public about the massacres of Jewish civilians in Minsk, Brest-Litovsk, Lvov and other places. However, since this information was only reported in the Yiddish press its impact was limited. In the autumn of that year the *New York Times* printed on its back pages reports by Hungarian soldiers of mass killings of Jews in Galicia and in the Soviet occupied territories. The Polish government-in-exile confirmed this information, reporting on atrocities which the Nazis and Ukrainians committed against Poles and Jews.

In the early spring of 1942 the details and frequency of information concerning the mass murders increased. Descriptions of the methods used were disclosed in the press. During these months and in the early summer of 1942, the reports quoted different sources (Hungarian soldiers, Swedish businessmen and others), stressing the deliberate massacre of entire Jewish communities executed by the special liquidation units, the *Einsatzgruppen*. Accounts from Romania disclosed the fate of the Jews in Bessarabia and northern Bukovina, and news of the expulsions to Transnistria followed almost immediately. The well-known Polish government-in-exile's report of 2 June 1942 added that the massacres were not restricted to the front line in the Soviet Union, but that in the interior in special death camps

Polish Jews were also being systematically murdered by the hundreds of thousands.

In August 1942, a cable written by Dr Gerhart Riegner, the representative of the World Jewish Congress in Geneva, and Richard Lichtheim, a representative of the Jewish Agency, reached Britain and the US State Department. It disclosed a plan to deport and concentrate 3½–4 million Jews from occupied Europe and exterminate them in the east. The stated method of killing was by the use of Prussic acid, and the plan itself originated in Hitler's headquarters; thus it would solve once and for all the Jewish problem in Europe.

This cable contributed primarily to an understanding of the motives and purposes behind what was already known by that time to the politicians and Jewish leaders. It connected the information on the killings with the deportations from France to 'unknown destinations'. These reports were received through the American Friends Service Committee (Quakers) in Vichy (unoccupied) France and appeared frequently in the American press during the summer of 1942.[1]

However, the formal declaration of the Allies on the systematic murder of the Jews – the Final Solution – did not come until 17 December 1942. It was released simultaneously in Washington, Moscow and London. This marked a turning point, the Allies' official acknowledgement that the Jews of Europe were being systematically annihilated. For many months previously the State Department refrained from disclosing this information to the press, and demanded that the heads of Jewish organizations and leaders of the community wait before revealing their knowledge to the public. This indicated both the dismay and inability to grasp the scope of the disaster, and the concern by State Department officials that the issue concerning the murder of the Jews would distract attention and resources from the main goals of the war. No less important was the fear that political opponents would present the war to the American public as a 'Jewish war', as Nazi propaganda claimed and anti-Semites agreed. These were the circumstances in which a policy was formulated towards the fate of European Jewry.[2]

THE ALLIES AND RESCUE ACTIVITIES

The Allied attitude towards the rescue of Jews after Hitler's Final Solution became public knowledge has been thoroughly detailed in a number of books. In the title of his book, *The Abandonment of the Jews*, David S. Wyman both coined a term and conveyed his moral stance. As he stated: 'Unwillingness to offer refuge [to those who could escape] was a central cause for the Western world's inadequate response to the Holocaust.'[3] Henry Feingold described the failure of the 'politics of rescue', A. Kraut and D. Breitman emphasized the politicians' ineffectuality in *The Refugee*

Problem and European Jewry, 1933–45. In his new book, *The Quadruple Trap*, Sh. Aharonson claims that it is ahistorical to view the 'abandonment' of the Jews from a moral perspective since the Jewish question was insignificant when weighed against general political and military considerations. B. Wasserstein, who studied Great Britain's policy towards European Jewry in the context of its conduct of the war and its policy in the Middle East and Palestine after the White Paper, found that Great Britain's rescue policy was determined predominantly by these political parameters.[4]

The political considerations of the western Allies were both internal and foreign: on the home front, anti-Semitism and the anti-immigration lobby, on the international scene, the blockade of occupied Europe and the delicate relationship with the Soviets who were extremely sensitive to any hint of talks with Nazi representatives.[5] Indeed, rescue never reached a high priority in the war policy of the democratic governments. This was already demonstrated in late 1942, when information concerning the Final Solution and what was known as the Transnistria Plan came to the attention of the western governments at the same time.[6]

The massacres of the Jews of Bessarabia and Bukovina from June to September 1941 and the deportations of the remnants to Transnistria, in the southern tip of the Ukraine between the rivers Dniester and Bug, from September 1941 to January 1942 were known in the west almost as soon as they occurred. The Romanian Jewish leaders headed by Wilhelm Filderman, Wilhelm Fisher, Rabbi Alexander Safran and Misho Benvenisti maintained contacts with Jewish organizations in neutral countries, with the Romanian and International Red Cross, and with the Roman Catholic Church in Romania. Jewish leaders in Romania and in particular Filderman were informed as early as the beginning of 1942 of the apprehensions shared by a few eminent Romanian politicians (among them Mihai Antonescu, the Prime Minister) concerning Ion Antonescu's pro-Nazi policy, and this too was transmitted to the west.

In December 1942, almost a year after the large-scale deportation of some 140,000 Jews to Transnistria ended, Romanian officials proposed a plan to allow the remaining 70,000 Jews who had been deported and were still alive to emigrate from Transnistria to Palestine. They demanded a payment of 200,000 Lei (some $400) per person for the expenses involved in transportation. The Jews saw in this plan an indication of a change of heart among Romanian leaders concerning their alliance with the Nazis in general and as a consequence a move away from the Nazi policy towards the Jews.

The British government opposed the offer and so did the US State Department. They considered it Romanian blackmail, and a Nazi effort to incite anti-British feeling among the Arabs, by encouraging large-scale immigration to Palestine under the White Paper. Humanitarian considerations and options for rescue were therefore ignored. The fact that the plan was leaked by the State Department to reporters indicated the Allies' intentions of stopping any negotiations and eliminating all hopes regarding the Transnistria Plan.[7] This episode, which occurred just as news of the Final Solution was disclosed publicly, was only one example of a real and basic conflict between rescue operations and the political considerations of the Allies.

PALESTINE: KNOWLEDGE OF AND REACTION TO THE FINAL SOLUTION

The press in Palestine had access to similar sources of information as the western press, as well as others. From the autumn of 1939 until the end of 1941, a number of Jews arrived in Palestine from Poland, among them a few Zionist leaders who had escaped from Poland at the beginning of the war. They described the first stages in the implementation of Nazi policy, the establishment of the Jewish Councils (*Judenräte*), the flight of many families and young people to Soviet territory. They told of the deportations from the Lodz area and other small villages to larger communities and the suffering that ensued. Information also reached Palestine through personal letters from Vilna, Yugoslavia and Romania, although in some respects this information impeded a full comprehension of the reality of Jewish life. Since the testimonies described both the suffering and the powerful will to survive, the radical and unprecedented situation was not understood even long after the beginning of the wholesale slaughter in the summer of 1941. Hopes that the Jews would somehow survive this terrible time and a deep sense of the temporality of the Nazi occupation prevailed during the first two years of the war, as expressed by many Jewish leaders and ordinary people in occupied Europe (and evidenced in diaries and testimonies of the time).

Despite close family ties and relationships with the Diaspora, the Jewish community in Palestine (*Yishuv*)* did not comprehend Nazi policy and intentions any earlier or more clearly than the Jewish public and its leaders in Britain and the USA. Only in November 1942, when a group of Palestinian Jews who had been trapped in Europe in 1939 at the outbreak of war were returned to Palestine (through an exchange scheme) from the ghettos and labour camps in Poland, where they had shared the fate of the Jews until the deportations, did the *Yishuv* come to realize that the mass murders had begun. The Jews of Palestine, like the nations who fought against Hitler, learned of the Final Solution only when most European Jews under Nazi rule had already perished.

The response of the leadership of the *Yishuv* to the Final Solution was

---

* The *Yishuv* numbered a little over 177,000 at the beginning of 1933 and some 500,000 when the war broke out in 1939. The rapid growth of the community was due to immigration of Jews from Poland, Germany and other parts of the Reich, and the Balkans.

one of sorrow and mourning, together with an intense effort to restrain these emotions in order to act effectively and realistically. Already at the time, many leaders voiced their strong feelings of guilt, re-evaluating with pain their actions and those of the Zionist movement, in particular the *Yishuv*, in aiding and rescuing European Jewry. They subjected their Zionist ideals to much soul-searching in view of the Final Solution. However, their immediate reaction was to act quickly and effectively to aid both the Jews under Nazi occupation and those in Axis countries who were under threat of either expulsion to the east or future Nazi occupation. Their plans aimed at increasing the number of Jews escaping from occupied Europe to neutral countries, in particular to Turkey and Spain, while promising their governments a supply of food for the Jewish refugees as long as the war lasted and immigration to a safe haven when it ended. They also set out to deter the governments in the Balkan countries from cooperating with the Nazis and allowing the expulsion of their Jews to Poland. A chief aim was to send food parcels and other assistance to Jews under Nazi occupation with the help of the International Red Cross. All these proposals, of necessity, depended on the Allies and the neutral countries whose ability and desire to offer refuge to European Jewry were the key to any large-scale rescue plans. It was quite evident that without such cooperation all rescue efforts would be extremely limited.[8]

Yishuv leaders closely followed the progress of the war and the military campaigns of the Allies, trying to predict future developments and their effect on Zionist aspirations.[9] The *Yishuv* leadership identified strongly with Allied war aims and the major strategies of the war, although some of these strategic considerations directly affected potential rescue and aid plans, for example the decision not to negotiate with the Nazis, and the blockade on Germany and occupied Europe. Contacts with the Balkan countries, where a large number of Jews still lived, were essential to the success of any rescue and aid programme.

David Ben-Gurion, Moshe Shertok (later Sharett) and other leaders shared the belief that, in the final analysis and regardless of political and economic interests, the democracies were responsive to the moral dimension of political issues. While they were not so naive as to think that its weight in the overall decision-making process was central, they felt it was not negligible. They thought that moral considerations would play a role in future peace arrangements. To that end a policy was carefully constructed that would strengthen the political power of the *Yishuv* in support of its moral claims. The leadership therefore worked to minimize the conflict of interest between Great Britain and the political goals of the *Yishuv*. Hence, Shertok and Ben-Gurion encouraged an atmosphere of compromise despite many disappointments and setbacks in working with the British.

These basic tenets of Zionist political policy existed when knowledge of the Final Solution – the scope of the annihilation and its systematic nature – reached the *Yishuv* and the issue of rescue was put to the fore.

From November 1942 to February 1943 and even until the spring, there was a short period of optimism about Allied reaction to the Final Solution. As early as January 1943, when the Allies rejected many of the practical demands of the *Yishuv* and other Jewish organizations, there was uncertainty as to the real intention of the Allies regarding rescue schemes. Between January and April 1943, when the Bermuda Conference on rescue efforts and relief for refugees was convened, the leaders of the *Yishuv* began to realize that there was very little hope of involving the Allies in substantial rescue plans.[10] Nevertheless, they ceaselessly presented the Allies with plans and appeals to their conscience. At the same time, the *Yishuv* itself launched an effort to aid European Jewry with the financial support of its own people and the Jewish communities in the free world. A rescue committee was formed in 1943, which established rescue and aid delegations in the neutral countries.

The two central delegations were located in Geneva and Istanbul and were different in character and field of action. In general, the Geneva centre was active in maintaining contact with the occupied territories. They kept contact with Jews – heads of communities or Zionists in west and central Europe – and had relatively good contacts with Slovakia and Yugoslavia. Lichtheim corresponded with most of these countries, and Nathan Schwalb, a representative of the Hehalutz movement (established after the First World War to train youth movement members aged 18–25 for life in Palestine), kept relatively close connections even with Poland. Their activities in Switzerland centred on political contacts with neutral and Allied representatives and with people who came from Germany and other parts of occupied Europe. Their working relations with representatives of the western Allies were quite routine and were used for transmitting information to Great Britain and the USA. The delegates in Istanbul maintained most of their contacts with the Balkans and through them with occupied Europe. They too focused on securing and transmitting information from one community to another and to Palestine. They had direct contact with Palestine and visited it frequently. On their visits they met with political leaders, reported to the Rescue Committee and to their affiliated organizations and gave public lectures. They were active mostly in sending money, food parcels and organizing immigration, legal and illegal, from the Balkan states to Palestine. They were also involved in a variety of plans to send *Yishuv* agents to occupied Europe, on which I shall elaborate later.

The delegates developed a network of couriers, initiated contacts with and administered aid to the European communities. They used many dubious types as couriers, sometimes underworld figures or double agents posing as merchants or industrialists. Others were low-ranking diplomats who moved freely and frequently from occupied Europe to the neutral

countries. Through them communication with Jews in the occupied territories was established and expanded. The couriers delivered money to
communities in Poland and in the Balkans, carried letters from Palestine
to the isolated Jews and brought back information on the fate of the Jews
in the European countries.

THE RESCUE ACTIVISTS

'Rescue activitists' is the term used to describe the group of people who
carried out a variety of aid and rescue tasks and missions to the Jewish
communities in Europe, and who acted in various capacities throughout
the war. The group was not homogeneous; its members did not belong to
one political organization or institution in Palestine. Some were representatives of the Rescue Committee, some were emissaries of Hamossad
Le'aliyah (Mossad), which was established in spring 1939 to bring in
immigrants in defiance of the Mandate immigration regulations, others
belonged to the political or *aliyah* (immigration) departments of the Jewish
Agency. They were divided into sub-groups according to their political
affiliation and formal assignments.

The emissaries who belonged to the labour movement, for example,
included members of the Hakibbutz Hameuhad (the union of *kibbutz*
which belonged to the labour movement in Palestine and was moderately
left-wing). They were motivated primarily by socialist-Zionist ideological
considerations, they were extremely loyal to the *kibbutz* movement, and
had strong emotional bonds with members of the youth movements and
labour Zionism in the Diaspora. Most of this sub-group came on *aliyah*
(immigration) in the late 1920s or early 1930s. Many had served as emissaries to Hehalutz sometimes only a few years after their own emigration to
Palestine, and some had returned to Palestine in 1939, just as the war
broke out. Among this sub-group of rescue activists were people who
were involved in illegal immigration operations before and during the first
two years of the war, when efforts to bring Jews from Europe to Palestine
secretly and illegally were still going on.

Another sub-group consisted of staff members of the Jewish Agency
aliyah department, among them representatives of Palestine Offices in
different European countries. They were involved in the selection of immigrants and in the distribution of *aliyah* certificates. After the war broke
out some were active in arranging the emigration of certificate holders
from Germany and Poland and in obtaining transit visas through the
neutral countries for individuals and groups. Haim Barlas, who headed the
Jewish Agency (JA) delegation in Istanbul, was a typical representative of
this sub-group. He set up two important *aliyah* operations in 1939 and
1940 for some 2,900 German Jews who held certificates in September 1939,
and for 1,200 Halutzim (youth movement members who went through

special training to live in Palestine), mostly from Poland, who had escaped to Vilna in the first months of the war.[11] In Geneva this sub-group was represented by Haim Posner, who was the representative of the Palestine Office, and, to some extent, by Richard Lichtheim of the Jewish Agency.

One more sub-group was composed of representatives of the World Jewish Congress, an organization closely connected to the Zionist movement, which was established in 1934 to help German Jews. The members of this group were not residents of Palestine and did not represent the *Yishuv*. Moshe Silberschein, who was of east European background but spent a number of years in Germany, and Gerhard Riegner were stationed in Geneva. Both were close to the General Zionists (a liberal non-socialist party in the Zionist movement) in their political views.

The rescue activists were not a central part of the political decision-making process, nor were they always in agreement with the *Yishuv*'s policy of rescue. They frequently criticized the leadership and the public for not being alert to the opportunities and the need for aid and rescue. They were also confronted by the shortcomings of the aid and rescue programme and the great needs of the suffering Jews. Since they were in almost direct contact with the Jewish communities in occupied Europe and the Balkans they had first-hand reports about the situation in different parts of Europe such as Transnistria, the deportations from Slovakia, and conditions in the labour camps. They could evaluate the pleas for help and felt that they were best equipped to identify the needs of the Jews with whom they communicated. The geographic location, the social background and past experiences of the rescue activists played an important role in shaping their attitudes towards rescue and its implementation in the difficult political situation.[12] Their direct contacts with representatives of the Allies in neutral countries and the often unpleasant negotiations with the couriers mentioned above (p. 273) were also major factors in forming their approach. The emissaries shared a rather pragmatic attitude in this trying state of affairs. Therefore, the point of view of these rescue activists holds special interest and merits a thorough examination.

Most rescue activists developed an ambivalent relationship with the Allies. They greatly depended on both Allied high-level policy and the diplomats in the countries in which they were based. They also developed a working relationship with a number of Allied representatives, most importantly with the lower political echelons: consuls, rank-and-file consular officials, military intelligence and others. In order to establish such a relationship the rescue activists concentrated on practical issues. Although they somewhat mistrusted the consular staff members and presumed some of them to be anti-Semitic, they tried to avoid making judgements. They ranked their contacts in a rather sophisticated hierarchy ranging from 'good' to 'bad' associates; i.e. more or less sympathetic to the Jewish cause and ready to render services or overlook dubious activities. The best working relationship evolved in the intelligence sphere. An example of this ability of the emissaries to differentiate between aspects of their working relationship was the positive opinion most held of Major Arthur Whitall who was both head of the Passport Control Office (PCO) of the British Consulate in Istanbul and part of the British Intelligence service. He was therefore responsible for entry permits to Palestine. The activists believed that he had a tolerant attitude to the immigrants who arrived in Istanbul in 1944 because he was aware of the services they could offer to the British.[13]

INTELLIGENCE COOPERATION AND RESCUE

The emissaries took advantage of the fact that the neutral countries, Turkey and Switzerland, were centres of intelligence work. A great number of couriers and business representatives were engaged in a variety of espionage activities.[14] Allied representatives in different capacities were in charge of many clandestine operations, so contacts with the Allied representatives were part of the daily agenda of some of the rescue activists.

From the summer of 1940, some of the rescue activists in Istanbul were involved in planning and conducting secret operations with British Intelligence in different fields of action. The British were interested in cooperating in three areas: propaganda warfare in Syria and other countries in the Middle East and the Balkans; re-establishing a network of informants to replace those lost in the Balkans and Mediterranean countries; acquiring first-hand knowledge about political organizations in the different countries, since support of anti-Nazis throughout the Mediterranean and in North Africa and the Balkans were high priorities. The third field of cooperation was the creation of a network of agents to assist British pilots shot down during operations in the Balkans. This became more important as the war advanced and larger numbers of British planes were shot down. The British airmen had to be instructed on where to hide after they landed and how to find assistance to escape from enemy territory. For that they needed the help and guidance of local people.

The *Yishuv* leadership and the British military command in the Middle East planned to cooperate on these issues. These plans were endorsed by the government in London. Different military bodies and agencies were responsible for this work. Among them was the Special Operation Executive (SOE) which was established to carry out sabotage efforts in occupied areas and the A Force, another intelligence unit, which was responsible for helping British pilots shot down in action in the Balkans to reach safe territory, and for planting disinformation in occupied and neutral countries to mislead the enemy. George Taylor, who headed the Balkan Section of the SOE, cooperated with the *Yishuv*, in particular with David Hacohen and Yehudah Arazi.[15] Both were assisted by the Hamossad Le'aliyah Bet

(Mossad), and central figures in illegal immigration efforts such as Zeev Shind and Zvi Yehieli worked with them.

The Mossad wanted to use dedicated and trustworthy Zionist youth movement members to do intelligence work for the British. Suitable members were intelligent, informed and ardently anti-Nazi, and could supply the British with reliable information and critical analysis. The youth movement members and veteran Zionists were also capable of organizing a network of informers and could spread disinformation. The Mossad claimed that Jews in the Balkans were the best source of information for the British. However, this suggestion was risky and dangerous, for the entire Jewish community would be blamed if the informers were discovered. Therefore, a proposal emerged which combined both the interests of the British and those of the rescue activists. People assigned to collecting information would establish a network of assistants who would be guided as to what information to compile and how to accomplish the task by the Mossad representatives, who would maintain contact with them. Also, agents from Palestine would be sent to the Balkans where they could be disguised as part of the community and lead the work. The information itself, however, would be delivered only when the informers had left the country. They would emigrate, as this was not completely forbidden (and in some cases was even officially permitted) by the Romanian and Bulgarian governments. Others in the network would continue to collect information and transmit it upon their departure. In this way a pattern was formed: gathering information and spreading disinformation, leaving the country and handing the materials over to the British in Palestine or Istanbul. This work was limited to the Balkans and to the emissaries in Istanbul for political and geographical reasons.

On 15 January 1943 an agreement was signed by Colonel Simonds of the A Force and Shind of the Mossad covering this matter.[16] It was quite clear that immigration was a necessary element in implementing the scheme, not merely immigration of a few individuals but a movement of immigration which would camouflage the informers. The strategy of cooperation with British intelligence agents alongside illegal immigration, which was a major means of rescue, was embodied in this agreement.

During 1943, another section was established to gather information. Gideon Ruper (Refael), a German Jew who was active in German Jewish immigration before the war and until 1940, headed the special section, the Haifa Interrogation Bureau which had been established as early as June 1940 as part of Royal Air Force (RAF) intelligence. His section investigated the situation of the Jewish communities under occupation.[17] In 1943 a branch of this office was established in Istanbul based on the assumption that a large flow of immigrants would soon begin.

The weakness of this strategy from the Mossad's point of view was obvious. The agreement with the A Force did not include the Mandate

Government in Palestine, which could deport the immigrants when they arrived in Palestine. Nor was the British Navy in the Mediterranean part of the agreement and it could continue to intercept the immigrants' boats as it had done in the past. The intelligence agencies could not promise the 'good behaviour' of the political bodies.[18] Shind and his colleagues had learned from past experience that the goals and methods of any specific operation should be defined in advance in explicit terms. They evidently succeeded with the A Force agreement. This activity became an important avenue in developing mutual interests between the *Yishuv* and a few other intelligence sectors in the British army: the Inter Service Liaison Department (ISLD) which had hosted the plan to send parachutists to Europe, and M.O.4, which was responsible for activities in the Nazi-occupied territories. For the delegation in Istanbul the cooperation with these intelligence sections was advantageous. There was greater security in using their agents for sending money and other aid to the Jewish communities. They obtained better contacts because of this relationship and the movement between the Balkans and Istanbul could operate with greater efficiency. However, the expectations of Shind and his associates that goodwill and working relations with Simonds and Taylor would result in greater assistance to immigration were not borne out. On a number of occasions when Shind and other delegates desperately needed British help to obtain a ship or to get the support of the International Red Cross, they were disappointed. From the British point of view the limits of these agreements were clear; they should not interfere with political decisions.

The work of the rescue activists, and in particular of the Mossad, was greatly assisted by agents of the Political Department of the Jewish Agency who either visited Istanbul, such as Eliyahu Epstein and Reuven Zaslani (Shiloah), or remained there for longer periods, such as Teddy Kollek and Ehud Ueberal (Avriel).[19] Kollek, a Viennese Jew who was active in bringing young Jewish children to Palestine and England in 1938 and who had come on *aliyah* shortly before the war started, was sent by the political department of the Jewish Agency to aid Shind. He had good contacts with the British in England and in the Mandate administration of Palestine, and he became instrumental in furthering relations with the British in Istanbul. At the same time he was involved in Shind's work as a Mossad emissary and assisted him in purchasing vessels for illegal voyages.[20] When Kollek left Istanbul in the summer of 1943 he was replaced by Ehud Avriel who was a Hehalutz member in Vienna and organized illegal journeys after Moshe Agami, the Mossad emissary in Vienna, was ordered by Eichmann to leave in May 1939. Avriel himself came on *aliyah* to Palestine in December 1939. Avriel had close ties with the British Consulate in Istanbul and in particular with Major Whitall because of his special intelligence tasks. Whitall was indeed interested in aiding the immigration of a certain number of Jews who could provide information about the Balkans and in particular about public opinion in Romania after the military setbacks and heavy casualties among Romanian soldiers in the battles of the winter of 1942–3. He wished to establish a branch of the Haifa Investigation Bureau in Istanbul and hoped to secure good results from the initial interrogations of the immigrants. From Whitall's point of view a limited number of immigrants was sufficient, yet the larger numbers of immigrants which were part of the *Yishuv*'s plan did not affect his readiness to collaborate.

In August 1943 the rescue activists suffered a serious blow. A well-constructed plan to transport 1,000 Jews from Bulgaria failed (for more details see p. 281). This was partially due to the British Embassy in Ankara's refusal to support a voyage planned and organized by Shind and Kollek. (The embassy's opposition to the plan was in part the result of a lack of coordination between the British Foreign and Colonial Offices.)[21] It is not clear whether the immigration of the 1,000 Jews received Major Whitall's support and whether he so informed the embassy in Ankara. He himself was in the British Consulate in Istanbul and the embassy was not part of his jurisdiction. But in August 1943, when it became clear that the plan had failed, he encouraged Avriel with what he knew was unprecedented news. The British government, he said, had decided to give entry visas to Palestine to all Jewish refugees who managed to escape to neutral countries. As Avriel recalled, Whitall called this decision the 'New Balfour Declaration' for the Zionist movement and Palestine.[22] It would relieve the neutral governments of the fear of having to support refugee camps in their territories during and after the war.

The fact that Whitall delivered this information to Avriel was quite significant. The British Cabinet had already adopted the new policy on 2 July 1943, yet not only was it withheld from Ankara and other neutral governments, but the British ambassadors were forbidden to disclose it.[23] In effect it remained officially unknown until March 1944. Nonetheless, Whitall was prepared to deliver this information to Avriel, breaking the orders of confidentiality, undoubtedly in the knowledge that Avriel and his associates would utilize it immediately. To Avriel this approach proved Whitall's honesty and true humanitarian interest in their work, above and beyond his interest in the information provided by the scheme.[24]

Examples of this kind explain why emissaries like Shind, Kollek, Avriel and others maintained a working relationship with the Allied representatives in the full awareness of the Allied governments' reluctance to shape and follow a real rescue policy.

ATTEMPTS TO COOPERATE WITH ALLIED AGENTS

The information about the Transnistria Plan was delivered to the Allies via rescue activists in Istanbul and Geneva. When the plan was publicized in the *New York Times* on 16 February 1943, thus ensuring its failure, the rescue activists were unwilling to forfeit the opportunity for Jews to emigrate, even when the governments rejected the plan outright.[25] The rescue activists were interested in taking advantage of the situation, even if the Allies would not cooperate. Therefore they compromised on partial goals: to move some groups of Jewish children or young adults from either Transnistria or Romania. In the meantime they had to provide the practical means to transport a number of children from Romania and other Balkan states in accord with a scheme which already had British approval.

They planned to transport the Jews from Romania to Istanbul and possibly further to Palestine, on two Romanian ships, the *Bessarabia* and the *Transylvania*, which had been captured by the British Navy in Istanbul in the summer of 1941. These two ships were adequate for human cargo and could accommodate a large number of immigrants on board. Both the Romanians and the Jews were interested in releasing them. The rescue activists hoped that their contacts with the intelligence community in Istanbul would help them acquire the boats. However, the British Ambassador Sir Hugh Knatchbull-Hugessen was opposed to the scheme since the Turkish Foreign Office was reluctant. Unlike the British Foreign Office in London, Knatchbull-Hugessen was less worried about the political implications this move would have in Palestine than about the difficulties of transportation in Turkey and its overtaxed railroad system, which Great Britain itself utilized heavily for transporting military supplies. He sympathized with the Turkish claim that they could not accommodate a steady flow of refugees unless the numbers were very limited.[26] Knatchbull-Hugessen and his staff were wary of upsetting the delicate relationship with the Turkish government, in particular during 1943. Nazi Germany was pressing Ankara to limit its services to the Allies and to join it in the war. As things stood, the rescue efforts and the extraordinary methods used by the team of rescue activists were often irritants. However, if these were to increase substantially, they could be detrimental to political relations with the Turks.[27]

In January 1943 Oliver Stanley, the British Minister for the Colonies, announced in Parliament that the 29,000 remaining certificates for Palestine would be reserved for the rescue and immigration of children. He mentioned the Bulgarian willingness to allow Jews to emigrate. The first stage, he said, would start with the emigration of 5,000 children from Bulgaria.

This was a springboard for the rescue activitists. They were ready to begin emigration from Bulgaria rather than Romania if it had a chance of success. In their unorthodox way they reached an agreement with a Bulgarian seaman Yordan Spassov, who had a close relative in the police headquarters in Sofia, to obtain an authorization to transport Jews from Bulgaria. (At that point the Nazis expressed their direct opposition towards Bulgarian intentions to allow Jews to emigrate and demanded their deportation to Poland. The Bulgarians removed the Jews of Sofia to the countryside to prevent the Nazis from deporting them.[28]) Shind and Kollek provided Spassov with a boat which would become his after he made three voyages. In July 1943, Spassov acquired a licence to convey 1,000 Jews in that month. Because of the time limit more than one boat was needed. Mindful of Britain's official policy of January 1943 and the promises given by the British in Ankara to Kaplan, Barlas, who headed the rescue delegation in Istanbul, and Shind turned to the British for assistance. Both went to Ankara with the Bulgarian permit and requested a ship which would take the immigrants. They did not disclose the way in which they had acquired the permit; nevertheless, the British understood. Knatchbull-Hugessen and his staff were not willing to tolerate the unconventional methods used by the Mossad. They opposed the plan more zealously than their counterparts in the Foreign Office in London and not only expressed hostility towards Barlas but cast aspersions on his character.[29] This attitude was a great blow to the rescue activists since the work of long months never came to fruition. The 1,000 immigrants never left Bulgaria.

Throughout 1943 the British authorities in Turkey and other neutral countries like Switzerland and Spain were uncooperative; they viewed the *Yishuv* emissaries in Istanbul as trouble makers.[30] Understandings reached by Eliezer Kaplan, the treasurer of the Jewish Agency, with the British in March 1943 to support plans for emigration from Bulgaria and Romania, and by Moshe Shertok, the head of the Political Department, who led the negotiations with the British in August of that year, were of no avail. The British refused to release the *Bessarabia* and *Transylvania* while a substitute vessel that had been promised was allocated by the navy but was never delivered to Shind and the emissaries.[31]

In September 1943 Laurence Steinhardt, the American Ambassador who supported the *Yishuv*'s emissaries but did not wish it to be publicized, rejected a plea by the Emergency Committee, a body established in the USA in July 1943 to promote a rescue policy by the administration, to send an envoy to Turkey to advance aid and rescue efforts. He claimed that too many emissaries from Palestine were already in Turkey and they caused great difficulties with the authorities. Turkey was limited in its capacity to serve as a base for large rescue operations, he added, and therefore the Jewish organization should refrain from sending more delegates.[32] Neither Steinhardt nor Knatchbull-Hugessen recognized the emergency which drove the emissaries during 1943. Their perspective was political and their horizons local (i.e. Turkish). Their indifference could therefore easily turn into hostility if the rescue emissaries' activities developed in a way that they considered detrimental.

TOWARDS NEW STRATEGIES

The failure to achieve the immigration of the 1,000 Jews from Bulgaria proved to the rescue activists that they could not ignore the negative attitudes of the political representatives, i.e. the ambassador and his staff. It was not enough to rely only on intelligence personnel. They had to overcome the opposition of the political administration to immigration and rescue efforts or at least prevent them from hindering these efforts. Shind and Avriel realized that because they were manoeuvring within a narrow framework of mutual interests with the British, they must use greater flexibility and more daring. They had to broaden the framework of mutual interests between the British and Americans and the rescue activists. Effecting this change was very difficult, and they thought that perhaps direct confrontation would clarify the issues and lead to a change in the British and American attitudes. They used the information which Whitall had revealed to create such a conflict and planned a new strategy.

The Mossad, in conjunction with the other emissaries, changed their strategy for transporting immigrants. Since they were not able to land in Turkey they created a rather difficult and dangerous alternative: transferring the immigrants on the high seas from boats that carried Bulgarian or Romanian flags and could not sail in the Mediterranean, to boats that carried neutral or Allied flags. They were promised the help of Colonel Simonds for such an operation. However, on July 1943, they lost in a storm the boat *Lily-Ayalah* which flew a Palestinian flag and which had been in the Mossad's possession since 1942.[33]

The new British policy enacted in July 1943 enabled the emissaries to use Turkey as a base to land immigrants, since Turkey agreed to provide transit visas for Jews who had an additional visa to another country.[34] These transport arrangements considerably eased the difficulties of the Mossad. It meant a much shorter sea voyage which could be accomplished with boats carrying either neutral or Balkan flags. From Istanbul the immigrants would reach Palestine by rail.

The rescue activists ignored their disappointments and anger over the Bulgarian affair and endeavoured to prevent another rejection of their plans by the British in Ankara. Since they had failed to push the British towards flexible and tacit cooperation with their work they chose a more vigorous course, forcing a confrontation which would embarrass the British and make them act according to their own secret policy. The idea was to bring immigrants to Istanbul without Turkish entry visas. The British, who would not be able to afford the publicity caused by Ankara refusing to allow them to land in Istanbul, would have to stamp Palestine entry permits on the immigrants' passports when they reached Istanbul. The Turkish authorities would then give them transit visas and the immigrants would continue by rail to Palestine.

When in April 1944, the *Maritsa*, with the first boatload of immigrants, left Constanza the rescue activists were fortunately able to reduce the risk they were taking. In February 1944 the War Refugee Board (WRB) was established after growing pressure in the US Senate and government regarding rescue efforts. The formation of the WRB signalled an important turn in American rescue policy. It added another source of pressure on the British and the Turks. Avriel, Shind and Venya Pomerantz (a member of the 'Histadrut Rescue and Relief Committee'), sceptical but determined, approached Ira Hirshman, a special emissary of the WRB, who arrived in Istanbul in February 1944. They were in the midst of a crisis concerning the voyage of the *Maritsa* to Istanbul and hoped to use Ira Hirshman's services to solve their problems. Their attitude was very pragmatic; for them Hirshman was a vehicle to advance the goals of rescue and immigration. They had little patience for waiting until Hirshman learned the lesson they had learned over long and painful months, that only unorthodox methods would bring success. They were not interested in his intentions and motivations unless they could be used to advance their own plans, which they believed to be the only practical ones in that situation. They had established the apparatus in Romania, and the right contacts with lower echelons in the government whom they generously bribed to be helpful.

They indeed succeeded; Hirshman soon realized that the rescue activists were advantageous to him as well. A formal legalistic approach was ineffective even when its representative was sent by the President of the US. The practical and bureaucratic obstacles were too great to overcome in a short time, and time was a decisive factor in all rescue plans, in particular after the Nazi invasion of Hungary (19 March 1944). The team of rescue activists could provide Hirshman with plans that were half completed and enable him to show progress in a relatively short period of time. Hirshman's political efforts created a more positive attitude towards the rescue work of the *Yishuv*'s delegation in Istanbul, and Steinhardt, the American Ambassador in Ankara, persuaded the Turkish Foreign Minister to allow the Jewish refugees to land in Istanbul and to allocate rail cars for the voyage to Palestine after Whitall stamped Palestine entry visas in their passports.[35]

Some 4,000 immigrants reached Istanbul in this way from March to December 1944. A report to the Jewish underground army in Palestine (*Haganah*) written on 11 December 1944 sums up the situation in Istanbul: 'The experience of our work in Istanbul has proved that rescue activities can be coupled with, and are often inseparable from, intelligence work.'[36] However, this evaluation was one-sided: without political assistance even the smallest rescue plans could not be successful.

CONCLUSION

The relationship between the rescue activists and the Allies was highly complex. The attitude of Allied political representatives in Istanbul moved from indifference to something approaching overt hostility and ended with limited cooperation. The rescue activists maintained a pragmatic and practical approach and moved to a more dynamic strategy of almost forcing Allied representatives to cooperate. In this respect they suppressed the suspicion they had towards different persons with whom they worked. Although they operated on a different level from the Zionist political leadership, their pragmatism resembled Zionist policy of the time. In a long report to the Jewish Agency in November 1944 Zaslani summed up the cooperation with British intelligence.

> I looked through my correspondence with the British . . . and I found how enthusiastic the British were about numerous plans and schemes that we offered. Although they told us that they could not give the final approval right away they encouraged us to go ahead and start preparing. Then, suddenly they would come up with a negative answer. A power behind the scenes – the Palestine Administration and the Colonial Office – intervened to obstruct the plans.[37]

In spite of the political impediments the rescue activists managed to accomplish some of their aid and rescue plans. However, all these operations were limited and in the larger context of the Holocaust were marginal. The Allies did not understand that the elimination of the Jews was a major war aim for the Nazis, thus all rescue efforts were under the category of 'humanitarian considerations' which had very limited impact in a time of a total war.

NOTES

1 For a thorough description of news and information about the slaughter of the Jews, see: Walter Laqueur, *The Terrible Secret: Suppressing the Truth about Hitler's Final Solution* (Boston and Toronto, Little Brown & Co., 1980); David S. Wyman, *The Abandonment of the Jews: America and the Holocaust 1941–1945* (New York, Pantheon Books, 1984), pp. 3–58; Deborah E. Lipstadt, *Beyond Belief: The American Press and the Coming of the Holocaust 1933–1945* (New York, The Free Press, 1986), pp. 159–97.
2 Wyman, *The Abandonment of the Jews*, pp. 42–78.
3 ibid., p. 98.
4 Henry Feingold, *Politics of Rescue* (New Brunswick, NJ, Rutgers University Press, 1970); Alan Kraut and Richard Breitman, *The Refugee Problem and European Jewry 1933–45* (Bloomington, Indiana University Press, 1987); Bernard Wasserstein, *Britain and the Jews of Europe, 1939–1945* (Oxford, Clarendon Press, 1979); Shlomo Aharonson, 'The quadruple trap' (work in progress).
5 This last point was demonstrated in the Brandt Affair. See: Yehuda Bauer,

American Jewry and the Holocaust: The American Joint Distribution Committee, 1939–1945 (Detroit, Wayne State University, 1981), pp. 356–99; Wyman, *The Abandonment of the Jews*, pp. 235–88; Wasserstein, *Britain and the Jews of Europe*, pp. 249–63.

6 For a general description of the Transnistria Plan, see: Wyman, *The Abandonment of the Jews*, pp. 80–103; Dina Porat, *The Blue and the Yellow Stars of David: The Yishuv and the Holocaust, 1939–1945* (Cambridge, Mass., Harvard University Press, 1991), pp. 164–74; Dalia Ofer, *Escaping the Holocaust: Illegal Immigration to the Land of Israel 1939–1944* (New York, Oxford University Press, 1990), pp. 187–94.

7 It is interesting to note that from the summer of 1942 the Romanian Jewish leadership was preoccupied by the endeavour to revoke the plans to deport Romanian Jews to Poland. They used all political means available inside and outside Romania in this attempt. The intervention of Cordell Hull, the Secretary of State, via the Swiss Embassy, against proceeding with the deportations was quite unusual. The Nazis' adviser on Jewish matters in Bucharest, Gustav Richter, believed that US intervention was largely responsible for the Romanians' change of mind regarding the planned deportations to the east. For further deliberations on this affair, see Jean Anzel, 'Plans for the destruction of the Rumanian Jews and their discontinuation in the light of documentary evidence (July–October 1942)', *Yad Vashem Studies*, vol. 16 (1984), pp. 381–420.

8 Central Zionist Archive (CZA) S25–259, 18 January 1943, Meeting of the Small Zionist Executive (SZE); Porat, *The Blue and Yellow Stars*, pp. 49–93.

9 Long deliberations on these issues were held in meetings of the Jewish Agency Executive, the Histadrut (Union of Workers), the Va'ad Leumi (the National Committee representing all Jewish inhabitants of Palestine) and Mapai (the Labour Party), throughout 1943, 1944.

10 Porat, *The Blue and Yellow Stars*, pp. 140–4; Ofer, *Escaping the Holocaust*, pp. 199–210.

11 Haim Barlas, *Hazalah Bimie Hashoah* (Hebrew) (Tel-Aviv, Beit Lohamie Hagetaot Hakibbutz Hameuhad, 1975), pp. 18–25, 37–8.

12 Numerous letters of the emissaries in Istanbul are found in *Haganah* Archive (HA) unit 14 the Files of the Mossad (Illegal Immigration Organization), CZA L15 in the Files of the Istanbul delegation and in S26 the Files of the Rescue Committee. Another important collection is in Moreshet Archive (Givat Havivah) D. in the Files of Menahem Bader.

13 HA 14/714, report by Shind; Testimony of Ehud Avriel, Oral History Centre Institute of Contemporary Jewry, Hebrew University, Jerusalem (OHC).

14 HA 14/714 – Shind report; 14–80 – Dani (Shind's cover name) to Yehieli, 12 June 1942; Barry Rubin, *Istanbul Intrigues* (New York, McGraw-Hill Publishing Co., 1989), pp. 148–201; Aharonson, 'The quadruple trap'.

15 David Hacohen of the *Haganah* clandestine *Yishuv* defence force was the creative mind behind the cooperation with the British in matters concerning intelligence which began at the outbreak of the war. He developed very good relations with the many British intelligence personnel. See his report, CZA S25–205; David Hacohen, *Time to Tell* (New York, Cornell Books, 1965). Yehudah Arazi a veteran *Haganah* activist was the major planner of the operation in the Balkans.

16 Yoav Gelber, *Jewish Palestinian Voluntarism in the British Army During Second World War*, vol. 3 *The Standard Bearers' Rescue Mission to the Jewish People* (Jerusalem, Yad Ben Zvi, 1983), p. 150, in particular Note 74; HA 14–148. It is worth noting that Colonel Simonds was one of Orde Wingate's men, known

for their support of Zionism and dedicated to cooperation between the *Yishuv*'s defence forces and the British military forces.

17 Gelber, *Jewish Palestinian Voluntarism*, vol. 3, p. 137; Report of Vilansky, on the work of the Investigation Bureau CZA S25/10630; CZA S25/7823, 'Din veheshbon 'al peulot hamisrad lehakirat mazav hayehudim bagolah hanazit 1943–45' (Hebrew).

18 A similar strategy based on cooperation with British Intelligence failed in 1940 in the notorious *Darien* affair. Then, the Mossad handed over the ship *Darien* to the British for purposes of sabotage in Romania. After a few months it became apparent that the plans were not working. The Mossad decided to take back the *Darien* for a necessary illegal voyage. When the British realized this, they demanded the return of the boat. Mossad agents in Istanbul, who had organized this voyage, refused to return the boat, and it accomplished its illegal voyage, but was confiscated by the British in Haifa. The operation caused great tension and embarrassment between British intelligence agencies and the Zionist political leaders, between the latter and the heads of the Mossad, and within the Mossad itself. For more details, see Ofer, *Escaping the Holocaust*, pp. 49–88.

19 For a detailed report on the work of these people, see: Haggai Eshed, *Mossad shel ish ehad: Reuven Shiloah; avi Hamodiyin shel Israel Intelligence* (Hebrew) (Jerusalem, Edanim publication, Yediot Aharanot, 1988); Teddy Kollek, *For Jerusalem* (New York, Random House, 1979); Ehud Avriel, *Open the Gates* (New York, Athenaeum, 1975); CZA S53–230 Epstein's diary of his visit to Istanbul, July 1943.

20 Ofer, *Escaping the Holocaust*, pp. 214–17, 227–34; Gelber, *Jewish Palestinian Voluntarism*, vol. 3, pp. 156–7.

21 Ofer, *Escaping the Holocaust*, pp. 218–26.

22 OHC testimony of Ehud Avriel, Ofer, *Escaping the Holocaust*, pp. 227–37.

23 Public Record Office (PRO) FO 371/36682 W9840, Halifax to Foreign Office (FO), 15 August 1943, and FO reply, 30 August 1943. Jewish Agency representatives in London and Jerusalem were informed officially of the Cabinet decision in July 1943; they were told that the decision would not be announced publicly to avoid Nazi and Arab negative reaction. For more details, see Ofer, *Escaping the Holocaust*, pp. 226–7, 235–7.

24 OHC testimony of Avriel; Kollek, *For Jerusalem*, pp. 37–53.

25 As the Mossad emissaries reported, the Romanians were ready to allow 1,000 Jews to leave every month on Romanian boats from Odessa to Istanbul. They demanded a promise that after each transport the boats would return to Romania. Labor Archive (LA) 3/28, 21 January 1943, Barpal talk; MAPAI Archive (MA) 24/23, 2 February 1943, Kaplan talk.

26 There was an agreement between the Turks and Barlas of the Jewish Agency that nine families per week could pass through Turkey with visas to Palestine. The total number was not to exceed fifty persons per week (Barlas, *Hazalah*, pp. 25, 233–4).

27 PRO FO 371/3667 W7309, Hugessen to Foreign Office, 17 May 1943.

28 For a detailed description of the fate of the Jews in Bulgaria, see *Korot yehudei Bulgaria* (Hebrew) (Tel Aviv, 1970), vol. 3, pp. 89–150.

29 Ofer, *Escaping the Holocaust*, pp. 218–35; Barlas cable to Shertok, 25 May 1943, in Barlas, *Hazalah*, p. 224.

30 It is important to note that Hugessen, who was uncooperative during 1943, acted in an unusually humane manner in January 1942, when the illegal ship *Struma* reached the harbour of Istanbul. Then he proposed that the Turks allow the ship to continue southward to the Dardanelles, and was condemned by Lord

Moyne, then Minister for the Colonies. This demonstrates that the political considerations were the major guide to his actions. About the *Struma* affair, see Ofer, *Escaping the Holocaust*, pp. 147–67. For Hugessen's attitude towards the rescue activists, in particular with regard to the Bulgarian immigration scheme, see ibid., pp. 225, 231–5; PRO FO 371/36679 W7309, 13 May 1943, Hugessen to Foreign Office.

31 CZA S25/531/6/Z, Kaplan's report, 28 March 1943; Shertok's report, August 1943.
32 CZA Executive Minutes (EM) 36II, Kaplan report, 28 March, 1943; ibid., S53/230, Epstein's diary of his visit to Istanbul, July 1943; National Archive (Washington DC) (NAR) 840.48 Ref/4460, Steinhardt to State Department, 7 September 1943.
33 Ofer, *Escaping the Holocaust*, pp. 214–17.
34 ibid., pp. 228–34.
35 Ofer, *Escaping the Holocaust*, pp. 270–80; Wyman, *The Abandonment of the Jews*, pp. 215–21.
36 CZA S25/8908, 'Switzerland as base of operation', unsigned.
37 CZA S25/205 Zaslani Report, 12 November 1944.

Part IV

HISTORIOGRAPHY

17

DOCUMENTS ON THE HOLOCAUST IN ARCHIVES OF THE FORMER SOVIET UNION

Shmuel Krakowski

Since there is no more Soviet Union, and obviously no more Soviet archives, we now have to talk about what were formerly Soviet archives and are now those of the Russian, Ukrainian, Byelorussian, Moldavian and Baltic states' republics. Most files in the Soviet archives were closed to historical research and had gradually been opened as a result of the policy of glasnost which began, as far as archives are concerned, only around 1989. We may only hope that with the final fall of the communist regime, the policy of free access to archives for historians will be respected in all the post-Soviet republics. Historians may now have great new possibilities for research into our troublesome twentieth century.

In spite of the involvement of many historians in research into the Holocaust, and the hundreds of books which have appeared until now, there is still a great deal left unknown. We still have very few works dealing with the Holocaust in the Nazi-occupied territories of east Ukraine, east Byelorussia and the occupied parts of the Russian Republic. The events in dozens of ghettos, and dozens of camps in these territories, still remain largely unknown. One of every four Jewish victims of the Holocaust was murdered in these territories. And yet, a short glance at the main publications dealing with the history of the Holocaust may be sufficient to indicate how inadequate was the space devoted to the plight of Soviet Jewry under German occupation.

For example, in Hilberg's monumental work *The Destruction of the European Jews*[1] numbering 1,274 pages, fewer than fifty pages are devoted to events in the Soviet occupied territories (within pre-Second World War boundaries). There is an obvious lack of proportion here between the description of events in smaller countries with a smaller Jewish population, and the treatment of Soviet Jewry. Likewise, Nora Levin in her very important two-volume work *The Jews in the Soviet Union since 1917*[2] treated the period of the Holocaust only marginally.

Somewhat more information concerning the events of the Holocaust in the east can be found in Leni Yahil's two-volume work *The Holocaust. The Fate of European Jewry 1932–1945.*[3] However, here too, the space devoted to the events in the Soviet occupied territories is insignificant. Even in the recently published *Encyclopedia of the Holocaust*[4] the entries devoted to the suffering of Soviet Jewry are disproportionately small in number and significance.

Of course, the authors are in no way to be blamed for devoting so little space to the history of the Holocaust in the German-occupied territories of the Soviet Union. The lack of documentation resulting from the policy of closing the archives created this situation. In the Soviet Union no research into the Holocaust could be undertaken because of brutal interference by the Communist Party and Soviet government in the work of historians.

There are also many other insufficiently elaborated subjects connected with the history of the Holocaust, not only regarding the occupied territories of the Soviet Union. The involvement in anti-Jewish activities of many German and satellite military and police formations, as well as many civilian institutions, is still mostly unknown or very little known. The participation of many units of collaborators in the murder campaigns against the Jewish population also remains largely concealed. Little has been written about the plight of survivors in many countries, and the difficulties which they encountered during the first years after the liberation. Until recently subjects connected with the attitudes of non-German or even anti-Nazi, but at the same time anti-Semitic, movements in Nazi-occupied countries have received marginal treatment.

We have very good reason to hope that in the newly opened archives historians will find plenty of material for fully developing all these as yet untreated or only marginally treated subjects.

There are, as yet, no catalogues or guides to the material in Soviet archives dealing with the Holocaust. Neither are there proper retrieval methods for material dealing with the general events of the Second World War. However, a lot has become known since 1989. Several working groups were sent from Yad Vashem to work in the Soviet archives. Copies of material, xeroxes and microfilm have been received, and so far amount to over 100,000 pages. Intensive work in the Soviet archives has also been carried out by the United States Holocaust Memorial Museum. Both institutions, Yad Vashem and the United States Holocaust Memorial Museum, work in close cooperation.

The documents dealing with the Holocaust are kept in many archives of the former Soviet Union – central, republican and city archives, and also in the archives of various institutions. The material is of different provenance, and may be divided into the following groups.

Material of Soviet provenance

The most important are the files of the Soviet Extraordinary Commission for the Investigation of the German-Fascist Crimes on the Temporarily Occupied Soviet Territories (thereafter SEC).

Also important are the files of the many trials of German Nazi war criminals and local collaborators. Many of the accused took an active part in the murder campaigns against the Jewish population.

We must also mention the files of the Soviet partisan movement, collections of testimonies kept in the Institute for History in Moscow, the material in former party archives and the film and photographic material kept in various places, and finally the files of various ministries of the Soviet government, principally the Ministry for Foreign Affairs.

Material of German provenance

Here we must differentiate three main groups:

a) Files of local German administrative bodies, which the withdrawing German Army failed to evacuate or destroy and were therefore left in many liberated cities and towns of the Soviet Union. These documents are kept mainly in a number of city archives, the most important being in Kiev, Kharkov, Odessa, Lvov and Minsk. However, material of significant importance is kept in dozens of other regional and city archives.

b) Military documents of the German armies, divisions and regiments destroyed in battle. These files are kept in the Soviet military archives.

c) Documents captured by the Red Army in the conquered territories of east Germany and east Austria. These include the documents of various German central and local administrative bodies, Nazi Party institutions, files of economic enterprises, and also files from the concentration camps. This material is without doubt of the greatest importance, comprising very large collections of German Nazi material, probably second only in amount and importance, or maybe even equal to, the very well-known Captured German Documents microfilmed at the National Archives of the United States. These documents are being held in what has been called until recently the 'Osobi', which means separate or special archives. Their existence was kept strictly secret for several decades, until autumn 1989, when a series of articles criticizing the policy of closed archives was published by Ella Maximova in the official Soviet daily *Izvestiya*. The first of these articles was published on 23 September 1989, and was then followed by others published on 17, 18, 19, 20 and 21 February 1990.

Material of Romanian provenance

These holdings kept in the Odessa Archive are the files of the Romanian occupation authorities in the region of Odessa, and the so-called Transnistria region.

Collections of collaborationist newspapers and magazines

These were published by, or supported by, the German occupation authorities, and published by local collaborators. Most are in the Ukrainian language. Collections are kept in many places.

Archives of the Jewish Anti-Fascist Committee

These files are of tremendous importance for Holocaust research. They include twenty-seven volumes of reports, diaries, testimonies and letters, mostly written by survivors or Red Army soldiers, describing the fate of Jews under the German occupation in very many localities of the Soviet Union. These files also include much information concerning the situation of the survivors after the liberation and the struggles of Jewish soldiers and partisans.

Archives of the newly independent Baltic states

Of special importance here are the large holdings kept in the Vilna and Riga archives. These may be divided into three major groups:

a) German-Nazi documentation, such as the files of the Reichsministerium für die besetzten Ostgebiete, Wehrmachtsbefehlshaber Ostland, Generalkommissar Riga, Stadtverwaltung Wilna and other German offices;
b) files of the local collaborators, mainly the Lithuanian and Latvian police;
c) files of the Vilna and Kovno ghettos, including the local *Judenräte* (Jewish Councils).

It is too early to know how far knowledge on the Holocaust will be extended by information derived from the documents in the newly opened archives. Neither can we say at present to what extent Holocaust historians will have to amend or add to their previous writings after they have studied the new documents. However, we can give some indication of the implications from some newly received files originating from the Soviet archives for which detailed catalogues are being elaborated in the Yad Vashem Archives.

The most important files are those of the SEC. The documents of the SEC in the Central Government Archive in Moscow are organized in a special record group of tremendous dimensions. It numbers over 40,000 files.[5] These files deal, among other things, in great detail with events in many dozens of ghettos, camps and killing sites all over the Nazi-occupied territories of the Soviet Union. We find here extensive information on life in the ghettos and camps; the activities of many German Nazi and collaborators' units and individuals involved in the murder campaigns against the Jewish population; the involvement of Romanian and Hungarian forces in anti-Jewish activities; the theft of Jewish property; anti-Jewish propaganda; the function of the *Judenräte*, resistance activities, and help by some non-Jews. These files include long lists of Jewish victims and also names of perpetrators, Germans and local collaborators.

The documents and reports of the SEC dealing with the anti-Jewish activities and the plight of the Jewish population under the German and Romanian occupation were microfilmed by the Yad Vashem Archives. They amount to about 80,000 microfilm frames. The Yad Vashem Archives is now preparing a very detailed catalogue of these microfilms.

In order to give a better understanding of the character and importance of the SEC files, I will cite a few examples from the forthcoming Yad Vashem catalogue.

From File 7021–16–8, dealing with the events in the Krasnodar region:

> The shooting of all Jews in the Cossack village (*stanitsa*) Piaginsk in December 1942; in the Cossack village Segiyevsk on 5.10.1942; in the Cossack village Dondukovsk of the Taginsk region on 17.8.1942; the execution of all the Jews in the Timoshevets sovkhoz of the Timoshevsk region on 20.8.1942 and the Jews of the Proletarskiy farm in the Timoshevsk region in October 1942; the shooting of all the Jews of the kolkhoz Boyevnik of the Udobnensk region, not far from the town Cherkessk on 16.10.1942. Shooting of Jews from the same region on 14.10.1942 near the Cossack village Udobnaya; shooting of Jews near the Cossack village Peredovaya (date unknown); the execution of about 3,000 Jews of the Temirgoyevsk region near the brickworks and the Cossack village Petropavlovskaya in September 1942; the shooting of 400 Jews near the Cossack village Ust-Labinskaya of the Temirgoyevsk region in December 1942; shooting of the Jews of Temirgoyevsk region in October 1942.

This file, numbering 118 pages, also contains hundreds of names of murdered victims, and names of German war criminals and members of the local police who participated in the murder campaigns with the Germans.

From File 7021–77–420, dealing with the events in the town of Kherson (209 pages):

> Anti-Jewish terror in July 1941; the establishment of the ghetto in August 1941; transfer of Jews from the ghetto to the prison in September 1941 and their execution near the village Zelenovka. The

murder of the mentally sick patients from the city hospital in October 1941. The establishment of three POW camps in the town and the mass executions of the prisoners of war in May 1942 and October 1943. Death march of Jews from Kherson in the direction of Niko-layev, and their execution.

From File 7021–61–25, dealing with events in the Pologovsk county of the Zaporozhe region (17 pages):

The forced registration of the Jews in the town Pologi after the town was conquered by the Germans on 5.10.1941; the Jews forced to wear a white armband with the red star on the left arm; the murder of almost all the Jews near the town in December 1941; the murder of the remaining Jews of the town Pologi during the period until 18.9.1943; names of the murdered Jews; testimony of a Russian woman, whose child from her Jewish husband was taken from her and murdered; testimony of a Russian whose Jewish wife and children were discovered and murdered in May 1943; testimony of a Russian woman whose Jewish husband and child were taken by local police-men and murdered; testimony of a Russian woman whose four children from her Jewish husband (at that time in the Red Army) were taken from her and murdered in June 1943.

It would take a full volume to list all the previously unknown or obscure camps, ghettos and mass killing sites described in the files of the SEC. Just to give an idea of the number of these killing sites, let me name the camps established in the villages of only one county, the Bershad county of the Vinnitsa *oblast*, documented in the files of the SEC. These are the camps: Voytovka, Potashnia, Krushinovka, Osiyevka, Pyatkovka, Shumilov, Man-kovka, Balanovka, Lugovoy, Sumovka, Birlovka.

Of major importance are the files of the Jewish Anti-Fascist Committee, which was established at the request of the Soviet government after the German invasion of the Soviet Union. Its task was to gather support from Jews in the free world for the Red Army's struggle against Nazi Germany. Thus the Committee became the only Jewish institution officially allowed to function, all others having been dissolved by the Soviet authorities long before the war. The Committee became known to Jews all over the Soviet Union. Jews who survived the German occupation, as well as Jewish soldiers on the front line and Jewish partisans, wrote to the Jewish Anti-Fascist Committee, sent them their diaries written during the occupation, and memoirs written after the liberation. Members of the Committee also gathered reports and testimonies from survivors. Thus, a great Holocaust archive numbering many thousands of pages bound in twenty-seven large volumes was created.

After the war, the Soviet authorities dissolved the Jewish Anti-Fascist

Committee. Most of its members were arrested and executed, and the archive was confiscated by the secret police. After some time the collection was transferred to the Central State Archives in Moscow, and its existence disclosed only two and a half years ago. Copies of its contents were recently received by Yad Vashem.

The files of the archives of the Jewish Anti-Fascist Committee contain information about events in many places, which were not sufficiently well documented, or may not have been documented at all except by the SEC. However, the importance of these files is much greater than just the information about events. They are indispensable for an understanding of the events, the plight of the victims under the most tragic circumstances, the severe dilemmas unique in human history, the scope of collaboration and the moods among various strata of the local population, the sadism and endless brutality of the perpetrators, Germans and some non-Germans, their complete moral deterioration, and the almost total absence of chances for survival for a Jew in the occupied territories of the Soviet Union. All this can hardly be learned from official documentation alone. The diaries, the memoirs and testimonies enable us to understand the events, and here lies the main importance of the files from the archives of the Jewish Anti-Fascist Committee. Without them one might know all the facts but yet fail to understand them.

I will illustrate this with just two examples. In her memoirs, sent to the Jewish Anti-Fascist Committee shortly after the liberation of Kiev, I. Belozovskaya describes how she became one of the very few Jewish survivors in the city. Her husband was Russian, and due to illness he was not mobilized into the Red Army like the husbands of her sisters. When the Germans ordered the Jews of Kiev to appear for what they said would be an evacuation, her vast Jewish family turned to her Russian husband as their saviour. The man volunteered to take the risk and went to find out what was happening to Jews who were turning up in accordance with the German demands. He returned to tell them about the mass murder at Babi Yar. So everything was clear. Now they knew that to obey German orders meant death. However, they soon learned that it was impossible to find a place where they could hide. The Germans and their Ukrainian collaborators were searching every hole, threatening to execute anybody who dared to help a Jew. All members of her family were captured and murdered. Only with the greatest difficulty did her husband succeed in hiding their son. The places where she herself hid were discovered one after the other, and only by some miracle did she manage to escape. Then her husband appeared and told her that he had sized up the situation, and come to the conclusion that all their efforts were hopeless. It made no sense to continue. He would not leave his wife and suggested joint suicide as the only reasonable solution. She agreed, but asked him to try just once more to find a hiding place. This time they were lucky, and so she became one of those few Jews who lived to see the Red Army liberate Kiev.[6]

Now for the second example. In a long report written in the form of a letter to the famous writer Ilya Ehrenburg, a member of the Jewish Anti-Fascist Committee, V. M. Sorina, a Jewish woman, describes how she survived the Nazi occupation with her three children while her husband was fighting the Germans in the Red Army. They ran away from the ghetto in the small town of Khislavichi in the Smolensk region. Her Russian friend helped them to obtain false papers as Russians, and establish themselves in a small village in the vicinity. Soon it became evident that even in this village police and collaborators were looking for fugitive Jews. They checked the identification documents of all suspect persons, and conducted careful interrogations. The family had a dilemma. The woman and her two daughters were of 'good' appearance, and could pass as Russians. But the boy had inherited his father's black eyes and black hair, and could therefore betray himself and also his mother and sisters. The Russian friend who helped them was also in danger. It was suggested that the woman, when interrogated, should insist that she and the daughters were Russians, while the boy was from a liaison with a Jewish man. By sacrificing the boy, as the Russian friend suggested, she would thus be able to save herself and the two girls. However, that suggestion was unacceptable. The woman knew that she could not live without her son. So the problem remained. The 6-year-old boy learned to stay in bed, making himself sick and covering his face whenever somebody entered the room. Luckily he was not discovered.

Once, one of the villagers came back from the town of Khislavichi and reported that the day before all the Jews of the local ghetto had been executed. The woman could hardly control her feelings and avoid betraying herself. However, she left immediately for the town where all her family lived. She became the only Jewish witness to describe the place of the mass murder carried out only the day before, and the plunder of the property of the murdered Jews which was still going on in the town.[7]

Copies of valuable documents have been received by the Yad Vashem Archives from a number of regional and city archives, mainly from Kiev, Minsk, Lvov and others. They include orders by the occupation authorities, correspondence of many German institutions concerning the Jewish population, reports of anti-Jewish activities and anti-partisan activities, details about the organization of various collaborationist units and personal data concerning many of the perpetrators, information about the involvement of German firms in the exploitation of Jewish slave labour, and the theft of Jewish property.

Yad Vashem Archives is working on the development of detailed retrieval systems for all these newly arrived files. At the same time, we are continuing to gather further information on the holdings of many other Soviet archives which are important for research into the Holocaust period.

In spite of the significant amount of material already received by the joint efforts of the Yad Vashem Archives and the United States Holocaust Memorial Museum, it must be stated that this is only the beginning. Enormous numbers of documents have still not been seen or studied by historians of the Holocaust period. The most important are obviously the holdings of the Osobi Archives. The documents in these archives are of the utmost importance not only for the study of the Holocaust in the Soviet occupied territories. They are of primary importance for general studies of the Holocaust, mainly general Nazi policy and events in all occupied countries, as well as many concentration camps. Until these documents have been studied, the research on many aspects of the Holocaust will have to be considered provisional.

NOTES

1 *The Destruction of the European Jews*, revised and definitive edn, 3 vols (New York, Holmes & Meier, 1985).
2 Nora Levin, *The Jews in the Soviet Union since 1917. Paradox of Survival*, 2 vols (New York, New York University Press, 1988).
3 Leni Yahil, *The Holocaust. The Fate of European Jewry 1932–1945*, 2 vols (Jerusalem, Yad Vashem, 1987, in Hebrew).
4 *Encyclopedia of the Holocaust*, editor-in-chief Israel Gutman, 4 vols (New York, Macmillan Publishing Company, 1990).
5 Tatiana Pavlova, Lecture delivered at the conference 'From Barbarossa to Wannsee' held at Yad Vashem, Jerusalem, 16 October 1991, in Russian (to be published).
6 Central State Archives, Moscow. File 8114/962, pp. 105–8. Copy in Yad Vashem Archives, file: M35/962.
7 Central State Archives, Moscow. File 8114/960, pp. 228–32. Copy in Yad Vashem Archives, file M35/960.

CONCLUSION
The significance of the Final Solution
Yehuda Bauer

I wonder whether the Holocaust has any significance at all, if by significance we mean a sense, purpose, meaning, in other words a significance that is intrinsic to the event itself. Does any historical event have an intrinsic significance? Does it have any meaning in and of itself (I am using the terms 'meaning' and 'significance' interchangeably)? I doubt it very much. A historical event is, I think, the result of the convergence of an infinite number of causal chains, the most important ones of which are analysed and examined by the historian, sociologist or psychologist, in the search for a plausible explanation for the occurrence of the event in the first place. The humans involved in the historical event may or may not have thought out the reasons for their actions, or they may have reacted unthinkingly or emotionally to the unfolding of the event, and for them there is a significance: in so far as they had aims or desires or yearnings and these were fulfilled or partly fulfilled or not fulfilled, the event has a meaning for them, in relation to their individual lives. But in itself, the event is meaningless. Historical events or the processes leading up to them have, I think, significance only in so far as one thinks of them as closed circles. The significance lies in the contribution we perceive, rightly or wrongly, that they make to the unfolding of other events in the chain of human history. In other words, the significance I can see in any historical event is how much it contributes to the explanation of motives, causes, factors, etc. leading up to it and on from it to subsequent events. An intrinsic meaning, a significance, a purpose, if you will, I cannot see.

If the Holocaust was caused by extra-human intervention from a god or a devil or both, then of course one can talk about significance. But most theologians dealing with the Holocaust, Christian and Jewish alike, oppose the idea that there was a divine or a satanic intervention, and the whole thrust of the arguments of important thinkers such as Eliezer Berkovits, Emil Fackenheim, Irving Greenberg and others on the Jewish side, or Franklin H. Littell, John Pawlikowski or Gregory Baum and many others on the Christian side, is that the Holocaust is the result of human evil and the hiding of God's face, whatever that may mean. Within the freedom of choice given to the human being by God, they would argue, this was made possible. To theologians, the non-intervention of God may be significant, but they leave the event itself firmly within the responsibility of humans. Their problem of course is that the freedom of choice was limited to the Nazis. The Jews caught by the Nazi juggernaut had no freedom of choice, and the non-intervention of an absolutely powerful and absolutely good and just God causes a number of moral problems that in my humble view are bridged over largely by verbiage.

Fundamentalists such as the Lubavicher Rebbe, Menachem Mendel Shneersohn and some others solve the problem by arguing that the Holocaust indeed is the work of God, for His own reasons and purposes, just as all of history is directly ordained by the divine. If you accept that view, then of course the Holocaust has significance in terms of divine punishment of Jews for their transgressions. The Nazis then become the instruments of the divine implementing of God's will. If, however, you reject this view as an internalization of antisemitism by Jews, and exclude God from the equation, then you return to humans and their aims, desires and passions. The Nazis, for historical reasons, developed an ideology that led them, in 1941, to decide on the annihilation of every Jew, man, woman or child, they could lay their hands on. The only significance in that is that it is what they wanted, and had they been more successful, I would not be here to talk about it.

In these thoughts I may be influenced, I readily admit, by a revulsion from the very idea that the mass murder of nearly six million Jews should have any significance at all, in and by itself. But of course there is the very valid emotional objection to this, namely that it means that the death of all these people, to me my fellow-Jews, with whom most Jews feel an emotional identification just as I do, was in itself meaningless, in other words that their suffering and death had no meaning in itself. Their death could only have a Nazi significance; in other words only if we accept the Nazi way of thinking could we find significance in the murder of absolutely innocent people. All of which does not mean that the victims and their heirs, Jews or non-Jews, do not desperately try to find significance for the event, the suffering and the deaths, at the time and *post factum*. Indeed, during the Holocaust itself, large but obviously undetermined numbers of people went to their deaths with the conviction that by the manner they met their fate they were giving significance to that fate, whether by prayer or by adherence to some ideology. They glorified God's name, or showed steadfastness in their belief that their ideology would ultimately win. They were submerged in a terrible flood that left their cries unheard by their fellow humans, with but a few exceptions, and the flood itself had no meaning: it was the result of a rationally explicable outburst of irrational lust for murder which turned against them for reasons which were external to them. If the cries and prayers were directed at God, the response obviously was silence. Nazi antisemitic delusions can be, as I just said, rationally explained, but they had only marginal contact with reality, and especially with the reality of the life of the Jewish people as a group or with the lives of Jews as individuals.

This unreal reality is exemplified rather convincingly, I believe, in the Wannsee meeting – it was hardly a conference. A group of bureaucrats at the level of secretaries of state were asked by Heydrich, who had an equivalent status as head of the security apparatus of the SS, to coordinate the execution of a Hitler order to murder all the Jews in territories within German reach that had evolved in the previous year. We have some oral testimony of what actually transpired there, but the protocol we have is doctored; it contains a censored version of what was said and does not deal with much that was said there. There is an aura of unreality about all that. It is a slanted version of past history, and, I think, of the plans for the future. Little of what was said there was executed in detail: Jews were not 'combed', as Heydrich put it, from western to eastern Europe, but were murdered in Poland from late 1941 on, and then in the summer of 1942 transports began to be sent from western Europe to the death camps, while murder by shooting in the occupied areas of the Soviet Union was proceeding in a parallel fashion. Most Jews were not worked to death in road building, as Heydrich promised, but by a variety of other means. The whole discussion about the *Mischlinge*, which took up so much of the time apparently, and the space in the protocol written up by Eichmann, was quite pointless, because without a Führer decision no solution could be agreed upon, and Hitler did not reach such a decision then or later, and policies in that regard fluctuated constantly. The purpose of the exercise was to make clear to the representatives present that the Führer had empowered the SS to take over the Final Solution of the Jewish question, that Heydrich was the man responsible (*federführend*), and to make sure they all collaborated when asked to do so. The transport people were not invited – their collaboration had apparently been assured already. Nor was the army there – perhaps because they might have caused problems. They would have to toe the line, in the name of the Führer, separately. The others were friendly, understanding, and dealt, as Heydrich surely must have hoped, with details. No wonder he drank to the success of the meeting after it was over.

Is there a significance in Wannsee? Yes, of course, there is a historical significance: in other words, it contributes to our knowledge of the processes involved in the design for mass murder, and it formed a step towards their implementation.

There is much *post factum* significance, of course. Psychologists tell us that the Holocaust is yet another example of the tremendous range of possibilities of human behaviour, from the saintly to the satanic, often if not always in the same personality. The problem, stated rather simply, is whether we can understand the Holocaust at all, the victims, the bystanders and, of course, the perpetrators. The argument is sometimes put forward that we cannot understand the Holocaust, that it is beyond human comprehension. If that were so, we would be wasting our time. I have been arguing against this mystical interpretation for decades but without much success. Let me repeat: if the Holocaust was caused by humans, and its horrors inflicted on other humans and watched by yet other groups of humans, then it is as understandable as any other historical event. If it was not a human event, then it was the result of an intervention by extra-human forces, and in that case there is no point in dealing with it, because it is no part of human history. Are human events understandable? Largely, yes; never completely, because, as I have tried to point out, history is the result of the convergence of infinite numbers of causal chains; hence it is not the case that if we knew all the causes we would know all the consequences: we cannot, in principle, know all the causes because there is an infinite number of them. But we can perhaps get at quite a number of causal chains, and achieve an approximation to understanding the historical event.

We cannot, of course, repeat history in our endeavour to understand; nor, I suspect, do we particularly want to. But then we cannot repeat very trivial things that have happened, or even fully reconstruct our own experiences. We certainly cannot feel other people's sufferings, although we can empathize with them because we have general knowledge, and many unfortunately have some experience of suffering. One of the fallacies of writers and thinkers dealing with the Holocaust is that they wrongly believe that what makes the Holocaust unique is the suffering of the victims. Very unfortunately this is not so, because mass murder, sadism, murder, especially of children, torture of all kinds – this has been with us since long before the beginning of recorded time. If, then, we cannot understand the Holocaust because we cannot feel the suffering of the victims, all history becomes a mystery. After all, history is suffused with endless suffering, and all of it would then be closed to us.

But we can understand the victims. In this special case, a very large and growing number of detailed accounts, and many thousands of testimonies that were not recorded in book form, bring us nearer to the experience. Beyond that, as I tried to point out, suffering is human and we are human, and while we can never feel what the victim felt, we can approach it vicariously, and come close enough to feel an approximation of understanding, as we do with other historical events.

The situation is, for obvious reasons, simpler when we consider the bystander. But what of the perpetrator? Can we understand the perpetrator in the sense that we can feel we are in his shoes? Can we feel ourselves in the shoes of people like Heydrich or Eichmann or Lohse at Wannsee, either before or afterwards? Indeed, I would claim we can, and the fact that most of us become very angry even at the thought that we could do so would seem to me to indicate that we protest too loudly. What the Holocaust has shown, and if you will there is an important *post factum* significance here, is that the range of possibilities of human behaviour is very wide indeed. We might have learned that from studying Genghis Khan or Nero or Caligula or the early Aztec kings, but we thought perhaps that the Enlightenment and the rise of democracy in some western countries in the nineteenth century might have changed all that. No, it didn't. We got decisive and overwhelming proof that the range remains. But then, if the psychologists are right, in different circumstances Adolf Hitler might have eked out a living as a nationalist speaker on the margins of society, and Himmler might have continued to raise chickens, and Eichmann would have made a career selling washing machines. The potential for what we call near-absolute evil would have remained untapped. On the other hand, there may be among us people with that potential, and if the circumstances arose, then . . . I think I had better not finish the sentence.

But if that is true, do we not have within us, within all of us, the same basic potential? If we do, we surely can understand Heydrich, because he is a human not unlike ourselves. We have criminals among us, murderers, evil men and women. Do we claim we do not understand them? We understand them very well; that is why we legislate to curb them, that is why we try to catch them and put them behind bars, and in many countries kill them after a judicial process of one kind or another. And we try to educate our children not to be like them – we try to educate, because we know they could become criminals.

In principle, therefore, the perpetrator can be understood, and if he can be understood, then we can understand the Holocaust, not completely, not absolutely, but approximately. Which of course is not to say that we actually do understand it. We can discuss the range of our lack of understanding in order to overcome as much of it as possible. That, again, is one of the *post factum* elements of the significance of it all.

I am often asked what are the lessons of the Holocaust. That of course is not the same as asking for its significance, but perhaps another *post factum* significance is that one may learn some lessons from it. However, I have to tell you honestly that I have great difficulties with the lessons. First of all, they will change: each generation will look at the event from its own perspective and will derive different lessons. That of course means that it is not the Holocaust itself that is the lesson, but the lesson is in the eye of the beholder, depends on his or her circumstances and will be applicable in an environment that will hopefully radically differ from that of the Holocaust. Second, some of the lessons may well be rather banal and self-evident. Obviously, our work is directed towards preventing a repetition of the Holocaust. The Holocaust was a historical event, and therefore can be repeated, simply because if it happened once it can happen again, though not of course in exactly the same way, and not necessarily to Jews and not necessarily by Germans, but to anyone by anyone. But I must say that I do not know many cases where people have learned from history – there may be some, but surely not many. Do we then strive in vain to contribute to preventing a repetition? I cannot tell, but I do know that if there exists even the slightest of chances that we can contribute to the prevention of that horror we are under a categorical imperative to try and do so.

Any number of false lessons have been drawn, false in the sense that people interpret the Holocaust in what Fackenheim has called an inauthentic manner, reading into it things that are demonstrably untrue.[1] Some Israeli politicians, when they make their obligatory speeches on Holocaust memorial days, say that all nations were against us during the Holocaust and that therefore we can rely only on ourselves. Then they add that the lesson of the Holocaust is that Israel must be strong.

This is patent nonsense. The *post factum* significance of the Holocaust lies in part in the fact that there were all kinds of people – in eastern Europe unfortunately mostly hostile or indifferent in an unfriendly way, but still there were small minorities who behaved differently, and there were indeed nations where the majority tried to help as best they could, or at least were not hostile to the Jews. Italy, Bulgaria, Serbia, Denmark, Belgium, Norway are obvious examples. Holland and France are more problematic, but still do not conform to the politicians' dictum. As to the other argument, if it needed the Holocaust to convince an Israeli politician that Israel must be strong, then, first, he must be rather obtuse, and, more importantly, if it needed six million murdered Jews to make Israel strong, then as an Israeli who has served in most of Israel's wars I would prefer to have six million of my people alive and no Israel.

These are of course not the only so-called lessons that show a tremendous capacity for misrepresentation. The Holocaust is being misused as a symbol for a wide range of current political situations. Israeli behaviour towards the Palestinians is compared to Nazi behaviour towards Jews, a comparison which tells us a great deal about the deep-seated antisemitism of those who present such comparisons but very little about either the Arab–Israeli conflict or indeed about the Holocaust. People will talk about the Holocaust of the Blacks in American society, or even about cultural Holocausts, surely a nonsense when you consider that the Holocaust is a form of mass murder. Cultural repression is not murder. Another type of comparison will equate the Holocaust with ecological disasters, mostly man-made, which again is an obvious misplacement, because the definition of Holocaust is a genocide that is total, involving a plan for the total annihilation of a people as defined by the perpetrator, and that has simply nothing to do with ecological disasters.

A much more serious attempt is a comparison between the Holocaust and nuclear disaster, often called nuclear Holocaust. A similar lesson is drawn from both cases, and the same significance is assigned to both. Again, I find the comparison weakens the *post factum* fight against repetition of these man-made disasters. The overall nuclear threat (which has only apparently been reduced by the collapse of the Soviet empire), or the threat of orbicide as it is sometimes called, does not target groups for destruction, but threatens all humankind. It is true, however, that Holocaust situations in the future may well involve nuclear bombing directed against a certain nation or a certain population with the aim of total annihilation of that group only, but such a course of action might well develop into a threat of orbicide. Yet we should keep in mind that in itself a Holocaust, defined as total genocide, is directed towards peoples or nations as defined by the potential perpetrator. To deal with both threats in the same way seems to me counterproductive: they may be the results of quite different historical processes, and therefore lumping them together will probably decrease the effectiveness of any counter-measures. At the base, of course, they are different forms of mass murder, and prove the correctness of the thesis about the range of human behaviour from near-absolute evil to near-absolute good.

What is most interesting about *post factum* significances accorded to the Holocaust is the way the Holocaust, and Wannsee within it, has become a cultural symbol of great potency. Contrary to warnings by many writers and historians, the Holocaust is not receding into the background; quite the contrary. Whether presented authentically or inauthentically, in accordance with the historical facts or in contradiction to them, with empathy and understanding or as monumental kitsch, the Holocaust has become a ruling symbol in our culture. I am not sure whether this is good or bad, but it seems to be a fact. Hardly a month passes without a new TV production, a new film, a new drama, new books, prose or poetry, dealing with the subject, and the flood is increasing rather than abating. Dead Jews, as contrasted with live ones, have very often been a subject of commiseration, sympathy, understanding, identification and soul-searching. The Holocaust appears to fit in with an unconscious antisemitic code in Christian and Muslim society that needs the Jews as the permanent victims and prototypical sufferers in order to prove the underlying ideological consensus of Christianity or Islam. On the other hand people, until now exclusively in the world broadly and incorrectly defined as Christian, who are sensitive to the dangers to which their societies are exposed, fight that code in their serious attempts to draw lessons of warning from the Holocaust. They will interpret the Holocaust, correctly I believe, as exemplifying an underlying failure of Christian society and/or Christian theology, some 2,000 years after the appearance of the Messiah who brought the message of love to the world. In other words, they will deal with the

universalistic aspects of the Holocaust without denying the Jewish speci-
ficity of it; indeed, they will argue that the two are inseparably intertwined.

From both sides of this particular fence, therefore, the Holocaust
becomes a central symbol for the problems and dangers facing contemporary society, and from different ideological perspectives significance is
accorded to it to answer real or imagined needs. There is a mixture there,
perhaps, of two trends: one in which the Holocaust becomes a didactic
instrument to pass a message or make a centrally important point; the
other that tries to deal with the Holocaust itself, not as a tool for something
else, and yet extracts from it Jewish or universal contents that mean something for contemporary society.

In a recent insightful chapter, Alvin H. Rosenfeld touches upon some
of these issues of significance and interpretation, in the case of the *Diary
of Anne Frank*.[2] He shows how the diary, in itself an authenic autobio-
graphical document, has become a tool to pass on messages that were not
included in it, or that were inconsequential in the eyes of the young diarist.
Anne Frank, Rosenfeld points out, was a girl who was very conscious of
her Jewish identity, and who at the same time wrote down simple and
very convincing observations which we may call universalistic, on the
nature of people as such, Jews or non-Jews. The play that was made from
the diary distorted all that. The German translation eliminated all references
to the Germans as perpetrators. The diary itself, as we know, was slightly
but significantly censored by the father, when personal matters relating to
intra-family affairs were concerned. Here we have a clear case of the use,
or rather misuse, of the Holocaust as a tool to present ideology. Yet, as
Rosenfeld points out, in many countries people became aware of the
Holocaust through the diary. It was the distorted diary that became an
important catalyst for the penetration of the Holocaust into the consciousness of many millions, being the most widely read book and one of the
most effective plays and films about the subject. It created the backdrop
for undistorted and authentic presentations. The awful question then is
whether we need kitsch and distortions in order to arrive at authentic
interpretations of the Holocaust or any other major turning points in
human history.

For the opposite example let me remind you of the last segment of
Claude Lanzmann's *Shoah*, when Simchah Rotem ('Kajik') and Yitzhak
(Antek) Zuckermann are interviewed about the last stages of the Warsaw
Ghetto rebellion. The story is rooted not in the past but in the present,
and the Holocaust is evoked as memory. Kajik tells the story of his descent
into the sewers and his emergence into the destroyed ghetto. He looks for
his comrades, but does not find them; all he hears is the wailing of a
woman whom he tries to find but fails. The film ends with Kajik saying
that he then felt totally at peace: he knew he was the last Jew alive, and
he would meet his fate the next morning. We know of course that that

feeling was utterly mistaken: Kajk was not the only Jew left alive, and he did not die the next morning. We also realize that he must have continued his testimony to relate what happened subsequently. So in that sense the film is, chronologically so to speak, inaccurate in its portrayal of what happened. But in the sense of leading us to the significance, *post factum*, of the events, it is most authentic, because we know instinctively that the feeling expressed by Kajik reflects what he felt then, and the destruction of European Jewry is an overwhelming fact that the survival of tens of thousands in Poland does not contradict but on the contrary emphasizes. Kajik expressed his version of the sense of total destruction by his story, and Lanzmann knew that that is where the film had to end: he could not have a happy ending to a film on the Holocaust, comparable to the kitsch NBC Holocaust series of 1978; in fact, he could not end it at the end of the war, because a film on the Holocaust could not end with the end of the war in 1945. The Holocaust had no end. We still live in a world in which the Holocaust took place. We do not deal with a past, but a present. That is, to my mind, an authentic presentation, and an authentic interpretation of the *post factum* significance that we legitimately may read into the event.

So we are back at Wannsee, and a conference on Wannsee, where colleagues will present us with the latest research on and around the topic, in order to deepen our understanding, and where we will argue points of historical interpretation. Some of the old arguments have become redundant. The intentionalist-functionalist controversy has, I believe, ended. Hitler emerges as the radicalizing factor, and Eichmann's protocol mentions that explicitly. Some will emphasize the role of Heydrich, others that of Himmler. There will be analyses of the background, the implementation, and other issues, and we will learn a great deal from it. In the background to all this will loom the discovery of a vast Russian archive containing German archival loot, so vast indeed that we may find ourselves at the next conference in more or less utter despair about the size of the task of integrating 27,000 metres of archival material into our work. We talk here as though the factual basis is already investigated and we can safely engage in arguments about significance and interpretation. But with the discovery of these archives in eastern Europe we might well be thrown back into basic research about additional facts that may impact on our interpretations in a rather radical way.

The fact of our conference, on the fiftieth anniversary of Wannsee, shows how public perceptions influence us. In the eyes of too many of our contemporaries, Wannsee was the place where the Final Solution was decided upon. We of course know better: Wannsee was but a stage in the unfolding of the process of mass murder. The significance that people read into Wannsee is quite different from that accorded to it, presumably, by the conference participants. And yet, a *post factum* significance can be read into the meeting which goes beyond the factual description and historical analysis: we know of few cases where high representatives of a modern government bureaucracy met to discuss the implementation of a plan of total mass murder. The *post factum* significance appears to be that given a murderous ruling elite, and the identification of large parts of the middle class and intelligentsia with the regime as such – not necessarily with the ideological underpinning of the murder itself – the machine of the state and the ruling party will coalesce to execute total mass murder. The fact that the victims were Jews was not accidental. It was preceded by a long history. But the framework and the type of decision making on the practical implementation of the programme that we see here can be repeated elsewhere. We live in a period when Wannsee meetings are possible, and as Raul Hilberg has taught all of us, the study of bureaucracies is an essential part of our craft, so that we and our descendants should perhaps take heed.[3] The significance which we read, rightly, into Wannsee is that combination of the specific Jewish with the universal that exemplifies all of the history of the Holocaust. Wansee could happen again, in a different place, and who knows who the Jews might be then? As I have often tried to say, the Holocaust can be either a warning or a precedent. It should be the former, so that it may not be the latter.

NOTES

1 Emil L. Fackenheim, *To Mend the World* (New York, Shocken, 1987), pp. 190–200; idem, *The Jewish Return into History* (New York, Shocken, 1978), pp. 19–42.
2 Alvin H. Rosenfeld, 'Popularization and memory: the case of Anne Frank', in Peter Hayes (ed.) *Lessons and Legacies – the Meaning of the Holocaust in a Changing World* (Evanston, Ill., Northwestern University Press, 1991), pp. 243–78.
3 Raul Hilberg, *The Destruction of the European Jews* (New York, Holmes & Meier, 1985).

INDEX

310

United States Holocaust Memorial
Museum 292
Ustasha: death camps (Croatia) 175–7;
murder of Serbs 180–1

Vatican, and Croatia 184–6
Vichy France: delaying tactics of on
Jews 203; denaturalization of Jews
205; foreign pressure on 201–2; and
Jews 18–19, 197–201; relationship
with Germany 195, 202; and
Wannsee Conference 194–214
victory, euphoria of in east:
Einsatzgruppen's knowledge of Final
Solution 139–40, 141–3; and Final
Solution 137–47; manpower
problems in Final Solution 138–40
Vilna (Lithuania) 17, 159–71 *passim*
Viton, Albert 230
Volk concept 33–4
völkisch ideology 3–4, 33–4; and anti-
semitic propaganda 40
Volksfeind, Jews as 34–5, 40, 41
Volksgemeinschaft (*Volk*-community)
33–50; and Germany labour service
36; and Operation Barbarossa 85, 99

Waffen-SS 74; and Operation
Barbarossa 94
Wagner, General Eduard 104, 109
Wagner, R. 78
Wannsee Conference (1942) 1–2, 8–9,
68; and Operation Barbarossa 85;
and significance of holocaust 302,
308–9; and Vichy France 194–214
passim
Wannsee Protocol 76
Warsaw Ghetto 15, 153–4, 157, 307
Warthegau 154
Wasserstein, Bernard 21–3, 270
Night of Broken Glass (*Kristallnacht*)
38, 39
Wehrmacht: and decision on Final
Solution 11–12, 104–6, 108, 111; and
Hitler, on Final Solution 90, 104;
invasion of Balkans 179;

involvement in genocide 119–36; and
Operation Barbarossa 90, 98–9, 108,
119–36; and war in Poland 87–8
Weimann, E. 66
Weizmann, Chaim 230, 231, 234, 238
Welles, Sumner 236
Weltanschauung of Hitler 34; and
Operation Barbarossa 89; and war
in Poland 87
Wheeler, Mark 179–80
Widmann, Albert 54
Wilhelm, Hans-Heinrich 10, 163
Winnitza massacre 220
Wipperman, W. 75–6
Wirth, Christian 54–5
Wise, Rabbi Stephen S. 228–9, 231–2,
235–6, 238, 252
Wurm, Archbishop Theophile 218
Wyman, David S. 21, 269

Yad Vashem Archive 25; on Lithuanian
Jews 160; on Soviet Union 292,
294–5, 297
Yahil, Leni 292
Yehieli, Zvi 277
Yishuv: co-operation with allies
279–81; growth of in Palestine
229–30, 241; intelligence and rescue
activities 276–9; knowledge of Final
Solution 271–2; reactions to Final
Solution 24, 233; rescue activities of
268–87
Yugoslavia 179

Zaslani, Reuven 278
Zionism 156; Biltmore Conference
234–5; and British White Paper on
Palestine 233–4, 237–9, 242; and
partition of Palestine 230–2;
reactions to Final Solution 24,
228–45, 272
Zionist Organization of America
(ZOA) 228, 230
Zuckermann, Yitzhak 160, 307
Zyklon B (poison gas) 112